"Ted Matamis has drawn on his life-long love for the Bible and his journey through the loss of his wife to bring together these warm-hearted devotions that consistently point to our Lord Jesus Christ and show how His grace is sufficient for all circumstances."

— **Colin S. Smith,** Senior Pastor
The Orchard Evangelical Free Church
Author and Bible Teacher on Unlocking the Bible

"For many years, Ted Matamis has been writing and sending out his SPIRITUAL NOTES FROM THE BIBLE to readers all over the globe. They are all doctrinally sound and a great source of helpful and devotional thoughts on many subjects. Those who read them will find them thought-provoking and a blessing to their souls. By putting some of them in a book, a person can now profit from many challenging thoughts accumulated over many years. I recommend that you get this book, *The Journey and Destiny of a Christian* and I am sure you will find many profitable ideas within."

— **Dr. James R. Hines,** Retired Senior Pastor
Author and Founder of Brentwood Baptist Church,
Christian School and Brentwood Baptist Senior Manor

"In the book, *The Journey and Destiny of a Christian* brother Ted Matamis has masterfully managed, through God's enabling, to give us in a simple and comprehensive way biblical truth which is both biblically sound and practical in its orientation."

— **John P. Kremidas, Ph.D.** Professor of Biblical Studies
Greek Bible College, Pikermi

"There are many Internet websites and books which seek to glorify the Lord. I have found brother Ted Matamis' SPIRITUAL NOTES FROM THE BIBLE and his book, *The Journey and Destiny of a Christian* to provide a variety of research on various topics which feed the soul. It has given me ample food for thought in seeking the Lord."

— **Larry Pieri,** Pastor, and Missionary to Italy

The

Journey

and

Destiny

Of a Christian

TED MATAMIS

DEDICATION

This book is dedicated
to my Savior and Lord Jesus Christ and for His glory,
also, in memory of my honorable parents who taught me
to love and fear the Lord,
and my beloved first wife, Georgia
who helped me to raise two wonderful
Christian children.

ACKNOWLEDGEMENTS

I would like
to thank with love and warm appreciation
my beloved second wife, Deanna
who has been a tremendous help in my ministry
over the years and in this book.
She helped in editing
and proofreading to bring this book
to completion

For the editing and proofreading process,
I want to give special recognition to
my daughter Magdalene and my son George
and their spouses Bryan and Tiffanie.
They went over the manuscript
because they love the Lord
and His work.

CONTENTS

CONTENTS

CONTENTS

CONTENTS

FOREWORD

The Journey and Destiny of a Christian presents basic biblical truths with practical ways to edify and disciple new believers in Christ and to challenge other Christians to go forward to greater Christ-likeness and spiritual maturity. It also helps unbelievers and challenges them to accept Christ by faith as their personal Savior, to experience forgiveness of their sins, and to receive the gift of eternal life.

I have known Ted Matamis for a long time, and have received his short biblical messages with different topics for many years through his international email ministry: "A SPIRITUAL NOTE FROM THE BIBLE." They are doctrinally sound and can be a great source of help to everyone. You will find them useful for personal study, devotional thoughts, small group Bible studies, and Sunday school lessons. They can also serve as an aid in the Christian school, home school teaching, and family devotions.

As a Greek educator and teacher of the original New Testament language, Mr. Matamis has the knowledge, ability, and talent to write and present great biblical truths, with the help of the Holy Spirit, in very practical and simple ways that even a small child can understand. He has lived on both sides of the coin and has had the experience of religion as a Greek Orthodox before his conversion, and then for fifty years as a Bible-believing Christian. The Lord used him through all these years to glorify the Lord by helping and encouraging Christians and winning souls for God's kingdom. God has done many miraculous things in his life, and he shares some of them in his "testimonies" sections.

By putting some of his Spiritual Notes in this book, you can now profit from many challenging thoughts accumulated over the years. You will find them to be thought-provoking and a blessing to your heart. I recommend that you get this book, and I am sure that you will find in it many truths that will bless your soul.

—Dr. James R. Hines, Retired Senior Pastor, and Author.
   Founder of Brentwood Baptist Church, Christian School and
   Brentwood Baptist Senior Manor, Des Plaines, IL USA

AUTHOR'S INTRODUCTION

The first and most important thing in our lives is to know Jesus Christ as our personal Savior. This is not the end for Christians, but only the beginning of our new life in Christ. Second, we must *"grow in grace, and in the knowledge of our Lord and Saviour Jesus Christ"* (2 Peter 3:18a). Third, we must faithfully and consistently serve the Lord until the time we meet Him in glory.

Since I accepted Jesus Christ as my personal Savior in 1970, I have been involved in many Bible-believing ministries and have faithfully attended church services. In all these years, I have met many Christians strong in the Lord who have become my heroes. I have also met other Christians who needed substantial improvement in Christian growth, Christian service, and Christian living. The good news is that this book contains many basic teachings from the Bible, which will be helpful to everyone.

This book is written in simple English for everyone to understand. It deals with 100 biblical topics, which include Bible verses, quotes, illustrations, true stories, and personal testimonies that teach biblical principles. I am confident that these short messages will be a blessing to you and become one of your best teachers and counselors.

I wrote thousands of these short messages with different biblical topics, and I used them in my free international email ministry, "A SPIRITUAL NOTE FROM THE BIBLE." This ministry is respected, shared, and recommended by many Christians and unbelievers from all around the world. They are free of political correctness, and they glorify the Lord by teaching the truth, encouraging Christians, and helping others.

In the past, as a religious person and as an educator, I used to teach the Bible with head knowledge. Now, after God saved me by His grace and as a new creation in Christ, I rely on the power of the Holy Spirit to teach His Word. My messages are not just from head knowledge, but they are from my Christian experience and from my heart. Many people call them "biblical messages from the heart that speak to the heart," and God uses them for His glory.

THE JOURNEY AND DESTINY OF A CHRISTIAN

The Lord gave me the unique and blessed Internet ministry of "A SPIRITUAL NOTE FROM THE BIBLE," written in the English language after my first wife unexpectedly passed away from a heart attack just before Valentine's Day in 1996. As a loving father, I comforted and encouraged my children by email with short biblical messages with the title, "A SPIRITUAL NOTE FROM DAD." Later, it expanded to the people we knew with the title "A SPIRITUAL NOTE FROM TED," and finally by God's grace it spread to people around the world with the title, "A SPIRITUAL NOTE FROM THE BIBLE." This was the way the Lord helped me to start this wonderful ministry that has blessed countless people around the world. The goal of these messages with different biblical topics is to encourage, comfort, teach, inspire, challenge, evangelize, and help people to walk with the Lord.

These biblical messages are the first part of each SPIRITUAL NOTE, and over the years, many people encouraged me to publish them, but I did not. Lately, the Lord laid it upon my heart to print 100 of these messages. Now, you have the opportunity to taste some of them in this book. I pray that the Lord will richly bless you as you read them, and if you are not yet saved, I encourage you to accept Jesus Christ as your personal Savior.

Welcome to *The Journey and Destiny of a Christian!*

1

LOVE GOD'S WORD

"And Jesus answered him, saying,
It is written, That man shall not live by bread alone,
but by every word of God."
Luke 4:4

*

Read, study, and meditate on God's Word!

The Bible is God's Word, which is spiritual food for each Christian. The knowledge of the Bible is essential for a productive and meaningful life. The Word of God brings spiritual life, spiritual strength, and spiritual growth. All of our journey and destiny depends upon how we deal with the Word of God. We must seek with our whole heart to learn how to use God's Word accurately. We have to read the Bible regularly, prayerfully, and meditate on God's Word. We must read the Word of God with both our heart and our mind. We must read it with a desire to be not only hearers but doers of the Word. Finally, we must love God's Word. President Ronald Regan said, *"Inside the Bible's pages lie all the answers to all the problems man has ever known. I hope Americans will read and study the Bible…The Bible can touch our hearts, order our minds, and refresh our souls."*

The Bible is not like other books. This book is inspired by God. Within the Bible, God reveals Himself to us. In the Word of God, we find out our sinful condition and the way to be saved. Only the Bible answers the great questions of our lives… Where did we come from? Why are we here? Where are we going? Other books inform, but the Bible transforms. The Word of God works like a lamp, map, and compass on our Christian journey. Also, it is like a telescope. If we look through His telescope, we see worlds beyond and not just dead letters. In the Bible, God speaks to us about His Son, or God speaks to us through His Son.

We must pay close attention to the Bible because reverence for God means reverence for the Scriptures, and serving God means obeying the Scriptures.

Psalm 1:2 states that we have to *"meditate day and night"* on the Word of God, and the person who does this *"shall be like a tree planted by the rivers of water, that bringeth forth his fruit in his season; his leaf also shall not wither; and whatsoever he doeth shall prosper"* (Psalm 1:3).

The apostle Paul wrote, *"Let the word of Christ dwell in you richly..."* (Colossians 3:16). The whole Bible talks about Jesus Christ, and it is essential for us, and especially if we are true believers, to read and meditate on His Word.

We will grow spiritually only:

- **By connecting to Jesus:**
  "Abide in me, and I in you. As the branch cannot bear fruit of itself, except it abide in the vine; no more can ye, except ye abide in me. I am the vine, ye are the branches: He that abideth in me, and I in him, the same bringeth forth much fruit: for without me ye can do nothing" (John 15:4-5).

- **By applying the Word of God:**
  "All scripture is given by inspiration of God, and is profitable for doctrine, for reproof, for correction, for instruction in righteousness. That the man of God may be perfect, thoroughly furnished unto all good works" (2 Timothy 3:16-17).

- **By walking in the Spirit:**
  "This I say then, Walk in the Spirit, and ye shall not fulfill the lust of the flesh. For the flesh lusteth against the Spirit, and the Spirit against the flesh: and these are contrary the one to the other: so that ye cannot do the things that ye would" (Galatians 5:16-17).

The Word of God also will help us to grow in various ways, and some of them are the following:

- **In successfulness in prayer:**
  "If ye abide in me, and my words abide in you, ye shall ask what ye will, and it shall be done unto you" (John 15:7).

- **In strength against temptation:**
  "I have written unto you, young men, because ye are strong, and the word of God abideth in you, and ye have overcome the wicked one" (1 John 2:14).

- **In wisdom, instructing, and advising one another. Also, singing joyfully with grace to the Lord:**
  "Let the word of Christ dwell in you richly in all wisdom; teaching and admonishing one another in psalms and hymns and spiritual songs, singing with grace in your hearts to the Lord" (Colossians 3:16).

LOVE GOD'S WORD

Let the Word of Christ dwell in us richly! Give the Word an honored and important place in our hearts and in our lives. If we desire the Word of Christ to dwell richly in us, we must regularly attend a Bible-believing church where the Word is preached without compromise. We must fellowship with believers centered in the Word of Christ, and we must establish a pattern of daily Bible reading and meditation.

The New Testament describes people in whom the Word does not dwell richly. *"Of whom we have many things to say, and hard to be uttered, seeing ye are dull of hearing. For when for the time ye ought to be teachers, ye have need that one teach you again which be the first principles of the oracles of God; and are become such as have need of milk, and not of strong meat. For every one that useth milk is unskillful in the word of righteousness: for he is a babe"* (Hebrews 5:11-13). The Word of God is like a seed. The seed will grow and produce more in our lives if we do not allow other worldly things to take over our heart and our attention.

All of us must be hungry and thirsty each day for the scriptures and enjoy them instead of enjoying the world and material things. We must have a desire each day to dig more and more to find the treasures of the Bible–knowing Christ, the Living Word, and receive more spiritual food. We must have a desire for the Lord to draw us closer to Him and reveal more of His wonders to us every time we read, study, and meditate on His Word. We must admit God's Word to be His message to us. We must submit to the authority of this book. We must commit the words of the scriptures to our memory, and we must transmit God's message to others.

I hope and pray for all of us to become stronger Christians who depend on, love and serve the Lord more and more as our life goes on. I hope and pray all of us will *"Read the Bible to be wise, believe it to be safe, and practice it to be holy."* — *Author Unknown*

❖ ❖ ❖

• "The more you read the Bible, the more you meditate on it, the more you will be astonished by it."
—*"Prince of Preachers," Charles Spurgeon*

• "The Scriptures teach us the best way of living, the noblest way of suffering, and the most comfortable way of dying." —*Minister, John Flavel*

• "The Bible will keep you from sin, or sin will keep you from the Bible." — *Evangelist, D.L. Moody*

• "If God is a reality, and the soul is a reality, and you are an immortal being, what are you doing with your Bible shut?"
— *Clergyman, Herrick Johnson*

2

THE LOVE OF GOD

"For God so loved the world, that he gave his only begotten Son, that whosoever believeth in him should not perish, but have everlasting life."
John 3:16

*

The love of God is the greatest message of the Bible!

One of our most essential needs is to be loved. When somebody is interested in us, we are delighted, especially when they help and love us with unconditional love. The Bible provides us the most wonderful news, that God is the one who cares and loves us in this way. His nature is to love us because *"God is love"* (1 John 4:8). Maybe you are skeptical about God's love and ask, "How can I know that God loves me?" Well, I could quote many verses from the scriptures to prove to you that God loves you, but instead, I will paint a picture for you.

In this picture, we see the begotten Son of God leave heaven to come to earth. He was born in poverty but was God in the flesh. He was treated as the lowest person in the world. He always did good to those all around Him. He healed many of them and showed kindness and mercy to them in many ways. The picture becomes awful, as we see, man (mankind) take Him and severely flog Him. We see man hit Him in the face and all over His body. We see man strike Him on the head with a stick. We see man put a crown of thorns on His head. We see man spit in His face. We see man mock Him. Finally, we see man lay Him on a cross and drive nails into His hands and feet. We then listen as He speaks with love and compassion these words, *"Father, forgive them; for they know not what they do..."* (Luke 23:34).

Jesus suffered to this level for only one reason, because He loves you! Yes! The Son of God loves because He wants you to spend eternity in heaven with Him. This is what John 3:16 precisely states: *"For God so loved the world, that he gave his only begotten Son, that whosoever believeth in him should not perish, but have everlasting life."* This verse is the most well-known verse in the Bible. This verse refers to "whosoever," and that includes you! This verse is a promise to you. If you believe in Jesus, His message, and His mission, He will give you eternal life. This verse reveals the depth of God's love for you!

It is impossible for us to make God love us any more or any less. He loves us entirely, regardless of how we act. God loves everybody unconditionally. God's love is much different than man's love.

GOD'S LOVE

is Unmeasured (Ephesians 3:18,19) (Jeremiah 31:3),
is Self-giving (Matthew 7:11) (James 1:17),
is Sacrificial (James 1:17) (Romans 5:8),
is Unconditional (Romans 5:10) (Colossians 1:21),
is Eternal (Jeremiah 31:3) (Romans 8:39),
is Holy (Hebrews 12:5,6),
is Comforting (1 John 4:18),
is Life-changing (Galatians 2:20),
strengthens and protects us (Romans 8:38,39),
disciplines us (Hebrews 12:6).

The Bible teaches us that God loves us unconditionally with an everlasting love! God's love is so amazing, so divine, it demands our soul, our heart, and our love. The hymn **"THE LOVE OF GOD"** states that *"The love of God is greater far Than tongue or pen can ever tell; It goes beyond the highest star, And reaches to the lowest hell."* When Frederick M. Lehman composed the words to this incredible hymn in 1917, he used his own words for the first two stanzas, but he took the third stanza from words written on the wall of an insane asylum. The inmate who wrote them apparently had a moment of incredible sanity when he penned:

> Could we with ink the ocean fill,
> And were the skies of parchment made,
> Were every stalk on earth a quill,
> And every man a scribe by trade,
> To write the love of God above
> Would drain the ocean dry.
> Nor could the scroll contain the whole,

THE JOURNEY AND DESTINY OF A CHRISTIAN

Refrain:
O love of God, how rich and pure!
How measureless and strong!
It shall forevermore endure
The saints' and angels' song.

— *Hymn by Frederick M. Lehman, 1917*

The apostle Paul tells us that we must know the love of God and experience it in our hearts. *"And to know the love of Christ, which passeth knowledge, that ye might be filled with all the fulness of God"* (Ephesians 3:19).

Many Christians have not experienced "The Love of God" in their hearts, and when going through trials, they doubt if God really loves them and sadly, they complain about it. This is not unusual because they do not experience "The Love of God." It is possible to be a pastor, a Bible school student, a seminary student, or a Christian who has gone to church their whole life, but has not experienced "The Love of God."

First, these Christians, need to know and believe what the Bible says about "The Love of God." Second, they must pray for God to direct them in His love. It is much different to hear, read, and learn about God's love than to experience God's love. Jonathan Edwards said, *"There is a difference between having a rational judgment that honey is sweet, and having a sense of its sweetness."*

John Wesley was a pastor who preached in England and in the United States, but something happened to him. He said:
"In the evening, I went very unwillingly to a society in Aldersgate Street, where one was reading Luther's preface to the Epistle to the Romans. About a quarter before nine, while he was describing the change which God works in the heart through faith in Christ, I felt my heart strangely warmed. I felt I did trust in Christ, Christ alone, for salvation; and an assurance was given me that He had taken away my sins, even mine, and saved me from the law of sin and death." — *Christian Classics Ethereal Library.org.*

Even though John Wesley was a pastor for many years, now he experienced the sweetness of God's love, and His life and ministry were revolutionized.

Blaise Pascal was a mathematician and a scientist. On November 23, 1654, he had a profound spiritual experience. The following text is a part of what is called the Memorial, a piece of parchment which was sewn into the lining of Pascal's coat.

THE LOVE OF GOD

"From about half-past ten in the evening until about half-past twelve, FIRE - God of Abraham, God of Isaac, God of Jacob, not of the philosophers and scholars. Certitude, certitude. Heartfelt joy, peace. God of Jesus Christ. My God and thy God. Thy God shall be my God." — *C.S. Lewis Society*

Blaise Pascal had an amazing experience of the love of God, and he did not desire to separate from Him. From that point, Pascal dedicated himself entirely to God and served the Divine Master with seriousness and accuracy. Jonathan Edwards, Dwight L. Moody, and many others had similar experiences of the flooding of God's love in their hearts.

God sent Jesus Christ, His only begotten Son, to die for you and me and to give us a chance for a new life. God finds great joy and receives great glory when we respond to His love, come into His fellowship, and do His will. Accept God's love even when you feel like you are most unacceptable. No matter how insane things look to you, place your hope in God. His love can be depended upon. You are not crazy to believe in God's love. God calls you to be His child through Jesus. Turn to Jesus and let Him bring you to the Father's arms. God's love cannot be explained, but can only be experienced. After you experience God's love, you will never regret it, and you will say along with the apostle Paul,

"For I am persuaded, that neither death, nor life, nor angels, nor principalities, nor powers, nor things present, nor things to come, Nor height, nor depth, nor any other creature, shall be able to separate us from the love of God, which is in Christ Jesus our Lord"
(Romans 8:38-39).

I hope and pray you have experienced the love of God in your heart. If you have not, pray and ask the Lord to point your heart into God's love and into the patience of Christ with apostle Paul's prayer: *"And the Lord direct your hearts into the love of God, and into the patient waiting for Christ"* (2 Thessalonians 3:5).

❖ ❖ ❖

- But God commendeth his love toward us, in that, while we were yet sinners, Christ died for us."— *Romans 5:8*

- "Love is truly the language of Heaven. It comes from the heart of God and is poured out into the heart of every believer."
— *Dr. Ray Pritchard*

- "When the time comes for you to die, you need not be afraid, because death cannot separate you from God's love."
— *Prince of Preachers," Charles Spurgeon*

3

FEAR AND LOVE GOD

"And now, Israel, what doth the LORD thy God require of thee,
but to fear the LORD thy God, to walk in all his ways,
and to love him, and to serve the LORD thy God
with all thy heart and with all thy soul."
Deuteronomy 10:12

*

Fear and love working together,
are like good and bad cholesterol in the human body!

The Bible requires us to fear and love God. To fear God means to hold Him in the highest regard. This means that we are to reverence, to respect, and to honor God. The fear of God is foundational for us as believers because respect and reverence of God influence the way we live.

To fear and love God are not separate and do not contradict one another as some Christians think. Maybe you struggle with this too. This can disappear when you realize what the Bible means. *The Jewish Encyclopedia* mentions that the fear of God is identical with the love and service that is mentioned in Deuteronomy 10:12.

To fear God does not mean we are afraid of Him because He will mistreat or hurt us. It means an awareness within ourselves of God's presence around us all the time. It means to honor God and follow His ways. It means respecting, obeying, submitting to God's discipline, and worshipping Him with admiration and respect. It means to have heartfelt respect and reverence for God because of His majesty and holiness.

Fear and love working together, are like good and bad cholesterol or like the red and white blood cells in our bodies. We need both cholesterols and blood cells for balance to have a healthy body. I feared my father while growing up, but I also loved him, and this kept me from trouble. Yes, if we fear and love at the same time, the blessings of our Heavenly Father will follow us. Today, many people love God but do not fear Him, and for this reason, their walk with the Lord is out of balance.

The Bible says, *"Let all the earth fear the LORD: let all the inhabitants of the world stand in awe of him"* (Psalm 33:8). God who created us also loves us and sent His Only Son to die for our sins. *"Herein is love, not that we loved God, but that he loved us, and sent his Son to be the propitiation for our sins"* (1 John 4:10). Because of this, we have to stop and thank God for loving us so much.

If we are Christians, we have to ask ourselves, "Do we fear and love God at the same time? Do we teach our children to fear and love God?" Our children do not have to learn God's commandments first. Even if they know them, they will break them without the fear and love of God. We have to teach them from when they are small ones, to put in their hearts and to practice the following and similar verses:

- *"Fear the Lord thy God, to walk in all his ways, and to love him, and to serve the Lord thy God with all thy heart and with all thy soul"* (Deuteronomy 10:12).

- *"Fear God, and keep his commandments: for this is the whole duty of man"* (Ecclesiastes 12:13).

- *"The fear of the LORD is the beginning of wisdom: a good understanding have all they that do his commandments: his praise endureth for ever"* (Psalm 111:10).

- *"Behold, the eye of the LORD is upon them that fear him, upon them that hope in his mercy" (Psalm 33:18).*

The fear of God is the inspiring and motivating factor for Christians to surrender to the Creator of the Universe in such a way that pleases Him. The fear of God is the basis for our Christian life for walking in God's ways, loving, and serving Him with devotion. Our society is in a big mess today because people do not have any fear of God. You do not have to follow others, but just pray and say, "Lord help me to live with reverence of You and care much more about what you think of me than what others think." *"Teach me Your way, O Lord; I will walk in Your truth; Unite my heart to fear Your name"* (Psalm 86:11).

❖ ❖ ❖

- "It is man's duty to love and to fear God, even without hope of reward or fear of punishment." — *Jewish Torah Scholar, Maimonides*

- "A person who fears God is one who has seen something of his glory, his judgment, and his love." — *Pastor and Author, Colin Smith*

4

FISH - ΙΧΘΥΣ

<:))))><

Ιησούς Χριστός Θεού Υιός Σωτήρ

Jesus Christ, God's Son, Savior

Many times you see the symbol of the fish on cars, jewelry, or in many other places. I wonder if you know the story behind this symbol, what it means, and what it represents. Most people, even many Christians who use it, do not know much about this symbol. They use it as others do simply because they believe it is a Christian symbol, and it tells others that they are Christians.

From the early Christian history of the church, we learn that the Christians were persecuted, especially by the evil emperors of the Roman Empire. At that time, when the believers faced intense persecution, they used this symbol of the fish to identify one another without exchanging verbal communication.

When two strangers met, they would be hesitant to reveal their faith. After a short time of conversation, one of them would take his foot or finger and draw the symbol of the fish or the letters **ΙΧΘΥΣ** in mud, dirt, sand, or on the walls of caves where they lived or hid. The other person, if he were a Christian, would do the same so they would know that both were believers in Christ and that it was safe to share their faith without the fear of being arrested.

Maybe you will ask why the early Christians used the symbol of the fish and the Greek letters **ΙΧΘΥΣ**? As a Greek educator, I will explain to you why. The Greek word ΙΧΘΥΣ (Ichthus) in the New Testament means fish. Jesus used the same word in Matthew 7:10, and His disciples used it in Matthew 14:17. Each Greek letter of ΙΧΘΥΣ declares a tremendous truth about Jesus Christ.

I — The first letter of ΙΧΘΥΣ stands for **Ιησούς** (Iesous), which is the Greek word for "Jesus" as we find in Matthew 1:21 *"And she shall bring forth a son, and thou shalt call his name JESUS: for he shall save his people from their sins."*

X — The second letter of ΙΧΘΥΣ stands for **Χριστός** (Xristos), which is the Greek word for "Christ," which means "anointed." As we know from the Bible, Jesus is God's *"Anointed One." "And the angel said unto them, Fear not: for, behold, I bring you good tidings of great joy, which shall be to all people"* (Luke 2:10,11).

Θ — The third letter of ΙΧΘΥΣ stands for **Θεού** (Theos -Theou) which is the Greek word for "God." Jesus is the Messiah, the eternal God who was revealed in human flesh. *"In the beginning was the Word [Jesus], and the Word [Jesus] was with God, and the Word [Jesus] was God."* (John 1:1), *"The great God and our Saviour Jesus Christ;"* (Titus 2:13).

Υ — The fourth letter of ΙΧΘΥΣ stands for **Υιός** (Hyios) that is the Greek word for "Son" and in the word ΙΧΘΥΣ, means Jesus is the Son of God. *"For God so loved the world that He gave His only begotten Son..."* (John 3:16).

Σ — The fifth letter of ΙΧΘΥΣ stands for **Σωτήρ** (Soter), which is the Greek word for "Savior." *"For unto you is born this day in the city of David a Saviour, which is Christ the Lord"* (Luke 2:11) and there is no other Savior besides Him. *"Neither is there salvation in any other: for there is none other name under heaven given among men, whereby we must be saved"* (Acts 4:12).

The next time you see the symbol of the fish displayed somewhere, remember that Jesus is the Son of God who gave His life to be the Savior for you and me. My simple question to you is, "Have you put your trust in Him to save you for all eternity?" If not, do it right now before your soul spends eternity in hell. With a sincere prayer, invite Jesus Christ to come into your life to become your personal Savior.

Dear God, I know that You love me and want to save me. Jesus, I believe You are the begotten Son of God, and you shed your precious blood and died on the cross to pay for my sins. I believe God raised You from the dead. Now I repent and turn from my sin, and by faith, receive You as my personal Savior. Come into my life, forgive my sins, and save me. In Your name, I pray. Amen.

If you are a Christian, proudly display ΙΧΘΥΣ every place you can, to tell other Christians that you are a follower of Jesus Christ.

5

TRUE PEACE

"Peace I leave with you, my peace I give unto you:
not as the world giveth, give I unto you.
Let not your heart be troubled, neither let it be afraid."
John 14:27

*

The gift of true peace can only be provided by the Lord!

There once was a King who offered a prize to the artist who would paint the best picture of peace. Many artists tried. The King looked at all the pictures, but there were only two he really liked and he had to choose between them. One picture was of a calm lake. The lake was a perfect mirror, for peaceful towering mountains were all around it. Overhead was a blue sky with fluffy white clouds. All who saw this picture thought that it was a perfect picture of peace. The other picture had mountains, too. But these were rugged and bare. Above was an angry sky from which rain fell and in which lightening played. Down the side of the mountain tumbled a foaming waterfall. This did not look peaceful at all. But when the King looked, he saw behind the waterfall a tiny bush growing in a crack in the rock. In the bush, a mother bird had built her nest. There, in the midst of the rush of angry water, sat the mother bird on her nest in perfect peace. "Which picture do you think won the prize?" The King chose the second picture. "Do you know why?" Because explained the King, "Peace does not mean to be in a place where there is no noise, trouble, or hard work. Peace means to be in the midst of all those things and still be calm in your heart. That is the real meaning of peace."—*Author Unknown*

Everyone wants peace, but not all find it because they are looking in the wrong direction. In the Old Testament, the Hebrew word for "peace" is "shalom." In the New Testament, the Greek word for "peace" is "ειρήνη" (eirene) which refers to rest, calmness, to be in agreement or harmony, security, and safety. A key focus of "eirene" is found in Luke 2:14. It was the time when the arrival of Jesus Christ was announced by the angels. *"Glory to God in the highest, and on earth peace, goodwill toward men!"*

In our sinful condition, *"we were enemies"* with God according to Romans 5:10. *"But God commendeth his love toward us, in that, while we were yet sinners, Christ died for us"* (Romans 5:8). The apostle Paul uses the word "eirene" (peace) with a deeper meaning in Romans 5:1: *"Therefore being justified by faith, we have peace with God through our Lord Jesus Christ."* Because of Christ's sacrifice, we are justified and have restored our relationship and fellowship with God, and we have peace with Him. This means "eirene" (peace) is spiritual harmony between God and us after the restoration we have with Him through salvation.

Isaiah predicted a long time ago that Jesus *"shall be called Wonderful, Counsellor, The mighty God, The everlasting Father, The Prince of Peace"* (Isaiah 9:6). The Prince of Peace is the One who is the leader of peace and offers it to others. The good news is that through Christ's work of justification, we can have that peace with God and that peace will keep our hearts and minds secure. *"And the peace of God, which passeth all understanding, shall keep your hearts and minds through Christ Jesus..."* (Philippians 4:7). Before His death, Jesus told His followers that He would give peace to them, which will be different from the peace of the world (John 14:27).

Following His resurrection, we read, *"Then the same day at evening, being the first day of the week, when the doors were shut where the disciples were assembled for fear of the Jews, came Jesus and stood in the midst, and saith unto them, Peace be unto you"* (John 20:19). Only Jesus can provide peace. God's peace is totally different from man's peace. God's peace was made through the blood of Jesus' cross. *"And, having made peace through the blood of his cross, by him to reconcile all things unto himself"* (Colossians 1:20).

True Christians have God's peace even when they go through hard times. I remember having peace when I went through tough and serious times with my cancer. I also remember the time when my first wife unexpectedly passed away at a young age because of a heart attack. One of my neighbors asked me to spend that night with his family. I told him, "Thank you, but I prefer to spend the night with my Lord." I did this because I believed that the peace Jesus gives is not the absence of loss and pain, but is rather the confidence that He is there with me always as He promised. Truly, His presence and peace were in my heart all that night. *"Peace I leave with you, my peace I give unto you: not as the world giveth, give I unto you..."* (John 14:27).

If you have not experienced God's peace in your heart and if you do not know Jesus Christ as your personal Savior, I encourage you to trust in Him today to experience His peace *"which passeth all understanding, shall keep your hearts and minds through Christ Jesus"* (Philippians 4:7).

❖ ❖ ❖

- "Peace is the smile of God reflected in the soul of the believer."
—*New Testament Scholar, William Hendriksen*

6

THE PRINCE OF PEACE

"For unto us a Child is born, Unto us a Son is given;
And the government will be upon His shoulder.
And His name will be called Wonderful, Counselor, Mighty God,
Everlasting Father, Prince of Peace."
Isaiah 9:6

*

The Prince of Peace is Jesus Christ
who is the leader of peace and offers it to others!

Sadly, every year, we witness the world in more turmoil and unrest. "The Personnel Journal reported this incredible statistic: since the beginning of recorded history, the entire world has been at peace less than eight percent of the time! In its study, the periodical discovered that of 3,530 years of recorded history, only 286 years saw peace. Moreover, in excess of 8,000 peace treaties were made - and broken." — *Today In The Word, MBI*

Maybe you ask, "Why?" Only God in His Word gives us the answer by making the solemn pronouncement to all men: *"And the way of peace have they not known"* (Romans 3:17). The Scriptures tell us the source from which this unrest and lack of peace came. There was an atmosphere of peacefulness and restfulness when God placed man in the Garden of Eden. In 1 Corinthians 14:33, we read, *"God is not the author of confusion, but of peace..."* By man, sin came in when Adam and Eve, by the influence of Satan, disobeyed the command of God and became unrighteous and lost God's peace. *"There is no peace, says the Lord, unto the wicked"* (Isaiah 48:22, 57:21). We sometimes wonder why peace treaties do not last long. It is because sin is involved in peace treaties.

In Isaiah 9:6, of the Old Testament, one of the names given prophetically to our Lord is "Prince of Peace." The Prince of Peace is the One who is the leader of peace and offers it to others. In the New Testament, the same person is the Child that was born in Bethlehem, the Son of God who brought *"on earth peace"* (Luke 2:14). He also is the "Lord of peace" (2 Thessalonians 3:16) and the "King of peace" (Hebrews 7:2). His sacrificial death on the cross has provided a way for all men, women, boys, and girls to be eternally set free from sin. This is because, through sin, they had lost their personal relationship and peace with God.

God now provides one way, and the only way for man to regain peace with Him. This way is through the cross of our Lord Jesus Christ as we read in Colossians 1:20: *"And having made peace through the blood of His cross..."* Therefore, the sin, sorrow, breakdown, and distance from God have been dealt with, to God's complete satisfaction, through the precious blood of Christ. Through the death and resurrection of Christ, Satan has been utterly defeated, and the day will arrive when he is banished to the lake of fire forever.

God commands us to seek peace. *"Depart from evil and do good; Seek peace and pursue it"* (Psalm 34:14). In Matthew 5:9, we read, *"Blessed are the peacemakers: for they shall be called the children of God."* We should make every attempt to do what leads to peace, according to Romans 14:19. As believers in Christ we have a responsibility to *"let the peace of God rule"* in our hearts (Colossians 3:15). This means we have to choose either to trust God's promises or to rely on ourselves and reject the peace He offers. *"Peace I leave with you, my peace I give unto you: not as the world giveth, give I unto you. Let not your heart be troubled, neither let it be afraid..."* (John 14:27). *"These things I have spoken unto you, that in me ye might have peace. In the world ye shall have tribulation: but be of good cheer; I have overcome the world"* (John 16:33). According to Galatians 5:22, peace is a fruit of the Holy Spirit, so we will experience His peace if we allow the Spirit of God to rule in our lives.

What is at the top of your wishlist this year? Do you secretly yearn for inner peace, because life is beginning to stress you out? This is a gift that money cannot buy, and friends cannot provide. The gift of true peace can only be provided by the Lord. If you do not know Jesus Christ as your personal Savior, and He has not filled your heart with peace, I have good news for you! Jesus desires to give you a peace that the world can never provide. Reach out to the Lord. Ask Him to reign in your heart. Put Jesus in charge and let Him bear your worries. Let the Prince of Peace bring you a present you will never want to exchange. The peace of God is different from comfort, joy, and rest. While comfort, joy, and rest may decline, your peace will still flow like a river. *"O that thou hadst hearkened to my commandments! then had thy peace been as a river..."* (Isaiah 48:18).

The problem is that the world wants peace without the Prince of Peace.

7

GOD'S GIFT

"Thanks be unto God for his unspeakable gift."
2 Corinthians 9:15

*

God promised His best gift-His Only Son-
in the Old Testament and gave it in the New Testament!

God created mankind to have fellowship with Him, but both Adam and Eve sinned against God by disobeying His command. God, being merciful, did not like to see any of His special creation perish. His eternal plan of love and mercy was to meet the need of man's soul and provide the best gift to fulfill and satisfy his empty heart. This is God's gift, the unspeakable gift of eternal life. *"For the wages of sin is death; but the gift of God is eternal life through Jesus Christ our Lord"* (Romans 6:23).

God made a promise and kept it. He promised His best gift in the Old Testament and gave it in the New Testament. Love always keeps promises. It was God's idea to come to earth and live as a man - Jesus - fully, man, yet fully God. He came for our sake. It was God's gift to us to redeem us from our sin and provide a way of salvation. *"For God so loved the world, that he gave his only begotten Son, that whosoever believeth in him should not perish, but have everlasting life"* (John 3:16). *"Herein is love, not that we loved God, but that he loved us, and sent his Son to be the propitiation for our sins"* (1 John 4:10). This is real love. His gift to us did not cost us anything, but it cost Jesus a lot, His death on the cross (Philippians 2:8). *"But he was wounded for our transgressions, he was bruised for our iniquities: the chastisement of our peace was upon him; and with his stripes, we are healed"* (Isaiah 53:5). During the Christmas season, we have to celebrate and concentrate on the real meaning of Christmas and not follow traditions.

Today, Christmas is expensive and involves hard work. We celebrate Christmas because it is a tradition. God does not command it. From Christian history, we learn that the Christians celebrated the resurrection and not the birth of Christ. They started to celebrate Jesus' birth by the fourth century when the Romans had their feasts—December 25 in the West, January 6 in the East. As Christians, we should not follow the world's traditions at Christmas. It is more meaningful when we celebrate because of gratitude, as we remember God's gift to us, and include it in our Christmas celebrations.

At the first Christmas, Jesus came a long way from heaven to earth. At this time, it is appropriate to tell you the following story: Some time ago there was an American missionary living in a very tiny African village. The young woman was a teacher who labored alongside the natives. One Christmas Eve a little boy from the missionary's class proudly brought her a crudely wrapped gift. The teacher was surprised. This little boy was poor. What could he possibly give? The teacher unwrapped the present and found within the crumpled brown paper an exquisite seashell. The missionary, knowing that the only place to find such shells was many rugged miles away, expressed her enthusiastic appreciation. "My goodness," she told him, "you've traveled so far to bring me such a wonderful present." At first the boy appeared surprised by her reaction, but his eyes quickly brightened and a wide smile crept across his small face. "Oh, teacher," he explained, "long walk part of gift." — *by the President of Focus on the Family, Jim Daly*

The scriptures tell us that the wise men came from far away. When they found Jesus after He was born, they did not give gifts to one another but gave Jesus the best gifts they had: gold, frankincense, and myrrh. Today, Jesus expect a gift from Christians, too. But the only gift He needs from us is our heart. If we truly think about it, Christmas is all about gift-giving. At Christmas, we celebrate the birth of Jesus Christ, the greatest gift ever given, by the greatest gift-giver of all, our wonderful God and Father. God gave the world a special gift at Christmas, His only Son.

During the Christmas season, it is essential that we remember the true meaning of Christmas. *"God our Saviour; Who will have all men to be saved, and to come unto the knowledge of the truth"* (1 Timothy 2:3,4), and He is *"not willing that any should perish, but that all should come to repentance..."* (2 Peter 3:9). This is God's desire and will for us, and so He offers us His Son *"His unspeakable gift"* (2 Corinthians 9:15).

God knows our *problem "For all have sinned, and come short of the glory of God"* (Romans 3:23). God knows that the penalty for our *sin is death. "For the wages of sin is death; but the gift of God is eternal life through Jesus Christ our Lord"* (Romans 6:23). Also, God knows that it is impossible for us to do anything to reconcile ourselves to Him. Because of that, and His unconditional love,

He chose to become one of us in the person of Jesus Christ. He did this to rescue us from our iniquity and keep us from being eternally separated from Him. He took our place voluntarily on the cross, where He died, and with His blood, paid the penalty for our sins. Because Jesus Christ satisfied all of the righteous requirements of the law with His death and resurrection, He now offers you the gift of forgiveness and eternal life. This is the Christmas message: *"For unto you is born this day in the city of David a Saviour, which is Christ the Lord"* (Luke 2:11). *"And she shall bring forth a son, and thou shalt call his name JESUS: for he shall save his people from their sins"* (Matthew 1:21).

God "walked" 2000 years with his people before sending the gift of Jesus. He has walked 2000 more years expressing the significance of Him. Remember, the gift God offers you does not become yours until you receive it. Millions of other people and myself included, have already received this gift and are eternally grateful for the blessings it has brought. Forgiveness of sins, eternal life, peace with God, and much more are all wrapped up in this valuable gift of God's beloved Son.

One year, a few days before Christmas, a shipping company delivered two big boxes to me. When I opened them, I found an expensive laptop computer and an excellent big monitor. After I read the message inside, I found out that it was a Christmas gift from my beloved son. At that time, I had two choices—send back this expensive gift or to keep and enjoy it. Because it was a gift, I never thought to send it back. I kept it and called my son and thanked him for his love and for his generous gift.

If you have never accepted Jesus by faith into your life, I am challenging you to accept Him as your very own Savior and start your personal relationship with Him. Today, you can reject God's gift or accept it. This is your choice. Just like the choice, I had to reject my son's gift or to accept it. I hope and pray you will accept the gift of love which you cannot find in the most expensive store. If you accept it, you will find Jesus Christ to be the best gift you have ever received. *"For by grace are ye saved through faith; and that not of yourselves: it is the gift of God"* (Ephesians 2:8,9).

❖ ❖ ❖

- "God walked down the stairs of heaven with a Baby in his arms." — *Dr. Paul E. Scherer* [His only Son, to provide eternal life to everyone who will receive it!]

- "I grew up in a Christian home but was nearly 17 before I realized I had to make my own decision to place my trust in Christ. Salvation cannot be earned by doing good works or going to church, and can't be automatically passed on from Christian parents. Salvation is a free gift from God, who sent His Son Jesus Christ to die in our place." — *Dr. Drew Pinsky*

8

CHRISTMAS

"And the Word (Jesus) was made flesh, and dwelt among us..."
John 1:14

"And she shall bring forth a son, and thou shall call his name JESUS: for he shall save his people from their sins."
Matthew 1:21

*

At the first Christmas, a Savior was born for you and me!

A television interviewer was walking streets of Tokyo at Christmas time. Much as in America, Christmas shopping is a big commercial success in Japan. The interviewer stopped one young woman on the sidewalk, and asked, "What is the meaning of Christmas?" Laughing, she responded, "I don't know. Is that the day that Jesus died?" — *by Donald Deffner, Seasonal Illustrations*

Many people celebrate Christmas without knowing much about it. As the years pass, people at Christmas time give more attention to traditional requirements such as decorations, songs, special meals and especially the exchanging of gifts with relatives and friends. All of these are wonderful, but this is not the true meaning of Christmas.

When the stores are in competition to put up better displays of decorations, and the pressure is increased on people to buy more expensive gifts, they easily lose sight of a meaningful Christmas. When we take away the commercialism and traditions of our culture that includes the celebration of Christmas, it becomes easier to see the true meaning of Christmas. The Christmas story from the Bible comes alive as we focus on Christ, *"For unto you is born this day in the city of David a Savior, which is Christ the Lord"* (Luke 2:11).There is nothing more fundamental at Christmas than to celebrate the birth of Jesus Christ, who is the Son of God. The message of Christmas is so important and such a blessing to each one of us, but it is often missed by many.

Sometimes, people think that the birth of Jesus is only an interesting fact of history and not related to our present life, but it has a direct effect on our lives. When the birth of Jesus was announced to the shepherds, the angel said to them, *"Fear not: for, behold, I bring you good tidings of great joy, which shall be to all people. For unto you is born this day in the city of David a Saviour, which is Christ the Lord"* (Luke 2:10,11).

Maybe you have never thought that the Lord was born for you. Perhaps you did not realize why God sent His Son into the world. He sent Him to become your Savior. Be careful and give special attention to what the herald angel said, *"for unto you is born...a Savior."* Yes! Jesus left His glory and came to be born for you because your greatest need was forgiveness, and you needed a Savior. Charles Sell wonderfully described our need as follows:

- "If our greatest need had been information, God would have sent us an **educator.**
- If our greatest need had been technology, God would have sent us a **scientist.**
- If our greatest need had been money, God would have sent us an **economist.**
- If our greatest need had been pleasure, God would have sent us an **entertainer.**
- But our greatest need was forgiveness, so God sent us a **Savior."** — *Unfinished Business, Charles Sell, 1989 pp. 121ff*

Jesus came to deal with the problem of sin, which separates every one of us from God. *"Christ Jesus came into the world to save sinners..."* (1 Timothy 1:15). Maybe you will say, "I'm not a sinner!" Have you ever lied or had a sinful thought? God's Word tells us that all of us are sinners. *"For all have sinned, and come short of the glory of God"* (Romans 3:23).

Usually, people do not realize that they are sinners, and *"every one of us shall give an account of himself to God"* (Romans 14:12). But the best good news is that God gives us the opportunity to solve the problem of sin by believing on His son. *"He that believeth on the Son hath everlasting life: and he that believeth not the Son shall not see life; but the wrath of God abideth on him"* (John 3:36). After all, the true meaning of Christmas becomes clear, and we are able to see that Christmas is all about God's special love for us and the precious gift that He offers us; the gift of eternal life. *"For the wages of sin is death; but the gift of God is eternal life hrough Jesus Christ our Lord"* (Romans 6:23).

The Baby, who was born in the manger, is the Lord of the Universe. Jesus was born fully human and was still fully divine. He is Emmanuel, God with us! When born in Bethlehem, Jesus did not just then become the Son of God, but He always was, is, and will be: *"Jesus Christ the same yesterday, and today, and forever"* (Hebrews 13:8).

"For unto us a child is born, unto us a son is given..." (Isaiah 9:6). We do not realize that this verse presents two important truths: The Son of God is fully human and fully God. In the first part of the verse, according to the prophet Isaiah, Jesus became a man: *"a Child is born."* Also, when the evangelist Luke wrote, *"For unto you is born this day in the city of David a Saviour, which is Christ the Lord"* (Luke 2:11), it brings the same message. In both Greek and Hebrew, the word for "born" means the same thing: "child-bearing."

The second part of the verse in Isaiah says that the *"Son is given."* He emphasizes and refers to eternal sonship, the relationship between a father and son. In Hebrew, the word "given" does not refer to birth, but to "bring" the Son, who is the Son of God, who already existed. *"In the beginning was the Word [Jesus] and the Word was with God, and the Word was God. The same was in the beginning with God. All things were made by him [Jesus], and without him [Jesus] was not anything made that was made. In him [Jesus] was life; and the life was the light of men"* (John 1:1-4). *"For God sent not his Son into the world to condemn the world; but that the world through him might be saved" (John 3:17).*

The sinless One, Jesus Christ, died on the cross to pay for our sins. He is risen from the dead, and to everyone who will confess their sins to Him, and trust Him as their Savior, He offers eternal life as God promises in John 3:16. This is explicit to the heart of Christmas. We have to think about how our lives would be if Jesus had never come. We would be unforgiven sinners without salvation, without hope, and with no prepared eternal home.

A few years ago a striking Christmas card was published, with the title, "If Christ had not come." It was founded upon our Saviour's words, *"If I had not come."* The card represented a clergyman falling into a short sleep in his study on Christmas morning and dreaming of a world into which Jesus had never come.

In his dream he found himself looking through his home, but there were no little stockings in the chimney corner, no Christmas bells or wreaths of holly, and no Christ to comfort, gladden and save. He walked out on the public street, but there was no church with its spire pointing to Heaven. He came back and sat down in his library, but every book about the Saviour had disappeared.

A ring at the door-bell, and a messenger asked him to visit a poor dying mother. He hastened with, the weeping child, and as he reached the home, he sat down and said, "I have something here that will comfort you." He opened his Bible to look for a familiar promise, but it ended at Malachi, and there was no gospel and no promise of hope and salvation, and he could only bow his head and weep with her in bitter despair.

Two days afterward he stood beside her coffin and conducted the funeral service, but there was no message of consolation, no word of a glorious resurrection, no open Heaven, but only "dust to dust, ashes to ashes," and one long eternal farewell. He realized at length that "He had not come," and burst into tears and bitter weeping in his sorrowful dream. Suddenly he woke with a start, and a great shout of joy and praise burst from his lips as he heard his choir singing in his church close by:

> O come, all ye faithful, joyful and triumphant,
> O come ye, O come ye to Bethlehem;
> O come and behold Him, born the King of Angels,
> O come let us adore Him, Christ, the Lord.

Let us be glad and rejoice today because "He has come." And let us remember the annunciation of the angel, *"Behold I bring you good tidings of great joy, which shall be to all people, for unto you is born this day in the city of David a Saviour, which is Christ the Lord"* (Luke 2:10, 11). — *by L.B. Cowman/ streams in the desert/ crosswalk.com*

Jesus is God's greatest gift of love. Jesus gave His life *"that they might have life, and that they might have it more abundantly"* (John 10:10). Without any question, love came down from heaven at Christmas. Jesus loved us so much that He came to die on the cross for our sins. What better Christmas gift could we give others than to share His love with them that they might have eternal life? Love is a gift our world desperately needs this Christmas season.

If you are not a Christian, and you have never made Jesus your personal Savior, it is time to do it now. If you do it, you can celebrate the true meaning of Christmas! Be mindful that Jesus came to be your Savior. He was born personally for *you*. He died on the cross to pay for your sins. Yes! He died personally for you. This kind of personal message of God's love, mercy, and grace also requires a personal response from you. Jesus Christ is God's gift to you, and He wants you to receive that gift. *"For God so loved the world, that He gave His only begotten Son, that whosoever believeth in Him should not perish, but have everlasting life"* (John 3:16).

To receive God's gift, you must by faith believe that Christ was born for you to be your Savior and that He died for you to pay for your sins. He has risen from the dead, and He offers you eternal life. Do not forget that Jesus died for all the sinners, but forgives only the ones who repent and by faith receive Him as their personal Savior. *"But as many as received him, to them gave he power to become the sons of God, even to them that believe on his name"* (John 1:12). Receive the gift of God this year if you desire this Christmas to be the best for all eternity. *"For by grace are ye saved through faith; and that not of yourselves: it is the gift of God"* (Ephesians 2:8,9).

Christmas is also a time to give and not only to receive. Christmas is not about the number of gifts purchased or how much money is spent to impress your relatives and friends. Christmas is the love in your heart. Share this love with those as Jesus Christ has shared it with you. Christmas is about the birth of Jesus, whom God sent to persuade the world how much He really loves us. He left His heavenly home in glory and came to die for us and pay our debt. If you have accepted Jesus by faith as your personal Savior, you now have secured a heavenly home for eternity. After this, from joy, let everyone know you have a friend in Jesus and show His love to others at Christmas and each day of your life! Because of His Love, I am who I am, and I am here to share these thoughts and truths of eternal value. *"Thanks be unto God for His unspeakable gift"* (2 Corinthians 9:15).

At Christmas time, do not be ashamed to loudly wish everyone "Merry Christmas" instead of "Happy Holidays." Let people know that you are one who has heard and received the good news of Christmas. Let people know you are not just shopping for a winter festival, but you are celebrating your Lord's birth. Christmas is not just a holiday - It is a birthday! By wishing a "Merry Christmas," the evil forces of darkness in our nation will be influenced. The Light of the World will be proclaimed. The hope of salvation will be announced, and the spiritual atmosphere will be brightened by the presence of God.

As a Christian, be careful what you watch over the Christmas season. When Jesus was born, God flooded the airways of the earth with special religious programming through a host of angels. Make sure you do the same. Turn to Christian radio and television stations this Christmas season and attend a Bible-believing church that presents Christ as God's Son and the Savior of sinful men. Let the message of Jesus be the "favorite" in your heart and on the button of your remote control this Christmas!

❖ ❖ ❖

- "The mystery of the humanity of Christ, that He sunk Himself into our flesh, is beyond all human understanding." — *Priest and Theologian, Martin Luther*

- The Son of God became a man to enable men to become the sons of God." — *Scholar and Author, C.S. Lewis*

- "You can never truly enjoy Christmas until you can look up into the Father's face and tell him you have received his Christmas gift." — *Dr. John R. Rice*

9

NEW YEAR-WILL OF GOD

"Boast not thyself of tomorrow;
for thou knowest not what a day may bring forth."
Proverbs. 27:1

"And the world passeth away, and the lust thereof:
but he that doeth the will of God abideth for ever."
1 John 2:17

*

Obedience to the will of God is of supreme value and is our only safety in the New Year!

Many people, even some Christians, live their own way and care only to fulfill their desires. They live by their will and not the will of God. They spend all their lives to satisfy themselves and pursue their own glory. They never realize the real purpose of their lives in this temporary and mortal world. They only start to think differently when tragedy happens to them, and they are disappointed when they find out that their will is not worth much compared to God's will.

A year untried before me lies.
What it shall bring of strange surprise,
Of joy, or grief, I cannot tell;
But God my Father knows well.
I make it no concern of mine,
But leave it all with Love Divine.

— By R.M.Offord

The magazine article summarized the life of a former winning NCAA basketball coach and network sports announcer. Throughout his colorful coaching career, he had been obsessed with the game and with winning. But years later, stricken with cancer, he came to realize the triviality of the goods and values to which he had been passionately devoted. "You get sick, and you say to yourself, 'Sports means nothing,' and that feels terrible." Because he had spent little time with his wife and children, he confessed, "I figured I'd have 20 years in the big time, who knows, maybe win three national titles, then pack it in at 53 or 54 . . . . I was going to make it all up to them, all the time I'd been away . . . . It sounds so silly now . . . . But it went on and on, that insatiable desire to conquer the world." — *Our Daily Bread, October 17, 1997*

Christians must not only grow and understand God's will, but they must also grow in obedience. Obedience is the key to God's heart. Obedience is one of the most critical responsibilities of the believer. The Lord rewards their obedience. *"Then spake Jesus again unto them, saying, I am the light of the world: he that followeth me shall not walk in darkness, but shall have the light of life"* (John 8:12), *"and to desire that ye might be filled with the knowledge of his will in all wisdom and spiritual understanding; That ye might walk worthy of the Lord unto all pleasing, being fruitful in every good work, and increasing in the knowledge of God"* (Colossians 1:9,10).

As long as we are close to God, we will be able to know His will. The apostle John tells us how important it is to follow God's will: *"And the world passeth away, and the lust thereof: but he that doeth the will of God abideth for ever"* (1 John 2:17). John expected that anyone who is born of God would obey the will of God. Throughout the epistle, he describes this kind of lifestyle. Obedience to the will of God is of supreme value, and it is not optional for the born–again believer. Preacher A.J. Gordon once said, *"If the Lord's business is made your principal business, I assure you that you will repeatedly have divine guidance in your Christian life."*

There are times we make a mistake when we think that God is not guiding us because we cannot see far ahead of us. However, this is not His technique. He only guarantees the steps which the Lord gives us, not the next mile. *"The steps of a good man are ordered by the LORD: and he delighteth in his way"* (Psalm 37:23). J. Oswald Sanders states: *"It is our duty to do our duty."* Our responsibility is only to do our duty, which will cover a large area of our life, and for the rest, we have to wait for God's guidance.

God shows His will to us, primarily in two ways. First, through His Spirit: *"Howbeit when he, the Spirit of truth, is come, he will guide you into all truth: for he shall not speak of himself; but whatsoever he shall hear, that shall he speak: and he will shew you things to come"* (John 16:13). Second, God makes known His will through His Word: *"Thy word is a lamp unto my feet, and a light unto my path"* (Psalm 119:105).

If you are a good man or woman of God, do not wonder what lies ahead in the New Year. Do not be confused or afraid. It is a matter of obedience to God's will because God is in control. You will be energized by God's power when you trust in grace while you obey in faith. Rest in God's sufficient power. Live like He asks, and you will face the future with confidence when you do what is right. You will never regret your actions as the NCAA basketball coach mentioned above.

• Once a country preacher was teaching his Sunday School class when Mrs. Smith appeared confused. "Pastor," inquired the elderly lady, "I am a little confused about the doctrine of election. Could you explain it more clearly?" The pastor cleared his throat and replied, "You know what an election is when we elect the President. It is the same in the Kingdom of God. There is always an election going on. Only three votes are cast. The Lord is always voting for you. The devil is always voting against you, but you have the deciding vote!" — *Author Unknown*

The Bible says, *"No man can serve two masters: for either he will hate the one, and love the other; or else he will hold to the one, and despise the other..."* (Matthew 6:24). In our lives, we have to make a decision to serve the Lord or the devil. Seeking the will of God will help us to make the right decisions. He is glad to reveal His will to those who are hungry and thirsty to follow His directions. *"Behold, the eye of the LORD is upon them that fear him, upon them that hope in his mercy"* (Psalm 33:18). When we make decisions, we must have the same attitude as Jesus when He said, *"not my will, but thine, be done"* (Luke 22:42).

• Former President Ronald Reagan once had an aunt who took him to a cobbler for a pair of new shoes. The cobbler asked young Reagan, "Do you want square toes or round toes?" Unable to decide, Reagan did not answer, so the cobbler gave him a few days. Several days later the cobbler saw Reagan on the street and asked him again what kind of toes he wanted on his shoes. Reagan still could not decide, so the shoemaker replied, "Well, come by in a couple of days. Your shoes will be ready." When the future president did so, he found one square-toed and one round-toed shoe! "This will teach you to never let people make decisions for you," the cobbler said to his indecisive customer. "I learned then and there," Reagan said later, "if you don't make your own decisions, someone else will" —*Today in the Word, MBI, August, 1991*

If we do not make the right decision, we will pay for it now and will regret it in the future. Our success or failure in life depends upon our decisions and choices. Every day we are making decisions. Our decisions form and build the complexity of our lives and the structure of our personality and character. The choices we make will affect the directions of our life, but the decision we make in this life about Jesus Christ will forever set our eternal destiny. For the ones who accept the Lord Jesus as Savior, the matter of making a choice is still open regarding how that Christian life shall be lived.

We have numerous examples in the Bible where people made right and wrong choices. For example, *Abram* made the right choice, but not *Lot.*

> *"And Lot lifted up his eyes, and beheld all the plain of Jordan, that it was well watered every where...Then Lot chose him all the plain of Jordan; and Lot journeyed east: and they separated themselves the one from the other. Abram dwelled in the land of Canaan, and Lot dwelled in the cities of the plain, and pitched his tent toward Sodom. But the men of Sodom were wicked and sinners before the LORD exceedingly"* (Genesis 13:10-13).

We also see the right choice *Moses* made. As a result of it, God used him. *"Choosing rather to suffer affliction with the people of God, than to enjoy the pleasures of sin for a season"* (Hebrews 11:25).

As a young man, I made the decision to follow and serve the Lord. Joshua 24:15 says, *"choose you this day whom ye will serve... but as for me and my house, we will serve the LORD."* This verse had a tremendous impact on my heart and daily life. I framed this verse, and I placed it above the door in the entryway of the kitchen in my house. On the way out, next to my front door is the verse, *"be strong in the Lord..."* (Ephesians 6: 10). Whenever people come to my home, these verses become visible to them and sometimes become a subject of discussion. Sometimes, people cannot leave without being convicted by God's Word - even if I may not speak a word to them.

In our lives, we have to make a decision to serve God or the devil. The question for you is: "Do you want to live closer to the Lord this year?" The choice is yours. God has promised to be with you and for you. You merely need to align your will with His. This is one election you need to be sure to vote for the winning party! This is the most important choice you have to make and follow this year and the years to come. God always honors the choices you make for Him. Remember, King David said, *"let us fall now into the hand of the LORD; for his mercies are great..."* (2 Samuel 24:14). David had sinned against God. However, by choosing to fall into God's hands, the Lord forgave him, uplifted him, and blessed him. David realized that God's arm is strong to strike, but His love is strong to save.

The strength, purpose, and effectiveness of your Christian life will depend upon what goes on in secret between you and God. You need to spend time in His presence day by day. May it be said of you, as it was said of Mary: *"Mary hath chosen that good part, which shall not be taken away from her"*

(Luke 10:42). The choice is yours. I hope and pray your choice will be for the Lord this year as King David and Mary chose, and you and your house will serve Him with all your heart. It is the only way to be a "shoe-in" for an abundant life! Remember, a life lived for self will end at the grave. A life lived for Christ by serving Him, will have an eternal impact!

❖ ❖ ❖

• "What the New Year brings to you will depend a great deal on what you bring to the New Year." — *Author, Vern McLellan*

• "God always gives His best to those who leave the choice with him." — *Missionary, Jim Elliot*

• "The center of God's will is our only safety."—*Author, Corrie ten Boom*

• "Every time you make a choice, you are turning the central part of you, the part that chooses, into something a little different from what it was before." — *Scholar and Author, C. S. Lewis*

**If you are a good man or woman of God,
do not wonder what lies ahead in the New Year.
Do not be confused or afraid.
It is a matter of obedience to God's will
because God is in control.
You will be energized by God's power
when you trust in grace while you obey in faith.
Rest in God's sufficient power.**

10

THE CROSS OF CHRIST

*"Christ hath redeemed us from the curse of the law,
being made a curse for us: for it is written,
Cursed is every one that hangeth on a tree [cross]."*
Galatians 3:13

*"When Jesus therefore had received the vinegar, he said,
It is finished: and he bowed his head,
and gave up the ghost [spirit]."*
John 19:3

*

**Jesus died on the Cross for us to pay our debt
which was impossible for us to pay and by His blood
to have redemption and forgiveness of our sins.**

In the New Testament, the Greek word for "it is finished" is "tetelestai" which means complete. Jesus meant that all the scriptures were fulfilled with His death. The word "tetelestai" was also written on receipts in New Testament times to show that a bill had been paid in full. The relationship between receipts and what Christ accomplished on the cross was clear to the apostle John. He used the Greek word "tetelestai" in his writings because for him, there was no doubt that Jesus Christ had died and paid in full for their sins.

When we celebrate Easter, it is appropriate for us to reflect on the importance of the death of Jesus on the cross. Do you ever ask yourself why Jesus suffered so much and died on the cross? The answer is simple — to pay for our sins. He suffered physically and emotionally. First, Christ suffered at the hands of his friends: Judas betrayed him, Peter denied Him, and all the disciples forsook Him. Second, He suffered at the hands of His enemies: they mocked Him, tortured Him, condemned Him, and crucified Him. Third, the deepest level of Christ's suffering was not at the hands of his friends or his enemies, but at the hands of God. I believe the twenty–seventh chapter of the gospel of Matthew is one that every Christian must frequently read to keep in his heart, mind, and soul the agony that Jesus went through. No one can imagine or describe the tragedy that happened on Calvary, where Jesus, the son of God, died for our sins.

• Many ask who crucified Jesus. A good answer comes from Dr. Adrian Rogers, "Well, you say the Jews crucified Jesus. Well, let me remind you that his apostles were Jews, the disciples were Jews. Well, you say the Romans crucified Jesus. Ha, well, the Roman soldiers were carrying out orders. Well, you say uh, we crucified Jesus. Now, you're getting closer to the truth. The truth of the matter is that we all had a part in the crucifixion of Jesus. We sing that song, 'Were you there when they crucified my Lord?' and that's a good question to ask. When Dr. R. G. Lee went for the first time to the Holy Lands, he went to that place that so many people love to go, that place called Calvary. When he stood there, the person who was giving the lecture asked this question. 'Have any of you ever been here before?' and Dr. Lee put up his hand. 'Oh,' he said 'When were you here before?' Dr. Lee said, 'One thousand years ago. He was there, I was there, we were there because our sins crucified Jesus. Our hands slapped him, our spit was the spit that defiled his face, our sins were the nails that sealed him to that cross, and our hard hearts were the hammers that drove those nails." — *hvf.org*

According to the following verses, Jesus died on the Cross for us, to pay our debt, which was impossible for us to pay and by His blood to have redemption and forgiveness of our sins. *"He [Jesus] humbled himself, and became obedient unto death, even the death of the cross"* (Philippians 2:8), *"Who his own self bare our sins in his own body on the tree [cross]"* (1 Peter 2:24a), *"In whom we have redemption through his blood, the forgiveness of sins, according to the riches of his grace"* (Ephesians 1:7), *"For God so loved the world, that he gave his only begotten Son, that whosoever believeth in him should not perish, but have everlasting life"* (John 3:16), *"For the preaching of the cross is to them that perish foolishness; but unto us which are saved it is the power of God"* (1 Corinthians 1:18).

When Jesus was crucified, only a few people that day understood the importance of his death. Some thought he was an innocent victim of political jealousies. Others saw Jesus as being justly punished for claiming to be the Messiah. The true meaning was prophesied centuries before by the prophet Isaiah that Jesus would give His life to save sinners. The cross is an emblem of Christianity and holds special meaning for every true believer. Whenever we see a cross, it reminds us that Christ died for us on Calvary.

In the twenty-seventh chapter of Matthew, we not only see who but more specifically, what crucified the Lord Jesus. On the cross, Christ gave His life to pay for my sins and yours, because He loves us. The question is: "Do you doubt God's love for you?" Have difficult circumstances caused you to wonder if He truly cares? Although the Lord may seem silent at this time, He reminds you of His love through the cross of Christ. The death of His Son is a constant reminder of His unconditional love for you.

When you feel He is far from you, let His hands do His talking. I hope you appreciate His sacrifice. Jesus came to pay a bill that He did not owe because we owed a bill we could not pay. He took upon himself our punishment so we can be set free from sin to serve God. If you never accepted Jesus as your Savior, do it now. He will rescue you from death and sin. What a privilege to know Him and be included in His words to His disciples that no longer He will call you servant but a friend (John. 15:15).

❖ ❖ ❖

- "The Cross of Jesus is the supreme evidence of the love of God." — *Evangelist and Teacher, Oswald Chambers*

- "There are no crown wearers in heaven who are not cross bearers below." — *Prince of Preachers," Charles Spurgeon*

- "We need men of the cross, with the message of the cross, bearing the marks of the cross." — *Evangelist, Vance Havner*

**Jesus died on the Cross for us,
to pay our debt,
which was impossible for us to pay and
by His blood
to have redemption and
forgiveness of our sins.**

11

THE LAMB OF GOD

"Behold the Lamb of God [Jesus], which taketh away the sin of the world."
John 1:29

Love Of God
For God, so loved YOU. (John 3:16)
He provided the Lamb. (Genesis 22:8)

The Precious Blood of Christ
"Without shedding of blood is no remission [of sins]."
Hebrews 9:22

During the Easter season, the verse above, John 1:29, is quoted in sermons, in Sunday School, and in Bible studies. These words came from the mouth of the last prophet, John the Baptist when he saw Jesus for the first time. In this verse, he proclaimed one of the greatest truths of the gospel. In the original Greek text, the word is "sin" in this verse. However, people, Christians, and religious leaders often misquote this verse and replace "sin" with "sins." You may wonder if it really matters and what is the difference. Yes, there is a difference, and it really matters, because it contradicts the teaching and meaning of the Word of God.

As we know, both the apostles Paul and Peter declared that the Lord Himself bore their sins upon the cross. *"So Christ was once offered to bear the sins of many; and unto them that look for him shall he appear the second time without sin unto salvation"* (Hebrews 9:28), and *"Who his own self bare our sins in his own body on the tree, that we, being dead to sins, should live unto righteousness: by whose stripes ye were healed"* (1 Peter 2:24). This assurance gives peace to each believer and a righteous basis to worship God.

Each Christian is encouraged to boldly enter into the presence of God by the blood of Jesus which has purged his sins according to Hebrews 10:19: *"Having therefore, brethren, boldness to enter into the holiest by the blood of Jesus."* Notice that this is only true for the believer and does not apply to the unbeliever. He is far off in guilt and condemnation. *"He that believeth on him is not condemned: but he that believeth not is condemned already because he hath not believed in the name of the only begotten Son of God"* (John 3:18). If Christ, as the Lamb of God takes away the "sins" of the world, all people would stand sinless before Him, but this is not true according to the Bible.

Yes, Jesus Christ is *"the Lamb of God,"* which takes away the sin of the world. Yes, Jesus died for all people, but He gives forgiveness of sins only to whoever believes in Him. This means "whoever" in the whole world will believe in Jesus Christ has forgiveness of his sins, but whoever rejects Jesus, must die in his sins. *"I said therefore unto you, that ye shall die in your sins: for if ye believe not that I am he, ye shall die in your sins"* (John 8:24). This is because "whoever" refused the message of God's grace. *"He that believeth on the Son hath everlasting life: and he that believeth not the Son shall not see life; but the wrath of God abideth on him"* (John 3:36).

The word "behold" in verse (John 1:29) means to look at, or watch carefully, or to take a closer look at Jesus. The prince of preachers, C.H. Spurgeon, tells us what the phrase, *"the Lamb of God"* means: "Nothing But The Best," "God's Appointed One," "God's Great Provision," and "God's Supreme Offering." Also, Christ is called *"the Lamb of God"* because He was provided by God. Jesus is the Father's only begotten Son and to all of us, *"His"* unbelievable and *"unspeakable gift"* (2 Corinthians 9:15).

God sent His only begotten Son to die for us. *"He that spared not his own Son, but delivered him up for us all..."* Romans 8:32). *"Herein is love, not that we loved God, but that he loved us, and sent his Son to be the propitiation for our sins"* (1 John 4:10). In the Old Testament law, men were required to provide the sacrifices. However, the one sacrifice in the New Testament is the gift of God, His own Son who died for our sins. C.H. Spurgeon said plainly, *"Now then, sinner, do you want to be rid of your sin? God's way of pardoning you is that your sin be laid on Jesus. As of old the Jew laid his hands upon the lamb and the lamb was his substitute, so lay your trembling hands by faith upon Christ, and He will be your Substitute! Oh that you were led to receive Him now to be yours forever!"*

If you are not a believer in Christ, I hope you will follow the advice above given by C.H. Spurgeon. Do not become a CARELESS SINNER or SELF-RIGHTEOUS SINNER, but a BURDENED AND BROKEN SINNER. Become a sincere, repentant sinner. Come with a broken heart and soul to him by faith to take away your sins, and do not ignore His encouraging invitation: *"And him that cometh to me I will in no wise cast out"* (John 6:37). Remember that all people are God's creatures, but not all people are children of God according to John 1:12: *"But as many as received him, to them gave he power to become the sons of God..."* It will be a blessing for you to become a CHILD OF GOD and FOLLOWER OF JESUS CHRIST.

All who become redeemed children of God by the blood of the Lamb are not only free from the guilt of sin but also from the power of sin. As we behold the Lamb of God as the foundation of our eternal hope, let us also follow His steps in all humility and patience, honesty, and holiness. Let us never forget that *"we are His workmanship, created in Christ Jesus unto good works, which God has before ordained that we should walk in them"* (Ephesians 2:10). If you have never received Christ by faith as your personal Savior, do it now. If you refuse His cleansing blood, you will die in your sins and be eternally lost!

❖ ❖ ❖

- "Either sin is with you, lying on your shoulders, or it is lying on Christ, the Lamb of God. Now if it is lying on your back, you are lost; but if it is resting on Christ, you are free, and you will be saved. Now choose what you want." — *Priest and Theologian, Martin Luther*

- "Salvation comes through a cross and a crucified Christ." —*Pastor and Author, Andrew Murray*

- "Salvation is so simple that we overlook it; so profound that we never comprehend it; so free we can't believe it." — *Dr. Paul White*

Jesus, the Lamb of God, gave His whole life for you. Such love demands your whole life. Give your all to Christ, who gave His all for you.

12

THE BLOOD OF JESUS

"Without shedding of blood is no remission."
Hebrews 9:22

*

The precious blood of Jesus Christ
is the foundation of our redemption!

People, even some Christians today, do not know the significant reason for the Easter celebration. One time before Easter, I had the opportunity to talk with a young lady and her two sons. She was a very nice religious lady, but she was not a spiritual person. She told me how she prepared for Easter with all the traditions of Easter eggs and the Easter Bunny without mentioning the real meaning of Easter—the resurrection of Jesus Christ. When I told her what is more important for me at Easter and why, she gave me the idea that she had never heard this in her church in all of her life, or she never gave proper attention to the preaching. She had never learned why Jesus Christ came to this world, why He shed His blood on the cross, why He died, why He was resurrected and what He offers to those who believe in Him.

Maybe you too have been going to church all your life and follow and practice all the Easter traditions, but you have never realized that the death sentence of an innocent man—Jesus Christ—changed not only the course of history but changed the course of eternity. From Jesus' arrest, trial, and execution came good news—salvation. From injustice came justice, and from His death and resurrection came the hope of eternal life. I will present to you a few interesting stories to explain to you more clearly why Jesus Christ, the Lamb of God, died and shed His blood. Also, I will present the importance and power of His blood for you and what you have to do to receive eternal life.

- In a little town in the Middle East, Ahmad and a friend were up high on some scaffolding repairing the side of a building. Ahmad lost his footing and fell. Horrified by the accident, his friend climbed down to his aid, expecting to see Ahmad's broken and fractured body. To his surprise, he found that Ahmad was not hurt! At the exact moment Ahmad fell, a shepherd was driving a flock of sheep under the scaffolding. Ahmad fell on the back of one of the sheep, killing it, but saving him. Ahmad got up and looked at the lifeless animal and sighed, "It died for me!" — *Source Unknown*

- The great English preacher Charles Spurgeon was preparing for a series of special meetings in the great Agricultural Hall in London. He visited the building the day before the crusade to test the acoustics. In a booming tone, Spurgeon's voice rang out over the empty building, *"Behold the Lamb of God, which taketh away the sin of the world."* A workman painting on a scaffold up in the ceiling, heard Spurgeon say just those few words and was convicted. The man promptly went home, knelt before the Lord, and found his salvation. *"Forasmuch as ye know that ye were not redeemed with corruptible things, as silver and gold...but with the precious blood of Christ..."* (1 Peter 1:18,19). — *Source Unknown*

- It is said that Luther, during a serious illness, seemed to see Satan coming to him with a great scroll on which were written all the sins and errors of his life. Looking at him with a triumphant smile, he unrolled it before the saint: "These are your sins. There is no hope of your going to heaven." Luther read the long list with growing consternation when suddenly it flashed upon his mind that there was one thing not written there. He said aloud, "One thing you have forgotten. The rest is all true, but one thing you have forgotten: The blood of Jesus Christ cleanseth from all sins." — *by H. Sayles, One Thousand Evangelistic Illustrations*

- G. Campbell Morgan was preaching to coal miners in Yorkshire, England. One miner doubted that forgiveness is won simply by faith. It was too cheap. Morgan asked the man how he got out of the coal pit each day. "The way I always do. I get into the elevator cage and go to the top," replied the worker. "How much do you pay to get out of the pit?" The astonished miner cried, "Pay? I don't pay anything, of course." Morgan said to him, "You weren't afraid to trust yourself in that cage? Wasn't it too cheap?" "Oh, no," he said, "It was free for me, but it cost the company a lot of money to build that shaft" — *Source Unknown*

- A young man was seriously injured in a two-car collision. He had a ruptured spleen, rib fractures, and a contused kidney. Surgeons said, "We must operate immediately." The young man and his wife said, "Go ahead." "You have lost a great amount of blood, and we cannot operate without a blood transfusion. Without it, you would probably die on the operating table!" said the surgeons. The patient and his wife flatly refused to allow blood transfusions. The surgeons argued and pleaded with the couple for hours, but the patient said, "My religion forbids me to submit to a blood transfusion!" The surgeons were helpless as they watched the man die. — *Source Unknown.*

The lamb died, and Ahmad's life was saved. Do you know that there is another lamb who gave its life so others could live? That was Jesus, the Lamb of God who died for us and paid our sins with His own blood. *"In whom we have redemption through his blood, the forgiveness of sins, according to the riches of his grace,"* (Ephesians 1:7) and *"Unto him that loved us, and washed us from our sins in his own blood"* (Revelation 1:5).

Has your sin cast you into a pit of despair? Do you know his forgiveness? God sent Jesus, His only Son, to die as a sacrifice for the sins of the world. He died for you on the cross, the just for the unjust. Do you know the path to God costs nothing? Salvation in Christ is free, but it is not cheap. Your forgiveness came at the price of Jesus' death on the cross. Remember, the way out of the "pit" cost your heavenly Boss a whole lot. Look to the Lamb of God to save you from an eternal fall. He died for you. Receive Him today as your Savior as I did when I was a young man. If you refuse His cleansing blood, you will die in your sin and be eternally lost! I hope and pray you will do as many others did and be eternally grateful.

Betty Cuthbert, the Australian athlete, said,
"My salvation was a free gift. I didn't have to work for it, and it's better than any gold medal that I've ever won."

Also, the gospel hymn by Edward More states:
"My hope is built on nothing less than Jesus' blood and righteousness."

Numerous theologians and Christian authors do not even talk about the blood or the power of "Jesus' blood" for man's redemption. Instead, they use other words that do not exist in the original text of the New Testament. Blood is very important and necessary to the doctrine of Christ's atonement and is mentioned over 300 times in the Bible. It is at the heart of the gospel, and it is through *"the blood of his cross"* that Jesus reconciled us to God (Colossians 1:20-23). In some Christian churches, they do not even sing hymns like "Saved By The Blood" and "Power In the Blood," because of their humanistic beliefs. They keep the real teachings of the Bible at a distance and do not allow the power of the

Holy Spirit to work in their lives, and they miss God's power and blessings. We are redeemed and *"justified by his blood"* (Romans 5:8,9). Never forget, only Christ and His sacrifice on the cross can redeem your soul. Do not be deceived by the fake "yellow gospel" of works that is powerless to save your soul.

Several years ago, a theologian with a Ph.D. and author of several books, translated the New Testament from the original Greek text into today's modern language. He asked me to check his transcripts since I was a Greek person and a Greek teacher with many years of education in the modern and ancient Greek language. I made many corrections, including those concerning the blood of Jesus. Every place that the original Greek text used the word "Jesus' blood" as mentioned in the verses above, he translated as just "death of Christ." We had debates about these kinds of areas because of the importance of Bible doctrine. Later, he called me and said that he honored 80% of my corrections. I told him that I did my part, and if he does not honor all of my revisions, he will be accountable to the Lord. I am very disappointed because some people try to make their own version of the Bible for their own reasons, away from the actual text of the original Holy Scriptures. Usually, the problem is not the translation to more plain English but changing the meaning of the Word of God. Today, there are available in the market so many English versions which create confusion for Christians and others.

Christian, keep in mind that you are redeemed, not with money, but with the blood of Jesus. You are God's very own, being redeemed by Him. Every Christian should wear a sign on his heart, "NOT FOR SALE."

❖ ❖ ❖

NOTHING BUT THE BLOOD

What can wash away my sin?
Nothing but the blood of Jesus.
What can make me whole again?
Nothing but the blood of Jesus.

Refrain:
O precious is the flow
that makes me white as snow;
no other fount I know;
nothing but the blood of Jesus

— *Hymn by Robert Lowry, 1876*

13

THE RESURRECTION

"And he saith unto them, Be not affrighted: Ye seek
Jesus of Nazareth, which was crucified:
he is risen; he is not here..."
Mark 16:6

*

The heart of Easter is the Resurrection of Jesus Christ!

Man deals with many things in this world, but he should never forget his three greatest enemies: Satan, sin, and death. Jesus came into this world to defeat these three strong powers of darkness. When we read the Bible, we discover Jesus defeated Satan in the wilderness, overcame sin by His sinless life, and conquered death by His victorious resurrection. The Bible gives more importance to the resurrection of Christ than to any other miracle because there is no Christianity without the resurrection. If this miracle can be proved to a man, he will have no difficulty with the rest of the Bible.

The resurrection of Jesus is the day that changed the world! The resurrection of Jesus from the dead is the greatest miracle of history and is one of the most undeniable facts of history. Every possible opposition raised against Christ's resurrection has been answered by the strong testimony of many who saw and died for Him like the apostle Peter. *"For we have not followed cunningly devised fables, when we made known unto you the power and coming of our Lord Jesus Christ, but were eyewitnesses of his majesty"* (2 Peter 1:16). The apostle Paul said Christ was *"declared to be the Son of God with power, according to the spirit of holiness, by the resurrection from the dead"* (Romans 1:4).

Paul declared Jesus to be the Son of God, whom God raised and exalted to His right hand. Even though some people crucified Him as a criminal, others believe in Him and enthrone Christ in their hearts. Ask yourself if you have done this very thing. *"That if thou shalt confess with thy mouth the Lord Jesus, and shalt believe in thine heart that God hath raised him from the dead, thou shalt be saved"* (Romans 10:9).

Jesus' resurrection certifies that God has removed the believer's sins *"As far as the east is from the west"* (Psalm 103:12) because *"He is the propitiation for our sins: and not for ours only, but also for the sins of the whole world"* (1 John 2:2). His death resolves the sin debt of every believer, and His resurrection is like a rubber stamp with the words *"paid in full"* on his bill, which he was not able to pay. *" [Jesus] was delivered for our offenses, and was raised again for our justification"* (Romans 4:25). The resurrection of Jesus Christ guarantees the Christian of his own resurrection that he will enjoy one day. *"And as we have borne the image of the earthy, we shall also bear the image of the heavenly"* (1 Corinthians 15:49).

In this world, we all carry the image of fallen Adam. We are helpless to sin and death, but in our resurrection, we shall be like Christ: sinless, adopted children of God and joint-heirs with Christ. We who have this blessed hope daily in this life are becoming more like Him. *"But we all, with open face beholding as in a glass the glory of the Lord, are changed into the same image from glory to glory, even as by the Spirit of the Lord"* (2 Corinthians 3:18).

The apostle Paul reminds us in Philippians chapter 3 of the importance of the resurrection of Christ. *"That I may know him, and the power of his resurrection..."* (Philippians 3:10). If we do not know the power of the resurrection of Christ, and if we do not see ourselves as dead in Christ, then the darkness of the cross is still upon our hearts. In this case, we do not breathe the fresh air of the resurrection of Jesus Christ. We are ignorant of our real liberty. To be alive with Christ, we must be dead to all that the flesh desires. We must know *"whosoever therefore will be a friend of the world is the enemy of God"* (James 4:4).

If we know the power of the resurrection of Christ, we must *"seek those things which are above, where Christ is, sitting at the right hand of God"* (Colossians 3:1). We must see ourselves as being raised up with Him, dead to sin, dead to the pleasures, and dead to the vanished glory of the world which crucified the Lord of Lords. The things of the world no longer exercise any influence over our thoughts and over our lives. His presence and divine love must shine on us with the assurance of our salvation and the joy of our redemption.

After all, we will no longer find any pleasure in things of this world. Satisfaction does not come any longer for us from the world, but from above, tirelessly serving, praising, and glorifying the risen Lord.

"For whether we live, we live unto the Lord; and whether we die, we die unto the Lord: whether we live therefore, or die, we are the Lord's" (Romans 14:8).

❖

HAPPY RESURRECTION SUNDAY TO YOU AND YOUR LOVED ONES!

❖ ❖ ❖

• In 1999, my wife and I had the privilege of visiting the Holy Lands— a wonderful place where our Lord spent His life on the earth. After that visit, our lives have not been the same. What the Bible says is all true. There is a Calvary, and there is an empty tomb. I have a picture of the empty tomb in my office. It always reminds me of my Lord's love, sacrifice, and power. We saw with our own eyes where our Lord was laid when He was buried and is now not there. Yes! He is Not There. He Is Risen. Hallelujah!

• Without Jesus' resurrection from the dead, life would be hopeless. Jesus is not a baby anymore in Bethlehem, an adult on the cross, or dead in a tomb. Instead, He is alive and sits at the right hand of His father. I know this because I talk to Him each day in my prayers, and through His Spirit, He answers me and reveals His existence as the Holy Scripture's prove it. I know my Redeemer lives. Hallelujah!

• The Risen Jesus has brought the gift of forgiveness and salvation to each Christian. Now, it is our responsibility as believers in Christ to share this good news with others without holding anything back.

HE IS RISEN

Let the heavens sing, and the earth rejoice!

14

IF CHRIST HAD NOT RISEN

"And if Christ be not risen, then is our preaching vain,
and your faith is also vain. And if Christ be not raised, your faith is vain; ye
are yet in your sins. If in this life only we have hope in Christ,
we are of all men most miserable."
1 Corinthians 15:14,17,19

*

The Empty Tomb (Mark 16:1-8)

Did you ever think about what would have happened if Christ had not risen? In the verses above, the apostle Paul tells us that without Jesus' resurrection, our preaching and our faith would be in vain. If we only have hope in Christ as Christians within this life, and not for all eternity, we will be the most miserable of all people. This means that everything depends upon the one and only important fact: a risen Christ. It is important that the resurrection of Jesus Christ is absolutely essential to everything we believe and hope for. It is the cornerstone of our salvation.

If Jesus had not risen, then none of Jesus' following claims and teachings would be fulfilled. *"Destroy this temple, and in three days I will raise it up"* (John 2:19). *"For as Jonas was three days and three nights in the whale's belly; so shall the Son of man be three days and three nights in the heart of the earth"* (Matthew 12:40), and *"I lay down my life, that I might take it again. No man taketh it from me, but I lay it down of myself. I have power to lay it down, and I have power to take it again..."* (John 10:17,18).

In reality, if Jesus had not risen, His work would not be finished. After His three years of public ministry, Jesus was crucified, one of His disciples betrayed Him, and another denied Him. Finally, the apostle Mark tells us: *"And they all forsook him, and fled"* (Mark 14:50). If Jesus had died and would not have risen, where would be the atonement? It would have been impossible for Him, through the Holy Spirit, to dwell in the heart of every believer to give him supernatural power in his daily life. The individual who trusts Jesus Christ shares His life, and that life changes him to break the bond of sin, and to set him free from all his transgressions. In other words, if Christ be not risen, the preaching is empty, our faith is in vain, we remain in our sins, and we are controlled by them. If Christ actually be not risen, His death was just another typical, natural death, and the doctrine of justification is nonsense—only a big joke.

Because some in Corinth did not believe in the resurrection of the dead, the apostle Paul in 1 Corinthians chapter 15 explains the importance of the resurrection of Christ and gives us a few terrible realities if there were no resurrection:

1. **Preaching Christ would be senseless, and faith in Christ would be useless:** *"And if Christ be not risen, then is our preaching vain, and your faith is also vain"* (v. 14).

2. **All the witnesses and all the preachers of the resurrection would be liars:** *"Yea, and we are found false witnesses of God; because we have testified of God that he raised up Christ: whom he raised not up, if so be that the dead rise not..."* (v. 15).

3. **No one would be redeemed from sin:** *"And if Christ be not raised, your faith is vain; ye are yet in your sins"* (v. 17).

4. **All former believers would have perished:** *"Then they also which are fallen asleep in Christ are perished"* (v.18).

5. **Believers in Christ would be the most miserable people on the earth:** *"If in this life only we have hope in Christ, we are of all men most miserable"* (v. 19).

"But now is Christ risen from the dead, and become the firstfruits of them that slept" (v. 20), assuring us that we will follow Him in the resurrection. *"And God hath both raised up the Lord, and will also raise up us by his own power"* (1 Corinthians 6:14). What a wonderful and glorious truth! The first evidence of the resurrection is the testimony of the disciples who saw Him in many of His various appearances. *"He [Jesus] rose again the third day according to the scriptures: And that he was seen of Cephas, then of the twelve: After that, he was seen of above five hundred brethren at once"* (1 Corinthians 15:4-6).

Even with their own previous unbelief, they preached and died for Him. The testimony of the apostle Paul himself is such a vital proof, and all of today's critics cannot explain what made him turn from persecutor of the church to a missionary. Paul saw Jesus and heard Him from heaven and the One whom he thought was dead, he found out was alive. As a result, he gave all his life to Jesus Christ by preaching the gospel and finally dying for Him. Paul believed and taught that *"It is Christ that died, yea rather, that is risen again, who is even at the right hand of God..."* (Romans 8:34).

The results of preaching about the risen Christ are that people experience forgiveness, peace, salvation, and supernatural power. The final line of evidence of actual resurrection from the dead is the church, a group of men and women and children, joined together from all nations. Before the resurrection of Christ, the Holy Spirit came upon individuals only at certain times and only for particular reasons. But now, after the resurrection, Christ through the Holy Spirit dwells in the heart of every believer to give him supernatural power in his daily life. Individuals who trust Jesus Christ share His life, and that life changes them.

I SERVE A RISEN SAVIOR

I serve a risen Savior, He's in the world today;
I know that He is living whatever men may say;
I see His hand of mercy, I hear His voice of cheer,
And just the time I need Him, He's always near.

He lives, He lives, Christ Jesus lives today!
He walks with me and talks with me along life's narrow way.
He lives, He lives, Salvation to impart!
You ask me how I know He lives? He lives within my heart.

Hymn, by Alfred Henry Ackley (1887-1960)

❖ ❖ ❖

• "I know the resurrection is a fact...Because 12 men testified they had seen Jesus raised from the dead, then they proclaimed that truth for 40 years, never once denying it. Everyone was beaten, tortured, stoned, and put in prison. They would not have endured that if it weren't true..." —— *Evangelist, Charles Colson*

• "The Gospel is the Gospel of the Risen Christ. There would be no Gospel for sinners if Christ had not been raised." — *Dr. H.A. Ironside*

God raised Jesus from the dead to free you and me from sin and bring the miraculous power of His kingdom into our world! Without Jesus' resurrection from the dead, life would be hopeless.

15

HOW TO REMOVE OUR SIN

"For all have sinned, and come short of the glory of God;
Being justified freely by his grace through
the redemption that is in Christ Jesus."
Romans 3:23, 24

*

There is only one way to remove our sin!

I was raised Greek Orthodox. In the Orthodox Church, I learned the first lessons of the Christian faith. Because the church taught about salvation more by works than by grace and because I was baptized as an infant, I thought I was a good Christian. I never realized that I was a sinner because I was a good moral person. I thought a sinner was only someone who had committed a big sin such as murder.

I had this mentality until a man of God sat down, and plainly talked to me about God's love and the price that Jesus Christ paid for me on the cross. He described God's simple plan and told me that Christ died for my sins and offered me eternal life. With all his boldness, he told me that I was a sinner because the Bible said, *"For all have sinned, and come short of the glory of God..."* (Romans 3:23). As he unfolded God's plan of free salvation, my spiritual eyes were opened. For the first time, I realized that I was a sinful man, and I needed a Savior. On March 17, 1970, I repented and by faith accepted Jesus Christ as my personal Savior and Lord. He forgave me and gave me eternal life, and at the same time filled all the emptiness I had in my heart. From that day on, my life has never been the same!

Sin is anything opposed to the law or the will of God. Sin is expensive. Do not keep paying, paying, and paying. If Satan got kicked out of heaven for sin, what makes us think we will make it to heaven with sin? The Bible tells us, *"He that covereth his sins shall not prosper: but whoso confesseth and forsaketh them shall have mercy"* (Proverbs 28:13).

The apostle Luke tells us what happened when Jesus called his disciples to follow Him. Peter was out fishing all night, and he did not catch any fish. Jesus told him to throw out the net one more time, and immediately, there were more fish in the net than he could pull. Peter realized that he was in the presence of the Lord, and he said to Jesus, *"Depart from me; for I am a sinful man, O Lord"* (Luke 5:8). Christ did not go away. Instead, he said to him, *"Follow me."* Christ came near to Peter because he wanted to give him a new life. If you feel an awareness of your own sin, do not be afraid. This will be a good sign that He is working in your life, and be thankful for that. When that happens, it will be the turning point in your life as it was in mine. Pastor and Author, Colin Smith, said, *"You are never closer to Christ than when you are most aware of your own sin."*

The Bible clearly teaches that all of us have sinned, and it is impossible for us to remove it. It is a permanent, irremovable stain, but He provided a way to erase our sin. PRAISE GOD! Only God can remove our sin through the sacrifice of His Son, Jesus Christ. He died on the cross for us. He rose again and offers forgiveness and eternal life to all who put their trust in Him. *"All have sinned..."* (Romans 3:23), *"We are all as an unclean thing, and all our righteousness are as filthy rags"* (Isaiah 64:6), *"Unto him [Jesus] that loved us, and washed us from our sins in his own blood"* (Revelation 1:5), *"Come now, and let us reason together, says the Lord: though your sins be as scarlet, they shall be as white as snow; though they be red like crimson, they shall be as wool"* (Isaiah 1:18), and *"Repent ye therefore, and be converted, that your sins may be blotted out..."* (Acts 3:19).

Always, remember that God hates sin, but He loves the sinner. We always have to preach this. Once, a young preacher, out of fear, preached what his people wanted to hear to not offend them. The only problem was that he had never experienced God's blessings in his life, his people, and his ministry. He came to the point of giving up from his disappointment. Around that time, an older preacher and saint of God gave him some advice which turned everything around. He told him, "God called you to serve and please Him and not to worry about the people being offended or not. Go back and preach about sin and tell them that the Lord died for sinners and loves them." The young preacher obeyed and put the new challenge into practice. In a few months, he was surprised when showers of blessings came from the Lord upon his life, his people, and his ministry.

- One of the earliest stories I ever heard about D. L. Moody, that great evangelist of the nineteenth century, took place when he was temporarily called away to another city and left a young English preacher named

Henry Moorhouse to speak during his absence. Upon returning from his trip, he asked his wife, "Well, what about the young preacher?"

"Oh," she said, "he is a better preacher than you are. He is telling sinners that God loves them."

"He is wrong!" said Moody, 'God doesn't love sinners."

"Well," she said, "you go and hear him."

"Is he still preaching?" asked Mr. Moody.

"Yes, he has been preaching all week and has only taken up one verse, John 3:16" was her reply.

When Mr. Moody went to the meeting, Moorhouse got up, and said, "I have been hunting and hunting all through the Bible, looking for a text, and I think we will just talk about John 3:16 once more." Mr. Moody always testified that it was on that night that he first got hold of a clear understanding of the gospel and the love of God. Think what it meant in Moody's life, and in the lives of tens of thousands who were reached through his ministry, to know that God loves sinners! — *Adapted-mwtb.org*

Do you realize that you are a sinner too, and you need a Savior? I am not saying that, but the Bible says:

- *"For all have sinned, and come short of the glory of God"* (Romans 3:23).

- *"If we say that we have no sin, we deceive ourselves, and the truth is not in us"* (1 John 1:8).

- *"For the wages of sin is death; but the gift of God is eternal life through Jesus Christ our Lord"* (Romans 6:23).

- *"For the Son of man is come to seek and to save that which was lost"* (Luke 19:10).

- *"Christ Jesus came into the world to save sinners..."* (1 Timothy 1:15).

- *"I came not to call the righteous, but sinners to repentance"* (Luke 5:32).

- *"But God commendeth his love toward us, in that, while we were yet sinners, Christ died for us"* (Romans 5:8).

- *"When Jesus heard it, he saith unto them, They that are whole have no need of the physician, but they that are sick: I came not to call the righteous, but sinners to repentance"* (Mark 2:17).

If you are not a redeemed sinner yet, it is time for you to come to the Lord and ask for His forgiveness from your sins to be able to receive His free gift of eternal life. Do not go to a Greek Orthodox or a Catholic priest or any other priest to forgive your sins. They are men like you with sins and not able to solve their own sins. How can they solve yours? Only God has the power to forgive sins. *"who can forgive sins but God only?"* (Mark 2:7).

ONLY Jesus can offer you forgiveness of your sins. ONLY Jesus can erase your sins, and not anyone else in heaven or on earth can. For this purpose, He died on the cross to pay for the sins of sinners like you and me, so that we will be able to spend eternity in heaven with Him. *"If we confess our sins, he is faithful and just to forgive us our sins, and to cleanse us from all unrighteousness"* (1 John 1:9).

We have to make sure all of us stay off the road of sin in our race to glory. We have to focus on Jesus as the goal of our lives and put everything else aside!

❖ ❖ ❖

- **Sin: Jesus Is The Answer**
  "The world's greatest need is not for a teacher,
  because the world's problem is not ignorance -
  it is not a patriot because our problem is not nationalism,
  not a philanthropist, because the problem is not poverty.
  But the world does need a Savior because the world's
  problem is sin!"
  — *Evangelist, Bailey Smith*

- **Three Marks**
  Pastor and Author, W. Tozer said that "People who are crucified with Christ have three distinct marks:
  They are facing only one direction.
  They can never turn back.
  They no longer have plans of their own."

God's Math: 1 CROSS + 3 NAILS = 4 GIVEN

16

THE PRICE OF YOUR SOUL

"For whosoever will save his life shall lose it;
but whosoever shall lose his life for my sake and the gospel's,
the same shall save it. For what shall it profit a man,
if he shall gain the whole world, and lose his own soul?"
Mark 8:35-36

*

What do you know about your Soul?

Most people are concerned about the value of their home, cars, stocks, bonds, and other possessions, but they never think about the value of their own soul. All their lives, they work hard to save for things they cannot take with them when they die. When they are on their deathbed and look back and say, "What is next now? Where will I go now?" I hope that you do not wait for your last breath to look for answers when you had all your life for that.

I will ask you a few very important questions: Do you know that your soul has tremendous value? Do you know what Jesus and the devil offer for your soul? Do you know that your soul can be lost forever in hell? Do you know that your soul can be saved forever in heaven? And finally, do you know that you must care, protect and feed your soul? Jesus himself said, *"For what is a man profited, if he shall gain the whole world, and lose his own soul? or what shall a man give in exchange for his soul"* (Matthew 16:26)? Your soul is you. It is your identity and what you are. Your body will decay and be destroyed one day, but your soul will live forever in one of two places: heaven or hell. C.S. Lewis said, *"You don't have a soul. You are a soul. You have a body."*

Two things can happen to your soul. It will be either saved, or it will be lost forever. Both Jesus and the devil bid for your soul. The devil, with all his power and his deceitfulness, tries to destroy your soul and take it to hell forever. Jesus Christ gave everything, even His life, to purchase your soul. All who trusts Him as their personal Savior will never be turned away, and every soul that has been entrusted to His hands will never be lost. Bishop John Charles Ryle said, *"It is the first step toward heaven to find out the true worth of our souls."* If you have a valuable possession in your life, you will do anything possible to protect it and save it. Maybe you protect your valuable possession by yourself, put it in your safe deposit box in the bank, pay guards to guard it or buy insurance for it. The same thing is true with your soul. Be wise and not foolish. Keep in mind, the soul that is given to Jesus Christ is the only one that is saved. Jesus is the best guard, safe deposit box, or insurance for your soul. If you do not protect your soul, it will be lost.

Picture this scene. You are standing before God on judgment day, and He looks you right in the eye and says, *"Depart from me, ye cursed, into everlasting fire, prepared for the devil and his angels"* (Matthew 25:41). I want you to think of the terror and fright that will overwhelm you with that ultimate death sentence. We read in 2 Thessalonians 1:6-9 the following: *"Seeing it is a righteous thing with God to recompense tribulation to them that trouble you; And to you who are troubled rest with us, when the Lord Jesus shall be revealed from heaven with his mighty angels, In flaming fire taking vengeance on them that know not God, and that obey not the gospel of our Lord Jesus Christ: Who shall be punished with everlasting destruction from the presence of the Lord, and from the glory of his power."* It is so critical that each of us understands that this life is temporary, and eternity follows, but we can be saved by the grace of God to spend eternity in heaven.

• A story tells about a little girl who lived in the slums of London. One day, dressed in rags, the child wandered quite far from her home searching for a shop where she might purchase some roses for her sick mother. When she came upon a beautiful garden surrounded by a fence, she noticed a young lady walking among the gorgeous flowers. Untying a corner of her ragged skirt, she drew out her few pennies and asked the lady if she could buy some flowers. "Come into the garden, and we'll talk it over," said the lady. The gate was opened, and the little one was shown through the lovely estate. "Choose the best you see for your mother," said her new-found friend. Soon, the little shopper had a magnificent bouquet. "Oh," said the child, "would you be willing to give me all of these for my few pennies?" "No," said the lady, "these roses belong to my father, who is the king. He does not sell his flowers, but he loves to give them away! Take them home to your mother, and tell her they are a gift from the king!" Wide-eyed with wonder the child realized that she had been walking in the Royal Gardens. — *Author Unknown*

All of us, like that little girl, come with our poor pennies, our "good works," thinking we can buy the blossoms of salvation. Not so! The blooms of grace have all been paid for by the King's Son, Jesus Christ. Realize that salvation is not something we achieve, but something we receive. If you are not a Christian, give proper attention. Today, there are two bidders for your soul. Satan and Jesus. Satan offers you what he cannot give. He is a deceitful liar and has been from the foundation of the world, but Jesus Christ is able to give all He offers as eternal life to every lost soul. *"The gift of God is eternal life"* (Romans 6:23). Who will have it? I hope and pray, you will accept the bid of Jesus Christ. I hope you will choose LIFE rather than DEATH. I hope you will choose HEAVEN rather than HELL. Jesus says to you today, *"For whosoever will save his life shall lose it,"* but then in love, He begs you: *"Whosoever will lose his life for my sake shall find it"* (Matthew 16:25).

If you really see the value of your soul, I encourage you to pray and say to Jesus Christ:

> *Dear Jesus, I realize without you, my soul will not make it. Without you, my soul will starve. I need you to be my Savior, my Lord, and the Master of my soul. I need you to save, protect, and feed my soul. I turn my whole life over to you. Forgive my sins and give me a new heart that loves you, yield to you, and serves you. AMEN.*

❖ ❖ ❖

- "The beginning of the way to heaven is to feel that we are on the way to hell." — *Evangelical Bishop, J. C. Ryle*

- "The greatest enemy to human souls is the self-righteous spirit, which makes men look to themselves for salvation." "Free will carried many a soul to hell, but never a soul to heaven."
— *"Quotes from "Prince of Preachers," Charles Spurgeon*

- "Souls are made sweet not by taking the acid fluids out, but by putting —something in—a great Love, a new Spirit—the Spirit of Christ."
— *Evangelist, Henry Drummond*

- "I will charge my soul to believe and wait for Him, and will follow His providence, and not go before it, nor stay behind it."
— *Pastor, Theologian and Author Samuel Rutherford*

- "There's not a single thing on offer in this all-too-temporary world for which you should ever sell your soul."— *Ambassador, Alan Keyes*

17

HEAVEN AND HELL ARE REAL

"In my Father's house are many mansions: if it were not so,
I would have told you. I go to prepare a place for you.
And if I go and prepare a place for you,
I will come again, and receive you unto myself;
that where I am, there ye may be also."
John 14:2,3

*

Have you reserved a heavenly home?

Many years ago, one of my students asked me, "What do I have to do to go to hell?" I told him, "Nothing." That is right. There is nothing more we need to do to go to hell. None of us are perfect. We all have sinned. There is, however, something that we all must do to go to heaven. The Bible says, *"He that believeth on the Son hath everlasting life: and he that believeth not the Son shall not see life; but the wrath of God abideth on him"*(John 3:36). Hell is not a joke.

Numerous churches today do not preach about hell and only preach about the love of God. Jesus himself warns that hell is a real place of darkness where *"there shall be wailing and gnashing of teeth"* (Matthew 13:42). This is bad news, but I have good news for you. God does not want anyone to spend eternity separated from Him in the darkness of hell. That is why God sent His Son to suffer the punishment for our sins, so we would be able to go to heaven. Heaven and hell are real, and they last for eternity. Heaven is to be with Christ! Hell is to be with the devil! Heaven or hell? It is your choice.

Everybody needs a heavenly home. Not everyone has one, but everyone sure does need one! D. L. Moody said, *"Heaven is a prepared place for a prepared people."* To make it to heaven does not depend on your efforts or good works. Heaven is God's home and is perfect because God is perfect, and nothing imperfect can ever enter heaven according to (Revelation 22:14-15). Romans 3:23 says, *"For all have sinned, and come short of the glory of God."* Still, God in His grace provided a way to bridge the gap between Him and us. John 3:16 tells us this, *"For God so loved the world, that he gave his only begotten Son, that whosoever believeth in him should not perish, but have everlasting life."* Jesus died for your sins and mine. He took our punishment for sin. He died for our sins, so we would not have to do it. Now, He offers forgiveness and a heavenly home for us.

Heaven is for all those who, by faith, receive Jesus Christ as Savior Lord. If you have never done this, today is the time to ask Jesus into your life. Heaven is for people like you!

- **FIRST,** to be saved, you must REALIZE that you are a sinner as the Bible warns us. *"All we like sheep have gone astray; We have turned, everyone, to his own way; and the LORD hath laid on him the iniquity of us all"* (Isaiah 53:6), *"For all have sinned, and come short of the glory of God"* (Romans 3:23), *"And as it is appointed unto men once to die, but after this the judgment."* (Hebrews 9:27).

- **SECOND**, you must REPENT. *"I tell you, Nay: but, except ye repent, ye shall all likewise perish"* (Luke 13:3), *"Repent ye therefore, and be converted, that your sins may be blotted out, when the times of refreshing shall come from the presence of the Lord"* (Acts 3:19).

- **THIRD,** you must RECEIVE. *"But as many as received him, to them gave he power to become the sons of God, even to them that believe on his name:"* (John 1:12), *"If thou shalt confess with thy mouth the Lord Jesus, and shalt believe in thine heart that God hath raised him from the dead, thou shalt be saved"* (Romans 10:9).

Accept Jesus today as your personal Savior. By accepting the Lord, you receive a one-way first-class ticket to heaven. Do not be a fool. Get on board! This way, you will enter heaven's Gates instead of hell's flames. You can accept Jesus as your personal Savior by praying something like this:

> *Lord, thank you for your Son Jesus who died on the cross to pay for my sins. Now I repent. I turn from my sin, and by faith, receive You as my personal Savior and Lord. Please forgive my sins, and save me and show me your will and help me become the person you want me to be. In Your name, I pray. Amen.*

Jesus in John 14:2-4 said, *"In my Father's house are many mansions: if it were not so, I would have told you. I go to prepare a place for you. And if I go and prepare a place for you, I will come again, and receive you unto myself; that where I am, there ye may be also."* Jesus reveals here that He is making preparations for us in His Father's house-heaven. Can you imagine that? Jesus Christ, the Lord of the universe, is going out of His way to prepare a unique place in heaven just for you and me. In heaven, we will experience eternal joy in the presence of the Lord!

According to the Lord, heaven is an actual destination, someplace where we will experience the absolute best of everything. Since Jesus Christ is preparing it for us, we can trust that it will be perfect. He can do nothing less. Heaven is a better place than earth. The great heavenly city that Jesus has prepared for us is just amazing. *"And the twelve gates were twelve pearls: every several gate was of one pearl: and the street of the city was pure gold, as it were transparent glass"* (Revelation 21:21). The Lord desires all of us who live on earth to be with Him in heaven. *"Whom have I in heaven but thee? and there is none upon earth that I desire beside thee..."* (Psalm 73:25). Additionally, the apostles Paul and John ensure what the Lord has for all of them who love Him. *"But as it is written, Eye hath not seen, nor ear heard, neither have entered into the heart of man, the things which God hath prepared for them that love him"* (1 Corinthians 2:9), *"Beloved, now are we the sons of God, and it doth not yet appear what we shall be: but we know that, when he shall appear, we shall be like him; for we shall see him as he is"* (1 John 3:2).

Most people want to go to heaven, but in reality, they do not want to die. Why? Because they do not know what the scriptures say about heaven or they do not believe them. They are scared to death when they think they might die. Sometimes we pray for the healing of sick Christians, to keep them out of heaven until a later time, instead of asking for God's will to be done.

Some years ago, one dear brother in Christ passed away from cancer and his wife asked everybody not to wear black clothes at his funeral, because this was a celebration. Her husband was in heaven with the Lord, and they walked together on the streets of gold. When we live with this kind of hope, we will never be scared of death. The day we die will be a blessed day because we will see the Lord face to face and be with Him forever.

WHEN WE ALL GET TO HEAVEN

When we all get to heaven,
What a day of rejoicing that will be!
When we all see Jesus,
We'll sing and shout the victory!

— *Hymn by Eliza E. Hewitt, 1898*

Christians must know that God is the center of all things in heaven, and that is why a person who lives wisely will make him the center of all things on earth, as well. *"If you read history, you will find that the Christians who did the most for the present world were just those who thought most of the next. It is since Christians have largely ceased to think of the other world that they have become so ineffective in this"* — *C. S. Lewis*

❖ ❖ ❖

• "I would rather go to heaven alone than go to hell in company."
— *Evangelist and Pastor, R.A. Torrey*

• "I would not give one moment of heaven for all the joy and riches of the world, even if it lasted for thousands and thousands of years."
— *Priest and Theologian, Martin Luther*

• "I have all that I need here and heaven hereafter! How much richer could anybody want to be?" — *Dr. Lester Roloff*

• "For the Christian, heaven is where Jesus is. We do not need to speculate on what heaven will be like. It is enough to know that we will be forever with Him." — *Theologian, William Barclay*

• "One reason some saints will have a greater fullness of heaven than others will be that they did more for heaven than others. By God's grace, they were enabled to bring more souls there."
— *Prince of Preachers," C. H. Spurgeon*

• "Those who go to heaven ride on a pass and enter into blessings that they never earned, but all who go to hell pay their own way."
— *Dr. John R. Rice*

By accepting Jesus as your personal Savior you receive a one-way first-class ticket to heaven. Do not be a fool. Get on board! This way, you will enter heaven's gates instead of hell's flames.

18

THE FOOLISH MAN

*"And I will say to my soul, Soul,
thou hast much goods laid up for many years; take thine ease, eat,
drink, and be merry. But God said unto him, Thou fool, this night
thy soul shall be required of thee: then whose shall those things
be, which thou hast provided?"*
Luke 12:19,20

*

**God tells us how we can prepare for the next life and
warns us if we do not!**

Years ago, I met up with Mike, a classmate of mine from college. He was an unbeliever. We held a short conversation, and it went a little like this:

TED: How are you doing, Mike?
MIKE: I am doing fine. Soon I will finish my Ph.D.

TED: This is wonderful! But, after that?
MIKE: I will pursue the president's job in the company where I am working.

TED: Excellent! But, after that?
MIKE: With all the money I will make, it will be easy to find a beautiful woman to marry. I will also be able to build a beautiful mansion in which to live.

TED: O, boy! But, after that?
MIKE: I will have some children, and I will send them to the best schools. I will also take expensive vacations and have a good time.

TED: Perfect! But, after that?
MIKE: I will have an excellent retirement with a good pension. I will spoil my grandkids and travel around the world for an adventure.

TED: Mike, all these sound fun. But, after that?
MIKE: I will die, and everyone will come to my funeral and say how I was such a successful and great guy.

TED: Fine! But, after that?
MIKE: What do you mean, "But, after that? But, after that?

Usually, most people are like MIKE. They know where they want to go in this short and temporary life, but they never think about eternity after the end of this life. The truth is in the Bible, where God tells us a lot about how we should live this life. Above all, He tells us how we can prepare for the next life and warns us. *"And as it is appointed unto men once to die, but after this the judgment"* (Hebrews 9:27).

Maybe you will say, "What judgment? I have lived a good life, not perfect, but I did not kill anybody or rob a bank. Why would I be judged?" You will be judged because the Bible says, *"For all have sinned, and come short of the glory of God"* (Romans 3:23). You cannot measure your perfection now or after you die with a perfect God. The Bible also says, *"But God commendeth his love toward us, in that, while we were yet sinners, Christ died for us"* (Romans 5:8). I hope you see that Jesus Christ died to take our punishment. By rising from the grave, He proved His power over sin and death. When by faith, we trust Him as our personal Savior, He will forgive us and give us eternal life. *"Verily, verily, I say unto you, He that heareth my word, and believeth on him that sent me, hath everlasting life, and shall not come into condemnation; but is passed from death unto life"* (John 5:24).

"Yes! I got it after all. Jesus loves me so much that He even died for me, but what do I have to do now?" The Bible tells us that the only thing we can do is to stop trusting ourselves and to put our trust in Jesus to forgive us and give us eternal life. *"He that believeth on the Son hath everlasting life: and he that believeth not the Son shall not see life; but the wrath of God abideth on him"* (John 3:36). Be sincere and pray and say something like this:

Lord, thank you for sending your Son, Jesus, to die on the cross for my sins. I now repent and place my trust in Him as my Savior. Thank You for Your love, forgiveness, and Your gift of eternal life. Amen.

The apostle John says, *"And this is the record, that God hath given to us eternal life, and this life is in his Son"* (1 John 5:11). If somebody asks you what happens after you die, you have the answer. You will step into eternity and live forever in the presence of your Savior and Lord. You have eternal life without any doubt in your mind because the promise comes straight from the lips of your Savior Jesus Christ, whom you have trusted. *"He that believeth on the Son hath everlasting life..."* (John 3:36).

❖ ❖ ❖

• "Saving faith is an immediate relation to Christ, accepting, receiving, resting upon Him alone, for justification, sanctification, and eternal life by virtue of God's grace.
— *"Prince of Preachers," C. H. Spurgeon*

• "Once a man is united to God, how could he not live forever?"
—*Scholar and Author, C.S. Lewis*

• "Don't let obstacles along the road to eternity, shake your confidence in God's promise. The Holy Spirit is God's seal that you will arrive."
— *Dr. David Jeremiah*

"He that believeth on the Son hath everlasting life: and he that believeth not the Son shall not see life; but the wrath of God abideth on him"

John 3:36

19

JESUS IS THE ONLY MEDIATOR

*"For there is one God,
and one mediator between God and men,
the man Christ Jesus;"*
1 Timothy 2:5

*"Jesus saith unto him,
I am the way, the truth, and the life:
no man cometh unto the Father, but by me."*
John 14:6

*

Use the One and only Mediator if you have never used Him!

In the Old Testament, Israel believed and worshiped the one true God of the Bible and did not worship the many gods that the heathen believed in and worshipped. In the New Testament and true Christianity, there is one mediator between God and men, the man Jesus Christ. Because of our sin, we cannot mediate between ourselves and God, but only through Jesus as He said,

*"I am the way, the truth, and the life: no man cometh
unto the Father, but by me"* (John 14:6).

Sadly, men in different Christian denominations over the centuries have added many mediators which dishonor God's Son. Instead of Christians going straight to Jesus Christ as the only mediator, they go and pray to other mediators. Angels are one of the mediators that people try to use. Other mediators Christians use are "saints," who are deceased souls in heaven. The most commonly used mediator is Mary, the mother of Jesus Christ. Even she said when told by an angel of the birth of the Savior,

"And my spirit hath rejoiced in God my Saviour"
(Luke 1:47).

Because Mary needed a Savior too, it is idolatry for people to share with her the glorious work of the one Mediator, Jesus Christ, the Only Son of God,

"Who gave himself a ransom for all, to be testified in due time"
(1 Timothy 2:6).

The apostle Paul wrote about Jesus that *"he is the mediator of a better covenant, which was established upon better promises"* (Hebrews 8:6). In the Bible, we have two covenants. One of them is in the Old Testament through Moses. The covenant of law required righteousness from man but did not give the ability to produce it. The other one in the New Testament was through Jesus. The covenant of grace attributes righteousness, where there is none. It teaches a man to live righteously and empowers him to do so with the help of the Holy Spirit. Also, it rewards him when he does it. This is the reason Jesus is the mediator of a better covenant than Moses.

Even though many people understand the seriousness of sin, they still ignore Jesus Christ, the One and only Mediator God has provided for the forgiveness of their sins. Jesus is the only Mediator who can promise to make us clear from guilt. Instead, many use other powerless mediators. It is time for you to use the One and only Mediator if you have never used Him. It is a time to call upon Jesus Christ today.

"Neither is there salvation in any other: for there is none other name under heaven given among men, whereby we must be saved"
(Acts 4:12).

❖ ❖ ❖

• "The redeemed are dependent on God for all. All that we have — wisdom, the pardon of sin, deliverance, acceptance in God's favor, grace, holiness, true comfort and happiness, eternal life and glory—we have from God by a Mediator; and this Mediator is God. God not only gives us the Mediator, and accepts His mediation, and of His power and grace bestows the things purchased by the Mediator, but He is the Mediator.

Our blessings are what we have by purchase; the purchase is made of God; the blessings are purchased of Him, and not so, but God is the purchaser. Yes, God is both the purchaser and the price; for Christ, who is God, purchased these blessings by offering Himself as the price of our salvation."
— *Pastor and Theologian, Jonathan Edwards*

• One is struck with the personality of this text (Matthew 11:28). There are two persons in it, "you" and "me" Jesus says, "Come to Me, not to anybody else but to Me." He does not say, "Come to hear a sermon about Me" but "Come to Me, to My work and person." You will observe that no one is put between you and Christ...Come to Jesus directly, even to Jesus Himself. You do want a mediator between yourselves and God, but you do not want a mediator between yourselves and Jesus...To Him, we may look at once, with unveiled face, guilty as we are. To Him, we may come, just as we are, without anyone to recommend us or plead for us or make a bridge for us to Jesus...You, as you are, are to come to Christ as He is, and the promise is that on your coming to Him, he will give you rest. That is the assurance of Jesus Himself, and there is no deception in it...You see, there are two persons. Let everybody else vanish, and let these one be left alone, to transact heavenly business with each other. "
—*"Prince of Preachers," C. H. Spurgeon*

Even though many people understand the seriousness of sin, they still ignore Jesus Christ, the One and only Mediator God has provided for the forgiveness of their sins.

20

ONLY JESUS IS GOOD ENOUGH

"For there is not a just man upon earth,
that doeth good, and sinneth not."
Ecclesiastes 7:20

"Not by works of righteousness which we have done, but according
to his mercy he saved us, by the washing of regeneration,
and renewing of the Holy Ghost;"
Titus 3:5

*

How good do we have to be to get into heaven?

I noticed a Christian book with the title, *"How Good is Good Enough?"* Maybe you will say, "I never thought of this. I do not know how good I have to be to enter God's heaven." When we review the Bible, we see there are many verses in the Old and New Testament that give us the answer. No one is good enough to gain eternal life. King Solomon wrote, *"For there is not a just man upon earth, that doeth good, and sinneth not"* (Ecclesiastes 7:20). The apostle Paul also wrote, *"For all have sinned, and come short of the glory of God"* (Romans 3:23). All of us deserve hell, *"but the gift of God is eternal life through Jesus Christ, our Lord"* (Romans 6:23). To enjoy the gift of eternal life is not based on man's goodness, but is based on the grace of God. *"I do not frustrate the grace of God: for if righteousness come by the law, then Christ is dead in vain"* (Galatians 2:21).

You have to receive Jesus Christ as your personal Savior to have eternal life today. The apostle Paul wrote, *"Christ died for our sins according to the scriptures; And that he was buried, and that he rose again the third day according to the scriptures: And that he was seen of Cephas, then of the twelve"* (1 Corinthians

15:3-5). This is the wonderful message of the gospel. *"For God so loved the world, that he gave his only begotten Son, that whosoever believeth in him should not perish, but have everlasting life"* (John 3:16). *"For by grace are ye saved through faith; and that not of yourselves: it is the gift of God: Not of works, lest any man should boast"* (Ephesians 2:8,9).

Bible teacher, J. Vernon McGee said, "When I hear Christians say, 'I don't do this, and I don't do that, and I am following a set of rules' I immediately recognize that they know very little about the grace of God. They are trying to live the Christian life in their own strength. But Paul says, *'Be strong in the grace that is in Christ Jesus'"* (2 Timothy 2:1). Yes! Even though the unspeakable gift of grace is offered to all people in the world, many do not know about it, and others have rejected it. Have you accepted God's gift? If you are a believer, I pray that all the verses above from the word of God, which teach about God's grace will cause you to stop and thank God for His grace and the gift of salvation. If you are an unbeliever, I encourage you to come to Jesus now, to accept and enjoy His eternal blessings, all as a result of God's grace.

You will never be "good enough" to go to heaven, but if you believe and trust in Jesus, He promises to allow you in.

"Let not your heart be troubled: ye believe in God, believe also in me. In my Father's house are many mansions: if it were not so, I would have told you. I go to prepare a place for you. And if I go and prepare a place for you, I will come again, and receive you unto myself; that where I am, there ye may be also. And whither I go ye know, and the way ye know. Thomas saith unto him, Lord, we know not whither thou goest; and how can we know the way? Jesus saith unto him, I am the way, the truth, and the life: no man cometh unto the Father, but by me" (John 14:1-6).

❖ ❖ ❖

GRACE + 0 = SALVATION

• "A man must completely despair of himself in order to become fit to obtain the grace of Christ... The law works fear and wrath; grace works hope, and mercy...Grace is given to heal the spiritually sick, not to decorate spiritual heroes" — *Priest and Theologian, Martin Luther*

• "Grace puts its hand on the boasting mouth and shuts it once for all." — *"Prince of Preachers," Charles Spurgeon*

- "All the grace contained in [the Bible] is owing to Jesus Christ as our Lord and Savior; and, unless we consent to Him as our Lord, we cannot expect any benefit by Him as our Savior."
— *Minister and Author, Matthew Henry*

- "As heat is opposed to cold, and light to darkness, so grace is opposed to sin. Fire and water may as well agree in the same vessel, as grace and sin in the same heart.
— "*Puritan Preacher and Author, Thomas Brooks*

- "When the mask of self-righteousness has been torn from us, and we stand stripped of all our accustomed defenses, we are candidates for God's generous grace."
— *Dr. Erwin W. Lutzer*

**Grace always humiliates the ego,
and salvation defeats the ego.
The ego always feels good to boast and
say I did it, and
I accomplished it all by myself.**

**In the scriptures, we realize that Salvation
is a FREE GIFT,
and we only have
to RECEIVE IT.
There is absolutely nothing
we can do to earn it.**

21

GOD'S PLAN OF SALVATION

Man's problem
is separation from the Holy God because of his sin.

Man cannot save himself.

God's solution
we find in the Bible, the Word of God, that there is only
one way to be saved and enjoy heaven!

Jesus Christ proclaimed
*"I am the way, the truth, and the life: no man cometh
unto the Father, but by me."*
John 14:6

Man cannot be saved with his own efforts, good works, or with religious ceremonies. No one can save you, except Jesus Christ. *"Neither is there salvation in any other: for there is none other name under heaven given among men, whereby we must be saved "* (Acts 4:12). *"For by grace are ye saved through faith; and that not of yourselves: it is the gift of God: Not of works, lest any man should boast"* (Ephesians 2:8,9).

If you are not a "born-again" Christian, turn immediately to Jesus Christ. Repent, turn from sin, and ask Him to save you. *"If thou shalt confess with thy mouth the Lord Jesus, and shalt believe in thine heart that God hath raised him from the dead, thou shalt be saved"* (Romans 10:9).

Do not postpone this decision, because tomorrow may be too late. *"Behold, now is the accepted time; behold, now is the day of salvation"* (2 Corinthians 6:2).

1. **Admit that you are a sinner.** *"There is none righteous, no, not one"* (Romans 3:10), *"For all have sinned, and come short of the glory of God"* (Romans 3:23), *"If we say that we have not sinned, we make Him a liar, and His word is not in us"* (1 John 1:10).

2. **Repent of your sins:** *"Except ye repent, ye shall all likewise perish"* (Luke 13:5), *"But now commandeth all men every where to repent"* (Acts 17:30).

3. **Believe that Jesus Christ died for you, was buried, and then rose from the dead.** *"For God so loved the world, that he gave his only begotten Son, that whosoever believeth in him should not perish, but have everlasting life "* (John 3:16), *"If thou shalt confess with thy mouth the Lord Jesus, and shalt believe in thine heart that God hath raised him from the dead, thou shalt be saved. For with the heart man believeth unto righteousness; and with the mouth confession is made unto salvation"* (Romans 10:9,10).

4. **With a sincere prayer, invite Jesus Christ to come into your life to become your personal Savior.** *"For with the heart man believeth unto righteousness; and with the mouth confession is made unto salvation"* (Romans 10:10), *"Whoever calls on the name of the LORD shall be saved"* (Romans 10:13). You can pray something like this:

   Dear God, I know that You love me and want to save me. Jesus, I believe You are the Son of God, You shed your precious blood, and You died on the cross to pay for my sins. I believe God raised You from the dead. I now turn from my sin and, by faith, receive You as my personal Savior. Come into my life, forgive my sins, and save me. In Your name, I pray. Amen.

Jesus promised that *"and him that cometh to me I will in no wise cast out"* (John 6:37). Also, by His Spirit, you will become a "born-again" Christian, a child of God and be added into His family forever. *"But as many as received him, to them gave he power to become the sons of God, even to them that believe on his name"* (John 1:12). *"Therefore if any man be in Christ, he is a new creature: old things are passed away; behold, all things are become new"* (2 Corinthians 5:17).

After you have received Jesus Christ as your personal Savior, there are four simple steps that you should follow in your Christian life to grow spiritually:

1. You must regularly read the Word of God to learn more about the Lord Jesus Christ and your new life. The Word of God must be your daily spiritual food.

2. Dedicate time to talk to God each day and have a conversation with Him through prayer.

3. Be baptized, worship, fellowship, and serve with other Christians in a Bible-believing church where the pure Word of God is preached without compromise. The Word of God must be your genuine and authentic guide for issues of faith and life. You must worship the Lord in spirit and in truth. Also, serve the spiritual and material needs of others as the Holy Spirit leads you.

4. You must give your testimony, as a child and ambassador of the Living God, to all the people you come in touch with. Your witness for Jesus will bring more souls to Him for His glory.

❖ ❖ ❖

Salvation is **GOD'S GIFT!**
It is not something we **EARN,**
but something we **RECEIVE.**

22

BIBLICAL REPENTANCE

"And saying, (Jesus) The time is fulfilled, and the kingdom of God is at hand: repent ye, and believe the gospel."
Mark 1:15

"The Lord...is longsuffering to us-ward, not willing that any should perish, but that all should come to repentance."
2 Peter 3:9

*

Have you ever come to true biblical repentance?

A lot of people today do not know what biblical repentance means and how important it is for our salvation. The Greek word for repentance is "Μετάνοια" (Metanoia.) This word comes from two words. The first is the word "Μετά" (Meta), which means "After." The second word is "Νοέω" (Noeo), which means "To think." Finally, the word " Μετάνοια " (Metanoia) means a fundamental change of mind, a spiritual conversion, and a fundamental change in one's beliefs. Maybe you ask, "Change our minds about what?" We have to change our minds about how we think about God, sin, and ourselves. We are called by God to turn from sin and commanded by God to repent of our sins. True biblical repentance for salvation is *"Repentance toward God, and faith toward our Lord Jesus Christ"* (Acts 20:21). This kind of repentance brings eternal salvation. This kind of repentance is TRUE, SAVING REPENTANCE. Some people have repented and have changed their minds about their past lives. They are sorry for their sins and realize they need a Savior, but they have not entirely changed their minds about Jesus Christ. This kind of repentance is NOT TRUE, SAVING REPENTANCE. It is because they have experienced "worldly sorrow," instead of "godly sorrow. *"For godly sorrow worketh repentance to salvation not to be repented of: but the sorrow of the world worketh death"* (2 Corinthians 7:10). The apostle Paul preached that the results of true repentance is a change of the old nature actions to godly deeds. *"they should repent and turn to God, and do works meet for repentance"* (Acts 26:20).

Peter's sermon on the day of Pentecost provides a clearer answer about the word "repent" from the saving view, *"Then Peter said unto them, Repent, and be baptized every one of you in the name of Jesus Christ for the remission of sins, and ye shall receive the gift of the Holy Ghost"* (Acts 2:38). When people heard Peter's request to repent, they might have asked, "Repent about what? " If they had listened carefully and closely to what Peter's sermon was all about, the answer to that question would have been clear.

FIRST, the apostle Peter spoke about Jesus of Nazareth: His life, His death, and His resurrection. *"Ye men of Israel, hear these words; Jesus of Nazareth, a man approved of God among you by miracles and wonders and signs, which God did by him in the midst of you, as ye yourselves also know: Him, being delivered by the determinate counsel and foreknowledge of God, ye have taken, and by wicked hands have crucified and slain: Whom God hath raised up, having loosed the pains of death: because it was not possible that he should be holden of it "* (Acts 2:22-24).

SECOND, Peter quoted from Psalm 16:8-11, in the following verses and reminded the crowds that the Messiah would be raised from the dead. *"For David speaketh concerning him, I foresaw the Lord always before my face, for he is on my right hand, that I should not be moved: Therefore did my heart rejoice, and my tongue was glad; moreover also my flesh shall rest in hope: Because thou wilt not leave my soul in hell, neither wilt thou suffer thine Holy One to see corruption. Thou hast made known to me the ways of life; thou shalt make me full of joy with thy countenance. Men and brethren, let me freely speak unto you of the patriarch David, that he is both dead and buried, and his sepulcher is with us unto this day. Therefore being a prophet, and knowing that God had sworn with an oath to him, that of the fruit of his loins, according to the flesh, he would raise up Christ to sit on his throne; He seeing this before spake of the resurrection of Christ, that his soul was not left in hell, neither his flesh did see corruption"* (Acts 2:25-31).

Peter told them that Jesus of Nazareth was the Messiah. It was also predicted by David in Psalm 110 that the Messiah would ascend to the right hand of God just as Jesus of Nazareth did, so Jesus must be the Messiah. In reality, Peter painted two pictures: one of the Messiah from the Old Testament and the other of Jesus of Nazareth. Specifically, he proved to them that Jesus is *"both Lord [God], and Christ [Messiah]"* *"Therefore let all the house of Israel know assuredly, that God hath made the same Jesus, whom ye have crucified, both Lord and Christ"* (Acts 2:36). After this, conviction came upon them, and they asked what they should do. Peter replied, *"Repent."* Change your minds about Jesus of Nazareth from what you thought about Him. Believe He is God and your Messiah who died on the cross and rose from the dead. With simple words, Peter told them that this is the kind of repentance that saves.

Biblical repentance is the only true saving repentance, but we must apply it in our lives. Michael Hodgin was right about this with the following illustration: A soap manufacturer and a pastor were walking together down a street in a large city. The soap manufacturer casually said, "The gospel you preach hasn't done much good has it? Just observe. There is still a lot of wickedness in the world, and a lot of wicked people, too!" The pastor made no reply until they passed a dirty little child making mud pies in the gutter. Seizing the opportunity, the pastor said, "I see that soap hasn't done much good in the world either; for there is much dirt, and many dirty people around." The soap man said, "Oh, well, soap only works when it is applied." And the pastor said, "Exactly, so it is with the gospel." — *Michael Hodgin, 1002 Humorous Illustrations for Public Speaking*

In this story, the pastor was right. If you have never applied the gospel in your life, do not expect to experience forgiveness of your sins and eternal salvation. Repent and believe today in Jesus of Nazareth. Admit you are wrong. God is waiting to heal your life. Repentance is the entrance to His intensive care unit and the first step to freedom. Confess your transgressions to the Lord. Honesty before God is one infection you want to catch. God is in the business of redeeming sinful people. No matter how bad you have been, Jesus will receive you just as you are. It is an offer only a fool will refuse. Open your heart to Jesus today. Do not forget that the gospel only works when it is applied.

❖ ❖ ❖

- "Repentance is to change your mind about sin, and Christ, and all the great things of God." "Repentance... makes the man love what once he hated, and hate what once he loved." — *Preachers, Charles Spurgeon*

- "Which comes first, repentance or faith? The two are so intimately related that you cannot have one without the other. The fact is, no man believes the gospel until he has judged himself as a needy sinner before God, and this is repentance." — *Dr. H.A. Ironside*

- In his book, *"I Surrender,"* Patrick Morley writes that the church's integrity problem is in the misconception "that we can add Christ to our lives, but not subtract sin. It is a change in belief without a change in behavior." He goes on to say, "It is revival without reformation, without repentance." — *Quoted in John The Baptizer, Bible Study Guide by C. Swindoll*

23

BIBLICAL FAITH

"Faith is the substance of things hoped for,
the evidence of things not seen."
Hebrews 11:1

"Without faith, it is impossible to please him [God]."
Hebrews. 11:6

*

Biblical faith is so important for our eternal destiny
and for our daily Christian life!

In the New Testament, the Greek word for "faith" is "πίστις" (pistis) which means assurance, confidence, trust, conviction, faith, belief, fidelity, and reliance. In the first verse above, faith, "πίστις" is the assurance of things we hope for, but have not yet received.
Faith is not feeling, it is believing. Faith is not doing, it is resting. Faith is more than mere belief. Faith is deep confidence in the One you trust. This confidence is demonstrated by your actions.

The second verse above tells us how important the Christian faith is. "Without faith, it is impossible to please God." It does not say "Without faith, it is difficult to please God" or "Without faith, you will not be able to completely please God," but it makes it crystal clear that "Without faith, it is IMPOSSIBLE to please God." When I read this text many years ago, I came to understand that faith is really important to my eternal condition and for my daily Christian life.

Many Christians have a hard time practicing faith in their daily lives, but without it, God cannot bless them. The Word of God states that *"the just shall live by his faith"* (Habakkuk 2:4) and we must *"walk by faith"* and *"not by sight"* (2 Corinthians 5:7). As Christians, we have to realize that without having faith in God, we cannot receive His blessings. Like anything else in our spiritual life, it is important to grow in faith. If we do not have money, we cannot buy material things. If we also do not have faith, we cannot please God and receive more blessings.

In our spiritual life, faith is the currency of exchange. People are missing blessings because of common misconceptions about faith. One is that faith is blind, but blind faith is really foolishness or superstition. Biblical faith is taking God 100% at His word and acting on it. Faith in action is the highest compliment that we can pay to God. If we do not exercise faith and believe what God says, we make Him a liar. *"He that believeth not God hath made him a liar..."* (1 John 5:10). When we do not exercise faith, we sin and miss God's blessings. We must ask ourselves, "Is there an area of my life that I am sinning against Christ by simply failing to trust Him?" If it is YES, we have to correct it.

I will mention an example from my own experience for you to see what happened when I had trusted the Lord. Several years ago, we gave our piano to my daughter so that she could teach her children to play. This way, her children could use their talents to serve the Lord as they grew. Because my wife played the organ in the church where we attended at that time, she needed an organ at home to practice. By faith, I told her that the Lord would give us a free organ for a Christmas present. I believed this because, first, we tried to help my daughter; second, we did not have thousands of dollars to buy an organ; and third, because my wife was going to use it to glorify the Lord. When some other people heard about this, they were skeptical and told me, "You are asking too much. Maybe the Lord will give you one for a good price, but not free."

Without giving those people any attention, I checked on the Internet and found a church in our area that wanted to give their organ away for free. They wanted to give it away because somebody had donated a brand new organ to them. I was the first to respond to their ad. Possibly others thought a free organ would not be worth anything. The organ was beautiful and in excellent condition, but it was too big for our living room. We talked to our pastor about the organ after we saw it. He told us that our church would take it and would give us the church's current smaller organ for free. Our church's smaller organ was like brand new. The church received the big organ; and the pastors, with a few other men from our church, delivered the smaller organ to our home without us having to pay a penny. The Lord not only blessed us—He blessed our church, too. PRAISE THE LORD!

We need to be encouraged that when we act in faith, God will bless us. Faith honors God, and God honors our faith when it is according to

His will, and not according to our fleshly desires. *"He is a rewarder of them that diligently seek him"* (Hebrews 11:6). Faith is so important; still, it is so misunderstood. Stop playing it safe and begin to live a little.

Life's greatest adventure comes when you follow Jesus in faith. More is unseen than is seen, and we should live our lives in light of the unseen reality instead of the visible reality. Faith is needed to see Christ and have a victorious Christian life. Jesus is everywhere if you only look through spiritual eyes. With just your natural eyes, "you get what you see!" Unfortunately, the more comfortable you are in this life with material things, the harder it is to live by faith.

The question to you is: "Are you living by faith or by sight?" Faith is not believing something hard enough to make it happen—that is positive thinking. Faith is not trying; it is depending on Christ alone if you are a child of God. Nothing is achieved without faith, and nothing is impossible with God. The Bible very clearly says, *"Without faith, it is impossible to please him [God]"* (Hebrews. 11:6) and *"we know that all things work together for good to them that love God"* (Romans 8:28).

Depend on God's promises. By faith, leave everything in God's hands and wait to see the surprises he has for you. Maybe the Lord will not do a miracle by opening the heavens to send you "manna" or to give you a free organ, but for sure He will find a way to *"supply all your need according to His riches in glory by Christ Jesus"* (Philippians 4:19). I recommend that you walk by faith and step out of the boat, and you will discover the thrill of walking on the waves as Peter did (Matthew 14:29). Remember, faith makes a Christian, life proves a Christian, and death crowns a Christian.

❖ ❖ ❖

- "Faith is to believe what we do not see, and the reward of this faith is to see what we believe." — *Theologian and Philosopher, Augustine*

- "Faith does not operate in the realm of the possible. There is no glory for God in that which is humanly possible. Faith begins where man's power ends." — *Evangelist, George Mueller*

- "God, our Father, has made all things depend on faith so that whoever has faith will have everything, and whoever does not have faith will have nothing." — *Priest and Theologian, Martin Luther*

- "Little faith will bring your soul to heaven, but great faith will bring heaven to your soul." — *"Prince of Preachers," Charles H. Spurgeon*

- "Faith sees the invisible, believes the unbelievable, and receives the impossible." — *Author, Corrie Ten Boom*

24

FAITH & WORKS

"For by grace are ye saved through faith;
and that not of yourselves: it is the gift of God:
Not of works, lest any man should boast.
For we are his workmanship, created in Christ Jesus
unto good works, which God hath before
ordained that we should walk in them."
Ephesians 2:8-10

*

Both FAITH and WORKS are divinely provided and are found in every true believer!

Countless people are confused about what the apostles Paul and James say about the relationship between FAITH and WORKS. If they do not take verses out of context, there is no contradiction between the two apostles' teachings. Both FAITH and WORKS are divinely provided and are found in every true believer, but each has its own place and use. When we read what Paul and James said about FAITH and WORKS, we find out that we are saved by faith and not by works. The works we did before we were saved, have nothing to do with our salvation. However, our saving faith produces good works after our conversion, which will be rewarded in heaven.

Let's look at a few scriptures to see what the Bible tells us about FAITH and WORKS.

FAITH

1. **What is faith?:** *"Faith is the substance of things hoped for, the evidence of things not seen"* (Hebrews 11:1). Faith, in other words, is the assurance of

things we hope for, but have not yet received. *"Abraham believed God," "He staggered not at the promise of God," "And being fully persuaded that, what he had promised, he was able also to perform"* (Romans 4:3,20,21). He took God's Word as promised.

2. **The significance of faith:** *"Without faith it is impossible to please him..."* (Hebrews 11:6). Without faith, we may be kind, friendly, and generous. We may please men, but without faith, we cannot please God.

3. **Saving faith:** Saving faith is to believe the evidence God gave of His Son. It is the faith which saves us, *"Thy faith hath saved thee..." (Luke 7:50)*. It is to believe with our heart for salvation in the Son of God and not only have knowledge of Him. *"And this is the record, that God hath given to us eternal life, and this life is in his Son"* (1 John 5:11). *"If thou shalt confess with thy mouth the Lord Jesus, and shalt believe in thine heart that God hath raised him from the dead, thou shalt be saved"* (Romans 10:9). Evidence of saving faith is a Christ-like and fruitful life in Christ.

4. **What faith does:** Only faith can accomplish the following: *"Faith hath saved thee"* (Luke 7:50), *"Saved through faith"* (Ephesians 2:8), *"He that believeth... hath everlasting life."* (John 6:47), *"Have everlasting life"* (John 3:16), *"Being justified by faith, we have peace with God"* (Romans 5:1), and *"That Christ may dwell in your hearts"* (Ephesians 3:17).

WORKS

1. **What works cannot do:** We cannot be saved by works: *"saved through faith...not of yourselves; [not of works]"* (Ephesians 2:8,9), *"If righteousness come by the law [works], then Christ is dead in vain"* (Galatians 2:21), *"Ye could not be justified by the law of Moses"* (Acts 13:39), and *"By the deeds of the law there shall no flesh be justified"* (Romans 3:20).

2. **The right place for good works:** After we are saved, God requires good works from us. *"For we are his workmanship, created in Christ Jesus unto good works, which God hath before ordained that we should walk in them"* (Ephesians 2:10). *"Be careful to maintain good works..."* (Titus 3:8).

3. **The profit of good works:** God has promised rewards for believers according to their good works. *"He will receive a reward..."* (1 Corinthians 3:11-15), *"He shall in no wise lose his reward"* (Matthew 10:42), and *"I will make thee ruler over many things..."* (Matthew 25:21). Believers are not saved

by works, but totally by faith. However, they are rewarded in heaven according to the works they did after they were saved. *"God hath before ordained that we should walk in them"* (Ephesians 2:8-10).

Grandpa Jackson once had a little rowboat. He carved the word "faith" over one oar and "works" over the other. One day while his grandson was boating with him, he asked about the words. Grandpa stopped rowing with both arms and then started to row with only one arm. As the rowboat moved in small circles, Grandpa told him, "This is exactly what happens in our Christian life. We need to have both faith and works. Works without faith are worthless, and faith without works is dead. This means we cannot go anywhere, like the rowboat when we use only one oar and not both. When faith and works are rowing together, they have balance, make progress, and bring blessing."

Remember that only faith is needed to be saved, and not works, but after salvation, you need to have both in your Christian life. FAITH and GOOD WORKS keep the believer in good balance. *"Ye shall know them by their fruits... so every good tree bringeth forth good fruit; but a corrupt tree bringeth forth evil fruit"* (Matthew 7:16,17).

Let all Christians obey the scriptures, do God's will, serve the Lord, and bring forth good fruit to glorify the Lord. *"And God is able to make all grace abound toward you; that ye, always having all sufficiency in all things, may abound to every good work"* (2 Corinthians 9:8), *"Let your light so shine before men, that they may see your good works, and glorify your Father which is in heaven"* (Matthew 5:16).

❖ ❖ ❖

- "Only through repentance and faith in Christ can anyone be saved. No religious activity will be sufficient, only true faith in Jesus Christ alone."
— *Christian Apologist, Ravi Zacharias*

- "The apostle Paul is abundant in teaching, *that 'we are justified by faith alone, without the works of the law!'* There is no one doctrine that he in sists so much upon and that he handles with so much distinctness, explaining, giving reasons, and answering objections."
— *Pastor and Theologian, Jonathan Edwards*

- "What is it about your own miserable works and doings that you think you could please God more than the sacrifice of His own Son!"
— *Priest and Theologian, Martin Luther*

- "Faith and works are bound up in the same bundle. He that obeys God trusts God; and he that trusts God obeys God. He that is without faith is without works; he that is without works is without faith."
— *"Prince of Preachers," Charles Spurgeon*

- "Regarding the debate about faith and works: It's like asking which blade in a pair of scissors is most important."
— *Scholar and Author, C. S. Lewis*

- "Faith without works is not faith at all, but a simple lack of obedience to God."
— *Theologian, Dietrich Bonhoeffer*

- "Faith is the deliberate confidence in the character of God whose ways you may not understand at the time."
— *Evangelist and Teacher, Oswald Chambers*

- **Good works will not bring salvation, but salvation will bring good works.**

- **Only faith is needed to be saved, and not works, but after salvation, we need to have both in our Christian life.**

- **FAITH and GOOD WORKS keep the believer in good balance.**

25

LAW AND GRACE

"Knowing that a man is not justified by the works of the law,
but by the faith of Jesus Christ, even we have believed
in Jesus Christ, that we might be justified by the faith
of Christ, and not by the works of the law:
for by the works of the law shall no flesh be justified."
Galatians 2:16

*

Are you living under the LAW or under GRACE?

The apostle John tells us, *"The law was given by Moses, but grace and truth came by Jesus Christ"* (John 1:17) and the apostle Paul tells us, *"I do not frustrate the grace of God: for if righteousness come by the law, then Christ is dead in vain"* (Galatians 2:21).

God gave us two covenants. On Mount Sinai, He gave us the old covenant, which is the LAW, and on Mount Calvary, He gave us the new covenant, which is GRACE. The old one commands "DO and LIVE," and the new one commands "BELIEVE and LIVE." Under the Law, righteousness is what we can DO for God, but under Grace, righteousness is what God has DONE for us. According to the New Testament, the believer is not under the Law, but instead under grace. Let us look at a few scriptures to see what the Bible tells us about LAW and GRACE.

LAW

1. **What is the Law?** The Law is the rules God gave to the children of Israel. These rules regulated almost every area of their lives in Old Testament times. God also gave Moses the Ten Commandments on

Mount Sinai. *"Thou shalt keep therefore his statutes, and his commandments..."* (Deuteronomy 4:40). (For more information read Exodus chapter 34). *"The law of the LORD is perfect, converting the soul: the testimony of the LORD is sure, making wise the simple. The statutes of the LORD are right, rejoicing the heart: the commandment of the LORD is pure, enlightening the eyes."* (Psalm 19:7,8), and *"the law is holy..."* (Romans 7:12).

2.   **What does the Law do for us?** The New Testament gives us a crystal clear answer. *"The works of the law are under the curse..."* (Galatians 3:10), *"For whosoever shall keep the whole law, and yet offend in one point, he is guilty of all"* (James 2:10), and *"Every mouth may be stopped, and all the world may become guilty before God..."* (Romans 3:19).

3.   **What cannot the Law do?** The Law cannot justify anyone. *"By the deeds of the law there shall no flesh be justified..."* (Romans 3:20), *"Ye could not be justified by the law of Moses"* (Acts 13:39), and *"The law made nothing perfect, but the bringing in of a better hope did; by the which we draw nigh unto God."* (Hebrews 7:19).

4.   **Why did God give the Law?** The Law was given for the following reasons: *"It was added because of transgressions..."* (Galatians 3:19), and *"The law was our schoolmaster to bring us unto Christ that we might be justified by faith. But after that faith is come, we are no longer under a schoolmaster"* (Galatians 3:24, 25).

GRACE

1.   **What is grace?** Grace is the freely given undeserving favor of God to the unworthy. God shows His love to those that are unlovely. He gives His peace and salvation by sending His only Son to die on the cross so those guilty ones might be reconciled to God. *"He might shew the exceeding riches of his grace in his kindness toward us through Christ Jesus."* (Ephesians 2:7), *"The kindness and love of God our Saviour toward man appeared, Not by works of righteousness which we have done, but according to his mercy he saved us, by the washing of regeneration, and renewing of the Holy Ghost"* (Titus 3:4,5), and *"His great love wherewith he loved us, Even when we were dead in sins..."* (Ephesians 2:4,5).

2.   **What does grace do?** Grace brings salvation and justifies man. *"For by grace are ye saved through faith; and that not of yourselves: it is the gift of God"* (Ephesians 2:8), *"For the grace of God that bringeth salvation..."* (Titus 2:11), and *"Justified freely by His grace through the redemption that is in Christ Jesus"* (Romans 3:24).

3. **Is Christianity a religion of law and grace?** Absolutely NOT! *"Now to him that worketh is the reward not reckoned of grace, but of debt. But to him that worketh not, but believeth on him that justifieth the ungodly, his faith is counted for righteousness"* (Romans 4:4,5) and *"Christ is become of no effect unto you, whosoever of you are justified by the law; ye are fallen from grace"* (Galatians 5:4). There is also a comparison between law and grace in Deuteronomy 21:18-21 and Luke 15:18-23.

The Bible teaches us clearly that the believer in Christ is no longer under the Law but under grace. *"For sin shall not have dominion over you: for ye are not under the law, but under grace. Wherefore, my brethren, ye also are become dead to the law by the body of Christ; that ye should be married to another, even to him who is raised from the dead, that we should bring forth fruit unto God"* (Romans 6:14, 7:4). The Law set man to try in his own strength to do what is right, and to keep the commandments. Under the Law, he is in bondage and tries to do what his old nature cannot do. He is never able to succeed.

The Law has no power to save anyone from sin, but helps all of us to compare ourselves with the character of God and acknowledges our sin. Augustine said, *"The law detects, grace alone conquers sin."* The Law is like a mirror. It informs us that we have a dirty face, but it cannot clean it. Only GRACE can clean our dirty face. Only GRACE can clean and wash our sins through the blood of Jesus Christ. *"The blood of Jesus Christ his Son cleanseth us from all sin"* (1 John 1:7). By the death of Christ, the believer is looked at as having died to the Law. Grace sets him free and wins his heart and motivates him to serve Christ.

The believer is not looking to do his own will and continue to sin, but to do the will of God. He finds the power to do this from the Holy Spirit who indwells him. *"Know ye not that your body is the temple of the Holy Ghost which is in you, which ye have of God, and ye are not your own?"* (1 Corinthians 6:19), and *"For the law of the Spirit of life in Christ Jesus hath made me free from the law of sin and death"* (Romans 8:2). When we yield more to God's Word for leading and guiding in our lives, everything the Law demanded will be produced in our lives by the Holy Spirit *"That the righteousness of the law might be fulfilled in us, who walk not after the flesh, but after the Spirit"* (Romans 8:4). This way, the person will find satisfaction, joy, and strength to be obedient to God's Word.

I hope you are free in Christ, and you are not still in bondage of sin and seeking justification by works of the Law. I hope you are saved according to Ephesians 2:8,9: *"For by grace are ye saved through faith; and that not of yourselves: it is the gift of God: Not of works, lest any man should boast."*

Remember, if you are a true believer in Christ, God's judgment is for you in JUSTIFICATION. God's power is for you in SANCTIFICATION. God's love is for you in ADOPTION. God's glory is for you in GLORIFICATION. God is entirely for you in CHRIST. Christ rescued you FOREVER. Your eternal security is purchased by CHRIST, promised by the FATHER, and sealed by the HOLY SPIRIT, and one day you will walk in heaven without hesitation but with boldness.

❖ ❖ ❖

Grace + Law = Law
Grace + Law = Anti-Gospel
Grace = The Gospel of the grace of God

The Law reveals our sin, but the Gospel is the cure.
The Law: "Be righteous." The verdict: "No one is righteous."
The Gospel: "Jesus is our righteousness."

**You can experience God's grace,
no matter who you are or
how much you have sinned!
The Lord Jesus Christ specializes
in complete restoration of your life
by His grace,
which is greater than your sin!**

26

SALVATION BY GRACE

"For by grace are you saved through faith;
and that not of yourselves: it is the gift of God:
Not of works, lest any man should boast."
Ephesians 2:8,9

*

Salvation is only by grace and not by works!

Grace + 0 = Salvation

Salvation is by grace: 100% from God and 0% from man.
We are saved by grace, or we are not saved at all.

The Bible very clearly teaches us that our salvation is by grace through faith in Jesus Christ. In the New Testament, the word "grace" in Greek is "χάρις" (Charis) which in the verse above focuses on the provision of salvation. Grace is the freely given undeserving favor of God to the unworthy. Grace is God's love in action to men who do not deserve it. In other words, grace is God's unconditional love to the undeserving. Grace is that God sent His only begotten Son to die on the cross so that we as sinners can be reconciled to Him. *"He [God] hath made him to be sin for us, who knew no sin; that we might be made the righteousness of God in him"* (2 Corinthians 5:21).

According to pastor and biblical scholar, Paul P. Enns, *"Grace may be defined as the unmerited or undeserving favor of God to those who are under condemnation."* Also, according to Bishop and author, R. P. C. Hanson, *"Grace means the free, unmerited, unexpected love of God and all the benefits, delights, and comforts which flow from it. It means that while we were sinners and enemies, we have been treated as sons and heirs."*

Grace + 0 = Salvation. We do not have to do works to earn salvation, as many people believe. Our salvation is totally a "gift of God." If it were by works, it would not have been necessary for Jesus to come to this world and die on the cross for our redemption. If it were by works, what would happen to people who are not able to do good works because of their physical, mental, or financial condition? It is straightforward, true, and biblical that God offers His free gift to all people: rich and poor, sick and healthy, as well as young and old by His grace through faith in Jesus Christ. *"And if by grace, then is it no more of works: otherwise grace is no more grace"* (Romans 11:6).

There once was a preacher who had departed from the truth. To justify his teaching of salvation by works, he told the following story: A frog one day fell into a bucket of milk. He tried to jump out but always failed. The only thing he was able to do was paddle and paddle and paddle some more in the milk. Finally, the milk turned to butter from which he was able to jump out and find his freedom. The preacher's conclusion was, "Just keep paddling, keep on working, keep on doing your best, and you will make it." According to the Holy Scriptures, this is wrong and laughable. This is not the "Good News" of the gospel of grace. This is the "false gospel" or the "yellow gospel," which many Christian churches and all non-Christian religions in the world preach today. They believe that you have to do the best you can in your life to earn salvation and make it to heaven. They ignore and reject the truth of justification by faith alone, through God's grace.

Most people know the hymn "Amazing Grace" and enjoy singing it, but they do not know what grace means. If you ask someone, "Do you know grace?" he may answer, "Grace, who?" He answers this way because he thinks you are talking about somebody's name and not about the grace of God. Another may know what you are asking about, and because he is aware of his sinful condition, he will respond, "I'm too undeserving for God's grace." He does not know that God's grace is for the undeserving, and Jesus died on the cross for him. The apostle Paul tells us Jesus Christ died for people *"who were dead in trespasses and sins"* (Ephesians 2:1). God offers grace that provides forgiveness and new life through Jesus Christ. *"For by grace are you saved through faith; and that not of yourselves: it is the gift of God: Not of works, lest any man should boast"* (Ephesians (2:8,9).

Clearly, we see that we are saved without good works, but the Lord requires good works from us after our salvation. We must do good works after we are saved as new creations in Christ. *"For we are his workmanship, created in Christ Jesus unto good works, which God hath before ordained that we should walk in them"* (Ephesians 2:10). The Lord does not require good works before our salvation to earn it through them because everything we have done is unclean as filthy rags: *"But we are all as an unclean thing, and all our righteousness are as filthy rags..."* (Isaiah 64:6). Augustine also said, *"For grace is given not because we have done good works, but in order that we may be able to do them."*

Christians must help others to understand that God's salvation is only for sinners like you and me according to the Word of God. *"All have sinned, and come short of the glory of God"* (Romans 3:23), but God's grace saves us.

AMAZING GRACE

Amazing grace! How sweet the sound
That saved a wretch like me!
I once was lost, but now am found;
Was blind, but now I see. — *Hymn by John Newton, 1779*

If you have not yet been saved by grace, I invite you to come to God today through the Savior, His Son Jesus Christ, who loves you and gave himself for you. To receive eternal life, you must admit that you are a sinner and that you do not deserve eternal life. Realize that you could not lift a finger to save yourself. Only God can take away your sin through the sacrifice of His Son, Jesus, who died on the cross for you, rose again and offers forgiveness to all who put their trust in Him. *"For God so loved the world, that he gave his only begotten Son, that whosoever believeth in him should not perish, but have everlasting life"* (John 3:16).

❖ ❖ ❖

- "If heaven were by merit, it would never be heaven to me, for if I were in it, I should say, 'I am sure I am here by mistake; I am sure this is not my place; I have no claim to it.' But if it be of grace and not of works, then we may walk into heaven with boldness."— *Charles H. Spurgeon*

God's
Riches
At
Christ's
Expense

Justice......getting what we deserve.
Mercy.......not getting what we deserve.
Grace........getting what we do not deserve.

- "And if by grace, then it is no more of works: otherwise grace is no more grace." — *Romans 11:6*

27

OBEDIENCE TO GOD

"Now when he [Jesus] had left speaking, he said unto Simon,
Launch out into the deep, and let down your nets for a draught.
And Simon answering said unto him,
Master, we have toiled all the night, and have taken nothing:
nevertheless at thy word I will let down the net.
And when they had this done, they inclosed a great multitude
of fishes: and their net brake."
Luke 5:4-6

"Let us hear the conclusion of the whole matter:
Fear God, and keep his commandments:
for this is the whole duty of man."
Ecclesiastes 12:13

*

Obedience is the key to God's heart!

One evening an evangelist preached with great zeal on the text, *"Thou shall not steal."* He impressed upon his listeners the necessity of absolute integrity in everything. The next morning, he boarded a bus and gave the driver a dollar bill for his fare. Counting his change, he found that he had received an extra quarter. Without hesitation, he approached the driver and said, "You accidentally gave me too much change." "It wasn't an accident," the driver replied. "I did it on purpose to see what you would do. Last night I was in your audience and wondered if you practiced what you preached. I made up my mind if you returned the quarter, I'd come and hear you tonight." — *Moody, quoted on preachhim.org*

Something similar happened to me some time ago. Just before Thanksgiving, my wife and I went to the grocery store to buy extra food because we were expecting company. After we checked out, I found out that the turkey and ham we purchased had been charged at the regular price instead of the sale price. I mentioned that to the manager of the store. He apologized and gave me back what I thought was the money they overcharged us. When I went to the car, I found out that he gave me a lot more money. I went back to the manager to tell him about the mistake he made, and to return the extra money. When I told him, he said, "I know. I gave you extra money to see if you are an honest man. You can keep the extra money and have a Happy Thanksgiving!" Wow! I never expected anything like that to happen. I told my wife afterward that if I had not tried to give the money back, every time the manager would see me, he would think to himself, "He is a dishonest man."

Obedience to God's commandments is essential for pleasing God and for our Christian growth. *"If ye love me, keep my commandments"* (John 14:15). Obedience in Greek is "υπακοή" (hupakoé) noun and "υπακούω" (hupakouo) verb. The Greek word "υπακούω" comes from two words: "hupo," which means "under" and "akouo," which means "to hear." The full word means "to hear under": to submit to any authority, absolute submission, obedience, and compliance.

The first humans to disobey God were Adam and Eve, and the first angel to disobey God was Satan; they all paid a price. Satan continues to disobey God even after his fall. Nevertheless, God is merciful, even after the fall of Adam and Eve, He gives us the opportunity to repent and ask for forgiveness. He is faithful, and through Jesus Christ, He provides forgiveness if we seek Him. Today, mankind can still restore his relationship with God through his obedience to Him. The key to God's heart is obedience. To enjoy the blessings of God, we must have obedience. Some think love or faith is the key to God's heart. No! The Holy Scriptures teach us that obedience is the most essential principle in our relationship with God. *"Jesus answered and said unto him, If a man love me, he will keep my words: and my Father will love him, and we will come unto him, and make our abode with him"* (John 14:23).

The apostle Peter obeyed Jesus' command and let down the nets again to catch fish and was blessed with many. When Peter heard the command of God, he took a great step of faith. That is where his journey of faith started. *"Master, we have toiled all the night, and have taken nothing: nevertheless at thy word I will let down the net"* (Luke 5:5). Real faith is not to say that you believe in God. It costs nothing to say that but obeying God is another thing. It is never easy to do and is always costly. Being a Christian involves walking in a daily life of costly obedience. The apostle Peter did everything as Jesus told him in Luke 5:4 and was blessed by catching a lot of fish. We have to obey and trust the Lord a lot more than we trust the captain of a boat or the pilot of an airplane. This happens only when we come to the point in our spiritual life when we will say as the apostle Thomas *"My Lord and my God,"* or as King David "The Lord is my shepherd."

Biblical obedience is when we seek God with our whole heart without questions. This kind of obedience counts and brings blessings. I remember one summer when I was a boy working with my father and older brother Mike at our farm. We ate under a big shade tree at noontime. I heard my father say with authority and warning in his voice, "Mike, run to me immediately." Because we were disciplined children, my brother ran into my father's arms. Afterward, my brother and I saw a deadly snake moving close to where my brother was eating. My father was able to kill the snake, but if my brother had questioned my father's command and did not obey, he would have possibly lost his life.

Another example of obedience comes from Evangelist Paul Rader, who had many a talk with a banker in New York. The banker would reply that he was too busy for religion. Time passed and the banker, seriously overworked, was sent to a sanatorium for complete rest. One day God spoke to Paul Rader; the message was clear: "Go and speak to the banker." Rader obeyed, catching a train and going with all speed to the sumptuous sanatorium. Arriving at the facility, Rader saw the banker standing in the doorway. "Oh, Rader," said the banker, "I am so glad to see you." "I received your telegram," said Rader. "That's impossible," said the banker. "I wrote a telegram begging you to come, but I tore it up. I didn't send it." "That may be," said Rader, "but your message came by way of Heaven."

Paul Rader found his friend under deep conviction of sin, and he pointed him to Christ as a perfect Saviour. That man accepted Christ, and his heart was filled with joy. "Rader," he said, "did you ever see the sky so blue or the grass so green?" Rader replied, "Sometimes we sing" 'Heaven above is softer blue, Earth around is sweeter green; Something lives in every hue Christless eyes have never seen.'" Suddenly the banker leaned against Paul Rader and fell into his arms, dead. — *Morning Glory, July 13, 1993*

When God is calling you to follow Him in faith, do not let fear keep you from obeying His orders. Go forward in faith. Obedience is all God requires. When the Lord is calling you to obey, make sure you respond quickly. You might not understand at that time but act in faith without questioning His wisdom.

In His Holy Scriptures, God gave us commandments and not suggestions. A Christian is only free when he does the will of God and obeys God's commandments. In the kingdom of God, this is as natural for God's child as the water is for the fish or the air for the bird. He must be obedient to His commandments! Obedience to God's commandments produces freedom while disobedience produces slavery. If he compares the cost of obedience, it is nothing to the cost of disobedience. Faith and obedience are unable to separate because obedience is evidence of true faith. The will of God never has been and never will be accomplished by those who are not entirely obedient to Him. If he is going to serve in an army, he must wear its uniform. If he is going to march in the parade, he must keep in step. The choice is his. Will he be obedient to God or to the devil.

Fear the Lord and do what He commands. It could be a matter of life or death! The evidence of knowing God is obeying God. *"Hereby we do know that we know him, if we keep his commandments"* (1 John 2:3). If God asks you to speak to someone about Him, obey the Spirit's direction. God's timing is perfect, so do not put it off. Someone's spiritual future may be at stake. Go and speak. Maybe it is your wife, your child, your parent, your sister, your brother, your friend, your relative, your co-worker, or your neighbor. If you do not speak to that person, and you learn that the person died and went to hell, you will regret it forever because you did not obey God's will. During the summer of 2018, my sister-in-law traveled from the state of Florida to the state of Wisconsin to visit a girlfriend who was dying from cancer. During the visit, she led her to the Lord. I am glad she did because a short time later, her girlfriend died, but not in her sins. She died in the Lord because she was saved (John 8:21) (Revelation 14:13). Praise the Lord!

TRUST AND OBEY

Trust and obey, for there's no other way
To be happy in Jesus, but to trust and obey.

— *Hymn by John H. Sammis, 1887*

❖ ❖ ❖

- "To obey is better than sacrifice..." —*1 Samuel 15:22*

- "It is the obedient soul who can lay hold of the precious promises of Scripture. The willful and lawless have no such opportunity."
— *Dr. H.A. Ironside*

- "People have a tendency to obey the Lord only as long as it suits them... God wants us to obey His Word, whether it suits us or not. That is the pathway to blessing." — *Minister and Author, William MacDonald*

28

SURRENDER TO JESUS

"I am crucified with Christ:
nevertheless I live; yet not I, but Christ liveth in me:
and the life which I now live in the flesh I live by the faith
of the Son of God, who loved me,
and gave himself for me."
Galatians 2:20

*

Surrender your life to Jesus and make Him the captain of your soul!

Surrender generally means, according to *en.wikipedia.org*, that a person completely gives up his own will and subjects his thoughts, ideas, and deeds to the will and teachings of a higher power. Surrender for a believer in Christ means that he completely gives up his own will to the will of God. To surrender is to die to self and allow Christ to live through the believer, as the verse above and the following verses teach:

- *"If any man come to me, and hate not his father, and mother, and wife, and children, and brethren, and sisters, yea, and his own life also, he cannot be my disciple"* (Luke 14:26).

- *"For to me, to live is Christ, and to die is gain"* (Philippians 1:21).

- *"For ye are dead, and your life is hid with Christ in God"* (Colossians 3:3).

- *"Now if we be dead with Christ, we believe that we shall also live with him"* (Romans 6:8).

THE JOURNEY AND DESTINY OF A CHRISTIAN

Today, more than ever, the church of Christ needs Christians who surrender to God. We often hear evangelists and pastors say, Christians need "absolute surrender" to the Lord Jesus Christ, but some people do not understand the meaning of these words. It means that, as Christ gave up everything to God, Christians must also give up entirely everything to Christ. Some agree, but some do not because they think this never can be done. Think about it. Jesus Christ entirely and absolutely gave His life to do nothing else but the will of God to please Him and depend on the Father absolutely and entirely. The same applies to Christians. They have to do nothing else but to seek the pleasure of Christ. Jesus Christ came to breathe His own Spirit into Christians to help them live entirely for God, just as He did. Now, each person who has the Holy Spirit, which means each Christian and redeemed child of God, must gladly live day by day, allowing Christ to do with him what He will.

In 1837, three Methodist ministers prepared to land on the Fiji Islands with their families. The captain of the ship that brought them pleaded with the missionaries to forsake their foolish endeavor. "You will lose your lives and the lives of your loved ones if you go to these savage islands," the captain appealed. One of the missionaries simply looked at the officer and said, "We died before we came here!" — *Source Unknown*

Just outside my office window, there is a high voltage wire which carries electricity to the house. If I lean out far enough to touch it, death would be swift, but the birds that sit on it are not harmed. The secret is that when they touch the high-powered wire, they touch nothing else besides the wire. My danger is if I touch the wire, I also contact the earth through the walls of my house and put my body in great danger. God wants to protect us from danger when we reach one hand to Him while keeping a hold on some earthly thing with the other hand. Our safety is complete only if we self-surrender to His power and love, and not depend on anything else.

If you have not surrendered to the Lord yet, my question to you is: "Are you fearful of landing on shore?" The three Methodist ministers did not fear to do so. Do not let the opportunity to love, obey, and serve the Lord be lost because of your worries. Surrender your life to Jesus and let him take the helm. God's peace will guide you when you make Christ the Captain of your soul. God can do more in one moment of your surrender than you can accomplish in a lifetime of being in control. Finally, remember the words of the Salvation Army founder, William Booth, *"The greatness of man's power is the measure of his surrender to the Lord."*

ALL TO JESUS I SURRENDER

All to Jesus I surrender,
All to Him I freely give;
I will ever love and trust Him,
In His presence daily live

Refrain:
I surrender all,
I surrender all.
All to Thee, my blessed Savior,
I surrender all.

— Hymn by Judson W. Van de Venter, 1896

❖ ❖ ❖

• "God is ready to assume full responsibility for the life wholly yielded to Him."
— Pastor and Author, Andrew Murray

• "Unless you have made a complete surrender and are doing his will it will avail you nothing if you've reformed a thousand times and have your name on fifty church records."
— Evangelist, Billy Sunday

• "Taking up my "cross" means a life voluntarily surrendered to God."
— Bible Teacher and Author, A.W. Pink

• "The man or woman who is wholly or joyously surrendered to Christ can't make a wrong choice - any choice will be the right one."
— Pastor and Author, A.W. Tozer

• "Surrender isn't about giving up. It's about letting go!"
— Unknown

• "When the will of God crosses the will of man, somebody has to die." *— Theologian Professor, Addison Leitch*

29

COMMITTED TO GOD

*"Commit thy way unto the LORD; trust also in him;
and he shall bring it to pass."*
Psalm 37:5

*"Let your heart therefore be perfect with the LORD our God, to
walk in his statutes, and to keep his commandments..."*
1 Kings 8:61

*

**Committed to God and His work.
He honors your commitment!**

Do not be a part-time Christian.
GOD is not a part-time SAVIOR!

According to the Bible, Christians must make commitments to many other people, yet the essential commitment of our lives must be to God. Jesus said, *"Thou shalt love the Lord thy God with all thy heart, and with all thy soul, and with all thy mind. This is the first and great commandment"* (Matthew 22:37,38). This means we must commit to placing God before everything else in our lives. This means as His disciples, we must be committed to Him before everything else, even our families and ourselves. *"If any man come to me, and hate not his father, and mother, and wife, and children, and brethren, and sisters, yea, and his own life also, he cannot be my disciple. And whosoever doth not bear his cross, and come after me, cannot be my disciple"* (Luke 14:26-27). *"If any man will come after me, let him deny himself, and take up his cross daily, and follow me. For whosoever will save his life shall lose it: but whosoever will lose his life for my sake, the same shall save it"* (Luke 9:23-24). Such commitment, obedience, and devotion will help us to go through the trials and suffering we will have in our lives.

We will have to pay the price to be God's man, woman, boy, or girl in a pagan world. If we are not paying the price, then we are not really serving Christ. Jesus alerted us that in our Christian life, we would not walk on streets of roses, but: *"Remember the word that I said unto you, The servant is not greater than his lord. If they have persecuted me, they will also persecute you..."* (John 15:20). The apostle Paul warns us, too. *"Yea, and all that will live godly in Christ Jesus shall suffer persecution"* (2 Timothy 3:12). The true commitment to Christ is to deny ourselves and take up his cross daily and follow Him. Our example for all of these is Christ himself. The apostle Paul followed the Lord's example and said, *"I am crucified with Christ: nevertheless I live; yet not I, but Christ liveth in me: and the life which I now live in the flesh I live by the faith of the Son of God, who loved me, and gave himself for me"* (Galatians 2:20). Complete commitment to God means that Jesus is everything to us in our Christian journey.

How we react to God's challenges shows the level of our commitment. Being committed to Christ means we live for Christ and not for ourselves as the apostle Paul states, *"For me to live is Christ..."* (Philippians 1:21). Christians are tested by hardship in many other countries, but in America, we are tested by freedom. The testing by freedom is much harder because we do not feel the pressures about our religion as much as in other countries. As a result of that, we relax, and we are not committed to Christ. We also do not concentrate on Christ, on His teaching, and how He wants us to live. God wants us to live by His ways and not our lifestyle, which does not support a godly life.

• We have many examples of totally committed Christians, such as **Missionary Hudson Taylor**. "It was a stormy night in Birmingham, England, and Hudson Taylor was to speak at a meeting...His hostess assured him that nobody would attend on such a stormy night, but Taylor insisted on going. 'I must go even if there is no one but the doorkeeper.' Less than a dozen people showed up, but the meeting was marked with unusual spiritual power. Half of those present either became missionaries or gave their children as missionaries, and the rest were faithful supporters of the China Inland Mission for years to come." — *by W. Wiersbe, Wycliffe Handbook of Preaching and Preachers, p. 242*

• **The Bohemian reformer, John Hus,** was a man who believed the Scriptures to be the infallible and supreme authority in all matters. He died at the stake for that belief in Constance, Germany, on his forty-second birthday. As he refused a final plea to renounce his faith, Hus's last words were, "What I taught with my lips, I seal with my blood."— *Sermonillustrtions.com*

• **Missionary Adoniram Judson,** sweated out Burma's heat for 18 years without a furlough, six years without a convert. Enduring torture and imprisonment, he admitted that he never saw a ship sail without wanting to jump on board and go home. When his wife's health broke, and he put her on a homebound vessel in the knowledge he would not see her for two full years, he confided to his diary: "If we could find some quiet resting place on earth where we could spend the rest of our days in peace. . ." But he steadied himself with this remarkable postscript: "Life is short. Millions of Burmese are perishing. I am almost the only person on earth who has attained their language to communicate salvation. . ." — *Regions Beyond, Vol. 37, No. 1, p. 2*

There are many Christians, churches, and Christian organizations in Burma today because of Judson, even though that country is under a Communist government.

Is your ministry discouraging? I know some pastors with small congregations that are disappointed even though they are faithful and work hard as God's ministers. If you are one of them, do not let the lack of numbers or results keep you from giving it your all. God will honor your commitment, although you do not see the blessings now. Stay faithful and be ready to walk through the open door, always knowing that *"your labour is not in vain in the Lord"* (1 Corinthians 15:58).

If you are a Christian, do people know that you are a Christian, or are you serving in the Lord's service secretly? Do not be afraid of announcing your spiritual commitment. People in your family, neighborhood, and workplace need to know about your relationship with the Lord. Knowing Jesus may not make you popular with all people, but boldly following Him will be a blessing to you. Jesus has committed to you. This kind of commitment deserves your commitment, too.

❖ ❖ ❖

• "Commitment is what transforms a promise into reality."
— *President, Abraham Lincoln*

• "Give me 100 men who hate nothing but sin and love God with all their hearts, and I will shake the world for Christ!"
— *Pastor, Theologian and Author, John Wesley*

• "Commitment is the enemy of resistance, for it is the serious promise to press on, to get up, no matter how many times you are knocked down." — *Professor, David McNally*

• "Today, Christianity seems to be less a matter of commitment and more a matter of convenience." — *Pastor, Al V. Hughes*

30

PRAY FOR REVIVAL

"And ye shall seek me, and find me,
when ye shall search for me with all your heart."
Jeremiah 29:13)

*

Seek the Lord with all your heart, then wait for revival!

The Lord can start a revival in your heart,
in your church, in your community
in your country and then in all the world.

After I got saved in 1970, I took my family to attend an American average-sized Bible-believing church where the people were on fire for the Lord. One time, we had a week of special revival meetings with an evangelist from out of state, who was a man of God and a dynamic preacher. The day before the meetings started, my pastor asked the men to go to the church to pray. When I arrived, I found the evangelist, my pastor, the deacons, and other men kneeling in prayer on the tile floor of the church's basement. As a new Christian, I had never experienced that before. They fervently prayed for a long time. They cried to the Lord with tears for revival in their own hearts and spiritual awakening in the hearts of the people in the community. I felt the presence of the Lord and heaven on the earth that night.

Over the next few days, the Lord did miracles in the hearts of many people in the community, and many got saved. For sure, I know the Lord started a revival in my own heart. I felt pain in my knees from praying that night for such a long time on the tile floor, but it was worth it. When I look back, I realize that night was the real turning point of my Christian life.

Later that week we had the evangelist in our home for dinner. After we finished eating, he asked me to show him the room where I worked. I will never forget what he told me, "I would like to picture in my mind your place when I pray for you. I will pray and ask the Lord to use you in a mighty way to serve Him and use you as He used Paul to reach the world with His gospel..."

A few years later, in the same church, my pastor preached a powerful sermon about the apostle Paul. At the end of the service, he gave an invitation. He asked all the people who wanted the Lord to somehow use them like Paul to preach the gospel, to come forward. I was one of them. The pastor prayed for us, and I went home that day without knowing the Lord's plans.

Even after I was involved in many different ministries, I never imagined that some years later the Lord would use the Internet miraculously for me to start my email ministry, "A SPIRITUAL NOTE FROM THE BIBLE" which has spread around the world. By the grace of God, this ministry has spread the gospel of Jesus Christ since 1996. This ministry glorifies the Lord and helps others by encouraging, comforting, teaching, inspiring, challenging, and evangelizing them. Through this ministry, many came to Christ and were saved. The Lord used my life because godly people prayed for me, and I attended good churches that preached the Word of God without compromise. The invitations that were given after the church services and the revival meetings every year in my church, also gave me the opportunity to make important spiritual decisions to please the Lord.

Today, some large churches boast of their big budgets, the number of attendees, and the many different programs they have. There is nothing wrong with that, but the problem is they do not preach about sin because they are afraid the people will be offended. They do not preach the gospel clearly, and they depend more on man's wisdom and power than God's. These churches become more like social clubs than New Testament churches. Author, Howard Spring was right when he wrote, *"The kingdom of God is not going to advance by our churches becoming filled with men but by men in our churches becoming filled with God."*

In these churches, the pastors may work hard to prepare sermons with good spiritual food for their flock, but they do not give them the opportunity to make personal and spiritual decisions by giving invitations. This happens Sunday after Sunday. I believe people can make decisions anywhere, but church invitations and revival services are cherished experiences for young and old Christians, alike. Unfortunately, invitations and revival meetings have become outdated and old-fashioned in many churches. They may support invitations at revival meetings and evangelistic crusades that happen outside of their churches, but they do not use them regularly in their services to encourage spiritual decisions.

Revival is so significant in our hearts and in our churches. Revival is the restoration of the first love of Christians and a new beginning of commitment, obedience, and devotion to God. In a revival, people see God in His holiness, turn from their sinful lifestyles and are transformed into God's likeness. The minds of the believers are concentrated on things of eternity, and nothing else really matters. It is never too late for a revival. Ask for God's will in your life and the strength to surrender all to Him. He waits for you and wants to bless you, abundantly.

We are humans and make mistakes. It does not matter how reasonable or logical our desires may seem; still, we need God's direction and guidance in our lives to find the perfect will of God. Remember, God's directions are always the best. Your prayers and the prayers of others are not in vain. Get desperate with God. Seek Him with your whole heart. Then, wait for a revival. *"And you shall seek me, and find me, when you shall search for me with all your heart"* (Jeremiah 29:13). *"Call unto me, and I will answer thee, and show thee great and mighty things, which thou knowest not"* (Jeremiah 33:3).

❖ ❖ ❖

- "A revival means days of heaven on earth."
— *Minister, Physician and Author, D. Martyn Lloyd-Jones*

- "The best way to revive a church is to build a fire in the pulpit."
— *Evangelist, D. L. Moody*

- "Revival is ultimately Christ Himself, seen, felt, heard, living, active, moving in, and through His body on earth." "Revival restrains the righteous anger of God, restores the conscious awareness of God, and reveals the gracious activity of God." "Revival is an invasion from heaven that brings a conscious awareness of God."
— *Quotes from Christian Leader, Stephen Olford*

- "Revival awakens in our hearts an increased awareness of the presence of God, a new love for God, a new hatred for sin, and a hunger for His Word."— *Evangelist, Del Fehsenfeld Jr.*

- "A revival is nothing else than a new beginning of obedience to God." "Revival is a renewed conviction of sin and repentance, followed by an intense desire to live in obedience to God. It is giving up one's will to God in deep humility." — *Quotes from Evangelist,, Charles Finney*

- Read 2 Chronicles 7:14

31

BORN AGAIN

"Except a man be born again,
he cannot see the kingdom of God..."
John 3:3

"A new heart also will I give you, and a new spirit will I put
within you: and I will take away the stony heart out of your flesh,
and I will give you an heart of flesh."
Ezekiel 36:26

*

To see God's Kingdom, make sure
you are "born again" with a heart of flesh
and not just religious with a heart of stone!

The word "heart" in the Bible is used 850 times, but only a few of them refer to the human heart. Otherwise, the "heart" is used to speak about our inner part, our thoughts, emotions, and will. The Bible teaches us a lot about this kind of heart.

In the Old Testament, we read about two kings, Saul and David, who were continually fighting. The Bible describes the hearts of these two kings. Saul was a religious man, but David was a spiritually reborn man. Saul, the old king, was rejected by God, but David, the new king, was anointed by God. The old king hated the new king, but the new king was gracious to the old king. David is a type of Christ, the anointed One who came to serve, and people refused Him. Saul is a type of sinner who hates Christ. Saul had a heart of stone, but David had a regenerated heart of flesh full of grace and love. In the New Testament in the third chapter of the gospel of John, we read about Nicodemus, who came to Jesus at night to talk to Him. He was a religious, moral, and respected man, but Jesus said to him, *"Ye must be born again"* (John 3:7), *"I say unto thee, Except a man be born again, he cannot see the kingdom of God"* (John 3:3). In other words, He told Nicodemus that he had to repent and believe in Jesus to receive a regenerated heart. This is the only way to see the Kingdom of God. You must become like David instead of like Saul.

• Only God can change a man's heart. I know a lady who had many marriage problems. After receiving godly counseling and witnessing, she accepted Christ and became a born-again Christian. Afterward, I asked her, "How are things at home?" "Things are just the same, but I am different," was her reply. Yes, she was different, a more loving and caring person for her family because God had changed her heart. Others and I noticed her extreme makeover!

• "I read that the prisons in the Canadian province of Quebec enforce a ban on smoking. With no cigarettes, the inmates have resorted to creative solutions. In place of tobacco, some use a mixture of tea leaves and residue from the nicotine gum provided to help smokers kick the addiction. The concoction is rolled up in a page from the Bible. The Bible is used because those pages reportedly burn slower than normal paper. An inmate named Robert told reporters, 'I smoked Matthew. I smoked Mark. I smoked Luke. When I got to John, I read about how God loves me. Now I don't smoke because now I am a Christian.'"

— *by http://www.redlandbaptist.net/sermon/the-bible-alone/*

• On the Internet, I read the true story about Chuck Shelton and Caleb Beaver. Chuck Shelton is a psychiatrist from Lexington, Kentucky. He became very sick from heart disease and received a heart transplant from Caleb Beaver on December 26, 2011. He wrote a letter to Caleb's parents to thank them, and the two families began communicating. Caleb was a young man with an arteriovenous malformation that put him in a coma, and doctors told his parents he was brain dead. When taken off life support, his parents donated his organs: heart, kidneys, lungs, liver, pancreas, and his skin tissue. His parents, April and Owen Beaver, later met Chuck and Amy Shelton and their sons at the Gulfport airport in Mississippi. Tears were streaming down everyone's cheeks. The Beavers then pulled out a stethoscope to hear their son's heart once again. "I can't even describe it," April Beaver said, her voice choked. "I can't even put it into words. I recognize it. It's such a strong heartbeat." Shelton said, "Thank you for this gift, it's given me life, so I can be with my wife and boys. Caleb still lives through me. Caleb's in Heaven, but he's still here."— *www.fox8live.com, Adapted*

Yes, each one of us is like Chuck Shelton. Initially, we have a sick heart. When we are converted, God gives a new heart. Our stone heart is replaced with a heart of flesh. Between the two people, there is all the difference in the world-the religious person from the born-again person. The person with a new heart has a love for Christ, a substantial spiritual appetite for God, as well as a desire to pursue a holy life in the power of the Spirit. The person with an old heart of stone is totally opposite.

Christianity is not just Christ in you, but Christ living His life through you. Only the One who made it can satisfy the human heart. Happiness is in the heart and not in life's circumstances. If you start the day with love in your heart, peace, and truth in your mind, you will not only benefit from their presence, but you also bring them to others, who cross your path that day.

If you are not truly "born again" according to the Bible, you are a failure as a human being. It is better never to have been born than to never be "born again." Nevertheless, the good news is that if you have never had an experience of a regenerated heart, God can give you one if you repent and ask Him for forgiveness. Tell the Lord you want to change. Ask Him to give you a new heart. He promises that the operation will be successful and you will be able to say like Chuck Sheldon, "Thank you for this gift, it's given me life..."

❖ ❖ ❖

• Jesus answered and said unto him, Verily, verily, I say unto thee, Except a man be born again, he cannot see the kingdom of God."
—*John 3:3*

• When a caterpillar turns into a butterfly, it becomes an entirely new creature. A metamorphose takes place. "Therefore if any man be in Christ, he is a new creature: old things are passed away; behold, all things are become new." — *2 Corinthians 5:17*

• "Being born again, not of corruptible seed, but of incorruptible, by the word of God..." — *1 Peter 1:23*

• "But as many as received him, to them gave he power to become the sons of God, even to them that believe on his name: Which were born, not of blood, nor of the will of the flesh, nor of the will of man, but of God." — *John 1:12-13*

• "O taste and see that the Lord is good: blessed is the man that trusts in him." — *Psalm 34:8*

32

NEW HEART

"A new heart also will I give you, and a new spirit
will I put within you: and I will take away the stony heart
out of your flesh, and I will give you an heart of flesh.."
Ezekiel 36:26

*

**The gospel of grace does not require us to give anything
to God. Only we have to receive what He offers us
with a thankful heart!**

In the Bible, especially in the King James version, the word "heart"
appears 850 times. Only a few times it refers to the physical organ,
while the rest of the time it refers to the inner part of us, like our
emotions, thoughts, and will. No one else can satisfy this heart except
God who made it.

Often, Christians, even Christian leaders, who teach and preach the
Word of God, use the phrase "give your heart to God." This phrase
usually passes without asking if it is biblically correct. Many people,
when awakened to their sinfulness, have a desire to get right with God.
As a result, they pray and seek to dedicate their hearts to Him. After
their prayer, the same people find that their hearts are just as bad as
before instead of being closer to God and loving Him more. Thinking
that their prayer was not good enough, they try to pray again and again to
give their hearts to God. Without accomplishing any good results, they
soon give up trying. Some people who go to Christian crusades repeat
the "sinner's prayer" with others. They then boast afterward that they are
Christians because they gave their hearts to God, even though they still
live an ungodly life.

It is regrettable to see souls misled in this way. To think that "giving
one's heart to God" will bring salvation is a big mistake, and it gives a

wrong idea of the gospel. The Bible plainly teaches that our human heart is naturally a source of every kind of evil. Think about it. As sinners, we "give our hearts to God." What kind of a present is that, to give to the Holy God who cannot behold iniquity? Our gift would never be accepted because it only deserves God's condemnation. When we examine our hearts under the light of the Holy Scriptures, they are absolutely worthless and useless.

Maybe some will say, the Bible says, *"My son, give me thine heart, and let thine eyes observe my ways"* (Proverbs 23:26). Yes, this is true, but notice the verse starts with the words *"My son."* This shows that the one addressed already belongs in a family relationship with the One who speaks. The questions to you are: "Can you claim that this kind of relationship exists between you and God? Are you really His child? Is God your Father?" Not everyone can say "yes" to these questions. Only the born-again believer who has trusted Jesus Christ as personal Savior and has received forgiveness of sins can say "yes." *"But as many as received him, to them gave he power to become the sons of God, even to them that believe on his name"* (John 1:12). *"For ye are all the children of God by faith in Christ Jesus"* (Galatians 3:26). If you are really a child of God then truly the verse above, *"My son, give me thine heart"* applies to you. In that relationship, the Lord as your heavenly Father asks you to give your life to Him, including your heart.

The law in the Old Testament says, *"Thou shall love God."* The law required love and obedience from man and cursed him because he did not produce it. The gospel of grace in the New Testament does not require us to give anything to God. In fact, it is just the opposite. The Gospel says, *"God loves you."* In the gospel, God does not demand anything from us. He only brings blessing, as the good Giver, *"For God so loved the world, that he gave his only begotten Son, that whosoever believeth in him should not perish, but have everlasting life"* (John 3:16). *"It is more blessed to give than to receive"* (Acts 20:35).

Our responsibility is only to receive what He offers us with a thankful heart. If you feel that you have a sinful heart of stone, do not worry, God can replace it with a new heart. You only have to repent and by faith receive Him as your personal Savior. He promises that He will remove your heart of stone and give you a heart of flesh and eternal life!

❖ ❖ ❖

• "Create in me a clean heart, O God; and renew a right spirit within me." — *Psalm 51:10*

• "God has two dwellings; one in heaven and the other in the meek and grateful heart." — *Writer, Isaac Walton*

33

FREE IN CHRIST

"If the Son therefore shall make you free,
ye shall be free indeed."
John 8:36

"Now the Lord is that Spirit:
and where the Spirit of the Lord is,
there is liberty. [Freedom]."
2 Corinthians 3:17

*

RELIGION sets rules. JESUS sets free!

When I talk with unbelievers, they usually think that Christians are in bondage, and they are free. However, this is not true. The scriptures tell us the opposite. Let us look at a few scriptures to see what the Bible tells us about the believer and the unbeliever.

THE UNBELIEVER IS NOT FREE

1.   **He is a slave to sin:** *"Verily, verily, I say unto you, Whosoever committeth sin is the servant of sin"* (John 8:34), and *"I am carnal, sold under sin"* (Romans 7:14).

2.   **He is a slave to self:** *"Bringing me into captivity to the law of sin..."* (Romans 7:23), *"Fulfilling the desires of the flesh ..."* (Ephesians 2:3).

3.   **He is a slave to Satan (the devil):** *"Who are taken captive by him at his will"* (2 Timothy 2:26), *"Your father the devil, and the lusts of your father ye will do..."* (John 8:44), *"Are the children of the wicked one"* (Matthew 13:38), *"In whom the god of this world hath blinded the minds of them which believe not ..."* (2 Corinthians 4:4).

THE BELIEVER IS FREE

1. **Through Christ***: "If the Son therefore shall make you free, ye shall be free indeed"* (John 8:36), and *"Christ hath made us free..."* (Galatians 5:1)

2. **From the law:** *"Christ is the end of the law..."* (Romans 10:4), *"But after that faith is come, we are no longer under a schoolmaster [law]* (Galatians 3:25), *"But now we have been delivered from the law..."* (Romans 7:6), and *"To redeem them that were under the law..."* (Galatians 4:5).

3. **From the bondage of sin:** *"Being then made free from sin..."* (Romans 6:18), *"Sin shall not have dominion over you..."* (Romans 6:14), and *"Christ Jesus hath made me free from the law of sin and death"* (Romans 8:2).

4. **From God's condemnation:** *"He that believeth on him is not condemned..."* (John 3:18), and *"There is therefore now no condemnation to them which are in Christ Jesus..."* (Romans 8:1).

5. **From the future judgment:** *"He that heareth my word, and believeth on him that sent me, hath everlasting life, and shall not come into condemnation..."* (John 5:24)

6. **From fear:** *"There is no fear in love; but (God's) perfect love casteth out fear..."* (1 John 4:18), *"And deliver them who through fear of death were all their lifetime subject to bondage"* (Hebrews 2:15), *"I will fear no evil..."* (Psalm 23:4), and *"For ye have not received the spirit of bondage again to fear..."* (Romans 8:15).

7. **From care:** *"Casting all your care upon Him, for he careth for you"* (1 Peter 5:7), *"Take no thought for your life..."* (Matthew 6:25), and *"Be careful for nothing..."* (Philippians 4:6).

When someone goes to jail, someone else must post a bond to set him free until the time of his trial. If not, he will remain locked up in chains. The same is true for us. We all are locked up in chains because of sin. A price must be paid by someone to set us free. The apostle Paul tells us in Galatians 4:3-5, *"Even so we, when we were children, were in bondage under the elements of the world: But when the fulness of the time was come, God sent forth his Son, made of a woman, made under the law, To redeem them that were under the law, that we might receive the adoption of sons."*

In reality, we were all in chains until Jesus came and paid the price to set us free. Jesus says in John 8:36, *"If the Son therefore shall make you free, ye shall be free indeed."* It is easy for you to understand that a big house, a fancy car, or a big bank account will not set you free. These things simply hide your chains, but it is impossible to break them. Only Jesus Christ can break the chains of sin and set you free. You do not have to try to unlock the chains when Jesus has already paid the price to make you free.

True freedom starts with the truth of God's Word by faith in Christ Jesus. In John 14:6, *"Jesus saith unto him, I am the way, the truth, and the life: no man cometh unto the Father, but by me."* There is no other truth. The truth is the "Word" of God, who is the "Son" of God. *"And ye shall know the truth, and the truth shall make you free"* (John 8:32). The longer you reject the truth of God and you live your life according to your will, the longer you will suffer from insecurity, unforgiveness, lust, lies, pride, jealousy, low self-esteem, a critical spirit, failure, confusion, discouragement, selfishness, worry, self-pity, anger, fear, blame, shame, bitterness, spiritual pride, worldliness, impatience and more.

If you have never allowed God to set you free, now is the time. There is no cost to you for the freedom God freely offers and has already paid. The only thing you have to do is believe on the Lord Jesus Christ and accept Him by faith. Let God set you free today by letting go and letting God. God set me free on March 17, 1970, and I continue to be free each day until I die. I encourage you to trust the Lord to set you free today. I promise you that the minute you place your entire trust and faith in God, new life will begin for you, and you will feel the chains dropping off of you. Remember, true freedom is found only in God alone. *"Blessed is the man that trusteth in the LORD, and whose hope the LORD is"* (Jeremiah 17:7).

❖ ❖ ❖

"But now being made free from sin, and become servants to God, ye have your fruit unto holiness, and the end everlasting life."
— *Romans 6:22*

"Stand fast therefore in the liberty wherewith Christ hath made us free, and be not entangled again with the yoke of bondage." — *Galatians 5:1*

There is power in the name of Jesus to break every chain that binds us. In Christ, we are SONS, not slaves.

34

CHRIST-LIKE CHRISTIAN

"Even so every good tree bringeth forth good fruit;
but a corrupt tree bringeth forth evil fruit.
A good tree cannot bring forth evil fruit,
neither can a corrupt tree bring forth good fruit.
Every tree that bringeth not forth good fruit is hewn down,
and cast into the fire.
Wherefore by their fruits ye shall know them."
Matthew 7:17-20

*

Bearing fruit is the evidence of a Christ-like Christian!

My father was a farmer, and as a young boy, I remember one time when he planted two fruit trees on different sides of our property. One was planted in a dry old landfill, and the other one was planted near a stream. In a few years, both trees grew and began to produce flowers and fruit.

When we tried the fruit of both trees, we found a big difference. The fruit from the tree in the landfill was irregular, extremely sour, and not suitable for eating. The fruit from the other tree near the stream was delicious, sweet, and juicy.

From what we understand, the fruit was affected by the nutrients absorbed through the roots. The tree that grew by the landfill produced sour fruit, while the other one by the stream produced sweet fruit. This means that the roots affect the quality of the fruit. The same principle applies to a Christian. He always has a choice to make. He can put his roots down into the soil of the landfill of fleshly desires and activities, or he can place his roots into the soil of the fresh stream of the person of Jesus Christ and His Spirit. Depending on his choice, he will produce different fruit.

Psalm 1 clearly describes the difference between the two men:

1. *Blessed is the man that walketh not in the counsel of the ungodly, nor standeth in the way of sinners, nor sitteth in the seat of the scornful.*

2. *But his delight is in the law of the Lord; and in his law doth he meditate day and night.*

3. *And he shall be like a tree planted by the rivers of water, that bringeth forth his fruit in his season; his leaf also shall not wither; and whatsoever he doeth shall prosper.*

4. *The ungodly are not so: but are like the chaff which the wind driveth away.*

5. *Therefore the ungodly shall not stand in the judgment, nor sinners In the congregation of the righteous.*

6. *For the Lord knoweth the way of the righteous: but the way of the ungodly shall perish.*

A Christian must develop a Christ-like character to bear fruit to please the Lord. He must walk not after the flesh, but after the Spirit. The apostle Paul uses seventeen specific words to describe the works of the flesh in Galatians 5:19-21 and nine specific words to describe the fruit of the Spirit in Galatians 5:22-23.

> *"Now the works of the flesh are manifest, which are these;* **Adultery, fornication, uncleanness, lasciviousness, idolatry, witchcraft, hatred, variance, emulations, wrath, strife, seditions, heresies, envyings, murders, drunkenness, revellings,** *and such like: of the which I tell you before, as I have also told you in time past, that they which do such things shall not inherit the kingdom of God"* (Galatians 5:19-21).

> *"But the fruit of the Spirit is* **love, joy, peace, longsuffering, gentleness, goodness, faith, meekness, temperance:** *against such there is no law"* (5:2 Galatians 5:22-23).

Paul encourages us in (Galatians 5:16-18, 24,25) to walk after the spirit and not after the flesh. *"This I say then, Walk in the Spirit, and ye shall not fulfil the lust of the flesh. For the flesh lusteth against the Spirit, and the Spirit against the flesh: and these are contrary the one to the other: so that ye cannot do the things that ye would. But if ye be led of the Spirit, ye are not under the law... And they that are Christ's have crucified the flesh with the affections and lusts. If we live in the Spirit, let us also walk in the Spirit"* (Galatians 5:16-18, 24,25).

I hope you belong to Christ and that you have crucified the flesh with its affections and desires. I hope you have found and enjoy the fruit of the Spirit, as stated above. These elusive qualities are only found in a person, Jesus Christ. If you do not know Jesus, get to know Him. Let His Spirit direct your life. This is the only proven way to reap a harvest of the fruit of the Spirit. *"There is therefore now no condemnation to them which are in Christ Jesus, who walk not after the flesh, but after the Spirit"* (Romans 8:1).

Pastor, theologian and evangelist, J. Sidlow Baxter said, *"What God chooses, He cleanses. What God cleanses, He molds. What God molds, He fills. What God fills, He uses."* It is good to pray and say something like this:

Lord, right now, I give up all my own plans, desires, and hopes, and I accept your will for my life. I give myself, my life, my all to you forever. Fill me and seal me with the Holy Spirit.

This means to be entirely controlled by the Holy Spirit. To be filled with the Spirit does not mean having more of the Spirit, but allowing the Spirit to have more or all of you. If you fill a glass with water, there is no more room for anything else in the glass. The same is true for the believer if he is filled with the Holy Spirit. There will be no room for pride, anger, selfish thoughts or any other works of the flesh.

❖ ❖ ❖

• "I cannot believe they are converts until I see fruit brought back; it will never do a sincere soul any harm."
— *Evangelist, George Whitefield*

• "Do not confound work and fruit. There may be a good deal of work for Christ that is not the fruit of the heavenly Vine."
— *Pastor and Author, Andrew Murray*

• "I believe firmly that the moment our hearts are emptied of pride and selfishness and ambition and everything that is contrary to God's law, the Holy Spirit will fill every corner of our hearts. But if we are full of pride and conceit and ambition and the world, there is no room for the Spirit of God. We must be emptied before we can be filled."
— *Evangelist, D. L. Moody*

• "Use me as Thou wilt. Send me where Thou wilt. Work out Thy whole will in my life at any cost, now and forever."
— *Missionary, Betty Scott Stam*

35

THE HOLY SPIRIT

*"And my speech and my preaching
was not with enticing words of man's wisdom,
but in demonstration of the Spirit and of power."*
1 Corinthians 2:4

*

Serve the Lord with the power of the Holy Spirit!

The Holy Spirit is the third person of the Trinity: God the Father, God the Son, and God the Holy Spirit. In the New Testament, the Greek word for the Holy Spirit Its "Ἅγιο Πνεῦμα" (Hagion pneûma). At other times, the names used are "Ἁγιο Πνεῦματι" (Hagion pneûmati), "Πνεύματι Θεοῦ" (Pneumati Theou), "Παράκλητος" (Paracletos), "Πνεῦμα της Αληθείας" (Pneuma tēs Aletheias), and "Πνεῦμα Χριστοῦ" (Pneuma Christou). The Holy Spirit is God, and He possesses the attributes of omniscience, omnipresence, and omnipotence. He was self-existent and played a role in the creation of the heavens and earth. *"And the Spirit of God moved upon the face of the waters"* (Genesis 1:2).

In the Old Testament, the Holy Spirit came for a limited time to people of God to accomplish God's plans. Soon after that, the Holy Spirit left them. In the New Testament, there is a close relationship between the Holy Spirit and Jesus during His earthly life and ministry. The deity of the Holy Spirit is supported in the Scriptures with facts. For example, He caused Mary's virgin birth of Jesus. He bore witness as a dove when Jesus was baptized, and He came as a comforter after Jesus ascended, as Jesus had promised His disciples. *"Nevertheless I tell you the truth; It is expedient for you that I go away: for if I go not away, the Comforter will not come unto you; but if I depart, I will send him unto you. And when he is come, he will reprove the world of sin, and of righteousness, and of judgment...I have yet many things to say unto you, but ye cannot bear them now. Howbeit when he, the Spirit of truth, is come, he will guide you into all truth..."* (John 16:7-13).

The Holy Spirit inspired the writing of the Scriptures, anointed Jesus for his ministry, played an essential role in Jesus' resurrection, and gave birth to the Church on the day of Pentecost. He is the source of all spiritual gifts for the Church, empowers those who preach the gospel, regenerates all those who become believers, and seals believers into the body of Christ.

In the New Testament, the word "Spirit" (Πνεῦμα) is mentioned around 390 times. Blasphemy against the Holy Spirit is the "unforgivable sin." The Holy Spirit is called by many other names such as the Spirit of God, the Spirit of Christ, the mind of Christ, the Spirit of the Lord, and the Spirit of life. Also, as the Spirit of adoption, the Spirit of promise, the Spirit of truth, the Spirit of liberty, the Spirit of Grace, the Spirit of godliness, and the Spirit of holiness. In Isaiah 11:4, He is also called the Spirit of wisdom, the Spirit of understanding, the Spirit of counsel, the Spirit of might, the Spirit of knowledge, and the Spirit of the fear of God. The New Testament tells us the Holy Spirit lives in every born again believer's body forever. *"What? know ye not that your body is the temple of the Holy Ghost which is in you, which ye have of God, and ye are not your own?"* (1 Corinthians 6:19).

The Holy Spirit, as a person according to the following verses, is connected to us with His mind, emotions, and will.

- *"And he that searcheth the hearts knoweth what is the mind of the Spirit, because he maketh intercession for the saints according to the will of God"* (Romans 8:27).

- *"And grieve not the Holy Spirit of God, whereby ye are sealed unto the day of redemption"* (Ephesians 4:30).

- *"*But all these worketh that one and the selfsame Spirit, dividing to every man severally as he will*"* (1 Corinthians 12:11).

The Holy Spirit helps us as believers in many ways. He makes us free from a life of bondage, convicts us of the sin in our lives, teaches us, comforts us, empowers us, brings us peace, gives us hope, helps us to do the Father's will, intercedes and guides our prayers, and directs us into the truth of God's Word. He seals us into the body of Christ, helps us to live a holy life, to tell others about our faith, to live by the fruits of the Holy Spirit to bear fruit, and fills us up on a regular basis. He gifts us for a ministry, and He sanctifies us to make us more like Christ.

The Holy Spirit is essential in the life of a believer in Christ. Once, "A lady went to a jeweler to fix her watch. He went to the back and very soon returned with it running. The lady was very surprised and asked him how he was able to fix it so quickly. He said, it only needed a new battery. What battery? Nobody said anything about a battery. I've been winding it every morning!" — *Author Unknown*

Sadly, a lot of Christians do not recognize the power of the Holy Spirit to control situations; they think they must handle themselves. If you serve God with your own strength and talent, you will burn out soon. Learn to serve Him with the power of His own Spirit. *Corrie Ten Boom* was right when she said, *"Trying to do the Lord's work in your own strength is the most confusing, exhausting, and tedious of all work. But when you are filled with the Holy Spirit, then the ministry of Jesus just flows out of you."*

Ask in prayer for the Lord to fill you with His Spirit. This means to be entirely controlled by the Holy Spirit. As the drunken person is controlled by alcohol, so the Christian must be controlled by the Holy Spirit. *"And be not drunk with wine, wherein is excess; but be filled with the Spirit"* (Ephesians 5:18). To be filled with the Spirit does not mean having more of the Holy Spirit, but allowing the Spirit to have more or all of you. On each believer, God has placed his mark of ownership, authority, and security by the sealing of the Holy Spirit. No one can remove the believer from his ownership until the day of redemption. Let God's Spirit direct our lives.

> Holy Ghost, with light divine,
> Shine upon this heart of mine;
> Chase the shade of night away,
> Turn my darkness into day.

— *Hymn by* Andrew Reed, 1817

❖ ❖ ❖

- "He [Paul] said unto them, Have you received the Holy Ghost since you believed?" — *Acts 19:2*

- "You might as well try to hear without ears or breathe without lungs, as try to live a Christian life without the Spirit of God in your heart." — *Evangelist, D. L. Moody*

- "Though every believer has the Holy Spirit, the Holy Spirit does not have every believer." — *Pastor and Author, A. W. Tozer*

36

JUSTIFICATION BY FAITH

"Knowing that a man is not justified by the works of the law,
but by the faith of Jesus Christ, even we have believed
in Jesus Christ, that we might be justified by the faith of Christ,
and not by the works of the law:
for by the works of the law shall no flesh be justified"
Galatians 2:16

*

"Justification
is the doctrine on which the church stands or falls."
Martin Luther

Justification is a gift and one-time act of God which lasts forever!

We hear government officials say a lot these days, "We will bring them to justice." This means the ones who are criminals and broke the human law will be punished accordingly. Besides human justice, there is another higher justice by which every one of us will be judged one day. This justice will be not according to human law, but according to God's standards, like His perfection and His sinlessness. The Bible says, *"All have sinned, and come short of the glory of God"* (Romans 3:23). This means that every man, woman, and child are guilty before God and will eternally be separated from God in hell. The only way to escape this kind of punishment is to be justified by faith in Jesus Christ.

The Greek word for "justify" in the New Testament is "δικαιώνω" (dikaiono). It means divine approval, be freed, to count righteous, and is credited as righteous, emphasizing Christ's full payment of the debt for sin which sets free the believer from all divine condemnation. In man's courts of law, when a person is proven innocent, he can be justified or proclaimed "not guilty."

The good news is that when mankind is in God's court, God's divine plan of mercy and love has made a way to justify the guilty sinner by punishing sin and upholding His righteous law. The question is: "How can God be 'Just' and the 'Justifier.' of sinners at the same time?" The Bible says, *"That he might be just, and the justifier of him which believeth in Jesus"* (Romans 3:26*)*. The answer is Jesus Christ, who died on the cross for the sins of the world, fully met the requirements of God's holiness. The blood that he shed as *"The Lamb of God"* paid and met all of God's claims for every sinner. He satisfied the demands of justice. Because of that, when each one of us believes in Jesus Christ exactly at that moment, he is justified by God. In other words, justification is God's answer to the faith of the sinner, who believes in Jesus. God proclaims him innocent and justified. The justification delivers the believer from the guilt of sin and declares him to be righteous.

The Bible says, *"And by him all that believe are justified from all things, from which ye could not be justified by the law of Moses"* (Acts 13:39). This is the wonderful news sent down from heaven to all of us. This verse does not say all who "do their best" or "give more money to the church and to the poor" NO! God's Word clearly says, *"All that believe"* and *"But believeth on him that justifieth the ungodly, his faith is counted for righteousness"* (Romans 4:5). *"Therefore we conclude that a man is justified by faith without the deeds of the law"* (Romans 3:28).

Each person on the principle of faith receives justification the moment he believes that Jesus Christ died for his sins. It is the only way He can be saved. It is essential to mention that the believer is saved not by his faith, but from the object of his faith, which is Jesus Christ. When one is justified, his relationship with God is changed. From a condemned sinner, he becomes a redeemed child of God. The justification is a gift and one-time act of God which lasts forever.

Justification is by faith and accomplished through the value of Christ's shed blood on the cross. Jesus died and paid for the sins of all men, but only those who believe are justified. If you are a believer in Christ, God's judgment is for you in justification. God's power is for you in sanctification. God's love is for you in adoption. God's glory is for you in glorification. God is entirely, for you in Jesus Christ. If you are not a believer, you must believe in Jesus Chris. Not only will you be forgiven, but you will also be justified. You will be cleared of every charge that could be brought against you: *"That through this man is preached unto you the forgiveness. And by him all that believe are justified from all things, from which ye could not be justified by the law of Moses"* (Acts 13:38,39). *"Therefore we conclude that a man is justified by faith without the deeds of the law"* (Romans 3:28).

❖ ❖ ❖

- "We are justified... by receiving from God, what Christ hath done for us." — *Clergyman and Author, William Gurnall*

37

RIGHTEOUSNESS OF GOD

"Blessed are they which do hunger and thirst
after righteousness: for they shall be filled."
Matthew 5:6

"For he hath made him to be sin for us, who knew no sin;
that we might be made the righteousness of God in him."
2 Corinthians 5:21

*

Our righteousness depends on what Jesus did on the cross!

One of the most significant challenges the leaders of the church have today is to communicate the gospel of Jesus Christ, and in such a way to speak the truths of the Bible in terms every person can understand. When leaders use deeply sophisticated, intellectual, and theological language, they cannot connect well with all of their audience. Because of this, some people have a hard time understanding simple words or doctrines of the Bible such as the word "righteousness" or "the righteousness of God" or how God transfers the righteousness of Christ to people who trust in Him to enjoy a restored relationship with God.

It is very simple. Only God is righteous. If someone feels righteous, it is because he is self-righteous. It is not because he is close to God. It is because he is close to himself. It is not possible for a man to achieve his own absolute righteousness, compared to the high standard of God. The Bible brings us wonderful news that true righteousness is possible for man, through the cleansing of sin by the blood of Jesus Christ and the permanent possession of the Holy Spirit. No man in the world is righteous in the eyes of the Lord, except the believer in Christ because he is counted righteous in God's eyes when he receives Jesus Christ by faith.

"And be found in Him, not having my own righteousness, which is from the law, but that which is through faith in Christ, the righteousness which is from God by faith" (Philippians 3:9).

Righteousness is not based on what man can do, but on what Jesus did on the cross.

"Who his own self bare our sins in his own body on the tree, that we, being dead to sins, should live unto righteousness..." (1 Peter 2:24).

The righteousness that is Christ's is counted to those that receive Jesus and are seen as righteous in God's eyes. *"For he hath made him to be sin for us, who knew no sin; that we might be made the righteousness of God in him..."* (2 Corinthians 5:21). Though they are actually worthy of eternal punishment in hell, now they are made righteous by Jesus' sacrifice on the cross.

"I will greatly rejoice in the LORD, my soul shall be joyful in my God; for he hath clothed me with the garments of salvation, he hath covered me with the robe of righteousness, as a bridegroom decketh himself with ornaments, and as a bride adorneth herself with her jewels" (Isaiah 61:10).

After all, they have the privilege to spend eternity with a righteous God. Jesus says in Matthew 5:6 that He will bless the ones who are hungry and thirsty for righteousness and not because they are righteous. This means they have to continue to feel hungry and thirsty for righteousness. Pastor, A. W. Tozer said, *"To have found God and still to pursue Him is the soul's paradox of love."* When we *"Seek ye first the kingdom of God, and his righteousness..."* (Matthew 6:33) and *"Blessed are they which do hunger and thirst after righteousness: for they shall be filled [satisfied]..."* (Matthew 5:6). I hope you are a Christian with this passion growing in you day by day, until the time you see Christ face to face: *"we shall be like him; for we shall see him as he is"* (1 John 3:2).

If you are not saved, you must know that Christ Jesus died for you on Calvary's cross that you might be saved. He offers you a pardon for all your sins. Now is the best time for you to tell God:

Thank you for loving me so much and sending your Son to die for me. I know that without Him, I would be separated from your love forever. I'm sorry for my sins. I admit that I am a sinner, and I repent of my sins. I trust and invite Jesus into my life as my Savior and my Lord. I'm thankful for Your mercy to me.

If you pray with sincerity, you will experience God's forgiveness of your sins. *"If we confess our sins, he is faithful and just to forgive us our sins, and to cleanse us from all unrighteousness"* (1 John 1:9), and have the assurance of eternal life, *"Whosoever believeth in him should not perish, but have everlasting life"* (John 3:16). You will be counted as righteous in the eyes of God" (2 Corinthians 5:21) and *"If Christ be in you, the body is dead because of sin; but the Spirit is life because of righteousness"* (Romans 8:10).

THE SOLID ROCK

My hope is built on nothing less
Than Jesus' blood and righteousness;
I dare not trust the sweetest frame,
But wholly lean on Jesus' name.

Refrain:
On Christ, the solid Rock, I stand;
All other ground is sinking sand,
All other ground is sinking sand

— *Hymn by Edward Mote, 1834*

❖ ❖ ❖

• "Know ye not that the unrighteous shall not inherit the kingdom of God? Be not deceived: neither fornicators, nor idolaters, nor adulterers, nor effeminate, nor abusers of themselves with mankind. Nor thieves, nor covetous, nor drunkards, nor revilers, nor extortioners, shall inherit the kingdom of God." — *1 Corinthians 6:9,10*

• "The righteousness of Jesus Christ is one of those great mysteries, which the angels desire to look into, and seems to be one of the first lessons that God taught men after the fall."— *Evangelist, George Whitefield*

• "We do not become righteous by doing righteous deeds, but having been made righteous, we do righteous deeds."
Priest and Theologian, Martin Luther

• "Self-righteousness is the devil's masterpiece to make us think well of ourselves." — *Preacher, Thomas Adams*

• "We shall never be clothed with the righteousness of Christ except we first know assuredly that we have no righteousness of our own."
— *Pastor and Theologian, John Calvin*

• "He hath covered me with the robe of righteousness..."
— *Isaiah 61:10*

38

LIVING HOPE

"Blessed be the God and Father of our Lord Jesus Christ,
which according to his abundant mercy
hath begotten us again unto a lively hope by the resurrection
of Jesus Christ from the dead,"
1 Peter 1:3

*

Are you a born again Christian with a living hope?

There was a terminally ill young man who went to the hospital every week for his usual treatment. One day, a new doctor was on duty, and cruelly said to him without any compassion, "Do you know you will not live out the year?" After the treatment, he stopped by the medical director's desk and with tears in his eyes and a broken heart said to him, "That doctor took away my hope," and the director replied, "I guess he did, but it is time to find a new one." He was right. There is hope even when the situation may seem hopeless. It is the Christian hope which God promises in the Bible.

Maybe today you feel down too, because you think there is no hope for you. My beloved, there is hope in Christ for everyone: for the family that has financial problems, for the father or child diagnosed with cancer, for the wife struggling to conceive, for the boy messed up with drugs, for the young girl considering an abortion, and for the many thousands who lost jobs and life savings. The holy scriptures tell us that each of us has been created by God, He loves us, and He wants us to have a full and fulfilling life. Jesus said, *"I am come that they might have life and that they might have it more abundantly"* (John 10:10). He meant a full life, an eternal life that goes beyond temporary existence, and a fulfilling life lived in harmony with His Creator now and forever.

The apostle John, inspired by the Holy Spirit, wrote that the purpose of this gospel is *"that ye might believe that Jesus is the Christ, the Son of God; and that believing ye might have life through his name"* (John 20:31). Also, the apostle Peter reminds us that *"God... hath begotten us again unto a lively hope..."* (1 Peter 1:3). This hope does not mean desire or expectation, but it means full confidence in Jesus, which dismisses all doubt, fears, and uncertainty about Jesus and His promises. The apostle Paul speaks about this hope as an *"anchor of the soul, both sure and stedfast..."* (Hebrews 6:19). This hope rests upon the solid rock of Jesus Christ, who is unchangeable (Hebrews 13:8). Christianity is not like other religions, but it is a relationship with a living person, our Lord Jesus Christ, who is on the throne of God. Our relationship is eternal. Jesus said, *"because I live, ye shall live also"* (John 14:19). Let us review some of the verses the apostle John wrote in his gospel about Jesus, which explains why Jesus came, what Jesus does, and what Jesus offers.

- *"For God did not send His Son into the world to condemn the world, but that the world through Him might be saved"* (John 3:17).

- *"The thief cometh not, but for to steal, and to kill, and to destroy: I am come that they might have life, and that they might have it more abundantly"* (John 10:10).

- *"I have come as a light into the world, that whoever believes in Me should not abide in darkness"* (John 12:46).

- *"I am the good shepherd: the good shepherd giveth his life for the sheep. As the Father knoweth me, even so know I the Father: and I lay down my life for the sheep"* (John 10:11,15).

- *"He that believeth on the Son hath everlasting life: and he that believeth not the Son shall not see life; but the wrath of God abideth on him"* (John 3:36).

- *"Verily, verily, I say unto you, He that heareth my word, and believeth on him that sent me, hath everlasting life, and shall not come into condemnation; but is passed from death unto life"* (John 5:24).

- *"Jesus said unto her, I am the resurrection, and the life: he that believeth in me, though he were dead, yet shall he live"* (John 11:25).

Finally, if you are not a Christian, you may ask, "How can I receive Jesus and what He offers?" Jesus answered this question for Nicodemus, who was a ruler of the Jews and a teacher of Israel when he came to Jesus at night. Jesus told him, *"Ye must be born again"* (John 3:7). "Born again" actually means "to be born from above." The new birth is essential, for salvation because man by nature is a lost sinner and must be born again by believing in God's Son, Jesus Christ. Nicodemus was a very religious person and sincere seeker of truth, and Jesus told him clearly, *"Except a man be born again, he cannot see the kingdom of God"* (John 3:3).

You have to receive Jesus by faith into your life to become "born again" to establish a relationship with Him and become a child of God. *"But as many as received him, to them gave he power to become the sons of God, even to them that believe on his name"* (John 1:12).

Admit that you are a sinner, and you need God's forgiveness. Trust only in Christ to save you. Believe that Jesus died on the cross for your sins. Turn (repent) from your sins, and accept Jesus into your life by faith as your Savior to receive eternal life and living hope. If you have never done this before, I pray for you to do this right now. This will be the most important decision of your life. I did this myself as a young man, and I have never regretted it. Because of God's love, mercy, and grace, I am here today to minister to you and to encourage you to become a blessed man which the Bible describes.

"Blessed is the man that trusteth in the LORD, and whose hope the LORD is. For he shall be as a tree planted by the waters, and that spreadeth out her roots by the river, and shall not see when heat cometh, but her leaf shall be green; and shall not be careful in the year of drought, neither shall cease from yielding fruit" (Jeremiah 17:7,8).

❖ ❖ ❖

• "Without Christ, there is no hope."
— *"Prince of Preachers," Charles Spurgeon*

• "Is there a hope when hope is taken away? Is there hope when the situation is hopeless? That question leads us to Christian hope, for in the Bible, hope is no longer a passion for the possible. It becomes a passion for the promise." — *Theologian and Author, Lewis Smedes*

• "When you say that a situation or a person is hopeless, you are slamming the door in the face of God" — *Pastor, Charles L. Allen*

• "Hope is called the anchor of the soul (Hebrews 6:19) because it gives stability to the Christian life. But hope is not simply a 'wish' (I wish that such-and-such would take place); rather, it is that which latches on to the certainty of the promises of the future that God has made."
—*Theologian and Author, R.C. Sproul*

• "God makes a promise. Faith believes His promise. Hope anticipates its fulfillment. Patience quietly waits." — *Author, Jack Countryman*

39

LIVING WATER

"In the last day, that great day of the feast, Jesus stood and cried,
saying, If any man thirst, let him come unto me, and drink.
He that believeth on me, as the scripture hath said,
out of his belly shall flow rivers of living water."
John 7:37-38

*

I hope rivers of living water flow out of you!

All Christians have the same experience. Before they came to Christ, they tried to find satisfaction in many different things around them. They were thirsty and hungry for happiness, for rest, peace, and joy, but they never found complete satisfaction in any of them. They thought they had discovered satisfaction for a moment, but it did not last long because it was not real. Nothing else can satisfy the human soul except Jesus. He is all-sufficient. Jesus said, *"If any man thirst."* He meant "Anyone!": the ones who are filthy with sin, as well as the ones whom all the world rejected. Jesus asked for only one qualification, and that was to be thirsty. He wants those to come to Him and believe in Him. Without a need for self-improvement or change in your life, come to the Lord. All you have to do is desire Him, lift your eyes to Him, and say:

JUST AS I AM

Just as I am, without one plea,
But that Thy blood was shed for me,
And that Thou bid'st me come to Thee,
O Lamb of God, I come! I come!
— *Hymn by Charlotte Elliott, 1835*

He promises that He will receive all who come to Him in faith. Jesus said, *"And him that cometh to me I will in no wise cast out"* (John 6:37). When thirsty souls come to Jesus, He gives them instant relief, washes, and cleanses with His shed blood. Also, He gives them the Holy Spirit, which provides many spiritual blessings that flow out as rivers of living water.

Jesus uses the phrase *"living water"* two times in the Bible. The first time in John chapter 4, when He asked for water from a Samaritan woman and said to her, *"If thou knewest the gift of God, and who it is that saith to thee, Give me to drink; thou wouldest have asked of him, and he would have given thee living water"* (John 4:10).

The second time is found in John chapter 7 when Jesus was in the Temple *"Jesus stood and cried, saying, If any man thirst, let him come unto me, and drink. He that believeth on me, as the scripture hath said, out of his belly shall flow rivers of living water (But this spake he of the Spirit, which they that believe on him should receive: for the Holy Ghost was not yet given; because that Jesus was not yet glorified)"* (John 7:37-39).

Jesus does not say on both occasions that He was the living water as He said at other times. *"I am the bread of life," "I am the light of the world,"* and *"I am the way, the truth, and the life."* Instead, He refers to the Holy Spirit, which will be given later to believers.

We see later that this happened in Acts 10:44-45, *"While Peter yet spake these words, the Holy Ghost fell on all them which heard the word. And they of the circumcision which believed were astonished, as many as came with Peter, because that on the Gentiles also was poured out the gift of the Holy Ghost"* (Acts 10:44-45). In each heart of redeemed children of God, the Holy Spirit becomes *"living water."*

Remember, if you believe in Jesus Christ, you are saved, and you have received the Holy Spirit. You cannot call Him "Lord" without the Holy Spirit, *"no man can say that Jesus is the Lord, but by the Holy Ghost"* (1 Corinthians 12:3). Believers of God have to put away sins which grieve the Holy Spirit. *"And grieve not the Holy Spirit of God, whereby ye are sealed unto the day of redemption"* (Ephesians 4:30).

When we glorify Jesus in our hearts and lives, the Holy Spirit fills us continuously with power. Jesus did not talk about *"a river of living water,"* but *"rivers of living water."* This means to be more than merely satisfied. When we receive the Holy Spirit, it is not only for our benefit, but it is used through us to minister the things of God to others.

I was impressed many years ago when I entered the men's room within a medical building. This was the first time that I did not find handles on the faucet. I wondered how to get some water. I cupped my hands and moved them back and forth under the faucet, thinking there might be an electric eye. In a few seconds, the water flowed automatically.

The soul needs living water as the human body needs water; it cannot live very long without it. The body needs eight to twelve cups of water a day to operate sufficiently. It helps to break up and soften food. The blood is slightly less than 80% water (H_2O), which carries nutrients to the cells. Also, it is a cooling agent which regulates the temperature of our body through perspiration. Without its lubricating effects, our joints and muscles would rub and squeak like unused parts of an old rusty machine.

The soul cannot survive without living water. There are several questions for you: "Are you spiritually thirsty? Do you need a drink of living water? Are you thirsty for more of God?" There are no techniques or gimmicks, only thirst, and faith in Jesus. Believe in God's promise. Soon, your faucet will begin to flow with rivers of living water and minister the things of God to others. From my own experience, I know this is true. If you have never believed in God's promise, I encourage you to do so to experience God's rivers of living water in your own heart. Pray and say something like this with faith and sincerity.

Lord Jesus, give me that living water. I want forgiveness of my sins. I want to know that I am going to heaven. I want a new life. I am tired of the old life I have been living. I want something else in life. I want the Living Water. I believe that you died for my sins and conquered death so that I can drink of the living water and have eternal life and a personal relationship with you. Amen.

❖ ❖ ❖

- I heard the voice of Jesus say, "Behold, I freely give
  The living water: thirsty one, Stoop down, and drink, and live."
  I came to Jesus, and I drank Of that life-giving stream;
  My thirst was quenched, my soul revived, And now I live in Him!
  — *Hymn by Horatius Bonar, 1808-1899*

- Fill my cup, Lord; I lift it up Lord;
  Come and quench this thirsting of my soul.
  Bread of Heaven, feed me till I want no more.
  Fill my cup, fill it up and make me whole.
  —*Hymn by Richard Blanchard, 1953*

- "If a spring has not been opened in a soul, a spring of living water from God's own Son, no waters can flow, and there is no life in you." —*Biblical Scholar and Theologian, G.V. Wigram*

40

ASSURANCE OF SALVATION

"And this is the record, that God hath given to us eternal life, and this life is in his Son. He that hath the Son hath life; and he that hath not the Son of God hath not life. These things have I written unto you that believe on the name of the Son of God; that ye may know that ye have eternal life, and that ye may believe on the name of the Son of God."
1 John 5:11-13

*

Do you have a biblical assurance of salvation?

There are some things in life that we want to be really sure about. One of them is our salvation. We especially want to know our eternal destiny. Maybe you have doubts about your salvation. The Bible warns that many are deceived about this crucial matter. Perhaps you are like the elderly man who said to Dr. H.A. Ironside, "I will not go on unless I know I'm saved, or else know it's hopeless to seek to be sure of it. I want a definite witness, something I can't be mistaken about!" Ironside replied, "Suppose you had a vision of an angel who told you your sins were forgiven. Would that be enough to rest on?" "Yes, I think it would. An angel should be right." Ironside continued, "But suppose on your deathbed Satan came and said, 'I was that angel, transformed to deceive you.' What would you say?" The man was speechless. Ironside then told him that God has given us something more dependable than the voice of an angel. He has given His Son, who died for our sins, and He has testified in His own Word that if we trust Him, all our sins are gone. Ironside read 1 John 5:13, "that ye may know that ye have eternal life..." Then he said, "Is that not enough to rest on? It is a letter from heaven expressly to you." God's Spirit used that to bring assurance to the man's heart. — *Dr. H. A. Ironside*

In the New Testament and especially in the Epistles, *"full assurance"* is mentioned three times.

FIRST: *"Let us draw near with a true heart in* **full assurance of faith***"* (Hebrews 10:22). It is the confidence of a believer that he is saved without any doubt. It is the result of believing what God says in the Bible. *"He that believeth on the Son hath everlasting life"* (John 3:36). He is absolutely sure that this promise of God is true because God does not lie. In other words, his confidence is based on God's promises and not on his emotional experiences.

SECOND: *"The* **full assurance of hope** *unto the end"* (Hebrews 6:11). The hope of the Bible is not the same as man's "wishing hope." The Christian's "hope" is *"an anchor of the soul, both sure and stedfast..."* (Hebrews 6:19). The full assurance of hope is the result of believing and accepting God's Word. This confidence will keep the believer to the end.

THIRD: *"All riches of the* **full assurance of understanding...** *"* (Colossians 2:2). This full assurance is God's reward to Christians who study His Word. It starts with His plan of salvation as proclaimed in the gospel of the grace of God. When one who believes and begins to understand God's Word, he comes to the point where he can enjoy all the blessings *and "riches of the full assurance of understanding."*

It is different knowing that you are saved than hoping that you are saved. The apostle John wrote to assure God's people about their salvation and eliminate any doubt they may have: *"These things have I written unto you that believe on the name of the Son of God; that ye may know that ye have eternal life, and that ye may believe on the name of the Son of God"* (1 John 5:13). He uses the Greek words "ἵνα εἰδῆτε," which mean to know, to see, to have surely seen. The verse gives you the assurance that you have eternal life. You are saved period.

You may ask, "How can I know?" Because God promised eternal life to all, who believe in Jesus Christ. He died not only to forgive your sins but to give you full assurance of going to heaven. The following are a few of God's promises:

- *"Jesus said unto her, I am the resurrection, and the life: he that believeth in me, though he were dead, yet shall he live: And whosoever liveth and believeth in me shall never die. Believest thou this?"* (John 11:25-26).

- *"And I give unto them eternal life; and they shall never perish, neither shall any man pluck them out of my hand. My Father, which gave them me, is greater than all; and no man is able to pluck them out of my Father's hand"* (John 10:28-29).

- *"For I am persuaded, that neither death, nor life, nor angels, nor principalities, nor powers, nor things present, nor things to come, Nor height, nor depth, nor any other creature, shall be able to separate us from the love of God, which is in Christ Jesus our Lord"* (Romans 8:38,39).

- *"Being confident of this very thing, that he which hath begun a good work in you will perform it until the day of Jesus Christ"* (Philippians 1:6).

- *"And this is the record, that God hath given to us eternal life, and this life is in his Son. He that hath the Son hath life; and he that hath not the Son of God hath not life. These things have I written unto you that believe on the name of the Son of God; that ye may know that ye have eternal life, and that ye may believe on the name of the Son of God"* (1 John 5:11-13).

- *"All that the Father giveth me shall come to me; and him that cometh to me I will in no wise cast out. And this is the Father's will which hath sent me, that of all which he hath given me I should lose nothing, but should raise it up again at the last day"* (John 6:37, 39).

- *"Verily, verily, I say unto you, He that heareth my word, and believeth on him that sent me, hath everlasting life, and shall not come into condemnation; but is passed from death unto life"* (John 5:24).

- *"Who was delivered for our offences, and was raised again for our justification"* (Romans 4:25).

- *"There is therefore now no condemnation to them which are in Christ Jesus, who walk not after the flesh, but after the Spirit"* (Romans 8:1).

- *"For ye have not received the spirit of bondage again to fear; but ye have received the Spirit of adoption, whereby we cry, Abba, Father. The Spirit itself beareth witness with our spirit, that we are the children of God"* (Romans 8:15,16).

We have to believe what God says to us. If we do not, we will pay the price. Evangelist Dwight L. Moody said, "Now, I find a great many people who want some evidence that they have accepted the Son of God. My friends, if you want any evidence, take God's word for it. You cannot find better evidence than that. You know that when the Angel Gabriel came down and told Zachariah, he should have a son, but Zachariah wanted a further token than the angel's word. He asked Gabriel for it, and Gabriel answered, *'I am Gabriel, who stands in the presence of the Lord.'*

Because Gabriel had never been doubted, he thundered out this to Zachariah. But Zachariah wanted a further token, and Gabriel said, *'You shall have a token: you shall be dumb till your son shall be given* you.'" — *CCEL*

Several years ago, our church had revival meetings with a famous evangelist. A Catholic Priest attended one of the meetings. He was an educated man and had even memorized all the New Testament, but he was lost spiritually. He admitted he was lost, but he did not have the courage to accept the Lord by faith as his personal Savior even though many leaders of our church encouraged him to do so. Sadly, he came and left a lost sinner, instead of a redeemed child of God. This happened because he did not believe what God said in the Bible even though he knew the scriptures and had them memorized.

It is wonderful to read and know the scriptures. However, even the devil knows the scriptures, as well as many people from other religions, but they are not saved. Regarding the story about the Catholic priest, we understand that only knowing the scriptures cannot save us. We have to believe and accept Jesus Christ as our personal Savior as the scriptures teach us very clearly.

"That if thou shalt confess with thy mouth the Lord Jesus, and shalt believe in thine heart that God hath raised him from the dead, thou shalt be saved" (Romans 10:9).

Numerous times, I ask people who claim that they are Christians, "Are you born again? Do you have the assurance of your salvation? Do you have a personal relationship with God?" The people who are not true Christians answer with many different statements that do not have anything to do with the question I asked. They say something like, "I have been baptized," "My parents were Christians, and I am," "I once said the sinner's prayer and I feel I am a Christian," "I am going to a Christian church," or "I think I am a Christian, but I have some doubts."

Sadly, all these people are not sincere followers of Jesus Christ, and we see them continue to live in sin, to love the world, and not obey God's commandments. These people deceive themselves and think that they are Christians, but they are not according to the Holy Scriptures. Pastor Steven J. Cole said, *"If you do not know God personally, you are not saved."* Many people know a lot of things about God but do not know God. It is much different knowing about God than to know God. It is much different, knowing Psalm 23 than to know the Shepherd.

I hope you have the confidence to say as the blind man who was healed by Jesus *"one thing I know, that, whereas I was blind, now I see"* (John 9:25). Joyful is the soul that can truly say, "One thing I know, is that I used to be blind (spiritually) and now I can see (spiritually)!" or "One thing I know, is that I used to be lost and now I am saved!" Apostle John used the word "know" 177 times in his writings because he dealt with the truth and reality. The gospel of John is the most assuring book in the Bible. Read it if you have doubts.

Christians must live by Bible principles and not by their feelings. They do not have to feel that their sins have been forgiven, but they have to know by faith that they have been forgiven because God says so in His Word. There is no more powerful testimony than that which is drawn from your own experience. I hope all of us have that experience so we can say, "I have the assurance of my salvation," "I know that I have eternal life," and "I know God personally through Jesus Christ." Also, to say as Job said in Job 19:25, *"I know that my redeemer liveth,..."* and with the apostle Paul in 2 Timothy 1:12, *"I know whom I have believed, and am persuaded that he is able to keep that which I have committed unto him against that day."*

BLESSED ASSURANCE

Blessed assurance, Jesus is mine;
Oh, what a foretaste of glory divine!
Heir of salvation, purchase of God,
Born of His Spirit, washed in His blood.

Refrain:
This is my story, this is my song,
Praising my Savior all the day long.
This is my story, this is my song,
Praising my Savior all the day long.

— *Hymn by Frances J. Crosby, 1873*

❖ ❖ ❖

- "I believe hundreds of Christian people are being deceived by Satan now on this point, that they have not got the assurance of salvation just because they are not willing to take God at His word."
— *Evangelist, D.L. Moody*

- "If any man is not sure that he is in Christ, he ought not to be easy one moment until he is sure. Dear friend, without the fullest confidence as to your saved condition, you have no right to be at ease, and I pray you may never be so. This is a matter too important to be left undecided."
—*"Prince of Preachers," Charles Spurgeon*

- "When you are not sure of your salvation, it is very easy to get discouraged and to backslide." — *Bible Teacher, Zac Poonen*

41

BIBLICAL CONVICTION

"Blessed is the man that walketh not in the counsel of the ungodly, nor standeth in the way of sinners... But his delight is in the law of the LORD...and whatsoever he doeth shall prosper."
Psalm 1:1-3

*

A biblical conviction is a belief that you will not change, because you believe God requires it of you!

Without strong biblical convictions of sin from the Holy Spirit, no one can be saved, and no one can live a victorious Christian life to please the Lord. A conviction is a belief that we will not change because we believe God requires it of us. Strong convictions based on the Word of God will act as a powerful rudder to steer our life during difficult times. True Christians must live with biblical standards and convictions. A true Christian must practice biblical convictions as a citizen of heaven on earth. Most of the time, people are more impressed by the depth of our conviction than the height of our logic. I will present to you a few true stories for you to review the deep conviction of Christians when they are committed to God.

• Levi Coffin is an unsung hero of the American anti-slavery movement. In the 1820s Coffin moved to Newport, Indiana and opened a shop. His home soon became a central point on the famous Underground Railroad, a pathway from slavery in the USA's South to freedom in Canada. People like Coffin would take an enormous personal risk to help fleeing slaves on their journey. Coffin provided refuge for up to 17 refugee slaves at a time at his house, and so active was he that three major routes on the Underground Railroad converged at his place which became known as Grand Central Terminal. Because of his activities, Coffin received frequent death threats and warnings that his shop and home would be burned. Yet he was undeterred. Like many of the whites he was undeterred. Like many of the whites involved in the underground Railroad, he was driven by his Christian convictions. Coffin was a Quaker and explaining his commitment said, *"The Bible, in bidding us to feed the hungry and clothe the naked, said nothing about color." — Readers Digest July 2001*

• Athanasius, an early bishop of Alexandria, stoutly opposed the teachings of Arius, who declared that Christ was not the eternal Son of God, but a subordinate being. Hounded through five exiles, he was finally summoned before emperor Theodosius, who demanded he cease his opposition to Arius. The emperor reproved him and asked, *"Do you not realize that all the world is against you?"* Athanasius quickly answered, *"Then I am against all the world." — sermonillustation.com*

• The Evangelist Rodney "Gipsy" Smith said, "When I was in South Africa, a fine, handsome Dutchman came into my service, and God laid His hand on him and convicted him of sin. The next morning he went to the beautiful home of another Dutchman and said to him, 'Do you recognize that old watch?' 'Why, yes,' answered the other. 'Those are my initials; that is my watch. I lost it eight years ago. How did you get it, and how long have you had it?' 'I stole it,' was the reply. 'What made you bring it back now?' 'I was converted last night,' was the answer, 'and I have brought it back first thing this morning. If you had been up, I would have brought it last night.'"— *Gipsy Smith, The Bible Friend*

• Dr. J. Wilbur Chapman tells of an incident in the life of President Lincoln that suggests a WEAKNESS in many a life and an efficient strength in the life of a few. He says Mrs. Pomeroy was counted a member of President Lincoln's household. One day when he had grown weary with the affairs of state, he asked her to accompany him to the theatre and occupy the president's box at the Ford Theater that night. Mrs. Pomeroy courteously declined. He gave her a subsequent invitation, and it was not accepted. Finally, with some degree of irritation, he said, "Mrs. Pomeroy, it is counted an HONOR to sit in the president's box. I should like to ask you why you have refused." Hesitating a moment, as if she feared to hurt the feelings of the president, she said "Mr. President, I am a Christian, and when I became such I PROMISED my Lord that I would go no place where I could not take him with me, or ask his blessing. I could hardly do this at the THEATER, and for that reason, I do not go." It is said that Abraham Lincoln never again asked her to accompany him to such a place, but it is known that again and again when they were driving together on some mission of MERCY in the various hospitals, he would say to his coachman, "Drive a little slower." And then he would say to Mrs. Pomeroy, "Tell me more of this Christ whom you SERVE." — *The Gospel Guardian, Vol.6, No.2, Pg.10,1954*

• John Smith had a profitable construction business. As a Christian, he tried to let his faith direct his work. One day, a wealthy builder asked John for dinner. During the meal, the builder offered John the main part of a massive government building project. When John asked for details, he learned that he would have to compromise his convictions if he took the job. Politely, he declined the profitable offer. The builder pressed John for his reason. "I am a Christian," replied Smith, "and I can only do business by Christian principles." Amazed, the builder responded, "Surely you do not want to mix two good things like business and religion." Looking across the table, John declared, "I have discovered that when I mix business with religion, I can prove my religion, and also improve my business."

• When I was a young man, the management of a well-known American sex magazine offered me a job to work for them as a commercial artist. Quickly, my answer was "No" because of my Christian convictions. The salary was five times more than the job I had. At that time, I worked for a well-known American Christian organization. My dream was always to make good money to help my family and enable my wife to stay home and take care of our children. In our case, one of us worked days, while the other worked nights. This arrangement enabled at least one of us to always be home with the children. Even though my wife would have benefited from my new job, she told me how proud she was of my godly decision. Being faithful to the Lord has made me feel rich, like a billionaire, from the spiritual blessings He has given me over the years. One of those spiritual blessings was to have a Christian family who served the Lord together without any compromise.

My first wife is with the Lord now. When I performed her funeral in 1996 with my senior pastor, the Lord gave me unbelievable comfort that is humanly impossible to imagine. He gave me positive thoughts and comfort in knowing how He will take care of her better than me, and also how proud He was for her faithfulness to Him. I know now more than ever that He is real and brings comfort and compassion in whatever happens in my life.

Levi Coffin did everything he believed and fought against the injustice he saw. Because of this, many slaves found their freedom. Bishop Athanasius, the converted Dutchman, Mrs. Pomeroy, and John Smith lived with strong biblical convictions and became good examples. The tragedy today is that some Christians practice religion and do not live with biblical convictions. As a result, they believe and do anything they please. True Christians must live with biblical standards and convictions. True Christians must fear God as much as they love Him. True Christians must obey God's commandments and believe God's promises. True Christians must support what they believe and not compromise in their daily lives. True Christians must practice biblical convictions as God's ambassadors on earth.

If you are a Christian, ask yourself how firm your Christian convictions are and whether your commitments draw others to Christ or not. Ask yourself if your integrity and convictions show in your daily life. Make sure the world sees that your Christianity is not just empty words. God wants your life to be a witness to your devotion to Jesus. We see today true and devoted Christians that prefer to be beheaded by terrorists rather than deny Christ. Be consistent and firm in what you know is right. Even your most critical friends will want to know what makes you such an Honest Abe. Always remember, putting the Lord and His Word first is an essential key to success in your life.

❖ ❖ ❖

- "Going to church doesn't make you a Christian any more than going to a garage makes you an automobile." — *Evangelist, Billy Sunday*

- "A conviction is a belief that is considered true and worthy of standing upon regardless of the consequences. However, because there are no real standards these days, our society has become worthy of God's judgment." — *Dr. Charles Stanley*

- "A conviction is not something that you discover; it is something that you purpose in your heart." — *Dr. David C. Gibbs, Jr.*

- "In the absence of biblical conviction, people will go the way of culture." — *Author, Sally Clarkson*

True Christians must live with biblical standards and convictions as God's ambassadors on earth.

42

BIBLICAL MEDITATION

"This book of the law shall not depart out of thy mouth;
but thou shalt meditate therein day and night,
that thou mayest observe to do according to all that is written
therein: for then thou shalt make thy way prosperous,
and then thou shalt have good success.
Have not I commanded thee?
Be strong and of a good courage;
be not afraid, neither be thou dismayed:
for the LORD thy God is with thee whithersoever thou goest."
Joshua 1:8, 9

*

Biblical meditation is the key to spiritual growth!

When Christians, especially young people, ask me to tell them the one thing that will help them to grow in their Christian journey and become successful in their ministries, my answer always is the same. A Christian's most important activity and the key to Christian growth is the continual private meditation on the Word of God and fellowship with the Lord.

One of the first indicators that we are maturing in our Christian walk is an increasing hunger to know God. By meditating on the Scriptures, we draw more truth and understanding from them. We enjoy and treasure the time spent alone with God. Our meditation brings wisdom, purifies our heart, develops a submissive and sensitive spirit to hear God's voice. It sharpens our judgment and clarifies our life's direction. In our biblical meditation, the Holy Spirit transforms our thoughts, feelings, and actions to please God rather than our sinful desires. The apostle Paul encourages us with the following verse:

- *"Finally, brethren, whatsoever things are true, whatsoever things are honest, whatsoever things are just, whatsoever things are pure, whatsoever things are lovely, whatsoever things are of good report; if there be any virtue, and if there be any praise, think on these things"* (Philippians 4:8).

The Christian who meditates on the Word of God and is not too busy to stay connected with God and listen to Him is always blessed.

- *"But his delight is in the law of the LORD; and in his law doth he meditate day and night. And he shall be like a tree planted by the rivers of water, that bringeth forth his fruit in his season; his leaf also shall not wither; and whatsoever he doeth shall prosper"* (Psalm 1:2,3).

- *"O how love I thy law! it is my meditation all the day. Thou through thy commandments hast made me wiser than mine enemies: for they are ever with me. I have more understanding than all my teachers: for thy testimonies are my meditation"* (Psalm 119:97-99).

In your biblical meditation, besides desiring God's fellowship, wisdom, and direction, a true indicator of spiritual growth is an awareness of your sinfulness before God. This awareness invites more of His grace into your life. The more you learn about God personally, the more you will appreciate His grace and accept His will in your life.

Stop being a typical Christian and start meditating on the Word of God day and night, filling your mind with God's Word. In your private time, instead of only listening to music, or reading newspapers, books, and magazines, or watching videos and TV shows, meditate on the Word of God. Spend time exclusively with God and be sensitive to His voice.

Stop being too busy with other unimportant things in your life and listen to God's directions. Your private meditations and personal devotions will make the difference in your Christian life. Remember not only to read the Bible but meditate on it; not only to think about God but fellowship with Him.

❖ ❖ ❖

- "O how love I thy law! it is my meditation all the day."—*Psalm 119:97*

- "Meditation will keep your hearts and souls from sinful thoughts. When the vessel is full, you can put in no more...If the heart be full of sinful thoughts, there is no room for holy and heavenly thoughts: if the heart be full of holy and heavenly thoughts by meditation, there is no room for evil and sinful thoughts." — *Preacher and Writer, William Bridge*

43

BIBLICAL GIVING

"All the tithe...is the LORD's."
Leviticus 27:30

"Every man according as he purposeth in his heart,
so let him give; not grudgingly, or of necessity:
for God loveth a cheerful giver."
2 Corinthians 9:7

*

Give to God with all your heart
generously, joyfully, and willingly!

Every-day we witness people making waste of everything: waste of food, clothing, furnishings, pleasures on self, and in many other ways. We also witness and think about how so many people waste their lives without Christ, without loving and serving Him sacrificially. In contrast, many others have laid down their lives for Him; spent their fortunes for Him; and given their two last mites for Him. Did any of them waste anything? NO! There is no waste in what is given to Christ. Many times, I ask the question: "Have we poured out our possessions as Christians, our time, our talents, our comfort, our legitimate enjoyments upon His blessed Person and service?"

Christ says, *"And every one that hath forsaken houses, or brethren, or sisters, or father, or mother, or wife, or children, or lands, for my name's sake, shall receive an hundredfold, and shall inherit everlasting life"* (Matthew 19:29). We have an example of giving from the Bible in 2 Corinthians 8:2,4,5 and 11, that the believers *"first gave their own selves to the Lord,"* and then they gave with *"joy"* without using their trials and poverty as excuses for not giving. Also, they gave *"with much intreaty (urgency),"* and *"perform (complete) the doing of it; that as there was a readiness to will, so there may be a performance also out of that which ye have." "God loveth a cheerful giver"* (2 Corinthians 9:7) and rewards his giving *"he which soweth bountifully shall reap also bountifully"* (2 Corinthians 9:6).

We must remember three things in Christian giving.

1. **To whom we give.** Everything we give is for the Lord.

    "Take ye from among you an offering unto the Lord..." (Exodus 35:5).
    "The things which were sent from you, an odour of a sweet smell, a sacrifice acceptable, wellpleasing to God" (Philippians 4:18).

2. **How we should give.** We must give according to God's instructions.

    A. We should give the Lord what is His.
    "And all the tithe of the land...is the Lord's: it is holy unto the Lord" (Leviticus 27:30).

    B. We have to give systematically, individually, proportionately, honestly, cheerfully, and sacrificially.
    "Upon the first day of the week..." (1 Corinthians 16:2).
    "Every one of you..." (1 Corinthians 16:2), with
    "a willing mind..." (2 Corinthians 8:12), and
    "willing of themselves" (2 Corinthians 8:3),
    "as God hath prospered him..." (1 Corinthians 16:2).
    "Wherein have we robbed thee? In tithes and offerings"
    (Malachi 3:8). *"God loveth a cheerful giver" (2 Corinthians 9:7).*
    "And he [Jesus] said, Of a truth I say unto you, that this poor widow hath cast in more than they all" (Luke 21:3,4).

3. **There is a reward for giving.**

    "Lay up for yourselves treasures in heaven..." (Matthew 6:20).
    "It is more blessed to give than to receive" (Acts 20:35).
    "For God loveth a cheerful giver" (2 Corinthians 9:7).
    "Bring ye all the tithes...and pour you out a blessing, that there shall not be room enough to receive it" (Malachi 3:10).

Some time ago, I had to clean my office cabinets and shred many personal records that I had accumulated over the years. These were not necessary for me to keep anymore. After going through all my personal records, I observed the many thousands of dollars paid to different services and God's work. I realized again that the money I spent for God's work was the best investment in my life. I believe it is the only investment which has an eternal impact.

I have never regretted that I do not have another house, a vacation home, a better car to drive, or other luxuries that I might have if I had kept and spent the money belonging to God. For me, there is no waste in what I gave to God, and I hope there is no waste for you either. We must realize that we do not currently live under the Law, and the tithe (10%) which no longer applies, but we must give to the Lord voluntarily. We now live under grace because Jesus fulfilled the Old Testament Law *"freely ye have received, freely give"* (Matthew 10:8).

"God loveth a cheerful giver." Today we must give Him not only tithes, but offerings with all our heart generously, joyfully, and willingly in appreciation for what He has done for us and for what He offered us as Christians. *"For ye know the grace of our Lord Jesus Christ, that, though he was rich, yet for your sakes he became poor, that ye through his poverty might be rich"* (2 Corinthians 8:9).

Today, some Christians give to the Lord like they are not living under grace. Some continue to give Him only a tithe, others less than a tithe, or entirely nothing. If you do not give, what is keeping you from giving to the Lord, generously and cheerfully? Are you afraid you will not have enough? Jesus is not poor. God promises to bless your finances as you obey Him. God really does not need your money, but He needs to see if you put Him first in your life. Remember that through giving, God invites all the believers to test His faithfulness. Make sure you put GOD first when it comes to giving.

What an opportunity we have in Christ for profitable investment with no possible chance of losing or danger of wasting! Today is the day of salvation for sinners, not tomorrow: *"Behold, now is the accepted time; behold, now is the day of salvation"* (2 Corinthians 6:2b). Today is also the day of spiritual investment for believers, not tomorrow. Jesus says, *"Be thou faithful unto death, and I will give thee a crown of life"* (Revelation 2:10), and we know He has the power both in heaven and on earth to make good every word out of His mouth.

❖ ❖ ❖

- "God judges what we give by what we keep."

— *Evangelist, George Mueller*

- *Captain Levy,* a believer, was once asked how he could give so much to the Lord's work and still possess great wealth. The Captain replied, "Oh, as I shovel it out, He shovels it in, and the Lord has a bigger shovel."

44

THE POTTER AND THE CLAY

"O LORD, thou art our father;
we are the clay, and thou our potter;
and we all are the work of thy hand."
Isaiah 64:8

*

Your life is like clay.
Do not let anyone mold it except the Lord!

There was a couple who used to go to England to shop in the beautiful stores. This was their twenty-fifth wedding anniversary. They both liked antiques and pottery and especially teacups.

One day in this beautiful shop they saw a beautiful teacup. They said, "May we see that? We've never seen one quite so beautiful." As the lady handed it to them, suddenly the teacup spoke.

"You don't understand," it said. "I haven't always been a teacup. There was a time when I was red, and I was clay. My master took me and rolled me and patted me over and over and I yelled out, 'let me alone,' but he only smiled, 'Not yet.'

"Then I was placed on a spinning wheel," the teacup said, "and suddenly I was spun around and around and around. 'Stop it! I'm getting dizzy!' I screamed. But the master only nodded and said, 'Not yet.'

Then he put me in the oven. I never felt such heat. I wondered why he wanted to burn me, and I yelled, and I knocked at the door. I could see him through the opening, and I could read his lips as he shook his head, 'Not yet.'

Finally the door opened, he put me on the shelf, and I began to cool. 'There, that's better,' I said. And he brushed and painted me all over. The fumes were horrible. I thought I would gag. 'Stop it, stop it!' I cried. He only nodded, 'Not yet.'

"Then suddenly he put me back into the oven, not like the first one. This was twice as hot, and I knew I would suffocate. I begged. I pleaded. I screamed. I cried. All the time I could see him through the opening nodding his head, saying, 'Not yet.'

"Then I knew there wasn't any hope. I would never make it. I was ready to give up. But the door opened, and he took me out and placed me on the shelf. One hour later he handed me a mirror and said, 'Look at yourself.' And I did. I said, 'That's not me; that couldn't be me. It's beautiful. I'm beautiful.'

'I want you to remember, then,' he said, 'I know it hurt to be rolled and patted, but if I just left you, you'd have dried up. I know it made you dizzy to spin around on the wheel, but if I had stopped, you would have crumbled. I know it hurt and it was hot and disagreeable in the oven, but if I hadn't put you there, you would have cracked. I know the fumes were bad when I brushed and painted you all over, but if I hadn't done that, you never would have hardened. You would not have had any color in your life, and if I hadn't put you back in that second oven, you wouldn't survive for very long because the hardness would not have held. Now you are a finished product. You are what I had in mind when I first began with you.' — *Author Unknown*

The Lord uses the potter's process in each of His children to develop a finished product, to develop a strong character, and faithful servant. Through life's painful trials and tribulations, the Lord's goal is to change His children from paper plates to beautiful and strong porcelains to use for His glory. If your Master has not yet told you, "You are what I had in mind when I first began with you" you are still in "The Refiner's Fire," and you need more purification. I know the situation is painful from my own experience, but hang on. The Lord who made you knows what is best for you and how to direct your life.

God is the potter, and you must be the clay, but the question to you is: "Are you the potter or the clay?" I hope you allow yourself to be the clay and yield to the Lord's hands. This way, you will become better than a beautiful teacup where the people say, "We've never seen one quite so beautiful."

HAVE THINE OWN WAY, LORD

Have Thine own way, Lord! Have Thine own way!
Thou art the Potter, I am the clay.
Mold me and make me after Thy will,
While I am waiting, yielded and still.

— Hymn by Adelaide A. Pollard, 1906

❖ ❖ ❖

- "Saith the LORD. Behold, as the clay is in the potter's hand, so are ye in mine hand..." *— Jeremiah 18:6*

- "You see, a potter can only mold the clay when it lies completely in his hand. It requires complete surrender." *Author, Corrie Ten Boom*

- "May we forever be clay that is willing to be shaped and reshaped..." *Botanist and Teacher, J. Royle*

**God is the potter; you are the clay.
When trials come in your life,
it is just another spin on the Potter's Wheel;
but the Lord who made you knows
what is best for you.
Just hang on!**

45

SACRIFICE FOR JESUS

*"And walk in love, as Christ also has loved us
and given Himself for us, an offering and a sacrifice to God
for a sweetsmelling savour."*
Ephesians 5:2

*

Sacrifice for others and for Jesus like He did for you!

In the Old Testament, the Israelites offered animals as sacrifices to God because it was required by Him. In the New Testament, Christians did not have to do this anymore because Jesus Christ, once and for all, offered himself as a sacrifice for us on the cross. His sacrifice was perfect, complete, and paid the penalty for all of our sins. As Christians, we are grateful for that and thank God for the sacrifice of Jesus on the cross for us. Now we have to sacrifice ourselves to God to please Him.

The apostle Paul said what kind of sacrifice we have to do, *"present your bodies a living sacrifice...and be not conformed to this world...be ye transformed by the renewing of your mind..."* (Romans 12:1,2). This sacrifice means we have to offer all of ourselves entirely to the Lord: our life, our time, our talents, our possessions, our emotions, and our attitudes. We must not love and conform to this world.

"Love not the world, neither the things that are in the world. If any man love the world, the love of the Father is not in him. For all that is in the world, the lust of the flesh, and the lust of the eyes, and the pride of life, is not of the Father, but is of the world" (1 John 2:15,16).

To accomplish this, we have to be *"transformed by the renewing of our minds,"* and we can do it through the power of God's Word. We have to fill our minds with the Word of God and not leave room for the things of the world.

- *"Wherewithal shall a young man cleanse his way? by taking heed thereto according to thy word. With my whole heart have I sought thee: O let me not wander from thy commandments. Thy word have I hid in mine heart, that I might not sin against thee"* (Psalm 119:9–11).

- *"But his delight is in the law of the LORD; and in his law doth he meditate day and night. And he shall be like a tree planted by the rivers of water, that bringeth forth his fruit in his season; his leaf also shall not wither; and whatsoever he doeth shall prosper"* (Psalm 1:2-3).

This kind of spirit helps us to be made *"complete, thoroughly equipped for every good work"* (2 Timothy 3:16). We have to pray and ask the Lord to help us make sacrifices that please Him. Once, I read about a Christian man who was suffering from kidney failure. He attended a church prayer meeting where he met another Christian man, and together they prayed about his health concerns. A week later, the suffering man received a call from the other Christian man who offered his kidney to him for a transplant. Later, when they asked him why he did it, he said, *"It was a desire to show how grateful I am for all Christ has done for me."*

Jesus died for us. When He gave His life, we were not a friend, a relative, or even a stranger. We were sinners and enemies of God. Let the extent of this gift of grace set deep into our hearts. We need to find a way today to demonstrate our gratefulness sacrificially for all He has done for us.

"For I say, through the grace given to me, to everyone who is among you, not to think of himself more highly than he ought to think, but to think soberly, as God has dealt to each one a measure of faith" (Romans 12:3).

- One summer, my wife and I went away for a few days to the state of Wisconsin. On Sunday, we visited a small church. We had a very blessed time in this little church. We strongly felt the presence of the Holy Spirit in the church services and the love of God's people. We had met the pastor and his family twenty years before in a more prominent church in another good-sized town. After Bible college, he started that church. In the beginning, it was a small church, and he earned a very small salary. He worked hard to help his church to grow, and he even helped to build a larger new church building on a large piece of property in a lovely location.

A few years later, when it was time for the church to give him a raise that would have provided him with a little better life without significant financial pressures, he resigned. He and his wife took over another smaller church with a small congregation in a town with a population of only ten thousand. The church building used to be a funeral home, and they lived in the rooms upstairs. We found out that this pastor was 62 years old, who in addition to serving his people, also had a job in his town's post office delivering mail for several hours a week. His wife told us that he was doing that to meet people, to give the gospel to them and at the same time, to help his church to grow. The first man the Lord enabled him to reach was the Post Master, who was an ungodly man with a filthy mouth.

• While my kids were teenagers, my family worked in our church bus ministry for six years. The bus ministry had seventeen buses. We worked many hours every Saturday and Sunday in a 20-mile radius around the church to bring kids to hear the gospel and learn of God's love. We knocked on many doors every Saturday to ask parents to allow us to take their kids to the church - from three-year-olds to young adults. I remember the hard work and sacrifice of my son George. He walked in one to three feet of snow and below zero temperatures to bring the kids to the bus and back to their homes - one by one - safely. On Sundays, the rest of my family worked on the bus to keep order. Usually, the kids were from broken homes and were unruly and undisciplined. Our bus brought about 50-75 kids a week to the church. Many of them got saved, and even some of their parents did as well.

Today, some of them are successful pastors, evangelists, Christian school teachers, missionaries, admirable business people, and many of them are good Christian parents. A few years ago, one of our former bus, kids who is now an adult with his own family, happened to see me in a Christian bookstore. Without hesitation, he gave me a big hug. With tears in his eyes, he told me how much he appreciated the sacrifices my family and I had made for him. He thanked us for the love and concern given to him and the other kids, at a time in their lives when even their own parents had not shown care.

Christian, when you are serving others, do it with the same zeal as you do for yourself.

"Let each of you look out not only for his own interests but also for the interests of others" (Philippians 2:4).

Never be weary in your service for the Lord. Never wonder if what you are doing will ever make a difference. If you put into practice what you have learned in the Bible, do not give up hope. With consistency and sacrifice, serve the Lord. He promises you a harvest, but it will come in His time and in surprising ways.

For a Christian, success is not to make only money, but to do God's will with sacrifices. Real happiness and satisfaction do not come from material things, but from the presence of God. To be a winner, you have to sacrifice yourself. Be a good example. Start to sacrifice for others and for Jesus like He did for you. He gave His life by dying on the cross to provide you with eternal life and a home in glory.

❖ ❖ ❖

- "If Jesus Christ be God and died for me, then no sacrifice can be too great for me to make for Him."
— *Missionary, Charles Studd*

- "I never made a sacrifice. We ought not to talk of sacrifice when we remember the great sacrifice that he made who left his Father's throne on high to give himself for us."
— *Missionary, David Livingstone*

- "Love is a verb. Love is something you do: the sacrifices you make, the giving of self. If you want to study love, study those who sacrifice for others. Love - the feeling - is a fruit of love the verb."
— *Educator and Author, Stephen Covey*

- "You cannot win without sacrifice."
— *Writer and Philanthropist, Charles Buxton*

- "Ministry that costs nothing, accomplishes nothing."
— *Preacher, John Henry Jowett*

- "Only a life lived for others is a life worthwhile."
— *Theoretical Physicist, Albert Einstein*

- **"The 7 Modern Sins**:
  Politics without principles, Pleasures without conscience
  Wealth without work, Knowledge without character
  Industry without morality, Science without humanity
  Worship without sacrifice."
— *Anglican Priest, Frederic Lewis Donaldson*

With consistency and sacrifice, serve the Lord.

46

SELF-DENIAL

*"I am crucified with Christ: nevertheless I live;
yet not I, but Christ liveth in me: and the life which I now live
in the flesh I live by the faith of the Son of God,
who loved me, and gave himself for me."*
Galatians 2:20

*

**The Christian life is not about self-promotion;
it is about self-denial which is painful but rewarding!**

"There are ministers who never speak
of repentance or self-denial.
Naturally, they are popular, but they are false prophets."
— Dr. J.I. Packer

Maybe you wonder, "Why is all the world in such a mess today?" The answer is because the majority of the people believe in self-righteousness, self-exaltation, self-love, self-assurance, self-confidence, self-worth, self-views, and many more self-beliefs. "Living for yourself is the world's philosophy, but the Word of God implies "dying to self." This expression is not found in the Bible but suggests self-denial and self-sacrifice, which we find in many verses in the Bible, such as the verse above in Galatians 2:20. In Philippians 1:21, the apostle Paul said, *"For to me to live is Christ, and to die is gain."* The minister and evangelist Charles G. Finney tells us what self-denial is: *"It is the denying of self, not for the sake of a greater good to self, but for the sake of doing good to others. This is really denying self."*

When we put God and others before ourselves, it is "dying to self," according to Matthew 22:37-39. *"Jesus said unto him, Thou shalt love the Lord thy God with all thy heart, and with all thy soul, and with all thy mind. This is the first and great commandment. And the second is like unto it, Thou shalt love thy neighbour as thyself."* As faithful Christians, we must genuinely care for others. It says in Philippians 2:3-4, *"Let nothing be done through strife or vainglory; but in lowliness of mind let each esteem other better than themselves. Look not every man on his own things, but every man also on the things of others."*

Jesus expresses the same thing in the following verse: *"If any man will come after me, let him deny himself, and take up his cross, and follow me"* (Matthew 16:24). When we do this, we not only follow God's will but also experience real life in Christ. *"For whosoever will save his life shall lose it: and whosoever will lose his life for my sake shall find it"* (Matthew 16:25). This verse is positive, not negative. With God, we have a better and real life, and we bring more fruit and can reach others with love and joy.

The moment we become a born again Christian, the old self dies, and the new one arises. We become a new creation: *"Therefore if any man be in Christ, he is a new creature: old things are passed away; behold, all things are become new"* (2 Corinthians 5:17). From the moment we become a new creation, we are indwelt by the Holy Spirit, *"But ye are not in the flesh, but in the Spirit, if so be that the Spirit of God dwell in you. Now if any man have not the Spirit of Christ, he is none of his"* (Romans 8:9). As believers in Christ, if we allow the Holy Spirit to work in our lives, He will help us to die to self, day by day, through the process of sanctification.

Dying to self is not optional for believers, as seen in the following verses.

"Verily, verily, I say unto you, Except a corn of wheat fall into the ground and die, it abideth alone: but if it die, it bringeth forth much fruit. He that loveth his life shall lose it; and he that hateth his life in this world shall keep it unto life eternal" (John 12:24,25).

"I beseech you therefore, brethren, by the mercies of God, that ye present your bodies a living sacrifice, holy, acceptable unto God, which is your reasonable service. And be not conformed to this world: but be ye transformed by the renewing of your mind, that ye may prove what is that good, and acceptable, and perfect, will of God" (Romans 12:1,2).

"God forbid. How shall we, that are dead to sin, live any longer therein? Know ye not, that so many of us as were baptized into Jesus Christ were baptized into his death? Therefore we are buried with him by baptism into death: that like as Christ was raised up from the dead by the glory of the Father, even so we also should walk in newness of life" (Romans 6:2-4).

"But God forbid that I should glory, save in the cross of our Lord Jesus Christ, by whom the world is crucified unto me, and I unto the world" (Galatians 6:14).

Jesus Christ must be our example. He denied himself and followed His Father's will. We can see this very clearly from the Scriptures. Following are a few verses with His words:

- *"Verily, verily, I say unto you, The Son can do nothing of himself..."* *(John 5:19).*

- *"I came down from heaven, not to do mine own will, but the will of him that sent me"* (John 6:38).

- *"I do nothing of myself; but as my Father hath taught me, I speak these things"* (John 8:28).

- *"Neither came I of myself, but he sent me"* (John 8:42).

- *"I seek not Mine own glory..."* (John 8:50).

- *"The words that I speak unto you I speak not of myself: but the Father that dwelleth in me..."* (John 14:10).

- *"The word which ye hear is not mine..."* (John 14:24).

These words teach us how Jesus' Father was able to work His mighty plans through Him. When Jesus was on the earth, God was everything, and Jesus was nothing. He gave everything to His Father. This is true self-denial to which our Savior calls us to follow.

With prayer and particular attention, please read and absorb the words of the following Christian hymn:

TAKE MY LIFE, AND LET IT BE

Take my life, and let it be consecrated, Lord, to Thee.
Take my moments and my days; let them flow in ceaseless praise.
Take my hands, and let them move at the impulse of Thy love.
Take my feet, and let them be Swift and beautiful for Thee.

Take my voice, and let me sing Always, only, for my King.
Take my lips, and let them be filled with messages from Thee.
Take my silver and my gold; not a mite would I withhold.
Take my intellect, and use every power as Thou shalt choose.

Take my will, and make it Thine; it shall be no longer mine.
Take my heart, it is Thine own; it shall be Thy royal throne.
Take my love, my Lord, I pour at Thy feet its treasure store.
Take myself, and I will be ever, only, all for Thee.

— *Hymn by Frances Ridley Havergal, 1874*

I am sure that many times you have sung this hymn in your church along with other believers. I wonder if you realize the meaning of the words of this hymn and practice them in your life. I hope you have died to self and are living for Christ. I hope you are a real follower of Jesus Christ and use everything for God's glory. I hope you are not only a part of the big Christian statistical numbers but a real child of the King. I hope you have experienced the joy of the Lord and His salvation in your heart. Remember, if you want TO LIVE, YOU MUST DIE TO SELF!

As Christians, we must keep in our minds daily that we belong to the Lord, and even if we are in the world, we should not live as if we are of the world. We should live to make our lives a witness and testimony to the lost and to our brethren. We should be different from those in this world. We should be worthy of our high calling. *"But ye are a chosen generation, a royal priesthood, an holy nation, a peculiar people; that ye should shew forth the praises of him who hath called you out of darkness into his marvellous light"* (1 Peter 2:9). The Bible clearly teaches us how to live our lives on this earth *"Whether therefore ye eat, or drink, or whatsoever ye do, do all to the glory of God"* (1 Corinthians 10:31).

My family and I always had a desire, by God's grace, to be close to the Lord, keep our eyes on Him, and do His will in our lives because we love Him and His work. For this reason, the verse above *"For to me to live is Christ, and to die is gain"* became part of our lives. When my first wife died in 1996, I designed her gravestone (which will also be mine one day) with this verse engraved on it. We believe this verse to be our testimony. I hope you also memorize, believe, and practice this verse.

❖ ❖ ❖

- "The first lesson in Christ's school is self-denial."
— *Minister and Author, Matthew Henry*

- "The most important qualification for a servant of God is that he does not seek his own." — *Bible Teacher, Zac Poonen*

- "If we do not die to ourselves, we cannot live to God, and he that does not live to God, is dead." — *Minister and Author, George Macdonald*

- "Those who determine not to put self to death will never see the will of God fulfilled in their lives."— *Missionary, Sadhu Sundar Singh*

- "Self-denial is painful for a moment, but very agreeable in the end." — *Poet and Novelist, Jane Taylor*

47

GOD'S PROMISES

*"And ye know in all your hearts and in all your souls,
that not one thing hath failed of all the good things which
the LORD your God spake concerning you; all are come to pass
unto you, and not one thing hath failed thereof."*
Joshua 23:14

*"For all the promises of God in him are yea, and in him Amen,
unto the glory of God by us."*
2 Corinthians 1:20

*

You will be blessed by believing all the promises of God!

In the Bible, we find God's promises, as well as God's commandments. God's promises are different than His commandments. God's commandments must be obeyed, while God's promises must be believed. Promises of God are absolute commitments made by God. Because God is faithful and does not lie, we have the full assurance and absolute confidence that what He has pledged He will do. *"God is not a man, that he should lie; neither the son of man, that he should repent: hath he said, and shall he not do it? or hath he spoken, and shall he not make it good?"* (Numbers 23:19).

According to the *Dictionary of Bible Themes*, there are 5,467 divine promises in the Bible. Some of the promises are for a specific person, but others are more general. Some promises are conditional, and others are unconditional. Some are popular, and some are not. All the promises of God are good and bring blessings if we believe them. If we do not believe them, they will not make any difference in our lives.

Some of the cherished and popular promises of God are for eternal life, believer's security, the Holy Spirit, resurrection, Christ's return, God's love, forgiveness, faithfulness, help in temptation, answered prayer, eternal blessings, provision, wisdom and guidance, strength, protection, comfort, peace, fear, healing, children, wives, husbands, family, marriage, and finances.

The following four examples are unpopular promises of God. These promises bring us blessings, even if we do not like them.

1. **"I said therefore unto you, that ye shall die in your sins:** *for if ye believe not that I am he..."* (John 8:24).

Our sin separates us from God, and many verses in the Bible warns us about the danger we are to face. *"The soul that sinneth, it shall die..."* (Ezekiel 18:20), *"For the wages of sin is death..." (Romans 6:23),* and *"For all have sinned, and come short of the glory of God"* (Romans 3:23). The interesting part of this promise is what we find when we read the rest of the verse. We die only when we do not believe who Jesus is. We have to believe that He is the Son of God. *"Jesus said unto them, Verily, verily, I say unto you, Before Abraham was, I am."* (John 8:58). When we believe this, we experience the blessed hope of our salvation, which comes from the second part of the verse Romans 6:23, *"but the gift of God is eternal life through Jesus Christ our Lord."*

2. **"All that will live godly in Christ Jesus shall suffer persecution "** Timothy 3:12).

Even if we do not want to be persecuted according to God's Word, we will face some kinds of persecution. Jesus said, *"Blessed are you, when men revile you and persecute you, and say all kinds of evil against you falsely for My sake"* (Matthew 5:11). If we read the whole chapter of 2 Timothy 3, we see that God one day, will not allow bad things to continue in the world, but will follow with blessings. As a result of that, the apostle Paul encouraged Timothy and us today to not give up. Until then, according to 2 Timothy 3:14,17, we need to continue to do what we are supposed to do as believers, reading and studying the Bible and doing good works.

3. **"In the world ye shall have tribulation:** *but be of good cheer; I have overcome the world..."* (John 16:33).

All of us experience and know that life is not easy. We wish it were the opposite, but like it or not, the Lord has promised us a life full of trials and tribulations. The interesting part of this promise we find when we read the rest of the verse with the Lord's comforting words: *"but be of good cheer; I have overcome the world."* This promise means it does not matter how many trials and tribulations we experience, Jesus, who has overcome them stands with us and helps us. Jesus went through worse trials and tribulations. He even died on the cross for us. He defeated death and overcame the world, and we as believers will one day be set free from all our trials and tribulations. Until then, *"Casting all your care upon him; for he careth for you"* (1 Peter 5:7).

4. *"Knowing this, that the trying of your faith worketh patience"* (James 1:3).

It is not necessary to pray for patience because of the above verse and the following verse *"but we glory in tribulations also: knowing that tribulation worketh patience"* (Romans 5:3). These verses inform us that patience is learned through the testing of our faith through trials and tribulations. God has His own ways to teach us patience for our benefit. Keep in mind that it is a process which takes time and is developed through our Christian life full of joys and trials. Both are needed, and the apostle James encourages us: *"But let patience have her perfect work, that ye may be perfect and entire, wanting nothing"* (James 1:4). After all, God's goal is to help us to grow from babies to mature Christians.

As Christians, we have to live day by day and wait on the Lord for tomorrow to direct our paths according to Proverbs 3:6, *"In all thy ways acknowledge him, and he shall direct thy paths."* We have to believe all the popular and unpopular promises of God in our daily lives. When we face mountains in front of us, it is impossible for us to reduce their size without God's help. Christians face adversity like everyone else in the world and sometimes more. No matter the difficulties we are facing, patient endurance will bring us success.

There is always sunshine after the thunderstorm. When we experience trials and tribulations, we do not have to overreact with panic, anxiety, and fear. We never need to question God. God always loves and cares for us, but He has a reason to have us go through all of these. God promises that He will use these trials to help us become stronger and depend more on Him, to grow our faith, increase our patience, and make us more like Jesus. Patience is one of the fruits of the Holy Spirit. It gives us the ability to do what we can do for today and trust God for tomorrow. Patience always grows in the soil of adversity and tribulation.

Our problem is on numerous occasions; we do not wait upon the Lord. We forget that it is through faith and patience we obtain God's promises. God's first concern is our growth, then our success. He is concerned that we learn patience. The Lord teaches us this needed lesson through the blessed discipline of delay. We do not have to be impatient and try to finish the mosaic of our lives in one day.

I have served the Lord all my Christian life, and I have had more trials and tribulations than many others, but the Lord has used them to grow my patience and faith. Now, every time any unexpected, unpleasant situation comes into my life, I do not worry and panic. With patience and a right attitude, I wait for the situation to pass and see what good will come from it for God's glory.

Early on in my Christian life, I learned to believe and claim the following promise of God. "*And we know that all things work together for good to them that love God, to them who are the called according to his purpose*" (Romans 8:28). When the Bible says "all things," it means "all," which includes the good and the bad. Praise the Lord! The above promise assures us that the Lord cares for and blesses the ones who love Him even when they are going through difficult times.

Before we become "promise believers," it is impossible to be what God wants us to be. The promises of God are greater than the threats of our enemy. When we focus on God's promises instead of the problems, we will notice our thoughts are healthier and filled with peace.

Christian, do you know you are rich? When you have trusted Jesus Christ by faith, you received more than the assurance of eternal life. God has provided you with the spiritual resources you need to live each day as an effective Christian. Faith is the key. Open a promise of God today!

❖ ❖ ❖

• "God makes a promise; Faith believes it; Hope anticipates it; and Patience quietly awaits it." — *D.L. Moody, Pleasure & Profit in Bible Study*

• "There is a living God. He has spoken in the Bible. He means what He says and will do all He has promised." — *Missionary, J. Hudson Taylor*

• "Every promise is built upon four pillars: God's justice and holiness, which will not suffer him to deceive; his grace or goodness, which will not suffer him to forget; His truth, which will not suffer him to change; his power, which makes him able to accomplish." — *Salter*

• "God didn't promise days without pain, Laughter without sorrow, sun without rain, But He did promise strength for the day, Comfort for the tears, and light for the way!" — *Author Unknown*

• "The secret of happiness is to count your blessings while others are adding up their troubles." — *Founder of the Province of Pennsylvania, William Penn*

48

GOD'S BLESSINGS

"Every good gift and every perfect gift is from above,
and coming down from the Father of lights..."
James 1:17

"Blessed be the God and Father of our Lord Jesus Christ,
who hath blessed us with all spiritual blessings
in heavenly places in Christ."
Ephesians 1:3

*

Do you realize who is behind all your blessings?

I know a lady who considers herself to be a good Christian. She calls me to pray and help her when she or one of her loved ones is in an emergency situation. She calls me from the hospital, from an auto accident location, when her children have problems with drugs and the law, or other similar circumstances. She only remembers God and me for help when she is in a difficult situation. She treats God like a fireman or policeman and then forgets Him after the fire or the troubles are over. She never calls to tell me about all the good things she receives each day from the loving hands of God. She never thanks the Lord when He answers prayers on her behalf or thanks Him for the many blessings He gives her and her family the rest of the time. She always complains. I never hear her praise God and be serious with Him but lives her life like God does not exist except when she is in trouble. Her attitude is insane, and she is not the only one who lives like this. It is especially sad to see Christians who have been blessed so much by God, and do not say, "Thank you Lord" or "Praise the Lord." It appears like it is not in their vocabulary, or they are embarrassed if they say it.

In life, we have to see all the blessings that come from the Lord and not stare only at the difficulties on our journey. Usually, we concentrate on the trials of life, instead of fixing our attention upon God's blessings. The Greek word in the New Testament for "blessing" is "ευλογία" (eulogía). It comes from two words "ευ-λογία" (eu-logía), which the first word, "ευ" means "good," and the second word, "λόγια" means "good words from somebody or provision of good things from somebody." Yes, the Lord provides many blessings every day for us from above. *"Blessed be the Lord, who daily loadeth us with benefits..."* (Psalm 68:19).

It would be wonderful to grow up in our Christian life with a thankful and a grateful heart. From early childhood and through our adult lives, we are usually exposed to a culture of critics and complainers. We complain about the food, work, weather, neighbors, church, government and just about everything else in life. We are especially ungrateful to God with our daily complaints against Him. It is sad when we receive so much from Him each day, and we are thankful for so little.

We have to realize that everything we have comes from God and is controlled by Him. Our health, our spouse, our children, our job, our house, our car, and everything else we have. All these came from the merciful hands of God and not ours. We have to depend on the Lord for all these blessings and not on ourselves. We can lose all of these blessings if God allows it. We can lose our health or our job because of illness, our spouse or children from an unexpected death, our house from fire, or our car from an accident. It is foolish to think that everything we have is because of us. No! In reality, we deserve nothing. It is only because of God's grace we have what we have. Job, a man of God, believed that. When he lost all the blessings he had, he said, *"the LORD gave, and the LORD hath taken away; blessed be the name of the LORD"* (Job 1:21).

Once a certified public accountant decided to open a journal with God. He created a debit and credit book where he would list everything that God gave him and that he gave to God. If someone did him a favor, he noted that as God's gift to him. Similarly, he credited God with his health, his friends, his food, his rescue from depression, and a thousand other undeserved blessings. He also put down what he did for God. In the end, though, he gave up the bookkeeping project, saying, *"It's impossible to balance the books. I find that God is completely my creditor and what I have done for God is next to nothing."* — *Author Unknown*

As Christians, we must be thankful for all the material blessings we receive from the Lord each day and especially for our spiritual blessings. Some of them are salvation, grace, forgiveness, righteousness, peace, joy, hope, deliverance, acceptance, and inheritance.

"When we are ungrateful, the heart of God is saddened, the Holy Spirit is grieved, and the joy of the Lord is quenched within us...our thanksgiving is always appropriate. It will gladden the heart of God to hear your heartfelt thanks being freely offered to Him today."
— *Roy Lessin co-founded DaySpring Cards, Inc.*

There is a story told about a young boy's dream that came true. He and his friend went to the local grocery store one hot day to buy an ice cream bar. When they entered the door, they noticed a tremendous commotion. Several workers, plus the manager, were scurrying around next to a large freezer unit. The manager saw them walk in and yelled for them to come by him. Unsure of what he wanted, they walked over to him. Immediately, he started to stick ice cream into their hands; pints of it. The freezer went out, and the ice cream was beginning to melt. Instead of wasting it, the manager decided to give it away. He and his friend waddled home, each with a shopping bag full of luscious treats. *"And of his fullness have all we received, and grace for grace"* (John 1:16).

We serve a generous God. Do not approach the Lord expecting too little. His blessings of grace have been piled upon us in Christ Jesus. The next time you pray, do not ask only for a single ice cream bar, ask for a full shopping bag.

COUNT YOUR BLESSINGS

Count your blessings, name them one by one,
Count your blessings, see what God has done!
Count your blessings, name them one by one,
Count your many blessings, see what God has done.

— *Hymn by Johnson Oatman, Jr, 1897*

❖ ❖ ❖

• "Not what we say about our blessings, but how we use them, is the true measure of our thanksgiving." — *Preacher and Scholar, WT Purkiser*

• "Pray for guidance and give thanks for your blessings every day."
— *Basketball player and head coach, John Wooden*

• "God has given you 86,400 seconds today. Have you used one to say, Thank You?" — *American boxer, William Ward*

49

COMFORT OTHERS

"Blessed be God, even the Father of our Lord Jesus Christ...
Who comforteth us in all our tribulation, that we may be able
to comfort them which are in any trouble, by the comfort
wherewith we ourselves are comforted of God."
2 Corinthians 1:3-4

*

The priceless comfort in our suffering is to know
that God is in control!

As Christians, we experience many different kinds of suffering. We suffer physically, we suffer heartbreak and loss, we suffer from the results of a fallen world, and we suffer from persecution. These happen every day among genuine believers. However, the God of the Bible who saved us eternally and gave us a living hope also comforts us in our daily storms. Comfort usually means to encourage and cheer up someone with different ways in times of need.

When my first wife passed away at a young age in 1996, a sweet Christian lady from my church told me, *"Brother Ted, through this storm the Lord will help you to comfort others as He comforts you now."* Those words have stuck in my mind just as the verses shown above in 2 Corinthians 1:3,4. John Henry Jowett said, *"God does not comfort you to make you comfortable, but to make you a comforter."* When I look back now, I see the Lord first used me to comfort and encourage my children with "A SPIRITUAL NOTE FROM DAD," afterward to the people we knew with "A SPIRITUAL NOTE FROM TED," and finally to people around the world with "A SPIRITUAL NOTE FROM THE BIBLE." This way, in 1996, the Lord helped me to start my free international email ministry, "A SPIRITUAL NOTE FROM THE BIBLE," which He continues to bless.

The Bible has many roles. Some of them are to teach, encourage, challenge, inspire, convict, evangelize, and reveal God. Another of its roles is to comfort Christians when they are going through times of suffering. God promises to provide comfort and gives a proper perspective when the world seems to be collapsing around them. Christians can also find comfort in God's Word and power to comfort others.

- *"For the LORD hath comforted his people, and will have mercy upon his afflicted"* (Isaiah 49:13).

- *"I will not leave you comfortless"* (John 14:18).

- *"I will never leave thee, nor forsake thee"* (Hebrews 13:5).

The Lord always uses His word and others to comfort us. I remember in one of my situations several years ago when I was suffering from cancer, many unbelievers and believers waited for my funeral. At that time, there was a sweet Christian lady who received the SPIRITUAL NOTES gave me the most significant encouragement. A retired Pastor also called me many times before one of my life-threatening surgeries. His calls were an encouragement to me. Both of these people were thousands of miles away from me. I never met them in person, and maybe I never will in this life, but I know I will see them in heaven. God gave them love and compassion and used them to comfort others like me. God can use anybody in these kinds of situations. He only needs their availability and willingness to go a little out of their way to brighten someone's day.

When Douglas Maurer, 15, of Creve Coeur, Missouri, was diagnosed with leukemia, "The doctors told him in frank terms about his disease. They said that for the next three years, he would have to undergo chemotherapy. They didn't sugarcoat the side effects. They told Douglas he would go bald and that his body would most likely bloat. Upon learning this, he went into a deep depression. His aunt called a floral shop to send Douglas an arrangement of flowers. She told the clerk that it was for her teenage nephew, who has leukemia. When the flowers arrived at the hospital, they were beautiful. Douglas read the card from his aunt. Then he saw a second card. It said: *"Douglas--I took your order. I work at Brix florist. I had leukemia when I was seven years old. I'm 22 years old now. Good luck. My heart goes out to you. Sincerely, Laura Bradley."* His face lit up. He said, "Oh!" It's funny: Douglas Maurer was in a hospital filled with millions of dollars of the most sophisticated medical equipment. He was being treated by expert doctors and nurses with medical training totaling in the hundreds of years. However, it was a sales clerk in a flower shop, a woman making $170 a week, who-by taking the time to care, and by being willing to go with what her heart told her to do-gave Douglas hope and the will to carry on." — *Bob Greene, "From One Sufferer To Another," Chicago Tribune, August 1987*

The same thing happened to me. The Christian lady and the pastor took the time to show love, concern, and compassion. When times are tough, and things just are not going our way, there is nothing like a hug, someone putting an arm around you, and saying, "*I will pray for you. The Lord will take care of you. Everything is going to be all right...*" Generally, all people need comfort, but we have to remember the priceless comfort in our suffering is to know that God is in control.

One time, I spent all night in the hospital comforting a family whose son was struck by a car on the way to church during the Christmas season. This family never forgot my presence and simple care. They even called me "God's angel." I have sometimes spent time in the hospital with people whose loved ones have had serious surgeries to comfort them and pray with them. None of these people have forgotten my simple comfort for them. Just my presence with them in these kinds of situations was worth more than anything else.

Christians appreciate comfort from others, but most of all, they are comforted in times of sorrow when they remember that the eternal suffering that they deserve has been replaced by eternal hope. Take heart, followers of Jesus Christ, your permanent citizenship is in heaven, and it does not matter what happens in this temporal life.

Finally, do you know people whose lives are falling to pieces? Reach Sometimes all that is needed during a crisis is your caring presence with a warm hand, a hug, a phone call, a small gift, or a greeting card. Let the Lord use you. Help others as much as you can to get their feet on the ground; maybe you will need the same one day.

❖ ❖ ❖

• "Wherefore comfort yourselves together, and edify one another, even as also ye do." — *1 Thessalonians 5:11*

• "One way to get comfort is to plead the promise of God in prayer, show Him His handwriting; God is tender of His Word." — *Puritan clergyman, Thomas Manton*

• "But they that wait upon the Lord shall renew their strength; they shall mount up with wings as eagles; they shall run, and not be weary; and they shall walk, and not faint." — *Isaiah 40:31*

50

THE POWER OF THE GOSPEL

"And he [Jesus] said unto them, Go ye into all the world,
and preach the gospel to every creature.
He that believeth and is baptized shall be saved;
but he that believeth not shall be damned."
Mark 16:15-16

*

The gospel of Jesus Christ is the power of God unto salvation!

The word gospel in Greek is "ευαγγέλιον" (euaggelion). This word comes from two words. The first word is "ευ," which means "Good," and the second word is "αγγέλιον," which means message, news. In this case, the gospel of Jesus Christ is "good news." All who receive it will have their lives changed forever. I know this from my own experience with my family members, friends, relatives, and many others. Even Charles Darwin, the father of modern evolution, admitted that the gospel could change lives because he was amazed at how people changed after hearing and accepting the gospel. As a result, "from 1867 until his death in 1882, Darwin made an annual subscription to the funds of the South American Mission Society (SAMS)." — *Church Mission Society*

As Christians, our responsibility is to spread the gospel everywhere. Some may question our beliefs, but they cannot debate the fact of a changed life. Once Charles Bradlaugh, a well-known atheist, challenged Rev. Hughes to a debate. Hughes accepted the challenge with the condition that he could bring along 100 men and women to share their testimonies. The minister invited his opponent to bring a group of non-believers to share how they were helped by their lack of faith. He even told him if you cannot bring 100, bring 50, or 20, or even 1. Because Charles Bradlaugh was not able to meet the request, publicly he withdrew

his challenge for the debate with great embarrassment and anger. —
Source Unknown

We are God's ambassadors in this world, and we have to work to benefit the kingdom of God. We must be bold Christians and not disobedient, careless, and lukewarm like the people in the following stories:

- A Christian was stopped by a long-time friend, who asked: "How long have we known each other?"

After a moment's thought he replied, "About fifteen years, I guess."

"You are a Christian, right?"

"Yes, I am."

Then his friend asked, "As a Christian, do you really believe I must accept Christ as my Savior?"

"Yes, I do. It's the truth."

Then came the more significant question: "Do you care whether or not I am saved?"

"Yes, of course, I do."

"Well," said the friend, "I don't believe that. As you say, we have been good friends for fifteen years, yet in all those years you have never once mentioned Jesus Christ to me. We have talked about everything else, and if you really cared the least little bit about my soul, you would have said something by now."

The Christian was stunned, and after confessing his failure to God, proceeded to share the Gospel with his friend. — *by MWTB*

- Some time ago, an 18-year-old girl from Washington state attended a worship service. For the first time in her life, she heard a gospel sermon. The following Tuesday, the pastor of the church received a letter from her. It read: "Dear Pastor: Last Sunday I attended your church, and I heard you preach. In your sermon, you said that all men have sinned and rebelled against God. Because of their rebellion and disobedience, they all face eternal damnation and separation from God. However, then you also said God loved men and sent his Son, Jesus Christ, into the world to redeem men from their sins and that all those who believe in him would go to heaven and live with God eternally. My parents recently died in rapid succession. I know they did not believe in Jesus Christ, whom you call the Savior of the world. If what you preach is true, they are damned. You compel me to believe that either the message is true, or that you yourself don't believe this message, or that you don't care. We live only three blocks from your church, and no one ever told us. You hypocrites! Signed:____ " — *PowerHouse, Vol. 5, No. 3*

- The president of a large company had to go overseas suddenly. He wrote a detailed letter of orders back to his staff. When he returned, they had a big party to welcome him back. He was thrilled. Then he asked if they got his letter. One of the VP's stood up and quoted page 3, paragraph 7. Another person quoted page 7, paragraph 2. The boss was overwhelmed; they had memorized the whole letter! Then the CEO asked, "How are you doing on the project?" The Executive Vice-President sadly replied, "Boss, we are still studying the letter." — *Author Unknown*

Jesus gave the church marching orders to follow while he was gone. *"Go ye into all the world, and preach the gospel [the good news] to every creature"* (Mark 16:15). God commanded us to take the gospel to all nations. This was not a suggestion, but a command. God is not as concerned with how well we know His Word as with how well we obey it. When the Boss returns, will you be following orders or still studying them? *"The proof of Christianity is not a book but a life"* — *W. Woodfin*

I hope and pray you never receive a letter from a friend questioning why you did not witness to him or that your pastor never receives a letter like the one above from a nearby neighbor. Hopefully, it will not happen if you and churches are praying and finding ways to touch their lives. The gospel is so powerful. The gospel is God's power to save sinners. I encourage you not to put off telling all the people around you about Christ. You will never regret it if you do!

❖ ❖ ❖

- Follow me, and I will make you fishers of men." — *Matthew 4:19*
- "A true witness delivers souls,"— *Proverbs 11:30*
- "Ye should go and bring forth fruit..." — *John 15:16*

- Angels cannot preach the gospel, only beings such as Paul and you and I can preach the gospel. "— *Evangelist and Teacher, Oswald Chambers*

- "We will have all eternity to celebrate our victories but only one short hour before sunset in which to win them." — *Missionary, Robert Moffat*

- "So, as much as in me is, I am ready to preach the gospel to you that are at Rome also. For I am not ashamed of the gospel of Christ: for it is the power of God unto salvation to every one that believeth; to the Jew first, and also to the Greek (the Gentile)." — *Romans 1:15,16*

- "The average Christian in America today will die without ever having shared his faith in Christ with another person." — *George Barna Seminar*

**All the people around us who have eternal souls,
will one day spend eternity in hell
if we do not obey God's command to preach the gospel to them.**

51

WITNESS FOR CHRIST

"For I am not ashamed of the gospel of Christ:
for it is the power of God unto salvation
to every one that believeth..."
Romans 1:16

*

**You might not be a good speaker or a polished
communicator, but the Holy Spirit can use your words
to bring people to God!**

As D. L. Moody walked down a Chicago street one day, he saw a man leaning against a lamppost. The evangelist gently put his hand on the man's shoulder and asked him if he was a Christian. The fellow raised his fists and angrily exclaimed, "Mind your own business!" "I'm sorry if I've offended you," said Moody, "but to be very frank, that is my business!" *(Source unknown)*

Once a macho man slammed his door on me when I took the opportunity to give him the gospel and talk to him about God's love. I felt sorry for him, not for me, because I was God's instrument. It was my business to bring God's message-the good news-to him.

Do you ever feel like you have little to offer the Lord? Do not cut yourself short. Do not let obstacles and disadvantages keep you from moving forward. Jesus is looking for people who will be willing to venture into unknown territories. Trust the Lord and commit yourself to the task in front of you. Be a trailblazer, pioneer, and explorer for God! The Lord seeks your willingness more than your resources. Give to the Lord the little you have. Watch Him multiply it far more than you could ever imagine. The next time there is a spiritual challenge, ask the Lord for help and direction for what you are supposed to do. Remember, God can do great things through small obedience.

When I was a new born-again Christian, I made a commitment to go to our church for soul-winning two times a week for a year. Sometimes, we had to knock on the doors of people to give us the opportunity to talk about the Lord. Other times, we had to visit people who had been to one of the church services. In both cases, I had a partner who was a good brother in Christ. He also spoke excellent English and was a good soul winner. One day, my visitation pastor told me that my partner had a serious situation and was not able to come. He asked me if I wanted to visit one family by myself. I had driven 17 miles to the church and would have to travel another 15 miles in the other direction to visit this family. I decided to go by myself even if my English at the time was poor. I had some fear in my heart and hesitation about how I would make it. On the way I prayed, "Lord, you know my situation, I leave everything in your hands, and I believe you will have blessings for me. Please help me."

Yes! He did it by putting His peace in my heart. When I knocked on the door, a 23-year-old young man, who was home alone, answered. After I introduced myself, he was very excited about meeting me and invited me in to talk to him. The Lord turned all the negative thoughts I had before into positive ones. Because he was a salesman in marketing and had to visit Europe, it was interesting for him to learn about Europe from me, even with my poor English. In addition to everything else, he asked me why I came to America. This gave me the opportunity to give my testimony. I shared the gospel with him and led him to the Lord-something his own Christian parents had not been able to do. *"A true witness delivereth souls..."* (Proverbs 14:25). The Lord taught me a lesson not to hesitate to talk to lost people about Him because He always keeps His promises. *"I am with you always, even unto the end of the world"* (Matthew 28:20).

It is one of God's miracles to see people come to the Lord and have their hearts change. Do not hold back the gospel. You might not be a good speaker or a polished communicator, but the Holy Spirit can use your words to bring people to God. The gospel is powerful and can change the lives of those who hear it. Your ability to communicate is secondary. What God wants is your availability. Put into practice what you already know. Do what you are able, with what you have, and right where you are. Be A KIND PERSON. PRAY for others. Use God's LOVE. GIVE to others. Be FAITHFUL and SURRENDER to the Lord. "The greatness of man's power is the measure of his surrender." — *William Booth, founder of the Salvation Army*

SOMEONE CARED

Someone cared enough to bring the truth to me.
Someone cared, and now my soul is free.
I know it wasn't easy to be bold enough to share,
But I'm so glad someone cared.

— *Song by Dave Thompson*

❖ ❖ ❖

"Every Christian is either a missionary or an imposter." "God save us from living in comfort while sinners are sinking into hell!" "We are not called to proclaim philosophy and metaphysics, but the simple gospel." "It is of no use for any of you to try to be soul-winners if you are not bearing fruit in your own lives. How can you serve the Lord with your lips if you do not serve Him with your lives? How can you preach His gospel with your tongues, when with hands, feet, and heart you are preaching the devil's gospel, and setting up an antichrist by your practical unholiness?" — *Quotes from "Prince of Preachers," Charles Spurgeon*

Do you ever feel like you have little
to offer the Lord?
Do not cut yourself short.
Do not let obstacles and disadvantages keep you from
moving forward.
Jesus is looking for people who will be willing
to venture into unknown territories.
Trust the Lord and commit yourself
to the task in front of you.
*
Be A KIND PERSON.
PRAY for others.
Use God's LOVE.
GIVE to others.
Be FAITHFUL and
SURRENDER to the Lord.

52

GOSPEL TRACTS

"Therefore, my beloved brethren, be ye stedfast, unmoveable,
always abounding in the work of the Lord, forasmuch as ye know
that your labour is not in vain in the Lord..."
1 Corinthians 15:58

"A true witness delivereth souls..."
Proverbs 14:25

*

Do you know the importance and power of gospel tracts?

Millions of people do not want to talk about politics or religion. Millions of people also do not listen to Christian radio or TV or go to church. How can we reach them with the gospel of Jesus Christ? The answer is with Christian tracts. Christian or gospel tracts are small pieces of paper with the message of the gospel printed on them. It is easy to carry. It fits in a man's pocket or a lady's purse. It is easy to distribute by handing it to people, by mailing it, or by placing it in popular or public places. People read them when found in a chair at the airport, in the hotel lobby, restaurant booth, doctor's waiting room, in a laundromat or in other various locations. They work as silent missionaries and evangelists. The Lord uses them in miraculous ways. The Holy Spirit works in the minds and hearts of individuals who have different attitudes about God and life after death.

Gospel tracts are an essential Christian tool to reach unbelievers who are close to us or far away. The printed page of a tract never shows lack of courage, never is tempted to compromise, never discourages, never loses its temper, and it works long after it has been received. A tract sticks to what it has said, and never answers back. You can destroy one, but the printing press will continue to produce millions more. It enters doors locked to the evangelist. It can be enclosed in a letter. It also preaches in the factory, in the streets, on trains, buses, and planes. It visits the prison, hospital, and nursing home. It can go everywhere, and if we pray for the Lord to bless, God is behind it. The tract ministry is so important. We hear testimonies each day of how people have been saved by a tract. A tract was used to save George Whitefield, preacher of the Great Awakening in America. After reading the tract, he wrote, *"God showed me I must be born again or be damned."* Even the famous missionary to China, Hudson Taylor was saved by a tract he found in his father's library when he was seventeen years old. One tract has the power to change a person, family, community, country, or even a continent. Joey Hancock of the American Tract Society said, *"Fifty-three percent of all who come to Christ worldwide come through the use of printed gospel literature."*

When we buy and distribute gospel tracts, we must make sure they contain a clear message of salvation and an uncompromised biblical message without political correctness. *"There are many tracts available. However, make sure they contain the whole counsel of God. The most popular of tracts fails to open up the Moral Law as Jesus did, to mention the fact of Judgment day, or the reality of hell. Instead, they promise a wonderful new life in Christ. The promise is one of happiness rather than righteousness."* — *Evangelist, Ray Comfort)*

Keep in mind that life is not in the sower but in the seed. As Christians, we do not need to be ashamed, to give a gospel tract to anyone. As God's ambassadors, we are commanded to work for God's Kingdom by spreading the gospel. It is the only time we have now to witness because we cannot witness in heaven. Someone said, "Tracts are everywhere!" not so. There will be none in hell. Only in this world do we have the opportunity to give tracts. When we give out tracts, we must glorify the Lord. We must follow God's guidance where and when we give tracts without disobeying government laws and damaging our Christian values and reputation.

Several years ago, I spent a morning visiting one of our hospitals in the area. Earlier, a Christian had thrown hundreds of gospel tracts on the ground trailing from the parking lot to the door of the hospital. It read, "If you died right now, are you 100% sure that you would go to HEAVEN?" What he did sounds crazy. However, out of concern or curiosity, the doctors, nurses, and patients who walked to the hospital that morning, picked up a copy and started to read it. Some of them put a tract in their pockets to read later. We always have to remember that to give tracts is our responsibility. The results belong to God, and eternity alone will reveal the results of our efforts.

THE JOURNEY AND DESTINY OF A CHRISTIAN

Some Christians know the value of gospel tracts and use them regularly, but some do not know anything about them. My wife and I once attended an outreach prayer meeting in a church within our community. One of my testimonies was to tell the group sitting at our table the importance of Gospel tracts. One man in the group, who has been a Christian for many years and served the Lord in his church, had no idea what a "gospel tract" was. I believe he is not the only one in many of today's liberal Christian churches.

When I visited my son out of state a few years ago, we had the opportunity to attend the Sunday morning and evening services of a large fundamental, Bible-believing church. We enjoyed the dynamic preaching and inspirational conservative music. The church has many wonderful ministries and has been blessed for many decades under the leadership of the pastor, who is a great man of God. In the morning service alone, ninety-five people were saved. The attendance ranges between 2500-3000 people. During October, the church had a goal to distribute 100,000 gospel tracts in their area by knocking on doors, witnessing, and inviting people to church. I was delighted to hear that the pastor, the assistant pastors, and deacons would meet in the church and afterward go out and knock on doors along with others. All these were very encouraging to me.

One of our most popular witnessing tools each year are the pocket calendars which we offer free worldwide to all recipients of the Spiritual Note. They have the gospel and a calendar that can be used all year to share the good news of Jesus Christ. We usually personally distribute them in our area before and after New Year's Day. During this time, people gladly receive them. Over the years, I have also found that another effective way to witness to people and give them the gospel is by mail. By checking the local newspapers, I see people who are going through happy and hard times like weddings, anniversaries, and deaths. By sending them appropriate greeting cards and Christian tracts, these people are very receptive. This allows God to work in their hearts to make spiritual decisions.

Every month, I also send tracts with my bill payments. One time after I sent my bill payment with a tract to my health insurance company, I received a beautiful handwritten letter from one of the employees. It was from the person who opens and processes the insurance premium payments. She thanked me very much for the tract. She told me that as a result of reading the tract, she trusted and dedicated her life to our Lord Jesus Christ! Praise the Lord! *"And let us not be weary in well doing: for in due season we shall reap, if we faint not"* (Galatians 6:9).

❖ ❖ ❖

- "Let each one of us, if we have done nothing for Christ, begin to do something now. The distribution of tracts is the first thing."

"When preaching and private talk are not available, you need to have a tract ready...But a touching gospel tract may be the seed of eternal life. Therefore, do not go out without your tracts."

"How many thousands have been carried to heaven instrumentally upon the wings of these tracts, none can tell ..."

"To be a soul-winner is the happiest thing in the world. And with every soul you bring to Jesus Christ, you seem to get a new heaven here upon earth."—*Quotes from "Prince of Preachers," Charles Spurgeon*

**Gospel tracts
are an essential Christian tool
to reach unbelievers who are
close to us or far away.**

53

SERVANT OF GOD

"But it shall not be so among you: but whosoever will be great among you, let him be your minister; And whosoever will be chief among you, let him be your servant: Even as the Son of man came not to be ministered unto, but to minister, and to give his life a ransom for many."
Matthew 20:26-28

*

God will honor your service when you stop snapping and begin shining!

I f we are followers of Jesus Christ, we have to obey and do His will. In the kingdom of God, there is no room for two Kings or two Lords to sit on one throne. Someone must surrender. In this case, we have to surrender and be His servants in every place He puts us. We must do any job He allows us to do without grumbling and complaining.

I know a young man that used to work on the staff of a large church where I was a member. Every time he talked with a church member, he would blow his own horn and say, "I serve the Lord." With a proud spirit, he put himself up while putting the other members down like he was the only one who served the Lord.

When it came time for the church to cut their staff, this man was one of them. Afterward, he started to complain and said, "Look what God has done to me. Now I cannot serve Him." When I heard that, I told him, "Son, Christians do not only serve the Lord in the church but everywhere God puts them. Submit to His will, and you will discover His wonderful plans for you." Even after my advice, he continued to complain. A.T. Pierson wrote, *"Service is, comprehensively speaking, doing the will of God. He is the object. All is for Him, for His sake, as unto the Lord, not as unto man. Hence, even the humblest act of humblest disciple acquires a certain divine quality by its being done with reference to Him. The supreme test of service is this: 'For whom am I doing this?' Much that we call service to Christ is not such at all...If we are doing this for Christ, we shall not care for human reward or even recognition...''*— *sermonillustrations.com*

There are Christians who serve the Lord with godly ways and others who do nothing but complain or look for man's recognition for all they do.

- The legendary country singer, Johnny Cash tells how a shoeshine man taught him a lesson for living back in 1956, but unfortunately, it took several more years for him to really understand the lesson. *"I was expecting a fast, snappy job like the young folks do,"* Cash said, *"and he was going about his job real slow. I said to him, 'You don't seem to be doing too much snapping.'* "That shoeshine man looked up at me sort of sideways and said, 'That's the problem with the world these days — there's too much snapping and not enough shining.'"— *Lesson for Living, Apple Seeds, May 1999*

- Hudson Taylor, the great missionary who carried the gospel to the interior of China, was approached by a man with one leg. This man said, "I want to go to China as a missionary." Rev. Taylor asked, "Why do you think you can be a missionary when you have only one leg?" The man replied, "Because I don't see any men with two good legs going.*" Author unknown*

- Some time ago, one businessman and a doctor, asked me, "How much do you charge people for your ministry?" My honest answer was, "Nothing." "Do you work fifteen hours or more a day for nothing?" and my response was, *"The work I am doing is for the Lord, and the kind of payment I receive every day from Him is worth a lot more than silver or gold."* Possibly, they thought I was crazy or stupid. The world will never understand how many people serve the Lord out of love and obedience and not for money.

- "A visitor saw a nurse attending the sores of a leprosy patient. 'I would not do that for a million dollars,' she said. The nurse answered, 'Neither would I, but I do it for Jesus for nothing'" *(Corrie Ten Boom)*. Today, most people are only concerned about receiving a Ph.D. from men rather than receiving a W.D. "Well Done!" from the Lord (Matthew 25:23).

If you do not serve the Lord according to His will, I have some advice for you. Never look for big opportunities in special places to serve the Lord. He will never give you big responsibilities before you are able to handle small ones with obedience and a servant's heart. I have known a man for fifty years who has always talked to others about his big ideas for things that could be done for the Lord. In reality, he has accomplished nothing significant - all his ideas were for others. From what I know, he still calls himself an obedient Christian and looks in his old age for significant opportunities to serve the Lord. Do not listen or follow these kinds of people. Surrender to the Lord! Roll up your sleeves and start to serve Him. God will give you peace through obedience. By serving Him, you will find His perfect and enjoyable will for your life. Do not let the need for recognition spoil your service for the Lord and the ministry He gives you, no matter how small it is.

Our purpose in life must be to serve God and others. The path to true greatness and success lies in being a servant! To serve, you do not need to have a higher education or to be a good communicator. You only need a heart loaded with grace and a soul motivated by love, compassion, and devotion. God desires a servant's heart that makes sure things are done right. The church is not the only place you can serve the Lord and others. Not everyone can work full-time for a church. Your profession does not matter. You can serve the Lord and others in every place He puts you. You must be God's ambassador and provide His message to those all around you.

I know doctors who pray with their patients. Recently, the surgeon who performed open-heart surgery on my nephew prayed before the surgery with him and his mother. I know good soul winners who are barbers, carpenters, plumbers, and electricians. Ladies and men from all professions are soul winners, encouragers, and comforters. Even if you are sick and lay in bed, you can serve the Lord and others by praying. It is time to ask yourself, *"Do I have two good legs that are not walking for God?"* Now is the time to make a start fulfilling your goals for Jesus. God will bless your service when you stop snapping and begin shining!

IN THE SERVICE OF THE KING

I am happy in the service of the King.
I am happy, O so happy!
I have peace and joy that nothing else can bring,
In the service of the King.

— *Hymn by A. H. Ackley, 1912*

❖ ❖ ❖

- "Before we can pray, 'Lord, Thy Kingdom come,' we must be (first) willing to pray, 'Lord, my kingdom go.'" — *Evangelist, Alan Redpath*

- "His lord said unto him, Well done, good and faithful servant; thou hast been faithful over a few things, I will make thee ruler over many things: enter thou into the joy of thy lord." — *Matthew 25:23*

54

ADJUSTING OUR PRIORITIES

"Thou shalt love the Lord thy God with all thy heart, and with all thy soul, and with all thy strength, and with all thy mind..."
Luke 10:27

"But seek ye first the kingdom of God, and his righteousness; and all these things shall be added unto you."
Matthew 6:33

*

Put God's priorities first and dream His dreams for your life!

The American author James W. Frick said, *"Don't tell me where your priorities are. Show me where you spend your money, and I'll tell you what they are."* Based on this principle, when I communicate with an individual in person, by phone, by mail, or by e-mail, it does not take me long to figure out what kind of person he is from his priorities. I will mention a few stories of people with right and wrong priorities below:

• A young Christian lady once told me, "I will not marry a good Christian man if he does not like my cats." Another lady who called herself a Christian told me, "I have made a commitment to my dog, and I will not marry anyone if he is not committed to my dog first." I saw a young lady walking on the sidewalk in front of my house one day with her small dog in her arms while her little daughter followed behind her like a dog.

• One of my friends had a high position in the police force. The first time I challenged him to accept Jesus Christ as his personal Savior, he told me, "I want to make a lot of money first, and then we will talk about it..."

- Milt Rood worked for years and years in Spokane as a car salesman. He was also very active with the Union Gospel Mission work with juvenile delinquents. Week by week he'd patiently teach the Word and pray with young boys in trouble. One week Milt went into the hospital for exploratory surgery. The doctors found he was full of cancer. They sewed him up again and sent him home. He died within a week. After the funeral, Ron Kinley remarked, "It's interesting that at the funeral no one ever asked how many cars he had sold!" — *by John Underhill, Spokane, WA/ Bible.org*

- In recent years the head coach of a football team divorced his wife, and he said winning football was his number one priority and his two sons were second. How tragic! In contrast to this, Tom Landry, former coach of the Dallas Cowboys, said "The thrill of knowing Jesus is the greatest thing that ever happened to me...I think God has put me in a very special place, and He expects me to use it to His glory in everything I do...whether coaching football or talking to the press, I'm always a Christian...Christ is first, family second and football third." — *Source Unknown*

- That great missionary to India, William Carey, became deeply concerned about the attitude of his son Felix. The young man, a professing Christian, had promised to become a missionary. But he broke his vow when he was appointed an ambassador to Burma. Carey requested prayer for him: "Pray for Felix. He has degenerated into an ambassador of the British government when he should be serving the King of kings." — *Our Daily Bread*

- Peter overheard his son George and several friends talking in the backyard. "My dad's got a million dollars," said one boy. "Well, my dad's got muscles like you couldn't believe," responded another. A third boy chimed in, "My dad's real smart. What's great about your dad, George?" Peter's son did not miss a beat. The young boy's response brought tears to the eyes of his eavesdropping father. "My dad knows God!"

- Over the triple doorways of the cathedral of Milan, three inscriptions are spanning the splendid arches. Over one is carved a beautiful wreath of roses, and underneath it is the legend,
"All that which pleases is but for a moment."

Over the other is sculptured a cross, and there are the words,
"All that which troubles us is but for a moment."

But underneath the great central entrance to the main aisle is the inscription,
"That only is important, which is eternal." — *Source Unknown*

Our priorities in life are essential. I admit that there is nothing wrong to have and care about pets. I like pets myself, and when I was growing up, we had dogs and cats. We took excellent care of them, but they did not control our lives - we controlled them. Without question, our first priority must be people and not our pets. We see people today who raise more dogs and cats than children. They spend more money and time on them than on things that are more important in life. It is much better to spend more time with your children and direct them to Jesus Christ.

The God who created us knows us very well, but how well do we know God? The person who knows God and has the Holy Spirit puts his priorities in God's order. He is not interested so much in the passing pleasures of the hour. By keeping his eyes on eternity, his priorities change. He lives for the permanent and the eternal. He is a spiritual person who puts his priorities right. For him, it is more important to go to church on Sunday than it is to go fishing or golfing. If we have a problem prioritizing our life, it is an excellent time to do a little spiritual housecleaning. Throw out those activities and involvements that take up our time and energy and the ones that do little for advancing the Kingdom of God. With a clean house, we will feel much better. Live with principles and not emotions. We have to put God and His priorities first and dream His dreams for our life. God's blessings will follow us as we follow the Lord. Let us make a life, not a living.

After twenty years of studying the careers of 1,500 business students, researchers tell us the following results: 83% of them had as their first priority to make as much money as possible while waiting until sometime later to decide on how to pursue other goals. From this group of business students, only one became a millionaire. Out of the remaining 17% whose first priority was to follow values and their dreams, 101 became millionaires. Do not let wealth, status, fitness, emotions, or other things keep us from what really matters. Our priorities are our character. Keep God as our priority. Grow daily in our relationship with Him. If we are going to brag, brag on the Lord.

- *"He that glorieth, let him glory in the Lord"* (1 Corinthians 1:31).

- *"Thus saith the Lord, Let not the wise man glory in his wisdom, neither let the mighty man glory in his might, let not the rich man glory in his riches: But let him that glorieth glory in this, that he understandeth and knoweth me, that I am the Lord which exercise lovingkindness, judgment, and righteousness, in the earth: for in these things I delight, saith the Lord"* (Jeremiah 9:23-24).

- *"And this they did, not as we hoped, but first gave their own selves to the Lord..."* (2 Corinthians 8:5)

I'D RATHER HAVE JESUS

I'd rather have Jesus than silver or gold,
I'd rather be His than have riches untold;
I'd rather have Jesus than houses or lands,
I'd rather be led by His nail-pierced hand.

Refrain:
Than to be the king of a vast domain
Or be held in sin's dread sway;
I'd rather have Jesus than anything
This world affords today.

— *Hymn by Oscar C. A. Bernadotte, 1888*

❖ ❖ ❖

- "One thing have I desired of the LORD, that will I seek after; that I may dwell in the house of the LORD all the days of my life..."
— *Psalm 27:4*

- "To be subjected to God's will is not only to give Him priority in our lives, it is but to give Him complete control."
— *Business Executive, Avery D. Miller*

- **Scriptural order of priorities:** 1. God, 2. Spouse, 3. Children, 4. Parents, 5. Extended family, 6. Brothers and sisters in Christ, 7 plus everyone and everything else.

- Give your children faith in Jesus Christ. "I have now disposed of all my property to my family. There is one thing more I wish I could give them, and that is faith in Jesus Christ. If they had that and I had not given them a single shilling, they would have been rich; and if they had not that, and I had given them all the world, they would be poor indeed."
— *Planter and Lawyer, Patrick Henry*

- "When you were born, you cried and the world rejoiced. Live your life in such a manner that when you die, the world cries and you rejoice."
— *Indian Proverb*

55

PURSUE EXCELLENCE

"And whatsoever you do, do it heartily,
as to the Lord, and not unto men."
Colossians 3:2

*

Whatever you do, do it with all your heart as to the Lord!

The Bible teaches us a lot about working hard and doing our best to glorify the Lord. We all know from experience when we have done our best on a project, we feel joy and satisfaction. The apostle Paul said to Christians, whatsoever they do they must do it with all their hearts as to the Lord, and not unto men. This principle applies to all believers. All believers should work and serve as if serving God Himself. Christians may perform different work depending on their professions. Maybe you work as a student or as a professor. Maybe you work as a mechanic or as a surgeon. Maybe you work as a plumber or as a pastor. Maybe you work as a mother or as a businesswoman. When you recognize that your work is for the Lord and not only for yourself and other people, it will give you a new perspective on what you do each day.

By keeping in mind all the above, the questions are: "Do you have a spirit of trying your best in everything you do? Do you pursue excellence? Do you strive for excellence?" This is something to think about. I am talking about your regular daily work routine. Do you only care to get things done and move on to the next task and just say what you did was good enough, or do you put 100% into every task you do? You should realize that when you work, you are not in competition with other people, but you are in a competition with yourself. More than that, you are in a competition to prove yourself to God. If you are a Christian, you are a child of the Lord of lords and King of kings, and you must not settle for second best. If you find yourself saying, "I probably could have done better," you did not give it your all..

Do you settle with just getting by? Do not be satisfied with being ordinary. God has redeemed you for His glory. He deserves the best. He deserves excellence. The missionary Jim Elliot once said, *"Wherever you are - be all there."* Make sure to use all your gifts and talents for the Lord! Andrew Carnegie said, *"The average person puts only 25% of his energy and ability into his work. The world takes off its hat to those who put in more than 50% of their capacity, and stands on its head for those few and far between souls who devote 100%."* Whatever the task is, say to yourself, "I serve the Lord Jesus. Is this the best I can do?" Do not be bored with your job. You need to see it as something more than a paycheck.

Do the best you can! Give 100% and reach even further on the next task. One day you will stand before the Lord. Which words would you like to hear? *"Well done, good and faithful servant; thou hast been faithful over a few things, I will make thee ruler over many things: enter thou into the joy of thy lord"* (Matthew 25:23) or *"Cast ye the unprofitable servant into outer darkness: there shall be weeping and gnashing of teeth"* (Matthew 25:30)

God is a great King and deserves excellence. Make Jesus the center of your performance. He is worthy of the best effort you can give. Make each day your treasure. When you do it for His glory, you will find yours. In case you have lost some excitement and enthusiasm for the work you are doing, ask the Lord to encourage you and refocus your heart, so that you are working for Him, and not just for men. Ask Him to help you to pursue excellence in everything you do for Him, and to help you to be powerful, useful, and fruitful to all you minister. You never know as a result of your excellent work, maybe they will stand on their heads. I pray that you will do the best for the Lord, and one day hear His words from Matthew 25:23 instead of His words from Matthew 25:30 ringing in your ears for eternity.

MAKE A COMMITMENT TO EXCELLENCE TODAY!

Lord, I will never give you my second best,
I will never do the minimum for you,
I will never give you my leftovers.
I will give you my best every day!

❖ ❖ ❖

• "I never had a policy; I have just tried to do my very best each and every day." — *President, Abraham Lincoln*

• "We have to do the best we can. This is our sacred human responsibility." — *Theoretical Physicist, Albert Einstein*

56

FOCUS ON THE THINGS ABOVE

"If ye then be risen with Christ,
seek those things which are above,
where Christ sitteth on the right hand of God.
Set your affection on things above, not on things on the earth."
Colossians 3:1,2

∗

Focus your mind on the things above where Christ is King!

American jurist Oliver Wendell Holmes, Sr. famously complained, *"Some people are so heavenly minded that they are no earthly good."* And there is an old expression that states, *"Do not be so heavenly minded that you are of no earthly good."* Both of these statements may sound clever, but they are unbiblical. The Bible says, *"Seek those things which are above... not on things on the earth"* (Colossians 3:2). The true followers of Jesus Christ must set their minds on things above, and faithfully serve the Lord. Their focus should center on Christ and on the eternal, not on the temporal. Opposite to popular opinion, being heavenly minded always inspires to be more earthly good. C.S. Lewis wrote, *"If you read history, you will find that the Christians who did most for the present world were just those who thought most of the next."*

People who tour the Death Valley Monument in the state of California notice many vultures and hummingbirds. The vultures are constantly circling the skies and looking down at dead animals to feast on their rotting meat. The hummingbirds look up toward the blossoms around them. They ignore the smell of death and zip around drinking the nectar of the cacti blooming. Each of these birds finds what it is looking for. Christians must always look up like the hummingbirds. In Romans 6:8, believers have *"died with Christ,"* in Colossians 3:1 they are *"raised with Christ,"* and in Ephesians 2:6: *"[God] made us sit together in heavenly places in Christ Jesus."* This is wonderful! Christians cannot have better promises than these. They only have to believe them to have overwhelming joy in their hearts. The believer is lifted up from the earth to find all the joys where Christ is and where their hearts should be. The question is: Do you have biblical faith to believe and claim all these promises? Remember, faith is to trust Christ by resting on His Word!

The Bible teaches that you must please God rather than men (Acts 5:29). Keep your eyes on Jesus Christ when dealing with daily circumstances, joys, and trials. Remember His grace and portions of His Word. Pray to Him throughout the day. Set your goals to glorify God. When you are in doubt, look up to Jesus, and He will let you know the answers to your walk of Life.

Learn to talk with the Lord daily. He will fill, encourage, and inspire your heart with faith, love, hope, peace, and joy. If you focus on the negative, you will find it. Stop being a vulture, but be a hummingbird instead. Fix your mind on the Lord. This world is passing away and to put your focus on the things of this life is an unwise investment of your life. LOOK UP, NOT DOWN. Focus on the things above where Christ is Lord of lords and King of kings! Things will work better if you do because His love will lift you!

LOVE LIFTED ME

I was sinking deep in sin, far from the peaceful shore,
Very deeply stained within, sinking to rise no more,
But the Master of the sea heard my despairing cry,
From the waters lifted me, now safe am I.

Love lifted me! Love lifted me!
When nothing else could help, Love lifted me!

— *Hymn by James Rowe, 1912*

❖ ❖ ❖

• "And as Moses lifted up the serpent in the wilderness, even so must the Son of man be lifted up: That whosoever believeth in him should not perish, but have eternal life." — *John 3:14,15*

• "The unbeliever looks down, the believer looks up." "Look and live - they go together - you cannot have eternal life without looking to Jesus, and you cannot look to Jesus without having eternal life." — *Glad Tidings*

• "If you look at the world, you'll be distressed. If you look within, you'll be depressed. If you look at God, you'll be at rest." — *Author, Corrie ten Boom*

GLORIFY THE LORD

*"Whether therefore ye eat, or drink, or whatsoever ye do,
do all to the glory of God."*
1 Corinthians 10:31

*"God in all things may be glorified through Jesus Christ,
to whom be praise and dominion for ever and ever. Amen."*
1 Peter 4:11

*

Glorify the Lord and not yourself, others, or idols!

In Bible-believing churches, God's glory is mentioned all the time. God's glory is celebrated in traditional hymns and in contemporary songs. Traditional worship services usually include the doxology: *"Praise Father, Son, and Holy Ghost!"* Sunday school teachers and preachers tell us we should seek to glorify God in everything we do. Do you ever wonder what the glory of God is and what it really means to glorify God? Would you know how to answer? If not, I will try to help you with some simple answers. The noun GLORY and the verb GLORIFY in the Hebrew are the words "kabad" and "kabowd"; and in the Greek, they are "δόξα" (doxa) and "δοξάζω" (doxazo). The noun GLORY means glorious, shine, riches, especially divine quality, splendor, to demonstrate, and to manifest the divine. In other words, glory represents the Lord's power, greatness, and presence. Throughout the Old and New Testament, God revealed Himself many times to His own people. For example, on Mount Sinai, *"And Moses went up into the mount, and a cloud covered the mount. And the glory of the LORD abode upon mount Sinai, and the cloud covered it six days: and the seventh day he called unto Moses out of the midst of the cloud. And the sight of the glory of the LORD was like devouring fire on the top of the mount in the eyes of the children of Israel"* (Exodus 24:15-17), on the tabernacle in the wilderness, *"Then a cloud covered the tent of the congregation, and the glory of the LORD filled the tabernacle. And Moses was not able to enter into the tent of the congregation, because the cloud abode thereon, and the glory of the LORD filled the tabernacle"* (Exodus 40:34,35), and in the New Testament when Stephen was stoned. *"But he, being full of the Holy Ghost, looked up stedfastly into heaven, and saw the glory of God, and Jesus standing on the right hand of God"* (Acts 7:55).

The verb GLORIFY means to adore, admire, honor, or worship a person or idol. We see in today's society, people who worship and give glory to themselves, to other people, or to many different idols. In the New Testament, "doxazo" refers specifically to worship, to praise, to honor, and to magnify the Lord. In other words, to glorify God means to give glory to Him by trusting Him, by shining in a dark world, and by bearing fruit.

> *"Let your light so shine before men, that they may see your good works, and glorify your Father which is in heaven"* (Matthew 5:16).

To glorify God means to proclaim everything that is about God. To glorify God is to highly praise His attributes. Some of His attributes include wisdom, holiness, faithfulness, righteousness, goodness, mercy, grace, love, majesty, sovereignty, infinity, power, omnipotence, omnipresence, trinity, self-existence, and justice. We need to recite these attributes over and over in our minds and tell others about them, as well as about the salvation He offers. We should always portray these attributes of the Lord instead of ourselves. We should never give glory to ourselves because everything that exists has its existence from God and for God.

> *"For of Him and through Him and to Him are all things, to whom be glory forever. Amen"* (Romans 11:36).

John Calvin was correct when he said that creation is *"The theater of God's glory."* Psalm 19:1 says, *"The heavens declare the glory of God..."* The glory belongs to the Lord only, as He reminds us that He never shared it with anyone, *"I am the LORD: that is my name: and my glory will I not give to another, neither my praise to graven images"* (Isaiah 42:8).

Today, many people have a goal to glorify themselves, other people, or idols, instead of glorifying God. This reminds me of a man who became proud because he rode a magnificent horse, wore a feather in his hat, and dressed in a beautiful suit of clothes. He did not see his foolishness. If there was any glory in such things, the glory belongs to the horse, the bird, and the tailor, but not to himself.

Remember that Jeremiah 9:23-24 summarizes the choice we always have before us:

> *"Thus saith the LORD,*
> *Let not the wise man glory in his wisdom,*
> *neither let the mighty man glory in his might,*
> *let not the rich man glory in his riches:*
> *But let him that glorieth glory in this, that he understandeth and*
> *knoweth me, that I am the LORD which exercise lovingkindness,*
> *judgment, and righteousness, in the earth:*
> *for in these things I delight, saith the LORD."*

When we choose to continue and follow what we desire over what God has told us to do, we will quench His Spirit that resides within us and promotes our image rather than His. *"So I gave them up unto their own hearts' lust: and they walked in their own counsels"* (Psalm 81:12). This kind of attitude will never bring anyone to the Lord, restore relationships, or heal marriages. Remember, Jesus warned us about this when He said, *"If I bear witness of Myself, My witness is not true"* (John 5:31). If Jesus says this about Himself, it is true for us, too. We always have to reflect Christ's image and glorify Him with our thoughts and actions. This way, people will be truly touched and changed.

Our purpose and goal as Christians must be to reflect the Lord and glorify Him. We must learn how to walk with His Spirit and show His likeness to the world, instead of our own. Self-denial will help us to accomplish this goal. Jesus must be our example. He always glorified His Father in heaven. Let us keep our eyes on the Lord and exalt only Him as the Baptist preacher Adoniram Judson Gordon did:

One night Gordon fell asleep while preparing his sermon and had a dream. In this dream, he was preaching to his congregation, when a man walked up the left side looking for a place to sit. He wondered who the man could be. The man did find a place and sat next to one of the regular attendees. After the sermon, the stranger left, and Gordon asked his parishioner who the man was. His answer . . . "don't you know him? That was Jesus of Nazareth. He has been here today, and he will come again."

When he awoke, Gordon realized that it was not important what men thought about his ministry, but only what the Lord Jesus Christ thought. It caused him to review how he preached, why he preached, and what he preached. He realized the most important person he had to please was Jesus Himself. His life and ministry would never be the same after that. He began to preach as he believed would honor Jesus. His church became one of the most vibrant, mission-oriented churches in the nation.
— *by healingandrevival.com*

If you are a Christian, start to serve and glorify the Lord with a renewed sense of intensity, passion, and conviction, just like Gordon. Do not let mediocrity rob you of the zeal for the Lord. Make Jesus the goal for all you do and glorify His Holy name. *"O magnify the LORD with me, and let us exalt his name together"* (Psalm 34:3).

❖ ❖ ❖

• "Our great object of glorifying God is to be mainly achieved by the winning of souls. Do not close a single sermon without addressing the ungodly." — *"Prince of Preachers, " Charles Spurgeon*

• "Man's true end is to glorify God and to enjoy Him forever." —*Historian and Author, Arnold J. Toynbee*

• "The person who fears God seeks to live all of life to the glory of God... All the activities of life should be pursued with the aim of glorifying God." — *Evangelical Author, Jerry Bridges*

• "I will praise thee, O Lord my God, with all my heart: and I will glorify thy name for evermore." — *Psalms 86:12*

• "Not unto us, O Lord, not unto us, but unto thy name give glory, for thy mercy, and for thy truth's sake." — *Psalm 115:1*

• "For ye are bought with a price: therefore glorify God in your body, and in your spirit, which are God's." — *1 Corinthians 6:20*

> **We should never give glory to ourselves because everything that exists has its existence from God and for God.**

58

WORSHIP THE LORD

"Give unto the LORD the glory due unto his name;
worship the LORD in the beauty of holiness."
Psalm 29:2

"For thou shalt worship no other god: for the LORD,
whose name is Jealous, is a jealous God:"
Exodus 34:14

*

God wants worship to be our lifestyle and not only on Sunday!

One Sunday, the great preacher, Henry Ward Beecher, became ill and could not fill his pulpit. At the last minute, his brother volunteered to give the sermon. At the beginning of the service, the auditorium of Plymouth Church was packed. When it became evident that the eloquent Beecher was not going to be there, many started to leave. The younger brother was not dismayed. Calling for silence he announced, "All who have come this morning to worship Henry Ward Beecher may leave now. The rest can remain to worship God." No one left after that. Sadly, this happens in many churches today.

The believer must worship the Lord and not man. Worship should be set aside for God only. *"Thou shalt worship the Lord thy God, and him only shalt thou serve"* (Luke 4:8). This was Jesus' reply when Satan tried to tempt Him. The Greek word in the New Testament for "worship" is "προσκυνέω" (proskuneo) which means "expression of profound reverence and adoration" and "deep love devotion and respect." The Greek word for worship is not synonymous with "music," as many have the misconception. Worship is your timeless devotion to God in spirit and truth.

- *"God is a Spirit: and they that worship him must worship him in spirit and in truth"* (John 4:24).

- *"Let us have grace, whereby we may serve God acceptably with reverence and godly fear"* (Hebrews 12:28).

- *"I beseech you therefore, brethren, by the mercies of God, that ye present your bodies a living sacrifice, holy, acceptable unto God, which is your reasonable service. And be not conformed to this world: but be ye transformed by the renewing of your mind, that ye may prove what is that good, and acceptable, and perfect, will of God"* (Romans 12:1,2).

True worship changes the heart of the worshipper and gives him more desire to love, obey, and serve the Lord. When we worship God, we must adore Him for who He is, and not just for what He has done. Worship is not only for church on Sundays, for a limited time, but it must be our lifestyle for the rest of the week.. True worship is constant internal praise to the Lord in prayer, in songs, in service, in giving, and in living.

Worship is often combined with the action of bowing *"O come, let us worship and bow down: let us kneel before the LORD our maker"* (Psalm 95:6), *"the king and all that were present with him bowed themselves, and worshipped"* (2 Chronicles 29:29), and *"I fell at his feet to worship him"* (Revelation 19:10). Worship must be connected with the heart because worship is an attitude of the heart. It is possible for a person to go through the outer motions and not be worshiping. *"And when thou prayest, thou shalt not be as the hypocrites are: for they love to pray standing in the synagogues and in the corners of the streets, that they may be seen of men. Verily I say unto you, They have their reward. But thou, when thou prayest, enter into thy closet, and when thou hast shut thy door, pray to thy Father which is in secret; and thy Father which seeth in secret shall reward thee openly"* (Matthew 6:5-6). God always sees the heart, and He desires sincere, worship with all our heart. *"The LORD seeth not as man seeth; for man looketh on the outward appearance, but the LORD looketh on the heart"* (1 Samuel 16:7).

In the New Testament, for example, we see Mary of Bethany devoted to Christ with all her heart. On three occasions, she is found at the feet of Jesus. On the first, she sat at His feet as a listener, *"Mary, which also sat at Jesus' feet, and heard his word"* (Luke 10:39). On the second, she is found at His feet as a mourner *"Then when Mary was come where Jesus was, and saw him, she fell down at his feet, saying unto him, Lord, if thou hadst been here, my brother had not died"* (John 11:32). On the third and last occasion, she is found at His feet as a worshiper *"Then took Mary a pound of ointment of spikenard, very costly, and anointed the feet of Jesus, and wiped his feet with her hair: and the house was filled with the odour of the ointment"* (John 12:3). On this last occasion, Mary worshiped Him with a loving heart and gave Him the best gift she had, an expensive ointment which she poured out upon His feet. Christ was everything to Mary. She forgot about herself and only thought of Him and worshiped only Him.

If you have been unhappy at church lately, take time to undertake an attitude check. Are you going to church to be entertained or to worship? Church services are meant to make God happy, not you. We will be blessed when we go to worship. We should lose sight of ourselves when we worship and see nothing except Jesus and His glory. It says in John 12:3 that *"The house was filled with the odour of the ointment."* Mary's act of worship was valuable and precious to the heart of Christ, and the pleasant sweet fragrance was a blessing to all around. That which gives honor to Christ also brings blessings to others. Worship God in spirit and in truth, not only in the church but everywhere. Worship is the key to drawing near to God. It invites us to experience the presence of God. Make it your point to worship God this coming Sunday with other believers. The preaching, music, and fellowship should seek to glorify Him. Do your part to please the Lord.

W - Wait upon the Lord
O - Offer our lives as a living sacrifice
R - Rest in His presence
S - Sing unto Him
H - Humble ourselves before Him
I - Intimacy with God
P - Pleasing Him

❖ ❖ ❖

• "The worship is to quicken the conscience by the holiness of God, to feed the mind with the truth of God, to purge the imagination by the beauty of God, to open the heart to the love of God, and to devote the will to the purpose of God." — *Bishop, William Temple*

• "The obligation of God's creation to give to Him all honor, praise, adoration, and glory due Him because He is the holy and divine creator. Worship is to be given to God only. (Exodus 20:3; Matthew 4:10)." — *Unknown*

• "Depend on it, my hearer, you never will go to heaven unless you are prepared to worship Jesus Christ as God." — *Preachers, Charles Spurgeon*

• "It is not enough for us to be where God is worshipped if we do not ourselves worship him." — *Minister and Author, Matthew Henry*

59

GOD'S FAITHFULNESS

"Know therefore that the LORD *thy God,*
he is God, the faithful God, which keepeth covenant
and mercy with them that love him and keep
his commandments to a thousand generations;"
Deuteronomy 7:9

*

Depend upon God's faithfulness!

Some people decide to give up on prayer or question God because they are confused when they wait and see their prayers go unanswered. In case you are one of them, instead of giving up on these kinds of situations, you have to look at them from a different perspective. The Bible says, *"God is faithful, by whom ye were called unto the fellowship of his Son Jesus Christ our Lord"* (1 Corinthians 1:9).

It is important to know that sometimes, your trust in God may be tested. This is part of a Christian's journey. Even though your circumstances change, the Lord and His Word remain the same. To encourage yourself and to regain confidence in God's faithfulness, you have to remind yourself of God's nature.

God is "Omniscient." He knows everything from our past, present, and future. *"Neither is there any creature that is not manifest in his sight: but all things are naked and opened unto the eyes of him with whom we have to do"* (Hebrews 4:13) and *"For if our heart condemn us, God is greater than our heart, and knoweth all things"* (1 John 3:20).

God is "Omnipotent." He is powerful. He has unlimited power. He created the heavens and earth by His word. *"Great is our Lord, and of* *great power...*" (Psalm 147:5), "*Ah Lord GOD! behold, thou hast made the heaven and the earth by thy great power and stretched out arm, and there is nothing too hard for thee*" (Jeremiah 32:17).

God is "Omnipresent." He is everywhere at the same time. "*Whither shall I go from thy spirit? or whither shall I flee from thy presence? If I ascend up into heaven, thou art there: if I make my bed in hell, behold, thou art there*" (Psalm 139:7,8).

God is "Immutable. "His character always stays unchangeable. "*For I am the LORD, I change not*" (Malachi 3:6) *and "Jesus Christ the same yesterday, and today, and forever*" (Hebrews 13:8).

God is "Faithful. " This is part of His nature and His character. "*If we believe not, yet he abideth faithful: he cannot deny himself*" (2 Timothy 2:13) *and "Faithful is he that calleth you, who also will do it*" (1 Thessalonians 5:24).

God never changes His plans or His promises unless the promise is conditional. "*And this is the confidence that we have in him, that, if we ask anything according to his will, he heareth us*" (1 John 5:14). This is a conditional promise. He promises that He will answer only if you ask, "*according to His will.*"

If we depend on God's faithfulness and believe in His promises, we will be able to defeat the enemies of doubt and discouragement in our Christian life, and we will never give up or question God in our Christian journey. The problems develop when we have doubts about the faithfulness of God and when we do not believe His promises.

The Bible promises that if we believe in Jesus Christ, we will have eternal life. "*For God so loved the world, that he gave his only begotten Son, that whosoever believeth in him should not perish, but have everlasting life.*" (John 3:16). It is very simple. If we do not believe in Jesus, we will not have eternal life. However, if we truly believe, we will have eternal life because it is an unconditional promise of God. This comes from an "omniscient," "omnipotent," "omnipresent," "immutable," and "faithful" God "*that cannot lie*" (Titus 1:2).

If you are not a Christian, I pray that you will become one today. "*O taste and see that the LORD is good: blessed is the man that trusteth in him*" (Psalms 34:8). I urge you to consider this invitation and take some time to get to know Jesus for yourself. He sincerely desires to have a personal relationship with you. Knowing about Him is not enough to get you to heaven. Head knowledge must be replaced by heart knowledge.

You can meet the Savior today. Only ask Jesus to come into your life, forgive your sins, and give you eternal life. If not, God will be faithful to you according to His promises: "*He who does not believe the Son shall not see life, but the wrath of God abides on him"* (John 3:36), *"And whosoever was not found written in the book of life was cast into the lake of fire"* (Revelation 20:15).

GREAT IS THY FAITHFULNESS

"Great is Thy faithfulness," O God my Father,
There is no shadow of turning with Thee;
Thou changest not, Thy compassions, they fail not
As Thou hast been Thou forever wilt be.

Refrain:
"Great is Thy faithfulness!" "Great is Thy faithfulness!"
Morning by morning new mercies I see;
All I have needed Thy hand hath provided —
"Great is Thy faithfulness," Lord, unto me!

— *Hymn* by *Thomas O. Chisholm, 1923*

❖ ❖ ❖

• "God's faithfulness means that God will always do what He has said and fulfill what He has promised." — *Theologian, Wayne Grudem*

• "Oh, blessed trust! To trust Him whose power will never be exhausted, whose love will never wane, whose kindness will never change, whose faithfulness will never fail, whose wisdom will never be nonplussed, and whose perfect goodness can never know a diminution!" "God writes with a pen that never blots, speaks with a tongue that never slips, acts with a hand that never fails." "The glory of God's faithfulness is that no sin of ours has ever made Him unfaithful."
—*Quotes by "Prince of Preachers," Charles Spurgeon*

• "All God's giants have been weak men and women who have gotten hold of God's faithfulness." — *Missionary, Hudson Taylor*

• "Trials should not surprise us or cause us to doubt God's faithfulness. Rather, we should actually be glad for them. God sends trials to strengthen our trust in him so that our faith will not fail. Our trials keep us trusting; they burn away our self-confidence and drive us to our Savior."
— *Pastor and Theologian, Edmund Clowney*

• "The promises of the Bible are nothing more than God's covenant to be faithful to His people. It is His character that makes these promises valid." — *Evangelical Author, Jerry Bridges*

60

MAN'S FAITHFULNESS

"Be thou faithful unto death,
and I will give thee a crown of life."
Revelation 2:10

*

Man's faithfulness to God is not optional!

The Bible talks a lot about faithfulness. To be faithful is to be loyal, truthful, obedient, trustworthy, honorable, steadfast, reliable, and unchanging. Faithfulness influences every human relationship we have, but the faithfulness that matters most is our faithfulness to God. God is faithful to us, and He does what He promises: *"For he is faithful that promised"* (Hebrews 10:23) and *"Thy faithfulness is unto all generations..."* (Psalm 119:90). Many Christians do not realize that without faithfulness to God, it is impossible to have a Christian life. We must have faith in God and faith in Jesus Christ to be forgiven, get saved, and become a Christian. After our salvation, our faithfulness to God is a commitment to Him that we will keep His commandments and do His will. Also, we trust Him as our heavenly Father and faithful Creator in all life's circumstances that we face, good and bad. *"Wherefore let them that suffer according to the will of God commit the keeping of their souls to him in well doing, as unto a faithful Creator"* (1 Peter 4:19).

When we receive Christ as our personal Savior, the Holy Spirit indwells within us and brings His fruit. One of them is "faith," which is a gift from God. *"But the fruit of the Spirit is love, joy, peace, longsuffering, gentleness, goodness, faith, meekness, temperance: against such there is no law"* (Galatians 5:22, 23). The Holy Spirit is always working within us to help us become more like Jesus. God anticipates that the believer will be faithful, too, because

He seeks people who are willing to carry out His will. *"And I will raise me up a faithful priest, that shall do according to that which is in mine heart and in my mind..."* (1 Samuel 2:35) and *"Mine eyes shall be upon the faithful of the land, that they may dwell with me: he that walketh in a perfect way, he shall serve me"* (Psalm 101:6).

Minister and author, *Oswald Chambers* said, *"The goal of faithfulness is not* We should all strive to be this kind of man or woman. The Lord's *that we will do work for God, but that He will be free to do His work through us."* servants are also good stewards. They control things in their own lives and in the lives of others who belong to God. *"Let a man so account of us, as of the ministers of Christ, and stewards of the mysteries of God. Moreover it is required in stewards, that a man be found faithful"* (1 Corinthians 4:1,2).

Dr. Adrian Rogers gives three "Reasons to be faithful."

"Be faithful in the small things. If you'll be faithful in the small things, the big things will take care of themselves *"He who is faithful in what is least is faithful also in much,"* (Luke 16:10). The big things in life are made up of little acts, little words, and little thoughts. Use integrity in the small things.

Be faithful in the secret things. What you are in secret is what you are. I'm talking to many who travel a lot and go into motels, and on the television are R-rated and X-rated films. Nobody is in there but you and Jesus. Be faithful in the secret things.

Be faithful in the sacred things. Be faithful to meet with God. Do you know how you have faithfulness? Not by resolution, not by gritting your teeth, but by abiding in Him. Come to Him; be committed to Him; surrender to Him; yield to Him, and God will make you faithful.

God—give us faithful men. I pray that You will give us some dads, husbands, teachers, and pastors who are faithful because, Lord, you have been faithful to us."

The faithful will not experience God's judgment and will be blessed here on earth according to the following verses:

- *"The LORD render to every man his righteousness and his faithfulness..."* (1 Samuel 26:23).

- *"A faithful man shall abound with blessings: but he that maketh haste to be rich shall not be innocent"* (Proverbs 28:20).

- *"My son, forget not my law; but let thine heart keep my commandments: For length of days, and long life, and peace, shall they add to thee"* (Proverbs 3:1,2).

- *"When a man's ways please the LORD, he maketh even his enemies to be at peace with him"* (Proverbs 16:7).

- *"Fear none of those things which thou shalt suffer:...be thou faithful unto death, and I will give thee a crown of life"* (Revelation 2:10).

Over the centuries, there have been many faithful men and women of God. For example:

Charles Spurgeon - was faithful in small things, and God trusted him with greater things

Paul and Barnabas - were given to us as examples of faithful servants in the New Testament.

Joseph - the son of Jacob, obeyed God even when faithfulness brought him difficulties, and because of His faithfulness, the Lord blessed him.

Moses - was *"faithful in all my [God's] house"* (Numbers 12:7). It means that he obeyed God in everything He asked of him. He was not a perfect man, but continually did God's will.

Daniel - was faithful to God even when he had reasons because of personal safety to disobey and deny God. Therefore, God blessed him for his faithfulness. Daniel is one of my heroes of faithfulness to God. From Daniel, we learn that God honors faithfulness even in the most ungodly of circumstances that may surround us.

- An unknown author tells us the story about a faithful pastor. An elderly preacher was rebuked by one of his deacons one Sunday morning before the service. "Pastor," said the man, "something must be wrong with your preaching and your work. There's been only one person added to the church in a whole year, and he's just a boy." The minister listened, his eyes moistening, and his thin hand trembling. "I feel it all," he replied, "but God knows I've tried to do my duty." On that day, the minister's heart was heavy as he stood before his flock.

As he finished the message, he felt a strong inclination to resign. After everyone else had left, that one boy came to him and asked, "Do you think if I worked hard for an education, I could become a preacher—perhaps a missionary?" Again tears welled up in the minister's eyes. "Ah, this heals the ache I feel," he said. "Robert, I see the Divine hand now. May God bless you, my boy. Yes, I think you will become a preacher." Many years later an aged missionary returned to London from Africa. His name was spoken with reverence. Nobles invited him to their homes. He had added many souls to the church of Jesus Christ, reaching even some of Africa's most savage chiefs. His name was Robert Moffat, the same Robert who years before had spoken to the pastor that Sunday morning in the old Scottish Kirk. Lord, help us to be faithful. Then give us the grace to leave the results to you. — *Source unknown-bible.org*

• There is a story that in the city of Edinburgh, a monument was raised in memory of a little dog named *Grey Friars' Bobby*. The story is this: A shepherd came in from the country district of Edinburgh to the city. He brought with him a dog, a little Cairn terrier. The man died while he was in the city. He was buried in Grey Friars' churchyard. The little dog made his way in through the iron Rockwood gates and lay down on the grave of his master. He did not lie there merely a week or a month or a year. He lay there for twelve years! Every day at one o'clock in Edinburgh they fired the gun in the castle. Everyone looked at his watch. The little dog would come out from the churchyard at that time each day and would receive a pie and a cup of water from one of the local bakers. Then the little dog would trot back to the grave again. He lay there until he died. In the Edinburgh museum, you can see the color plaid of that little dog that is called in Scotland, Grey Friars' Bobby!

This story helps to remind us how faithful we should be to our Master. Are we committed to spending the rest of our lives following His will? Jesus gave His whole life for us. Such love demands our whole life. If a little dog could show such love and fidelity to a dead master, how much greater love should God's children show to a living Master! I pray that all of us at the end of our lives can say what the apostle Paul said with confidence: *"I have fought a good fight, I have finished my course, have kept the faith: Henceforth there is laid up for me a crown of righteousness, which the Lord, the righteous judge, shall give me at that day: and not to me only, but unto all them also that love his appearing"* (2 Timothy 4:7,8). I also pray that the Lord will find us faithful and say, *"Well done, thou good and faithful servant: thou hast been faithful over a few things, I will make thee ruler over many things: enter thou into the joy of thy lord"* (Mathew 25:21).

I WANT TO BE FAITHFUL

So many times I've failed,
And I have turned away,
But I will never leave,
For You are so faithful.

Refrain:
I want to be faithful to You,
I want to be true, Lord.
Whatever You say I will do,
I will obey.

— *Hymn by Frank Garlock, 1930*

❖ ❖ ❖

● "You cannot see faith, but you can see the footprints of the faithful. We must leave behind "faithful footprints" for others to follow."
— *Dr. Dennis Anderson*

● "A wife who is 85% faithful to her husband is not faithful at all. There is no such thing as part-time loyalty to Jesus Christ. "
— *Evangelist, Vance Havner*

● "Don't waste your time waiting and longing for large opportunities which may never come. But faithfully handle the little things that are always claiming your attention." — *Pastor and Evangelist, F. B. Meyer*

● "God's faithful servant has no desire for people to say or to give to him, or what he likes to hear or see, for his first and greatest aim is to hear what is most pleasing to God." — *Theologian and Philosopher, Augustine*

● "My legacy doesn't matter. It isn't important that I be remembered. It's important that when I stand before the Lord, he says, 'Well done, good and faithful servant.' I want to finish strong." — *Dr. James Dobson*

61

BIBLICAL PRAYER

*"But without faith it is impossible to please him:
for he that cometh to God must believe that he is, and that he is
a rewarder of them that diligently seek him."*
Hebrews 11:6

*

Pray, according to God's promises and requirements!

More than 55% of Americans say they pray every day, according to a 2014 Pew Research Center survey, while 21% say they pray weekly or monthly, and 23% say they seldom or never pray." Many of them who pray have doubts and ask the following questions: "Does prayer actually work? Has prayer been scientifically proven? Does prayer make you healthier? Do prayers help healing? Can prayer block and even reverse disease? Can prayer improve your relationships? Can prayer increase your happiness and achievements?" These are genuinely heartfelt questions but do not look to the mainstream media for answers. Seek first in the Word of God for answers.

Researchers have found power in prayer. Additionally, today's science even supports God's Word. There are at least forty-seven scientifically proven health benefits of prayer. Some of these are: protecting against stress; increased peace of mind; boosting your resistance to illness and disease; increasing your memory and mental function; lowering blood pressure; reducing risk for diabetes; minimizing the risk of death from heart attack and stroke; improved immune function; reduced impact from chronic pain; reduced or eliminated panic attacks, anxiety, and depression; becoming more forgiving; improving family relationships; having a happier marriage; having a more positive and happy outlook on life; achieving goals more effectively; living a healthier, and longer life.

All who believe in Christ do not have doubts about the benefits of prayer because they already have experienced them in every part of their lives. For true followers of Christ, prayer is more than words. It is our way of communicating with our Creator. It is spiritual communication between man and God. This means a two-way relationship. We must not only talk to God, but we also must listen to Him. Praying to God is like a child speaking with his father. It is logical and natural for a child to ask his father for the things he needs. People who have doubts about prayer must learn to pray according to God's promises and requirements.

Prayer is a fruit of faith. It is an evidence of faith, an expression of faith, and there is no true prayer without faith. We must pray to the Father, through Christ, and in the Holy Spirit. We must ask for everything according to God's will, and He will answer us according to His promises. God has given us amazing promises regarding prayer. I will mention nine of these promises. The first six promises are from the lips of Jesus Christ Himself, and the other three are found in the New Testament letters of the apostles, Peter, John, and James:

1. *"If one of you shall agree on earth as touching anything that they shall ask, it shall be done for them of my Father which is in heaven"* (Matthew 18:19).

2. *"And whatsoever ye shall ask in my name, that will I do..."* (John 14:13).

3. *"If ye shall ask anything in my name, I will do it"* (John 14:14).

4. *"Whatsoever ye shall ask of the Father in my name, he may give it you"* (John 15:16).

5. *"Verily, verily, I say unto you, Whatsoever ye shall ask the Father in my name, he will give it you"* (John 16:23).

6. *"And all things, whatsoever ye shall ask in prayer, believing, ye shall receive"* (Matthew 21:22).

7. *"For the eyes of the Lord are over the righteous, and his ears are open unto their prayers..."* 1 Peter 3:12).

8. *"And this is the confidence that we have in him, that, if we ask anything according to his will, he heareth us"* (1 John 5:14).

9. *"Is any sick among you? let him call for the elders of the church; and let them pray over him, anointing him with oil in the name of the Lord: And the prayer of faith shall save the sick, and the Lord shall raise him up; and if he have committed sins, they shall be forgiven him. Confess your faults one to another, and pray one for another, that ye may be healed. The effectual fervent prayer of a righteous man availeth much."* (James 5:14-16).

Have you used any of these prayer promises? If not, why not? If you desire God to answer your prayers, you must learn to pray according to His promises and requirements. You must pray and ask with faith, in Jesus' name, and according to God's will. You must pray with sincerity, respect, and reverence because you are talking to God, the creator of the universe. At the same time, you have to open your heart and talk to God with simple language as a child talks to his father. The power of prayer can change your life, your family, and your community.

When you pray, you must have a clear heart. If there is any iniquity in your heart that you have not confessed, the Lord will not hear your prayer. The Bible says, *"If I regard iniquity in my heart, the Lord will not hear me"* (Psalm 66:18). Some people memorized prayers, using only their lips, and they do not use faith and sincerity. They do not believe that God is powerful enough to fulfill their prayers. These prayers do not go further than the ceiling of their home. These prayers never reach the heavens and are never rewarded by the Lord as He states, *"And when thou prayest, thou shalt not be as the hypocrites are: for they love to pray standing in the synagogues and in the corners of the streets, that they may be seen of men. Verily I say unto you, They have their reward"* (Matthew 6:5).

Be wise to ask for things that are in God's will and for His glory. If you ask in your prayers for things to fulfill your lustful desires, your prayers will never be answered. This is clear in God's Word. *"Ye ask, and receive not, because ye ask amiss, that ye may consume it upon your lusts"* (James 4:3). Do not pray only for yourself, but pray more for others. Ask in your prayers for things that you are not able to fulfill yourself, but for things that are beyond your power. A millionaire once prayed for a man who needed some money. After his prayer, his son asked him, *"Daddy, why do you pray when you have money to help him?"*

Unbelievers do not believe in prayers. However, people of God believe in God's power to answer prayers. God always answers believers' prayers with YES, NO, or WAIT. He sometimes answers our prayers quickly. Other times, He may take many years to answer our prayers, including some that may even be answered after we will be in glory. In other words, the Lord will answer our prayers one way or another. I have many examples in my life when the Lord answered my prayers when no one else was able to help me, and He answered in surprising ways. I hope you have these kinds of experiences, too. If not, when you are facing tough times in your life, have faith in God and His promises. Always remember that the man who kneels before God can stand up to anything!

SWEET HOUR OF PRAYER

Sweet hour of prayer! sweet hour of prayer!
that calls me from a world of care,
and bids me at my Father's throne
make all my wants and wishes known.
 In seasons of distress and grief,
my soul has often found relief,
and oft escaped the tempter's snare
by thy return, sweet hour of prayer!

— *Hymn by W. W. Walford (1845)*

In a time of prayer, your spirit touches the heavens, and you feel the presence of God. Prayer keeps you young in spirit. I encourage you to take advantage of your access to God. Remember that the cost of admission was the precious blood of Christ, His Son. Make sure you let the Father know it was worth His investment. Each day is a gift to be opened with prayer. As a child of the King, you can enter into His presence to seek His help in time of need and thank Him for all the blessings He has already given without you asking for them. The Lord never stops answering prayers.

God is real and personal. I know this is true because I talk to Him every day. God honors boldness, so ask with confidence when you pray. Prayer can accomplish miracles if you pray in faith. If you want to be used by the Lord, dedicate yourself in prayer today and be willing to follow Him, no matter what the cost. Remember to pray as often as you can with sincerity and faith.

❖ ❖ ❖

• "When we rely upon organization, we get what organization can do...When we rely upon prayer, we get what God can do."
— *Minister and Evangelisrt, A.C. Dixon*

• "Jesus and all the genuine saints throughout history had spiritual power, and they had a deep prayer life. We must, therefore, believe that there must be some connection between their prayer and their power."
— *Missionary and Author, Sherwood Eddy*

62

BE MERCIFUL LIKE GOD

"Blessed are the merciful: for they shall obtain mercy."
Matthew 5:7

"What doth the LORD require of thee, but to do justly,
and to love mercy, and to walk humbly with thy God?"
Micah 6:8

*

Do not just cry for mercy; give mercy as well!

In the New Testament, the Greek words for "mercy" are "ελεημοσύνη, ελεήμων, οικτιρμός, and οικτίρμων," which mean to love tenderly, to sympathize, and to have compassion. Mercy also includes showing kindness to those who do not deserve it and forgiving those that deserve punishment. Jesus teaches us about "mercy" in the parable of the Good Samaritan in Luke 10:30-37 when a lawyer asked Him, *"Who is my neighbour?"* Jesus told him that the priest and the Levite passed by on the other side when they saw the wounded man, but the Samaritan had compassion when he saw him. He stopped and helped him. Jesus then asked the lawyer, *"Which now of these three, thinkest thou, was neighbour unto him that fell among the thieves? And he said, He that shewed mercy on him. Then said Jesus unto him, Go, and do thou likewise"* (Luke 10:36,37).

A few years ago, an American woman that I know, was on a business trip in the capital of a European country. During the trip, she became sick while staying at a hotel. Her husband back home in the United States contacted a pastor and a missionary that he knew in that city by phone. He asked them if they could visit his wife at the hotel and offer any help that she might need. Unfortunately, both of them provided subtle excuses and denied her husband's request. Finally, he contacted another person he knew in that city who held a secular job but was also involved in several ministries. With gladness, that person offered to help. He and his wife visited the American woman at the hotel. Afterward, they took her to their own home and helped her with everything she needed during that difficult time. These people showed mercy to her.

Based on the stories above regarding the Good Samaritan and the American woman, we see that mercy has two parts. One part is the tenderness of heart, and the other part is action. The Good Samaritan and the couple above both opened their hearts to a person in need and did something to help regardless of the circumstances. Both of them did not sit down and ask many questions about why or how things had happened. Instead, they rolled up their sleeves and started to offer proper help. In these situations, Christians do not have to ask too many questions before doing something. Usually, there is criticism from the world when Christians are involved and glorify the Lord. "Prince of Preachers," Charles Spurgeon said: *"I recommend you, brothers and sisters, always to have one blind eye and one deaf ear. My blind eye is the best eye that I have, and my deaf ear is the best ear I have."*

It is possible to be grateful for the help you receive from others, but not be serious about helping others. It is also possible to be thankful for your own salvation, but not seriously concerned about the salvation of others. We see this in Jonah's story in the Bible. Jonah was far from the heart of God. Jonah received God's mercy, but he did not care about the 120,000 people of Nineveh. When the Lord showed mercy to all these people, Jonah became angry and said: *"I knew that thou art a gracious God, and merciful..."* (Jonah 4:2). Jonah was not a gracious and merciful prophet. He was only concerned about the vine that gave him comfort and not the salvation of other people. God's and Jonah's heart were miles apart. One was merciful, and the other one unmerciful. Let us pray to not be like Jonah.

HELP SOMEBODY TODAY

Look all around you, find someone in need,
Help somebody today!
Though it be little — a neighborly deed —
Help somebody today!

Refrain:
Help somebody today,
Somebody along life's way;
Let sorrow be ended, the friendless befriended,
Oh, help somebody today!
— *Hymn by Mrs. Frank A. Breck, 1904*

God is merciful, and He offers His mercy to all who ask for it. If you are not a Christian, the Lord Jesus Christ is trying to reach out to you in mercy today. With a tender heart, He cares for you, and He is ready to help and do good for you. You do not need to have fear to come to Jesus for help or for salvation. You may have messed up like the apostle Peter or like the prodigal son. You may have felt beaten like the man on the Jericho road. You may have even felt like people ignore you or have had a hard time trusting anyone. However, you do not have to fear to come to Jesus. He is the merciful God who lived like you and me. He has had His own experiences and knows exactly what it means to be beaten and ignored.

Come to Jesus and trust Him. His mercy is not for a limited time, but for a lifetime. Remember, God's justice condemns us, but His mercy redeems us. *"It is of the LORD's mercies that we are not consumed, because his compassions fail not. They are new every morning: great is thy faithfulness."* (Lamentations 3:22-23). The ones who know Him can say,

> *"Surely goodness and mercy*
> *will follow me all the days of my life,*
> *and I will dwell in the house*
> *of the Lord forever."* (Psalm 23:6)

❖ ❖ ❖

- "God gave to sinful mankind the greatest gift of mercy when He sent His only begotten Son Yeshua to the Cross on our behalf."
—*Rabbi. Mike Short*

- "This is the first work of God—that He is merciful to all who are ready to do without their own opinion, right, wisdom, and all spiritual goods, and willing to be poor in spirit."
— *Priest and Theologian, Martin Luther*

- "God's mercy is his tenderhearted, loving compassion for his people. It is his tenderness of heart toward the needy."
— *Theologian and Author, Millard Erickson*

- "God is pleased to show mercy to his enemies, according to his own sovereign pleasure. Though he is infinitely above all and stands in no need of creatures; yet he is graciously pleased to take a merciful notice of poor worms in the dust." — *Pastor and Theologian, Jonathan Edwards*

63

FORGIVE OTHERS

"And be ye kind one to another, tenderhearted,
forgiving one another,
even as God for Christ's sake hath forgiven you."
Ephesians 4:32

*

To forgive others is a gift to ourselves!

Lora had a fight with her twin sister Alexandra. At bedtime, Lora still refused to even speak to her sister. The mother told her angry daughter, "Don't you think you should forgive your sister before you go to sleep? The Bible says we should not 'let the sun go down on our anger.'" The little girl thought for a moment and replied, "Mom, how can I keep the sun from going down?" This story may make you laugh, but a lot of people act this way. They hang on to their resentments and do not forgive others before they lose the light of day and before they go to sleep.

There may have been people in your life who have hurt you so much, and you refuse to forgive them. When you do that, your unforgiving heart can make you feel powerless. Your angry and bitter spirit disconnects you from others. God requires us to live in peace with others, but it is impossible to have peace if you keep resentment for others. Forgiveness always makes you free when you seek God's call of peace in your life. *"If it be possible, as much as lieth in you, live peaceably with all men"* (Romans 12:18), *"Follow peace with all men, and holiness, without which no man shall see the Lord"* (Hebrews 12:14). To forgive the unforgivable, we must follow Jesus' example when He forgave His enemies from the cross. He said, *"Father, forgive them; for they know not what they do..."* (Luke 23:34). Instead of seeking payback to those who hurt us, we must forgive them as the Lord forgave us. *"Forgiving one another...even as Christ forgave you, so also do ye"* (Colossians 3:13).

Forgiveness is hard, forgiveness hurts, and forgiveness costs, but we can do it by the power given to us by the Holy Spirit. Jesus gave us freedom by delivering us from our sin on the cross and freedom to forgive others. Galatians 5:1 tells us, *"Stand fast therefore in the liberty wherewith Christ hath made us free, and be not entangled again with the yoke of bondage."* As Christians, we must follow our Lord's example and forgive others. Even though you may think a person does not deserve forgiveness, you must forgive them because you deserve peace. "Not rendering evil for evil..." (1 Peter 3:9). Here are a few stories about forgiveness showing how God empowers Christians to forgive others.

• It was Communion Sunday, and the pastor finished preaching on the importance of forgiveness. Before the Lord's Supper, one of the deacons, an 87-year old man, stood up. He began, *"For eighty-four years I have hated a little boy who came riding up to me on his bike and said, 'Ha ha, your mother is dead.' This is how I learned my mother had died. Today, I want to forgive that boy."* The congregation was deeply moved. Soon, others stood and declared forgiveness. That day began a revival of the Holy Spirit, and it swept through the church.

• Chuck Swindoll reports that a seminary student in Chicago faced a forgiveness test. Although he preferred to work in some kind of ministry, the only job he could find was driving a bus on Chicago's south side. One day, a gang of tough teens got on the bus and refused to pay the fare. After a few days of this, the seminarian spotted a policeman on the corner, he stopped the bus and reported them. The officer made them pay, and then he got off the bus. With the officer gone, the gang robbed the seminarian and beat him severely right after the bus rounded a corner. He pressed charges, and the gang was rounded up. They were found guilty. As soon as the jail sentence was given, the young Christian saw their spiritual need and felt pity for them. He asked the judge if he could serve their sentences for them. The gang members and the judge were dumbfounded. "It's because I forgive you," he explained. His request was denied, but he visited the young men in jail and led several of them to faith in Christ.

• On October 2, 2006, Charles Roberts brutally attacked a one-room schoolhouse in an Amish community in Lancaster County, Pennsylvania. His attack left five young girls dead and five others wounded before Roberts killed himself. Later, in an amazing display of forgiveness, dozens of Amish neighbors joined Marie Roberts and her children at the funeral of her deceased husband. Marie Roberts wrote an open letter to her Amish neighbors afterward thanking them for their forgiveness, grace, and mercy.

- Charlie Hainline is a layman at Coral Ridge Presbyterian Church in Fort Lauderdale, Florida. He is a man who radiates the love of Christ and is serious about sharing his faith with others. One year, his goal was to lead 1,650 people to Christ (5 a day)! One day, he was out witnessing with a couple of other folks. Even though he did not share the gospel, he sat there and smiled broadly as a teammate did. When the teammate was finished and asked if the person would like to trust Christ and receive the gift of eternal life, the person replied, *"If being a Christian would make me like him (pointing to Charlie), I want it!"* Charlie's life was not a bed of roses by any means. His daughter was kidnapped, killed, and her head was found floating in a canal. When the murderer of his daughter was caught and convicted, Charlie went to jail in order to witness to the man.
— *Source unknown*

- One time, my dentist was doing a root canal on one of my teeth, and a small instrument he was using broke off in my tooth. Instead of removing it, he left it in the tooth. He never told me what happened. Later, I had to see a specialist. After taking an x-ray, he told me what was in my tooth. He gave me an extra copy of the x-ray. I sent it to my previous dentist and asked him why he never told me about it. He and his son, who also worked in his office, never sent back my x-ray, and neither one apologized.

As a Christian, I never thought about seeking revenge for their actions in any way; instead, I chose to forgive them even though they have ignored me and hurt me emotionally and physically for some time. I did not wait for them to apologize, but I forgave them first because God commands it of us. I forgave them by accepting the apology I never received. Forgiveness is indeed a gift you give yourself. It is not something we do for others. We do this for ourselves to get well, to have peace, and to move forward. If we do not forgive, we remain wounded inside, and we damage our own physical health.

If someone has hurt you lately, do not let him put you down. Lean on God's grace and share forgiveness. Forgiveness is an amazing form of love that returns peace and satisfaction. Let forgiveness ignite divine healing. Do not let negative attacks get the best of you. With Jesus' love in your heart, nothing can keep you from going forward. Act in forgiveness and let the Lord do the rest!

We have all sinned, but there is complete forgiveness in the Lord Jesus Christ. This is the good news that the gospel offers us. God was merciful to you by forgiving your sins even when you were an enemy of God. Now you must also be merciful and be willing to forgive others; it does not matter how bad you have been hurt. Our Lord must be your best example, and your obedience to the Holy Scriptures must be your first priority. *"And be ye kind one to another, tenderhearted, forgiving one another, even as God for Christ's sake hath forgiven you"* (Ephesians 4:32). *"He will turn again, he will have compassion upon us; he will subdue our iniquities; and thou wilt cast all their sins into the depths of the sea"* (Micah 7:19). *"I will be merciful to their unrighteousness, and their sins and their iniquities will I remember no more"* (Hebrews 8:12).

If God forgave you and wiped your sins out of His mind, you must do the same thing to others. Your forgiveness stops their bad behavior from destroying your heart. Your forgiveness, in reality, is a gift to your heart. I hope, as a Christian, your life is filled with peace and the power of God. The question is: "God forgave you-but do you forgive others?"

If you are not a Christian, and your heart is filled with hatred, bitterness, and anger, I have the best news for you. Jesus is not only willing to forgive you entirely, but He also gives you the power and desire to forgive others. You can walk in freedom today. Turn to Him today, repent of your sins, and trust Him by faith for your salvation.

❖ ❖ ❖

- "To be a Christian means to forgive the inexcusable because God has forgiven the inexcusable in you."
— *Scholar and Author, C.S.Lewis*

- "Forgiveness is me giving up my right to hurt you for hurting me."
— *Anonymous*

- "Forgiveness is unlocking the door to set someone free and realizing you were the prisoner! "
— *Pastor and Author, Max Lucado*

- "Forgiveness is the key that unlocks the door of resentment and the handcuff of hatred. It is a power that breaks the chains of bitterness and the shackles of selfishness."
— *Author, Corrie Ten Boom*

- "When you forgive, you in no way change the past, but you sure do change the future."
— *Radio Host, Bernard Meltzer*

64

TELL THE TRUTH

"These are the things that ye shall do;
Speak ye every man the truth to his neighbour..."
Zechariah 8:16

"But he that doeth truth cometh to the light, that his deeds may
be made manifest, that they are wrought in God."
John 3:21

*

Always tell the truth and shame the devil!

A n old man was walking down the street when he met a group of young boys surrounding an old dog. The old man asked the boys what they were doing. "We were trying to decide who will take the dog home by seeing who can tell the best lie!" one boy explained. Appalled, the old man said, "You boys should not be telling lies. At your age, I never told a lie." With a look of concession, the youngest boy threw up his hands and said with a sigh, "All right, give him the dog."

The boy was correct because the only place truth exists is in God and in His Word. *"Jesus saith unto him, I am the way, the truth, and the life: no man cometh unto the Father, but by me"* (John 14:6). On the other hand, the devil is just the opposite of God. He is not the truth; he is a liar. *"He was a murderer from the beginning, and abode not in the truth, because there is no truth in him. When he speaketh a lie, he speaketh of his own: for he is a liar, and the father of it"* (John 8:44). When we become God's children, Satan's misleading power is broken, and believers can be free from wrong thinking and lies.

The Bible talks a lot about truth, and in the New Testament, the Greek word for truth is "αλήθεια" (aletheia), which means "un-hide" or "hiding nothing." Many people never apply biblical truth, but instead, remain captive to the world's lies. Some Christians even fear to change their ways to follow God and reject to seek and serve Him by living a faithful and true Christian life. They allow fear, apathy, and laziness to defeat them. They do not make wise decisions or follow God's ways to succeed. We cannot begin to build a truth-based Christian life until we accept God's way as the only way. Christians who follow, defend, and fight for the truth win.

Several years ago, I went to my neighborhood store to buy an anniversary card for my wife the day before our wedding anniversary. When I drove to the store, a young policeman stopped me and gave me a speeding ticket for $75.00. His reason was that he thought I was driving 50 miles per hour in a 35 miles per hour zone. I did not argue with him, but I followed his instructions, even though I did not agree with his charges.

After I received the ticket, I had two options. One was to pay the ticket, and the state would record it on my driving records. The other option was to appear in court before the judge, the policeman, and the state's attorney to defend myself. This option would enable me to keep my good driving records and save the $75.00. Without hesitation, I chose the second option. In the meantime, my wife and I prayed for the situation, and we believed that the Lord would deliver me from the policeman's mistake. *"And call upon me in the day of trouble: I will deliver thee, and thou shalt glorify me"* (Psalm 50:15).

I appeared in court three weeks later. I told the judge that I respect the law enforcement people and thanked them for trying to protect us and even sometimes giving their lives for us. However, I believed the policeman had made a mistake and stopped the wrong car in this specific case. I told the judge that I had lived in that neighborhood for thirty-five years, and sometimes I drove several times a day on that street and had never been stopped by a policeman for speeding. To prove my words, I challenged them to look at my driving records. I also showed them my insurance papers, which revealed the discounts I received every year during all of my years of being a safe driver.

Because my records were clear for many years, the judge asked the policeman and state's attorney if they had anything to say. Both of them were speechless in front of 400 people in the courtroom. The judge then said to me, "You are dismissed." After that, I left the courtroom with joy in my heart and praised the Lord, who had given me the victory.

Do you feel like you are on the edge of defeat? Do not throw in the towel yet. Jesus is still in charge. Even though things look dark now, God will ultimately triumph. Hang on and trust the Lord. Do not allow adversity to get you down, except to get you on your knees. *"If thou faint in the day of adversity, thy strength is small"* (Proverbs 24:10).

Remember that God sends the winds to make the trees grow strong. God is looking for people who will stand firm to the standards of His Word in an age of permissiveness. Always stand firm for what is right, even when others oppose you. Victory comes only to those who are prepared for battle. Tell the truth, shame the devil, and win the battle. Make sure you always tell the truth.

A study of the American Psychological Association proves that by telling lies, you affect your relationships, as well as your mental and physical health. If you lie, people will lose their respect for you and your faith. Remember that it is more important to win their hearts and lose the dog. By the way, it is also good for your relationships and your mental and physical health if you do not lie!

❖ ❖ ❖

● "The lip of truth shall be established for ever: but a lying tongue is but for a moment." — *Proverbs 12:19*

● "Son, always tell the truth. Then you'll never have to remember what you said the last time."
— *43rd Speaker of the U.S. House of Representatives, Sam Rayburn*

● "You're never so easily fooled as when you're trying to fool someone else." — *Author, La Rochefoucauld*

● "What upsets me is not that you lied to me, but that from now on, I can no longer believe you." — *Philosopher, Friedrich Nietzsche*

● "The Truth is heavy, therefore few care to carry it."
— *Prime Minister, Winston Churchill*

● "Sometimes, you have to be mean and hurt someone's feelings to help and save their heart. The truth hurts, but lies kill."
"I respect those that tell me the truth, no matter how hard it is.",
"Hurt me with the truth, don't comfort me with a lie."
— *Quotes from Unknown*

65

TRUE GODLINESS

"But thou, O man of God, flee these things; and follow after righteousness, godliness, faith, love, patience, meekness."
1 Timothy 6:11

"But godliness with contentment is great gain."
1 Timothy 6:6

∗

Work on developing true godliness!

In our culture today, people put great emphasis on physical fitness. There is nothing wrong in being interested in being healthy and physically fit, but the Word of God says, *"For bodily exercise profits a little, but godliness is profitable for all things"* (1 Timothy 4:8). To grow in godliness in our personal and professional life, we have to give the proper place to the Word of God in our heart with our reading and meditation. This will provide us with more satisfaction than from any other pleasures. The more we allow biblical principles to shape our decisions, the more we will be able to overcome problems and trials in our lives, as well as enable us to produce more spiritual fruit.

When we become mature in godliness, we will accept God's pruning to have more fruit. With patience, we must follow God's plans and His will. We must be investing our lives for the benefit of others. We should not worry or fear in any of our circumstances, but always rest in God's faithfulness. As a result, we will be able to say along with the apostle Paul, *"I can do all things through Christ which strengtheneth me"* (Philippians 4:13).

When we drive by a highly polluted area, we wonder what can be done to stop people from dumping their garbage. According to a

Reuters news story in January 2001, "Peru city authorities tried a novel approach. Some of the streets in the capital city were scarred by terrible littering-people, even stopping to urinate in the streets. The authorities responded by placing pictures of Jesus and Mary on the walls of buildings lining the most polluted streets. Why? Because the people of Peru are, on the whole, committed to Roman Catholicism. The authorities have found that people are far less likely to litter the streets under the gaze of Jesus and the Virgin Mary." If we are really mature Christians with true godliness, Jesus is with us all the time, and we do not need pictures to remind us of Jesus' presence to live godly lives.

Doctor Fred Smith said, *"I don't think God is interested in our success. He is interested in our maturity."* He had a point. As followers of Jesus Christ, we must be mature, godly, bold, and not compromisers. Several years ago, I worked for a large corporation. One day, the Lord allowed me to witness to people in the lunchroom and talk to them about God's love, why the Lord died, and how He provided salvation for them. A little later, a man who said he was a Christian came up to me and warned me, "Don't talk to them about that. You will offend them."

Another time in 1975, a small church in Chicago was without a pastor. The church asked me to be their temporary pastor even though I had a full-time job. I agreed to do it without pay until they found a pastor. The members liked me as long as I preached what they wanted to hear. However, one time, when I preached about sin, during the midweek service, the Holy Spirit began to convict some of them. Two deacons afterward said to me, "Don't preach about this now..." After that, I resigned. From what I heard, three more pastors served this church and did not last long. Finally, most of the people left, and the church did not survive.

Today, numerous churches within the United States and other countries have turned the house of God into "Social Clubs." These churches are spiritually dead because most of the members are not "born again" Christians and their pastors never preach about sin, but only what the people like to hear. In some churches, a church committee tells the pastor what to preach. In these churches, the pastor is afraid to lose members and income, so they become servants of their own pockets and not servants of the Lord. In other words, they pretend they have godliness. *"Having a form of godliness, but denying the power thereof: from such turn away"* (2 Timothy 3:5).

In the United States, Christianity is the largest religion, with around 78% of the population. There are approximately 253,500,000 professing Christians, but only about 18% of them "Walk the Walk." The rest are not going to church regularly, and many of them do not believe the Bible is actually the Word of God. We have been called a "Christian" nation, and we have believed that because it was founded as a Christian nation. Now, most of the Christians in this nation have let their faith and lifestyles become "lukewarm," and they have lost their "salt" and their power.

The devil is the god of this world. Because of the apathy of many weak Christians, he can do his job easily. They have allowed the Communists, Socialists, and Marxists to invade their publicly funded school systems and indoctrinate their children. They permitted politicians to support abortion, homosexuality, and same-sex marriage – all with public funds. They have also allowed the Islamic extremists, liberal media, and politicians to use their own political system to elect "their men." Some Christians have allowed the devil to destroy their minds, the minds of their children, and their own country.

When lukewarm Christians support ungodly politicians who are against their own Christian values, they invite the wrath of God. We saw some hope for this nation after 9/11 when we saw people praying and turning to God. How soon they forgot! After that, the Lord allowed this nation to suffer pain and sorrow through catastrophic hurricanes, floods, earthquakes, and fires to remind them that He exists. The devil has blinded people's minds and hearts. For this reason, they are not able to see the face of God. Even they do not use the word "God" because it might offend somebody. Instead, they use "Mother Nature." Sadly, this nation has become a nation of many fools.

Few years ago, one person who said he was a "born-again Christian" wrote to me and complained about specific elected politicians. At the same time, he also admitted that he did not vote. I answered him with the quote from Plato: *"Those who are too smart to engage in politics are punished by being governed by those who are dumber."* God has warned his children. There is only one hope: *"If my people, which are called by my name, shall humble themselves, and pray, and seek my face, and turn from their wicked ways; then will I hear from heaven, and will forgive their sin, and will heal their land"* (2 Chronicles 7:14).

This country and all the world needs men and women who love and fear the Lord, who practice Christianity, and who follow godliness. Christianity is a relationship with Jesus Christ and is not a religion. *Charles H. Spurgeon* said, *"I would not give much for your religion unless it can be seen."* Yes! Lamps do not talk, but they do shine. We need to keep praying for this country and our families. We always have to keep our eyes on the Lord and let our lives be more beautiful with godliness. *"Looking unto Jesus the author and finisher of our faith; who for the joy that was set before him endured the cross, despising the shame, and is set down at the right hand of the throne of God"* (Hebrews 12:2)

If you are a Christian, the questions for you are: "Are you a real follower of Christ? Do you stand BOLDLY for truth and righteousness? Do you read the Bible, pray, and witness? Do you love and fear God? Are you faithful to the Lord? Are you a lukewarm Christian who compromises on everything and who cares only for your bank account and for the things of this world?" The Lord is not mocked. One day, sooner or later, you will stand before Him to give an account of yourself and what you have done with your life. When that time comes, the Lord will not be interested in your bank account or how successful you have been in this world with material things. He will ask you how much you loved Him and how faithful you were to Him-the King of kings and the Lord of lords.

I WOULD BE LIKE JESUS

Be like Jesus, this my song,
In the home and in the throng;
Be like Jesus, all day long!
I would be like Jesus.

— Hymn by James Rowe, 1911

❖ ❖ ❖

• "The world sees successful individuals as powerful and self-sufficient, but Jesus didn't care about these qualities. Instead, He wants people to be aware of their own brokenness. This is the foundation for godliness."
— Dr. Charles Stanley

• "Stale godliness is ungodliness. Let our religion be as warm, and constant, and natural as the flow of the blood in our veins. A living God must be served in a living way." "Nearness to God brings likeness to God. The more you see God, the more of God will be seen in you."
— Quotes from "Prince of Preachers," C.H. Spurgeon

• "If truth were told, most of us spend longer each day on personal cleanliness than on practical godliness." *— Pastor, Alistair Begg*

• "True godliness does not turn men out of the world, but enables them to live better in it and excites their endeavors to mend it."
— Founder of the Province of Pennsylvania, William Penn

66

BIBLICAL HOLINESS

"Follow peace with all men, and holiness,
without which no man shall see the Lord."
Hebrews 12:14

*

Holiness is not an option,
it is God's requirement
for anyone who wants to enter His kingdom!

Evangelist, D.L. Moody wrote: *"It is a great deal better to live a holy life than to talk about it. We are told to let our light shine, and if it does, we won't need to tell anybody it does. The light will be its own witness. Lighthouses don't ring bells and fire cannons to call attention to their shining – they just shine."*

For Christians, holiness is a requirement of God. The Bible says, *"Without holiness, no man shall see the Lord"* (Hebrews 12:14). Holiness is also a command from God. The Bible says, *"Be holy, for I am holy"* (1 Peter 1:16). "Holiness" is an essential characteristic of God's nature. With respect to God, it means absolute purity and moral perfection. With respect to man, holiness means conformity to the character of God. We must be holy because God is holy. It means thinking as God thinks, loving what He loves, hating what He hates, and acting as Christ would act.

"Holiness" is "sanctus," in Latin; "agios," in Greek; and "qôdesh," in Hebrew. These words are all related to one another. In the New Testament, the Greek word is "Άγιος" ("agios," "saint") which means to separate from evil and every possibility of sin. To be "agios" is to not only be set apart for God but to be free from sin itself. In the Old Testament, holiness is usually associated with God's perfection, but we cannot become Holy and perfect like God. God is naturally holy and perfect. We only become holy when we have a relationship with Christ. We can only pursue practical holiness in this world, according to the New Testament when we mature spiritually. The ultimate achievement of holiness will be in heaven when we meet the Lord in glory.

When we come to Christ, the pursuit of holiness does not end. It just begins. There is positional holiness that we receive when we become "born again" and practical holiness which we must sincerely pursue. God waits for us to develop a lifestyle of holiness: *"As obedient children, not fashioning yourselves according to the former lusts in your ignorance: But as he which hath called you is holy, so be ye holy in all manner of conversation; Because it is written, Be ye holy; for I am holy"* (1 Peter 1:14-16), and commands us to *"cleanse ourselves from all filthiness of the flesh and spirit, perfecting holiness in the fear of God"* (2 Corinthians 7:1). As a result, we seek holiness and decline to go back to our former lifestyles, making us become honorable instead of dishonorable vessels for Him.

As born-again Christians, the Holy Spirit separates us from the world for godliness: *"And be not conformed to this world: but be ye transformed by the renewing of your mind, that ye may prove what is that good, and acceptable, and perfect, will of God"* (Romans 12:2). Even as we become more holy in this life, we will never be perfect because we still sin sometimes as the apostle Paul wrote, *"For to will is present with me; but how to perform that which is good I find not. For the good that I would I do not: but the evil which I would not, that I do"* (Romans 7:18-19). Only in heaven will all sin be removed from our lives, and we will be made perfect.

When we develop a lifestyle of holiness, we are free from the law. We live according to the guidance of the Holy Spirit. *"I say then: Walk in the Spirit, and you shall not fulfill the lust of the flesh. For the flesh lusts against the Spirit, and the Spirit against the flesh; and these are contrary to one another so that you do not do the things that you wish. But if you are led by the Spirit, you are not under the law"* (Galatians 5:16-18).

On the other hand, we do not have to rebel and grieve the Holy Spirit for our own spiritual growth: *"And do not grieve the Holy Spirit of God, by whom you were sealed for the day of redemption"* (Ephesians 4:30). Because of God's mercies, we should present our bodies a living sacrifice, *"holy acceptable to God"* (Romans 12:1). It is only in heaven, we will be free from sin and be perfectly holy in the presence of God. Until then, we have to keep running our race and looking to Jesus. *"Looking unto Jesus the author and finisher of our faith; who for the joy that was set before him endured the cross, despising the shame, and is set down at the right hand of the throne of God"* (Hebrews 12:2).

It is crystal clear that God is divine, holy, and morally perfect, but man is a sinful human. Biblical holiness is separation from sin and worldliness. It is also a dedication to God and His will. Holiness does not mean that we are sinless, but that we are set apart for God to live by following His purposes. We do not have to excuse our sins, but we must confess, repent, and choose to obey the Lord.

To become holy and pursue biblical holiness, you must believe and accept Jesus Christ as your personal Savior. If you have not placed your faith in Jesus Christ to save you from your sins, then your pursuit of holiness is worthless. Therefore, you must first make sure you are a born again believer. (To learn more, read chapter 3 of the gospel of John also the "Born Again" and "New Heart" topics in this book.)

If you are truly a believer, you must acknowledge that your position in Christ, without any doubt, sets you apart from the world, and makes you holy. *"But you are a chosen generation, a royal priesthood, a holy nation, His own special people, that you may proclaim the praises of Him who called you out of darkness into His marvelous light; who once were not a people but are now the people of God, who had not obtained mercy but now have obtained mercy"* (1 Peter 2:9-10). You have a relationship with the living God. You are not an unforgiven sinner. You have to recognize that you are a saint, and God has given you everything you need for a successful life of godliness. *"His divine power has given to us all things that pertain to life and godliness, through the knowledge of Him who called us by glory and virtue"* (2 Peter 1:3). You must daily live a life set-apart to honor and obey Him. You must not try to become like the world, but you must live according to God's Word.

As we desire to follow God's will each day, we can progressively become more holy as we become more and more like Christ. Our goal should be to imitate Christ as the apostle Paul said, *"Imitate me, just as I also imitate Christ"* (1 Corinthians 11:1).

❖ ❖ ❖

• "Nothing lies between holiness and sinfulness. You are either one or the other." — *Charles F. Stanley*

• "I believe the holier a man becomes, the more he mourns over the unholiness which remains in him." — *Preachers, Charles Spurgeon*

• "Every man is as holy as he really wants to be."
— *Pastor and Author, A.W. Tozer*

• "A holy life will make the deepest impression. Lighthouses blow no horns, they just shine." — *Evangelist, D. L. Moody*

• "The secret of Christian holiness is heart occupation with Christ Himself." — *Dr. H. A. Ironside*

67

LOVE YOUR ENEMIES

"But I say unto you which hear, Love your enemies,
do good to them which hate you, Bless them that curse you,
and pray for them which despitefully use you."
Luke 6:27-28

"Therefore if thine enemy hunger, feed him; if he thirst, give him
drink: for in so doing thou shalt heap coals of fire on his head."
Romans 12:20

*

Love and treat your enemies as the Lord directs!

Throughout our lives, there will come times when some people will be against us and become our enemies for a number of different reasons. Even Jesus makes it clear that some people will be against us and make our life difficult. It might be a jealous person at work, a rude relative, a bad neighbor, or an intimidating bully that makes our lives difficult. All these kinds of people have a negative influence on our lives. Sometimes they are "a pain in the neck." Our lives would be happier without them, but we do not have a choice. When they are gone, other difficult people will take their place. Whether big or small, evil monsters will continue to get in our way. We have to deal with them. Jesus teaches us in His Sermon on the Mount how we have to deal with our enemies.

1.   **We have to be careful with our deeds.**
"Do good to them which hate you" (Luke 6:27). If somebody is mean, nasty, hurtful, and evil to us, it will hit our nerves, and we will feel hatred towards him. Ultimately, we do not have to let it get this far. Instead, do

good to those who hate us. We will not be surprised how it will melt their hearts, and they will soon become our friends. As a young man and a new Christian, I once worked for a company that was under a Labor Union. At that time, I was not aware of how Unions operated. The leader of the Union did not like me and gave problems because I was a hard worker and did twice as much work as others. I found out that he liked to travel, so I bought him an oversized travel atlas and gave it to him with a nice note. That was the solution. His spirit of hatred turned to kindness. Instead of him continuing to be my enemy, he became my friend.

2. We have to be vigilant with our words when we talk.

"Bless them that curse you" (Luke 6:28). If somebody mistreats us and talks badly to us, we will be hurt and want to speak hurtful words in return. However, we should not do that. I remember a time when one of my neighbors first moved next door. The lady of the house came to our fence and threatened me using bad words while I was planting some vegetables. She told me, "If you touch my fence, I will call the police." First of all, she did not know that the fence was mine. Second, her attitude was silly because even if I had to touch the fence, it would not be damaged.

Quietly, I heard what she said without responding to her. After she went inside her house, I went over there and calmly asked her if we could speak. She allowed me to talk. I explained all the facts about the fence. I kindly reminded her that as neighbors, we have to be friends and not enemies. I also offered to help her if she needed it. To my surprise, I saw her start to cry and say, "You are such a nice man, but I acted stupidly..." We have since been good neighbors for over twenty years. If I had done what she did, who knows what kind of relationship we would have today. It never helps when we put fuel on a fire that somebody else has started. We have to remember: *"When a man's ways please the LORD, he maketh even his enemies to be at peace with him"* (Proverbs 16:7).

3. We have to pray for our enemies.

"Pray for them which despitefully use you" (Luke 6:28). If someone mistreats us, we will want to mistreat him, too. We do not have to do the same. Pray for those who mistreat us. I had another neighbor who was an alcoholic with a filthy mouth. He thought he owned the whole neighborhood. I tried for fifteen years to be kind to him. I also tried to witness to him on several occasions. Nevertheless, because of his hateful spirit and his personality, I stopped communicating with him. Instead, I prayed and waited to see what the Lord had in store for him. A short time later, the other neighbors also stopped communicating with him. As a result, he decided to sell his house. He left, and another good neighbor arrived.

Numerous people do not want to hear about their enemies. They only want revenge, but this is not the best solution. Others ask how we can break free from revenge when we experience hatred, cursing, and anger? How can we break free from that? The answer is:

First, find out the enemy.
"For we wrestle not against flesh and blood, but against principalities... against spiritual wickedness in high places" (Ephesians 6:12). The power of evil is involved in every war we have with people. We have to overcome the evil, not the person. The person who mistreats us and wounds us with words is not our enemy. Our enemy is the one who tells the person to do it.

Second, admit the problem.
"The wages of sin is death..." (Romans 6:23) and *"He that covereth his sins shall not prosper: but whoso confesseth and forsaketh them shall have mercy"* (Proverbs 28:13). All the hateful words and evil attitudes are nothing else, but the power of sin in him. He will be delivered from this awful power only if he repents and calls on the mercy of God and becomes a new creation in Christ. If not, that power will direct that person to hell. The negative, destructive words, and bad attitudes of a person who wounds us arises from the darkness of evil. This darkness must be destroyed. If not, it will continue forever.

Third, do not take revenge on your enemies but trust in the justice of God.
"It is written, Vengeance is mine; I will repay, saith the Lord." (Romans 12:19). It is hard for people to show mercy to their enemies because they believe that there may not be any justice for them. For this reason, they try to carry out revenge for themselves. This is wrong. Revenge belongs to the Lord and not to us. God's justice is best. Keep in mind, each sin that has ever been committed will eventually either be covered by the blood of Jesus, or it will be destroyed in hell.

When I was not able to handle the people with evil spirits who were against me, I gave them over into the hands of God. Later, I saw with my own eyes how God's justice worked in their lives. We never have to change our Christian nature because of our enemies.

● In "Context," *Mary Marty* retells a parable from the *"Eye of the Needle"* newsletter: A holy man was engaged in his morning meditation under a tree whose roots stretched out over the riverbank. During his meditation, he noticed that the river was rising, and a scorpion caught in the roots was about to drown. He crawled out on the roots and reached down to free the scorpion, but every time he did so, the scorpion struck back at him. An observer came along and said to the holy man, "Don't you know that's a scorpion, and it's in the nature of a scorpion to want to sting?" To which the holy man replied, "That may well be, but it is my nature to save, and must I change my nature because the scorpion does not change its nature?"—*Joseph B. Modica*

• In the book *"The Grace of Giving,"* Stephen Olford tells of a Baptist pastor during the American Revolution, Peter Miller, who lived in Ephrata, Pennsylvania, and enjoyed the friendship of George Washington. In Ephrata also lived Michael Wittman, an evil-minded sort who did all he could to oppose and humiliate the pastor. One day Michael Wittman was arrested for treason and sentenced to die. Peter Miller traveled seventy miles on foot to Philadelphia to plead for the life of the traitor. "No, Peter," General Washington said. "I cannot grant you the life of your friend." "My friend!" exclaimed the old preacher. "He's the bitterest enemy I have." "What?" cried Washington. "You've walked seventy miles to save the life of an enemy? That puts the matter in a different light. I'll grant your pardon." And he did. Peter Miller took Michael Wittman back home to Ephrata--no longer an enemy but a friend. — *Lynn Jost / The Grace of Giving, Stephen Olford*

Because of my faith, one of my enemies sent me a negative letter. It was sent at the time I was diagnosed with several cancerous tumors, and my surgeon told me, "Even God cannot help you." After the Lord delivered me from cancer, this person is unable to face me or talk with me. On another occasion, a relative from Greece sent me a letter attacking me and putting me down because my faith was different than his. All these people tried to hurt me. They did not realize that the Lord was and continues to be with me. The Holy Spirit helps me to overcome these kinds of attacks. He also gives me the strength to forgive, pray, and treat them according to His will.

Some Christians know so little of victory today because they have failed to recognize conflict. Arthur Bloch said, *"Friends come and go, but enemies accumulate."* If you have an enemy who makes your life miserable, do not respond in hatred. You might not be able to stand them. Perhaps, you want revenge. I understand, but this is an attitude of the old human nature. When you become a new creation in Christ and grow in your spiritual life, you will discover over time that you can forgive and pray for those who mistreat you. You will also learn to seek blessings for those who curse you. Do not let negative attacks get the best of you. Look for ways to show them the love of God. Jesus wants you to love your enemies and treat them with kindness. Displaying such love is a powerful way to witness to them and show the reality of your faith. Give love when it is least expected. Watch the Holy Spirit work in their lives and give them the lesson they deserve. You may even find that you can do good to those who hate you just like Pastor Peter Miller when he walked seventy miles to save his enemy. *"Be not overcome of evil, but overcome evil with good"* (Romans 12:21).

❖ ❖ ❖

• "The good man has his enemies. He would not be like his Lord if he had not. If we were without enemies we might fear that we were not the friends of God, for the friendship of the world is enmity to God."
—*"Prince of Preachers," Charles Spurgeon*

• "In Jesus and for Him, enemies and friends alike are to be loved."
—*Author, Thomas a Kempis*

• "When we are privileged to meet the need of one who despises us, we might just see an amazing change in his life."
— *Dr. Charles Stanley*

• "You have enemies? Good. That means you've stood up for something, sometime in your life."
—*Prime Minister, Winston Churchill*

• "Pay attention to your enemies, for they are the first to discover your mistakes."
— *Greek philosopher, Antisthenes*

**Never revenge your enemies.
Instead look for ways to show them
the love of God.
Displaying such love is a powerful way to witness
to them and show the reality of your faith.**

68

CONTENTMENT

"But godliness with contentment is great gain.
For we brought nothing into this world,
and it is certain we can carry nothing out.
And having food and raiment let us be therewith content."
1 Timothy 6:6-8

*

Be content and take the time to count your blessings.

Contentment is not to get what we want and desire, but to appreciate what we already have. Sadly, according to *experian.com*, discontentment has caused the American household debt to rise to $13 Trillion in 2018. This was the most significant jump in a decade. The burden of debt has led to bankruptcy for over 250,000 Americans. Many people cannot control their spending. I will provide a few examples of people who evaluate contentment in different ways.

• On one national TV show, a woman who was addicted to spending said when she liked a pair of shoes, she did not buy only one pair, but ten of them. She did the same thing for dresses and other things. Her husband had two jobs, but she still put him $200,000 in debt. There are even more severe consequences for this type of financial problem which brings pressure at home and causes 56% of all divorces.

• One year, on an annual home improvement show in a Chicago suburb, many modern kitchens were on display for the public. All were professionally done with beautiful granite countertops, cabinets, and expensive appliances. One woman said, *"Last year we redid our kitchen, and my husband allowed me to spend only $50,000. I wish I had married a rich man to have better things in my life."*

CONTENTMENT

- Soon after a baby was born to a young couple, a tornado ripped through Will County, Illinois, USA. After the tornado hit, the man's house was gone and also his baby. Fortunately, the father discovered his child alive and well in a field near his house. When a reporter asked the young father if he was angry that he had lost everything he owned, the man replied: *"No, I just thank God I have my baby and my family. Some people don't even have that. Nothing else is important."*

- During World War II, Eddie Rickenbacker was on a tour when his plane made a forced landing in the Pacific Ocean. Rickenbacker and Army Captain Hans C. Adamson, along with the rest of the 8 crewmen, drifted in a lifeboat for 24 days. At one point, the desperate and starving crew prayed to God for food. After the prayer, a seagull landed on Rickenbacker's head. He warily and cautiously captured it. The seagull provided enough nourishment until they were rescued. Later, Rickenbacker wrote: *"Let the moment come when nothing is left but life, and you will find that you do not hesitate over the fate of material possessions."*

- A pastor told a story about how, as a young boy, his parents started a new church. They had only seven poor church members in the beginning. His parents struggled financially. When Thanksgiving Day was approaching, he asked his mother if they would have enough money for a Thanksgiving turkey. His mother, a faithful woman of God, looked at her young son and just said, *"My son, the Lord will provide."* On the last church service before Thanksgiving, during the offering, a stranger entered the church and dropped a twenty-dollar bill in the offering plate and left. There was more than enough for the Thanksgiving dinner. The Lord was faithful and did provide. This was a blessing and an encouragement to the young boy and future pastor.

If you are a Christian, are you struggling with discontentment? Consumerism and advertising breed the desire to always want more. Do not let your greed and your thirst for instant gratification put you in financial bondage. Publilius Syrus said, *"Debt is the slavery of the free."* God desires that you be financially free so you can help others.

Do not try to keep up with your neighbors. Do not let the pursuit of possessions take your eyes off of serving the Lord. Focus on things in life that are more important than material things. World statistics show that if you have food in the refrigerator, clothes on your back, and a roof over your head, you are richer than three-fourths of the people in the world. In the year of 2018 in the United States, credit card debt averaged $9,333 per household, and still, people are discontented. King Solomon, the wisest and richest man that ever lived, said, *"He that loveth silver shall not be satisfied with silver; nor he that loveth abundance with increase: this is also vanity"* (Ecclesiastes 5:10).

Trust and have confidence in God. He will satisfy your condition according to His promises regardless of your circumstances. Be faithful to God as He is always faithful to you. *"Be content with such things as ye have: for he hath said, I will never leave thee, nor forsake thee"* (Hebrews 13:5) and *"And we know that all things work together for good to them that love God, to them who are the called according to his purpose"* (Romans 8:28). God has promised to be with you and meet your legitimate needs in life. Learn to rest in God's adequacy. *"Humble yourselves therefore under the mighty hand of God, that he may exalt you in due time: Casting all your care upon him; for he careth for you"* (1 Peter 5:6-7). Do not let what you do not have blind you to the One you do have. The power of Christ is the secret to being content in any and every situation. The Lord will provide you with everything you need in your life, even a seagull on the head. Jesus said, *"Therefore I say unto you, Take no thought for your life, what ye shall eat, or what ye shall drink; nor yet for your body, what ye shall put on. Is not the life more than meat, and the body than raiment? Behold the fowls of the air: for they sow not, neither do they reap, nor gather into barns; yet your heavenly Father feedeth them. Are ye not much better than they?"* (Matthew 6:25,26).

Always remember the testimony of the apostle Paul:

"Not that I speak in regard to need, for I have learned in whatever state I am, to be content."— *I know both how to be abased, and I know how to abound: everywhere and in all things I am instructed both to be full and to be hungry, both to abound and to suffer need. I can do all things through Christ which strengtheneth me"* (Philippians 4:12-13).

A person can never be happy until the time he learns to enjoy what he has and stops worrying about things he does not have. Learn to be content. Take time to count your blessings. Real happiness is not getting more things, but getting more of Jesus. If you are facing a need, you cannot meet, trust the Lord. *"My son, the Lord, will provide."*

Guilt is concerned with the past.
Worry is concerned about the future.
Contentment enjoys the present.— *Unknown*

❖ ❖ ❖

- "Contentment makes poor men rich; discontent makes rich men poor." — *One of the Founding Fathers of the United States, Benjamin Franklin*

- "It is right to be contented with what we have, never with what we are." — *Doctor and Politician, James Mackintosh*

- "I complained that I had no shoes until I met a man who had no feet." — *Arabic Proverb*

69

BIBLICAL WISDOM

"The fear of the LORD is the beginning of wisdom..."
Psalm 111:10

*"If any of you lack wisdom, let him ask of God,
that giveth to all men liberally, and upbraideth not;
and it shall be given him."*
James 1:5

*

Are you wise like the owl?

One of the finest hotels in the USA, the El Cortez Hotel in San Diego, California, needed another elevator due to its popularity. Educated architects and engineers came up with an idea and designed a plan to put in another elevator. The plan required tearing holes in each of the floors, which would cost a lot of money, make a mess, and also lose customers in the process. However, with God's wisdom, one of the janitors offered the idea of building the elevator on the outside. As a result, they made the first exterior elevator, which saved a lot of money and trouble.

This teaches us that today, there is a lot of knowledge, but little wisdom. *"But God hath chosen the foolish things of the world to confound the wise; and God hath chosen the weak things of the world to confound the things which are mighty...That no flesh should glory in his presence. But of him are ye in Christ Jesus, who of God is made unto us wisdom, and righteousness, and sanctification, and redemption: That, according as it is written, He that glorieth, let him glory in the Lord"* (1 Corinthians 1:27, 29-31).

The architects and engineers used knowledge, information gained through school, and experience to solve the problem, but their results were not the best. The janitor used good judgment, which produced a better solution. In the present days, our knowledge has increased much faster than our wisdom. Wisdom is not just human knowledge, experience, or intelligence. Wisdom is an invaluable gift from God, the ability to know how to use knowledge to make sound judgments, decisions, and choices that will be helpful, effective, productive, lasting, and valuable. Knowledge can exist without wisdom, but not wisdom without knowledge and understanding. For example, knowledge is knowing how to use a hunting gun, but wisdom knows when to use it and to keep it safe.

When I was in high school, the male students were required to wear a special hat with an emblem of an owl in the front. At that time, I learned that the owl was a symbol of wisdom. Sometimes a person describes another as being "wise as an owl." The owl is a good size bird, but different from others. It has a large head and big wide-open eyes. At night, the owl is able to see much better than in the day. During the day, it hides from its enemies for safety reasons.

We need knowledge, but wisdom is what we most desperately need to solve the everyday challenges we face within ourselves while at home, at work, in conflicts with friends, relatives, or strangers. To solve all these challenges and problems, we need God's wisdom, and a lot of this is taught to us in the book of Proverbs and in the epistle of James. All of us need to continually ask the Lord to give us the gift of wisdom to see at night like the "owl."

We live in a world that produces spiritual darkness. The darkness is so great when we compare it to the *"Light of the world"* who is Jesus Christ. Jesus said, *"That light is come into the world, and men loved darkness rather than light, because their deeds were evil"* (John 3:19). We can see and operate normally in the darkness of this world with eyes wide open only if we have trusted Jesus Christ as our Savior. Then we will be able to say with the blind man who Jesus healed, *"One thing I know, that, whereas I was blind, now I see"* (John 9:25).

"For the LORD giveth wisdom: out of his mouth cometh knowledge and understanding" (Proverbs 2:6).
In this verse, according to King Solomon, wisdom is gained from God. With God's wisdom, we will be able to find success and happiness in life, and we will also be able to help others. If we are believers in Christ, we believe and depend on God's power and God's wisdom and not on human wisdom, which is foolish. *"For the wisdom of this world is foolishness with God"* (1 Corinthians 3:19).

"The fear of the LORD is the beginning of wisdom..."
(Psalm 111:10).
In the Bible, this is the perfect explanation of wisdom. This is why we must know the God of the Bible. We must know the scriptures, love, and fear the Lord. This way, His Spirit will help us to become wise and make good judgments on our Christian journey. Spiritual wisdom is not just about knowing

what is best, but also applying that knowledge into our everyday life. When we do that, this is when we know that we are truly wise.

Today, we need men and women with wisdom and especially within the church. We need men who have a fear of the Lord and knowledge of the Holy Scriptures. We do not need men who have ignorance of the scriptures and present or support false doctrines of the Bible. False teachers are a stumbling block. They damage the body of Christ and confuse both new believers and unbelievers. Instead of bringing people closer to the Lord, they pull them farther and farther from Him. Be careful of false teachers.

"If any of you lack wisdom, let him ask of God, that giveth to all men liberally, and upbraideth not; and it shall be given him" (James 1:5).
We need to ask the Lord to give us the gift of wisdom and trust His guidance to safely hide us in the day like the "owl." When we are saved by the grace of God, we have a spiritual enemy the devil, who continuously *"as a roaring lion, walketh about, seeking whom he may devour "* (1 Peter 5:8). We are not a match with his power or his deceitfulness, and we need a refuge for protection, which is the Lord Jesus Christ. Under the wings of the Lord is the perfect place to hide and find safety and security. *"Under his wings shalt thou trust..."* (Psalm 91:2). And *"Thou art my hiding place; thou shalt preserve me from trouble; thou shalt compass me about with songs of deliverance. Selah"* (Psalm 32:7).

Be Wise! If you are not a Christian, come to the Lord Jesus Christ now, just as you are. Admit you are a sinner. Repent, and by faith, receive Him as your personal Savior. *"Believe on the Lord Jesus Christ, and thou shalt be saved..."* (Acts 16:31). Then, you will have Jesus Christ, a light in the darkness, and a hiding place from danger and judgment for time and eternity.

"Verily, verily, I say unto you, He that heareth my word, and believeth on him that sent me, hath everlasting life, and shall not come into condemnation; but is passed from death unto life" (John 5:24).

❖ ❖ ❖

- "Wisdom is the power to see and the inclination to choose the best and highest goal, together with the surest means of attaining it." —*Theologian, J. I. Packer*

- "Wisdom is the right use of knowledge. To know is not to be wise. Many men know a great deal and are all the greater fools for it. There is no fool so great a fool as a knowing fool. But to know how to use knowledge is to have wisdom." —*Preachers, Charles Spurgeon*

70

DIVINE GUIDANCE

"I will instruct thee and teach thee in the way which thou shalt go: I will guide thee with mine eye."
Psalm 32:8

*"And thine ears shall hear a word behind thee, saying,
This is the way, walk ye in it, when ye turn to the right hand, and when ye turn to the left."*
Isaiah 30:21

*

Never ignore God's divine guidance!

One time, a traveler on foot came to a crossroads. He picked up a small stick and threw it into the air, watching where it landed. He repeated it two more times. A bystander watched and asked what he was doing. The traveler looked at the man and said, "I am throwing a stick to help me decide which way to go." "Why did you throw it three times?" inquired the observer. "I didn't like the directions it gave me the first two times," was the honest reply. This kind of wisdom is foolish. *"Where is the wise? Where is the scribe? Where is the disputer of this age? Has not God made foolish the wisdom of this world?"* (1 Corinthians 1:20). Other people seek guidance by consulting mediums, witches, or other places not allowed by God. (Leviticus 19:31; 20:6; Deuteronomy 18:14). To find God's wisdom and guidance for our lives, we have to go to Him. We have to seek His advice and consultation with all our hearts. *"And ye shall seek me, and find me, when ye shall search for me with all your heart"* (Jeremiah 29:13).

To claim the promise mentioned above, we must have a personal relationship with God through His Son. Jesus said, *"I am the way, the truth, and The life: no man cometh unto the Father, but by me"* (John 14:6). We must become children of God: *"But as many as received him, to them gave he power to become the sons of God, even to them that believe on his name"* (John 1:12). We must trust the Lord: *"Trust in the LORD with all thine heart; and lean not unto thine own understanding. In all thy ways acknowledge him, and he shall direct thy paths"* (Proverbs 3:5–6). We must ask for God's guidance in order to receive: *"Yet ye have not, because ye ask not"* (James 4:2). We must ask for wisdom: *"If any of you lack wisdom, let him ask of God, that giveth to all men liberally, and upbraideth not; and it shall be given him"* (James 1:5). We must have fellowship with the Holy Spirit as born-again Christians to receive help and guidance: *"When he, the Spirit of truth, is come, he will guide you into all truth: for he shall not speak of himself; but whatsoever he shall hear, that shall he speak: and he will shew you things to come"* (John 16:13).

Finally, as children of God, we must surrender to God's will and obey God's guidance. Some people want to know God's will, but afterward, they question God and do not obey and follow His guidance. Because God knows their resistant heart, He does not reveal His plans to them. We must understand that our life is like a prescription pill that contains many different ingredients. If we take the whole pill, it will help us. If we take the ingredients separately, it will damage us or even cause death. Only God knows how to mix the ingredients of the pill for our life. He expects us to follow His guidance. If not, tragedies can follow in our life.

Several years ago, I heard a young man's testimony in our church. He got saved before he was ten years old and was called to serve the Lord as a missionary. He told the Lord that he would go anywhere, but not to Africa. He waited several years for an answer from the Lord, showing him where to go as a missionary, but he never received a response. Finally, the young man gave up and told the Lord that he would be committed to going anywhere the Lord wanted, even to Africa. A short time afterward, the Lord opened the door for him to go as a missionary to Japan. Remember, never bargain with the Lord. He knows what is best for you. Always be open to His leading and obey Him. Finding God's way begins with giving up your will. You can find God's will by listening to His voice and obeying and following His directions!

In August of 2001, tests showed that I had three tumors in my neck and nearby chest area. My surgeon at that time told me in his office, "Even God can't help you." After I lost hope and all confidence in him, I went and talked with the specialist doctor who had recommended him. Before I met with the specialist, I asked the Lord to help me and give me His wisdom and guidance as I faced this serious situation. First, I asked the specialist to recommend someone for a second opinion, so he suggested an excellent surgeon who was a professor of surgery at a well-known university. Second, I asked if there was any other way, besides using only his eyes, for the surgeon to possibly see if there were more tumors in addition to those that were on the CAT SCAN. His answer was not satisfactory. It was almost the same response as my first surgeon when I asked him the same question. I then told him that the day before I had the CAT SCAN in the hospital, they had given me a radioactive pill to help them see the tumors in the pictures. I asked him why not talk to the surgeon and ask him to consider giving me two or more radioactive pills the day before the surgery. I told him I believed that these pills would help the surgeon to see more clearly, not only these tumors but also others if they existed.

My doctor and my second surgeon discussed my suggestion and decided to give me ten radioactive pills the day before my surgery. Because of that, the surgeon found and removed a total of 35 tumors and lymph nodes. Eighteen of them were malignant. Now, everything is history. By God's grace, I am alive, and my doctor and surgeon now use the same surgical procedure to do surgeries to help save the lives of other people.

The Lord's desire is always to give His guidance to those who seek Him with a heart to obey. Trust and obey the Lord to direct your paths. *"He shall direct thy paths"* (Proverbs 3:6). Realize that the Lord is in control of everything. He works behind the scenes to accomplish His will. Nothing happens without divine permission. The questions for you are: "Which way is the stick pointing for you? Is it pointing to your will or God's will?" Remember that it is not wise to ignore the directions God is giving you. He has promised to instruct and counsel you in the journey of life.

I hope you have experienced seeking, receiving, and following divine guidance with a humble heart. You can receive it through the Word of God, through the Holy Spirit, through your prayers, through other believers, through circumstances, and through meeting God's conditions as you follow in faith. When it comes to divine guidance, there is no room for a second opinion!

❖ ❖ ❖

- "An idol is anything you turn to for help when God told you to turn to him for help." — *Pastor and Author, Henry Blackaby*

- "God knew that we could never grasp the whole of His greatness with our finite human minds. It is for this reason that He provided us with a divine Teacher-the Holy Spirit." — *Dr. Charles Stanley*

- "God does not guide those who want to run their own life. He only guides those who admit their need of His direction and rely on His wisdom." — *Author and Speaker, Winkie Pratney*

71

CLEAR CONSCIENCE

"I exercise myself, to have always a conscience void
of offence toward God, and toward men."
Acts 24:16

"Speaking lies in hypocrisy;
having their conscience seared with a hot iron;"
1 Timothy 4:2

∗

Keep your conscience clear before God and man!

Our conscience is part of our soul. It is a wonderful gift from God. It is the inner voice of a man. It is our wise counselor and teacher. It gives us self and moral awareness and the knowledge of right and wrong. The conscience reacts when our thoughts, words, and actions conflict with our moral values. Conscience divides the good from the evil and is the referee in the game of life. The Greek word for conscience is "συνείδησις" (suneidesis) which literally means "knowledge with oneself." The following are three short stories for you to see how a good conscience works in a person's life.

• A farmer drove to town to buy some food supplies. When he got home, he found a $20 bill stuck to the bottom of an item he had purchased. The man went to sleep, believing that he was indeed lucky, but all night long, the farmer tossed and turned. Two voices kept shouting within him. One voice said, "Keep it!" while the other said, "Return it!" The next day, he decided to return the money. The grateful store clerk thanked him and asked what made him bring the money back. The old farmer sighed, "Two voices shouted inside me all night. I could not sleep. Now they are quiet, and I will sleep again."

- A man took his young son with him to help steal corn from his neighbor's field. Before pilfering the corn, the man looked to his right and then his left. Not seeing anyone, he started to fill his bag. Suddenly, his son yelled, "Daddy, there is one way you have not looked yet!" Panicking, the man looked quickly around himself again. "No, Dad," called the boy. "You have not looked up!" The conscience-stricken man took his son by the hand and returned home without any of the corn.

- The Internal Revenue Service received a letter from a man who was struggling with the fact that he had cheated the government. His letter read: "Dear Sirs: I underpaid my tax bill for last year. I cannot sleep at night, and my conscience is bothering me. Enclosed is a check for $600. P.S. If I still cannot sleep, I'll send the rest!"

Each of the previous stories teach us something important about a conscience. The Bible says, *"If any man be in Christ, he is a new creature"* (2 Corinthians 5:17). This does not mean that when a person becomes a born-again Christian and becomes a new creation that his body, hair color, or his voice changes. It means his mind, heart, will, and conscience work differently. The apostle Paul says in Acts 24:16 that he strives always to keep his conscience clear before God and man.

Our conscience gives us the ability to know what is right and what is wrong. It works like a fire detector. It keeps quiet when there is no danger of fire detected. It makes a noise when it needs to warn us when there is a danger of fire. When our conscience is on the right track, we are at peace. The Bible says, *"Let the peace of Christ rule in your hearts..."* (Colossians 3:15). This is the way our conscience is supposed to work, but it does not always work that way. Like any other part of our soul, the conscience can become dysfunctional. Just as a fire detector can malfunction and make noise when it should be quiet, it can also be silent when it should make a noise. At other times, it stops working when the batteries are dead. The same thing happens to our conscience when it is corrupted because of our sin.

"Unto the pure all things are pure: but unto them that are defiled and unbelieving is nothing pure; but even their mind and conscience is defiled" Titus 1:15). This is an example of a corrupted conscience. Picture a very good teenage boy that becomes involved with bad boys who influence him to become addicted to drugs. His conscience loses power, is weakened, and becomes less sensitive to do the right thing. His conscience is really distorted and becomes seared over time." *Speaking lies in hypocrisy; having their conscience seared with a hot iron"* (1 Timothy 4:2).

This story is an example of a seared conscience. In ancient times, doctors usually used a hot iron on the flesh as an anesthetic or to stop the bleeding. Sometimes, the bleeding stopped, or the patient recovered from the pain. However, the patient discovered later that he had lost all the feeling in that area of the skin because all the nerves had been killed. A person who does evil things and stops feeling guilty for them most likely has a seared conscience. This is precisely what Paul talks about when he says, *"having their conscience seared with a hot iron."* In this case, the conscience has lost all sensitivity: *"Who being past feeling have given themselves over unto lasciviousness, to work all uncleanness with greediness"* (Ephesians 4:19).

Some people say, *"Follow your own conscience."* Somebody said, that *"The trouble with the advice, 'Follow your conscience' is that most people follow it like someone following a wheelbarrow—they direct it wherever they want it to go, and then follow behind"* (Source unknown). This means the conscience is set by wrong values. Therefore, it approves the wrong things because the conscience is never the final judge of right and wrong. Paul *says, "For I know nothing by myself; yet am I not hereby justified: but he that judgeth me is the Lord"* (1 Corinthians 4:4).

After all, the question is: "Is it possible for us to get and keep a clear conscience?" The apostle Paul in Acts 24:16 says that he strives always to keep his conscience clear before God and man. How can we do that if our conscience has become corrupt, seared, and insensitive, just as burnt skin or like a fire detector without batteries? The answer is that the conscience can become sensitive and functional again through the power of the Holy Spirit: *"When he is come, he will reprove the world of sin, and of righteousness, and of judgment"* (John 16:8). Jesus is speaking about the Holy Spirit. When the Holy Spirit arrives into our life, it is like the fire detector getting new batteries and starting to work again.

The Holy Spirit convicts of guilt regarding sin, righteousness, and judgment. This means if you want to know more about your sin and you are looking for more of God's mercy to walk with God, you must say like King David: *"Search me, O God, and know my heart: try me, and know my thoughts: And see if there be any wicked way in me, and lead me in the way everlasting"* (Psalm 139:23-24). A good conscience is also well-established by the Word of God and cleansed by the precious blood of Jesus Christ. *"The blood of Christ, who through the eternal Spirit offered himself without spot to God, purge your conscience from dead works to serve the living God?"* (Hebrews 9:14). I hope and pray all of us will follow the apostle Paul's testimony to strive always to keep our conscience clear before God and man.

When I was a new Christian, I was once led by the Holy Spirit to give a gospel tract to the manager of the gas station where I bought gas for my car. Because of my hesitation, I did not give it to him. When I drove home, I did not have peace in my heart. My conscience was not clear. The Holy Spirit continued to convict me for my disobedient attitude. I knew that night I would not be able to have a good night's sleep. For this reason, I drove back to the gas station and gave the tract to the manager. I explained to him exactly what happened, and he promised me that he would read the tract. The title of the tract was, *"Am I going to Heaven?"* That was a good lesson for me. I should not resist the conviction of the Holy Spirit anymore. Instead, I should try to do what is needed to have a clear conscience. *"There is no peace, saith my God, to the wicked"* (Isaiah 57:21). There is no substitute for a clear conscience!

❖ ❖ ❖

- Conscience tells us that we ought to do right, but it does not tell us what right is – that we are taught by God's word.
— *Clergyman and Author, Henry Trumbull*

- "A good conscience is powered by the Holy Spirit, set by the Word of God and cleansed by the blood of Jesus Christ."
—*Pastor and Author, Colin Smith*

- "The one thing that keeps the conscience sensitive to Him is the habit of being open to God on the inside."
— *Evangelist and Teacher, Oswald Chambers*

- Cowardice asks, "Is it safe?"
- Experience asks, "Is it proven?"
- Pride asks, "Is it popular?"
- Greed asks, "Is it profitable?"
- Doubt asks, "Is it practical?"
- But conscience asks, "Is it right?"
— *Pastor, Emery Hovarth*

- "The torture of a bad conscience is the hell of a living soul."
— *Pastor and Theologian, John Calvin*

- "It is better to have a sore than a seared conscience."
— *Puritan Preacher and Author, Thomas Brooks*

- "There's no pillow as soft as a clear conscience." — *French Proverb*

72

TRUE HUMILITY

"By humility and the fear of the LORD are riches,
and honour, and life."
Proverbs 22:4

"God resisteth the proud, but giveth grace unto the humble."
James 4:6)

*

The power of humility invites God's grace!

D o you ever wonder what humility is? Thinking negatively or lowly about yourself is not true humility. True humility is thinking truthfully and accurately of yourself. True humility is when you agree with what God says about you. *C.S. Lewis* said, *"Humility is not thinking less of yourself but thinking of yourself less."*

The Bible describes humility as lowliness, meekness, humbleness, lack of pride, lack of vanity, and absence of self. The Greek word for humility is "ταπεινοφροσύνη" (tapeinophrosune), which comes from two words. The first word is "ταπεινός" (tapeinos), which means inner lowliness. This illustrates the person who depends on the Lord rather than self. The second word is "φροσύνη" (phrosune). This means right-mindedness, sound judgment, common sense, practical understanding, wisdom, prudence, and intelligence. "Ταπεινοφροσύνη" (tapeinophrosune) is translated "humility" in Colossians 3:12: *"Put on therefore, as the elect of God, holy and beloved, bowels of mercies, kindness, humbleness of mind, meekness, longsuffering:"* In this verse, and in others, it translates to "lowliness of mind." This clearly means that humility is a heart attitude, and it is not an outward attitude or appearance. For example, someone might show outward humility but still continues to have a heart full of pride and self-admiration.

Humility is the opposite of pride. Pride is like the foot that presses the gas pedal to get us as far from God as possible. Humility develops in us a capacity for the closest possible intimacy with God. Pride makes us fake and phony, but humility makes us real. Pride is power out of control. Humility is power under control. Humility is the root of every virtue. If we have pride, we exalt ourselves and place ourselves in resistance to God. God opposes the proud and gives grace to the humble: *"All of you be subject one to another, and be clothed with humility: for God resisteth the proud, and giveth grace to the humble"* (1 Peter 5:5). God hates pride because it exalts ourselves and not His mighty name. As a result, we miss his grace and all the spiritual blessings He promises.

When we have humility, we depend on God. When we accept God's plans instead of ours, we will be leaving our pride behind. When we humble ourselves, God gives us more grace and exalts us: *"For whosoever exalteth himself shall be abased; and he that humbleth himself shall be exalted"* (Luke 14:11). You might have known this verse as a small child. You might have even memorized it. However, have you ever experienced it in your own life? I hope and pray that you have.

Jonathan Edwards said, *"We must view humility as one of the most essential things that characterize true Christianity"* We must reject pride and seek to humble ourselves. With our dependence on the Holy Spirit, humility will grow in our souls. When we are growing in humility, Christ is increasing, and we are decreasing. *"I am crucified with Christ: nevertheless I live; yet not I, but Christ liveth in me: and the life which I now live in the flesh I live by the faith of the Son of God, who loved me, and gave himself for me"* (Galatians 2:20). This is true humility. If we have it, people will notice it..

Jesus made it crystal clear that the kingdom of heaven is for those who are *"poor in spirit."* These are the ones who admit a total bankruptcy of spiritual value. In other words, humility is an essential requirement for the Christian. When we come to Christ for salvation as sinners, we must come in humility and with a broken heart. We admit and acknowledge that we are not worthy and cannot offer anything to Him. We also recognize that we cannot save ourselves. When God offers us grace and mercy, we must accept them with humble gratitude and commit our lives to Him. In doing so, we become a new creature in Christ *"Therefore if any man be in Christ, he is a new creature: old things are passed away; behold, all things are become new"* (2 Corinthians 5:17).

Jesus is the greatest example of humility in history. He came to serve and not to be served: *"The Son of man came not to be ministered unto, but to minister, and to give his life a ransom for many"* (Matthew 20:28). Therefore, we must serve others with humility as Jesus did: *"Let nothing be done through strife or vainglory; but in lowliness of mind let each esteem other better than themselves"*

(Philippians 2:3). Jesus was humble as a servant, even unto death on the cross. *"And being found in fashion as a man, he humbled himself, and became obedient unto death, even the death of the cross"* (Philippians 2:8). Christ's humility showed how He was always obedient to the Father. This is precisely what each humble Christian must do. True humility must be our best friend. It increases our hunger and thirst for God's word and opens our hearts to His Spirit

Along with Jesus, good examples of genuine humility are John the Baptist, who was the forerunner of the Messiah and the apostle Peter who laid down his desires and selfishness for Christ. The apostle Paul must also be our example of humility. He called himself the *"least of the apostles...because I persecuted the church of God"* *(1* Corinthians 15:9), as well as the *"chief of sinners."* According to 1 Timothy 1:15, *"Christ Jesus came into the world to save sinners; of whom I am chief."*

If you are not saved, you must know that without humbling yourself as a little child in the sight of the Lord, you will never enter into the kingdom of God. *"Humble yourselves in the sight of the Lord, and he shall lift you up"* (James 4:10). The decision is exclusively yours to make. Will you live for your glory and continue your course and invite God's opposition, or will you humble yourself and live for the glory of God? If you are wise, it is not much of a decision, after all. Therefore, take a good look at your priorities and ask God to reveal any areas driven by pride.

Christian, remember that humility is like a powerful dynamic magnet that draws God's grace. The power of humility invites God's grace. True humility is total obedience and dependence on Almighty God. Let us remember what the apostle Paul said: *"Let nothing be done through strife or vainglory; but in lowliness of mind let each esteem other better than themselves. Look not every man on his own things, but every man also on the things of others. Let this mind be in you, which was also in Christ Jesus"* (Philippians 2:3-5).

❖ ❖ ❖

- "The fear of the LORD is the instruction of wisdom; and before honour is humility." — *Proverbs 15:33*

- "Humble yourselves therefore under the mighty hand of God, that he may exalt you in due time." — *1 Peter 5:6*

- "Humility is the root, mother, nurse, foundation, and bond of all virtue," — *Early Church Father, John Chrysostom*

73

NO COMPROMISE

"How long halt ye between two opinions?
if the LORD be God, follow him: but if Baal, then follow him.
And the people answered him not a word."
1 Kings 18:21

"No man can serve two masters:
for either he will hate the one, and love the other;
or else he will hold to the one, and despise the other.
Ye cannot serve God and mammon."
Matthew 6:24

*

Christians must not compromise on issues of faith!

Jesus teaches us to follow and obey the principles of the Kingdom of God. We have to live with convictions and not compromise God's principles. As believers in Christ, we must accept God's Word as absolute and inerrant. *"All scripture is given by inspiration of God, and is profitable for doctrine, for reproof, for correction, for instruction in righteousness"* (2 Timothy 3:16).

We must fully obey His Word. *"If ye love me, keep my commandments"* (John 14:15). We must acknowledge that His Word must not be compromised by anyone or for any reason. I am talking about compromise when it comes to issues of faith. *"According to the sentence of the law which they shall teach thee, and according to the judgment which they shall tell thee, thou shalt do: thou shalt not decline from the sentence which they shall shew thee, to the right hand, nor to the left"* (Deuteronomy 17:11). The Word of God warns us:

"For the time will come when they will not endure sound doctrine; but after their own lusts shall they heap to themselves teachers, having itching ears; And they shall turn away their ears from the truth, and shall be turned unto fables" (2 Timothy 4:3,4).

Compromise is not always bad. For example, my wife wants to paint our living room white, but I want to paint it off-white. If I compromise to paint it white, it will not be the end of the world. It will also not break any of my principles of faith. Since the beginning of the world, we have a history filled with inspiring stories featuring people of principle. These individuals were blessed because they refused to compromise on their beliefs. Here are a few examples:

When **Joseph** was in Potiphar's house, Potiphar's wife offered a sexual opportunity to him. Joseph immediately fled from the tempting offer to avoid sin. Joseph's wisdom considered the future consequences of his choices. Joseph understood that by satisfying his flesh, he would not please God whom he loved so much.

Shadrach, Meshach, and **Abednego** were Jews of the Babylon province who did not worship the golden image provided by King Nebuchadnezzar because of their faith in the living God. As a result of that, they were cast into the burning fiery furnace, but their God delivered them from it.

The prophet Daniel did not obey the King's orders and was cast into the den of lions because of his faith. However, Daniel, being a servant of the living God, was delivered from the lions. Daniel was a man without compromise.

The early 1st century Christians often offered themselves to be fed to the lions or burned at the stake in front of the Roman Emperor rather than worship him and denying their Lord Jesus Christ.

Christians around the world today still suffer in prisons because they will not compromise their faith. For example, Christians in "shipping container" prisons in Eritrea would be released if they would only sign a document to denounce their commitment to Jesus Christ. However, they prefer to suffer for the cause of Christ than deny Him.

Laura Fotusky, a town clerk in Barker New York, resigned from her position to avoid being forced to sign marriage licenses for same-sex couples. She wrote: "The Bible clearly teaches that God created marriage between male and female as a divine gift that preserves families and cultures. Since I love and follow Him, I cannot put my signature on

THE JOURNEY AND DESTINY OF A CHRISTIAN

something that is against God." She also wrote: "I would be compromising my moral conscience by participating in licensing same-sex couples. I had to choose between my job and my God."
— *religioustolerance.org, July 2011*

The actress Stephanie Stephenson had her big chance at stardom but turned it down. She landed a leading role in the touring cast of the musical, "Les Miserables." She ended up quitting rather than playing a role that compromised her Christian values. Her role would have required her to dress like a prostitute and let male actors inappropriately touch her. "There's a fine line between the morals and going over that line, and I didn't want to go over that line," stated the actress

In the United States, 78% of people claim that they are "born-again" Christians. This means that from a population of 325 million people, 253 million are Christians. From all these millions of people, only 23% or 58 million, go to church every Sunday. The remaining 77% or 194 million, do not go to church at all and do not practice their Christian beliefs. These people compromise on their beliefs by voting for ungodly government, state, and local legislators who govern them and then support their evil actions. God help us!

"When I was a boy, my father, a baker, introduced me to the wonders of song," tenor **Luciano Pavarotti** relates. "He urged me to work very hard to develop my voice. Arrigo Pola, a professional tenor in my hometown of Modena, Italy, took me as a pupil. I also enrolled in a teachers college. On graduating, I asked my father, 'Shall I be a teacher or a singer?' "'Luciano,' my father replied, 'if you try to sit on two chairs, you will fall between them. For life, you must choose one chair.' "I chose one..." —*Guideposts / Sermon Illustrtions.com*

I wish all Christians were like the men and women I mentioned above. They stood firm in their beliefs and did not compromise. Instead, they glorified their Lord and Savior. We need Christians to stand for what is right. Our country and the world today are in a mess. It is not only because of ungodly individuals and many politicians, but because of "Christian compromise." The gospel of Christ is mocked just like 2 Peter 2:2 says: *"And many shall follow their pernicious ways; by reason of whom the way of truth shall be evil spoken of."*

The blame for all the evils we see today does not belong only to the White House and the State House. It sits squarely at the church house and specifically in the pulpits of some church houses. In these church houses, lies and deceptions have been spread for different reasons, which destroy our homes and our nation. They have spread false teachings, such as being able to live in sin day and night and still go to heaven. This is "easy believism." They falsely believe that this way, they will get into the kingdom of God! *"But though we, or an angel from heaven, preach any other gospel unto you than that which we have preached unto you, let him be accursed"* (Galatians 1:8)

Because of false doctrine taught by many "experts" in our society, we now have more immorality, murders, violence, and drugs than ever before. In public schools, the new generation has been brainwashed with all kinds of humanistic teachings and ideas. We see our society collapse day by day. There is less and less righteous leadership in many churches in America today and around the world. Because of the so-called "Christian compromise," we see evil spreading every day all around us. Like it or not, any Christian who lives contrary to the truth of God's word is not truly a Christian. Very sadly, our nation, our society, our homes, and our children's lives have been destroyed by Christian compromise. The destruction of the nation, churches, and our children sit totally and entirely on the shoulders of "compromising" parents and church leaders (Hosea 4:6-7, Jeremiah 2:8, 10:21, 12:10).

The majority of Christians have never caught a glimpse of the face of God. For this reason, they fear man more than they fear God. Christians have the power to turn everything around for good. They can do so if they would just not allow the devil and their own interests to deceive them. The powers of darkness put them to sleep with apathy. This is the most deceptive technique of the devil. They are not involved in fulfilling their own responsibilities as Christians to glorify the Lord!

"Christian compromise" became the cancer of Neo-Evangelicalism. What the Lord said to the church of Laodicea holds true today:

"I know thy works, that thou art neither cold nor hot: I would thou wert cold or hot. So then because thou art lukewarm, and neither cold nor hot, I will spue thee out of my mouth" (Revelation 3:15-16)

Is evil getting the best of you? Are you tempted to compromise your faith or morals? Do not give in. Do what is right. Tell all the world that you are a Christian and take Jesus with you everywhere. God calls His children to walk the highway of holiness. Tough choices may be required when you "walk the talk," but you will never regret doing what is right. Do not let injustice and immorality bully you into surrender. Although you are one person, the Lord can use your courage to make needed changes in our world. Sit tight in God's power and let Satan take a back seat in your life's car.

Finally, are you sitting on two chairs? Do not waver between the Lord's will and yours. When it comes to issues of faith, you are expected to stand for Christ and His kingdom and never compromise on God's principles! Your love for Christ should be so strong that you would rather die than sin against Him. Maybe this is not very popular today, but you will never win by compromising. Choose God's kingdom and do what He tells you to do. Why settle for sitting on anything less than a throne?

❖ ❖ ❖

- "Compromise is but the sacrifice of one right or good in the hope of retaining another – too often ending in the loss of both."
— *Theologian, Tryon Edwards*

- "One of the truest tests of integrity is its blunt refusal to be compromised."
— *Writer and Teacher, Chinua Achebe*

- "No compromise with the main purpose; no peace till victory; no pact with unrepentant wrong."
— *Prime Minister, Winston Churchill*

- The English preacher, *John Bunyan*, was jailed because he preached. Later a judge promised Bunyan immediate release if he only promised not to preach again. His answer was: *"If you release me today, I shall preach tomorrow!"*

- The great English preacher *John Wesley* once said, "Give me a hundred men who fear nothing but sin and desire nothing but God...Such men alone will shake the gates of hell and set up the kingdom of heaven on earth."

- "It is a great deal easier to do that which God gives us to do, no matter how hard it is than to face the responsibility of not doing it."
—*Author and Editor, J. R. Miller*

74

DO NOT LIE

"A righteous man hateth lying:
but a wicked man is loathsome, and cometh to shame."
Proverbs 13:5

"A false witness shall not be unpunished,
and he that speaketh lies shall perish."
Proverbs 19:9

*

Do not lie, but be truthful in all you say and do!

A little girl came very early one morning to her mother, saying: "Which is worse, Mamma, to tell a lie or to steal?" The mother replied that both were so sinful she could not tell which was the worse. "Well, Mamma," replied the little one, "I've been thinking a good deal about it, and I think it is ever so much worse to lie than to steal." "Why my child?" asked the mother. "Well, you see, Mamma, it's like this," said the little girl. "If you steal a thing you can take it back 'less you've eaten it; and if you've eaten it, you can pay for it. But" -- and there was a look of awe in her face -- "a lie is forever." — *sermoncentral.com*

Even though the little girl had a point for her logical debate with her mom, biblically, to lie and steal are sinful actions. They both displease God. One of God's Ten Commandments given to Moses was the following: *"Thou shalt not bear false witness against thy neighbour"* (Exodus 20:16). The first sin committed in this world involved a lie told to Eve by the devil. He is the Father of lies. In the early church, Ananias and Sapphira lied regarding a donation. The apostle Peter rebuked him: *"Ananias, why hath Satan filled thine heart to lie to the Holy Ghost, and to keep back part of the price of the land?"* (Acts 5:3). God's judgment came on them. The couple died because of their sin of lying.

The apostle Paul in the New Testament tells us not to lie one to another. *"Lie not one to another, seeing that ye have put off the old man with his deeds"* (Colossians 3:9). The Bible also says that liars are ungodly and will be judged in the end. *"But the fearful, and unbelieving, and the abominable, and murderers, and whoremongers, and sorcerers, and idolaters, and all liars, shall have their part in the lake which burneth with fire and brimstone: which is the second death"* (Revelation 21:8). As Christians, we have to tell the truth and not lie because the source of truth is God who cannot lie. The Bible says, *"In hope of eternal life, which God, that cannot lie, promised before the world began"* (Titus 1:2). The Bible also says, *"it was impossible for God to lie..."* (Hebrews 6:18).

People think that if they say a few white lies, it is harmless, but not so. *"We found that the participants could purposefully and dramatically reduce their everyday lies and that in turn was associated with significantly improved health,"* said Anita Kelly, study author and professor of psychology at the University of Notre Dame, in a statement. Kelly presented her findings at the annual meeting of the American Psychological Association in Orlando. *"I think lying can cause a lot of stress for people, contributing to anxiety and even depression,"* Dr. Bryan Bruno, acting chairman of the department of psychiatry at Lenox Hill Hospital in New York City, told Health Day. *"Lying less is not only good for your relationships but for yourself as an individual. People might recognize the more devastating impact lying can have on relationships, but probably do not recognize the extent to which it can cause a lot of internal stress."* — *healthland.time.com, Aug. 06, 2012*

Studies one after the other show that a person who does not lie improves his health and his relationships. The person who lies will pay the price not only on judgment day but in this life, too. The following stories teach us precisely this:

- A shepherd-boy, who watched a flock of sheep near a village, brought out the villagers three or four times by crying out, "Wolf! Wolf!" and when his neighbors came to help him, laughed at them for their pains. The Wolf, however, did truly come at last. The Shepherd-boy, now really alarmed, shouted in an agony of terror: "Pray, do come and help me; the Wolf is killing the sheep;" but no one paid any heed to his cries, nor rendered any assistance. The Wolf, having no cause of fear, at his leisure lacerated or destroyed the whole flock. There is no believing a liar, even when he speaks the truth. — *Aesop's Fables: The Shepherd Boy and the Wolf*

- A USA Today poll found that only 56% of Americans teach honesty to their children. And a Louis Harris poll turned up the distressing fact that 65% of high school students would cheat on an important exam.

"Recently a noted physician appeared on a network news-and-talk show and proclaimed, 'Lying is an important part of social life, and children who are unable to do it, are children who may have developmental problems.'" — *Our Daily Bread, September 23, 1991*

- The book *"The Day America Told the Truth"* says that 91 percent of those surveyed lie routinely about matters they consider trivial, and 36 percent lie about important matters; 86 percent lie regularly to parents, 75 percent to friends, 73 percent to siblings, and 69 percent to spouses. — *pastorhistorian.com*

- Stuart Briscoe tells of being hired by a bank. He was young, new, and just learning the business. One day his boss told him, "If Mr. _____ calls for me, tell him I'm out." Briscoe replied, "Oh, are you planning to go somewhere?" "No, I just don't want to speak to him, so tell him I'm out." "Let me make sure I understand--Do you want me to lie for you?" The boss blew up at him. He was outraged, angered. Stuart prayed, and God gave him a flash of insight. "You should be happy, because if I won't lie for you, isn't it safe to assume that I won't lie to you?" — *Moody Bible Institute Founder's week, 1986*

Are you the prisoner of a lie, or are you tempted to lie? Stretching the truth will not make it last any longer. Distorting the truth for your own sake will only force you to lie more often in the future. A lie has no legs. It requires other lies to support it. Do not give in to the lie, and thinking that telling the truth does not matter. Our society might not put a premium on integrity, but God does. Try hard to be truthful in all you say and do. Make a break for freedom and come clean with the truth. If you only tell a lie once, all your truths after that become questionable.

I have to admit that when Christians and other people lie to me, I have a hard time believing them again. I also lose my respect for them. Do not be like most of the politicians who lie to us every day. Be an honest person if you want to have a clear conscience and win the trust of others. Any lie is an abomination to the LORD and will be judged:

- *"Lying lips are abomination to the LORD: but they that deal truly are his delight"* (Proverbs 12:22).

- *"But ... all liars, shall have their part in the lake which burneth with fire and brimstone: which is the second death"* (Revelation 21:8).

- *"My son, forget not my law; but let thine heart keep my commandments:... It shall be health to thy navel, and marrow to thy bones"* (Proverbs 3:1,8).

Every lie is a sin and "is forever" as the little girl said to her mom. Be wise and not a fool. Stay away from lying for better relationships. It also helps with mental and physical health. At the same time, you will escape God's judgment. Never forget that in this day of spin and media image, honest people are the real heroes!

❖ ❖ ❖

- "All the trouble in the world began with one lie."
— *Unknown Author*

- "Speaking lies in hypocrisy; having their conscience seared with a hot iron." — *1 Timothy 4:2*

- "When regard for truth has been broken down or even slightly weakened, all things will remain doubtful."
— *Theologian and Philosopher, Augustine*

- "I would not tell one lie to save the souls of all the world."
— *Pastor, Theologian and Author, John Wesley*

- "He who tells little lies will soon think nothing of great ones, for the principle is the same."
— *"Prince of Preachers," C.H. Spurgeon*

- "Exaggeration" is actually a proud, unbroken word for "lying."
— *Christian Radio Host and Author, Nancy Leigh DeMoss*

- "No man has a good enough memory to make a successful liar."
—*President, Abraham Lincoln*

- "Those who think it's permissible to tell white lies soon become color-blind."
— *MD and University Professor, Austin O'Malley*

75

MAKE NO EXCUSES

"And he said unto another, Follow me. But he said, Lord,
suffer me first to go and bury my father. Jesus said unto him,
Let the dead bury their dead: but go thou and preach the kingdom
of God. And another also said, Lord, I will follow thee; but let me
first go bid them farewell, which are at home at my house. And
Jesus said unto him, No man, having put his hand to the plough,
and looking back, is fit for the kingdom of God."
Luke 9:59-62

*

Do not let your excuses keep you from answering God's call!

We have to realize that when God gives us directions, He expects cooperation and not excuses. Excuses are as old as the first human couple in the Garden of Eden. We know from the Bible that the first sin ever committed, came with excuses: *"And the man said, The woman whom thou gavest to be with me, she gave me of the tree, and I did eat...and the woman said, The serpent beguiled me, and I did eat"* (Genesis 3:11-13). We also know that the Bible mentions numerous cases where the Lord blessed the people who answered and obeyed His call while others lost His blessings because of their rejection. If we are wise for our benefit, it is better to respond to God's invitation and not make excuses to avoid it..

● A radio news series about honesty in America talked about excuses. The commentator said that people use three types of excuses when guilty of wrongdoing.

The first is outright denial–a rejection of any involvement. Sometimes, this is done even though the person is obviously guilty.

The second is the "It's not my fault" excuse. The person looks around for someone he can blame. (Often it is a loved one - a husband or wife or parent. Sometimes, it's the boss.)

The third form of excuse is the "I did it, but...." approach. In this instance, the person blames circumstances for his shortcoming. Either he's been struggling with some illness or the assignment wasn't clear, or the car's been giving him trouble." — *Source Unknown*

All of us know that these three types of excuses are real. They happen to all of us when we deal with people. Usually, all excuses have one thing in common: they enable us to avoid facing the truth.

- I had a married neighbor lady. She suffered from depression. Several times she said to me, *"I wish I could have what you have."* I challenged her to get what I had by trusting the Lord by faith as her personal Savior. Yet, she always gave me different excuses. She once wanted to commit suicide, but first came to talk to me. She told me God led her to speak with me about it. I was more than happy to help her. I prayed with her and asked the Lord to help her to stay away from this terrible decision, and He did. I then asked her again to accept the Lord as her personal Savior. However, she declined again with more of her excuses. With her excuses, she missed the gift of eternal life and a Christ-centered life in this world.

- Even though I was a born-again Christian serving in many Christian ministries, I still made mistakes. One mistake was my desire to make a lot of money. I hoped to help in God's work and to give to missions. At first, that sounds like a reasonable desire or excuse to work hard and make a lot of money, but that was not God's will for me. I started two businesses with the hopes of becoming successful and making a lot of money. However, He never gave me more than what I needed. I was disappointed. I felt deep in my heart that something was missing. When I looked for answers, the Lord revealed to me that He did not want my money. He wanted me. The Lord has all the money in the world, but He wanted all of me - my body, soul, and spirit. He wanted me to serve Him by using my education, abilities, talents, and life experiences. When I realized His will for me, I surrendered to Him. My spiritual life and His work through me were richly blessed.

Non-believers, even Christians, frequently do not respond when the Lord calls them to do the right thing and follow His will. What about you? Are you putting off responding to the Lord? Do not allow your excuses keep you from answering God's call. Do not fool yourself. The Lord wants obedience. He does not want defenses and justifications. Jesus does not accept excuses. He hates excuses. Make today the day you stop making excuses. When you follow God's call, He will be with you, and His hand will be upon you. The Lord told Moses: *"Certainly I will be with thee..."* (Exodus

3:12). God's blessings always follow you when you obey the Lord. Otherwise, you will lose them.

It is better to be solving problems in God's work than to make excuses and lose the job God has for you. Think about Moses and the apostle Paul. What if Moses and Paul had not gone God's way? What if they had refused in the end to follow? They would have lost the joy that came from living God's way, but they did not refuse. Instead, they were used by God in unbelievable and miraculous ways.

Christian, do you realize that the same choice is before you? Are you making excuses, so you do not have to obey, do what God wants, or go where He wants? Are you making excuses why you do not trust Him to direct your life? Excuses only keep you from becoming better and more blessed. Be honest with yourself and make some adjustments. Decide to be a learner this year and not a whiner. Do not just work for God. Work with God.

If you are not a Christian, what excuse do you have for not making a decision to trust Jesus Christ? Do not be like the people the Bible mentions in Luke 14:15-20 who did not attend the banquet and gave different excuses. In other words, they rejected the invitation. *"And they all with one consent began to make excuse"* (Luke 14:18). If you want to be substantially used of God, you must first accept Jesus' invitation without excuses. *"Come unto me, all ye that labour and are heavy laden, and I will give you rest"* (Matthew 11:28). Second, after you receive forgiveness of your sins and the gift of eternal life, be willing to follow wherever He leads you.

It is wise and time to stop hiding behind the excuses that you are so good at creating. Excuses are worse than lies. They come from fear, laziness, lack of faith, and disobedience. If you have a problem with excuses, I suggest you stop avoiding and rejecting Jesus and start following Him with all your heart. It is time to stop saying, "I cannot" and start saying, "He can." It is time to stop arguing about faith and start practicing it in your life. Step out of the boat. You will discover the thrill of walking on the waves as Peter did (Matthew 14:29).

❖ ❖ ❖

- "The blood of Jesus was not shed to remove excuses."
— *Author, Corrie ten Boom*

- "An excuse is worse than a lie, for an excuse is a lie, guarded."
— *Poet, Alexander Pope*

- An EXCUSE is something said to hide the real reason for wrong actions. It is an attempt to cover up a shortcoming or sin."— *Pastor, Rodelio Mallari*

76

BE NOT DECEIVED

"He [The devil] was a murderer from the beginning,
and abode not in the truth, because there is no truth in him.
When he speaketh a lie, he speaketh of his own:
for he is a liar, and the father of it."
John 8:44

"Let no man deceive you with vain words:
for because of these things cometh the wrath of God
upon the children of disobedience."
Ephesians 5:6

*

There is always a price to pay when we are deceived!

Today, all the world is experiencing confusion and difficulties financially and spiritually because of the corruption and immorality of people and political leaders. We know that our government has put America in unimaginable financial debt. Our country spends money we do not have and borrows money with high-interest rates. They put the responsibility to pay for these debts on future generations. Our government has created this, and nobody has the courage to step up and fix it.

When some decent politicians try to fix the problems, they find resistance from others who usually work to protect their own interests while having a good time at the expense of the tax payers. My parents taught me while growing up, that I should spend less than what I had and not a penny more. For many today, this is an old-fashioned mentality. Because we do not operate with this mentality, there are spending problems everywhere with countries, families, and individuals. I do not have a debt problem because my old-fashioned mentality works. This mentality is the only right and safe way to live. The financial problems America has today are nothing compared to the spiritual and moral issues she faces.

Numerous extremist teachers in public schools have brainwashed the new generation, and most parents do not discipline their children as they should. You do not hear much any more about individual and personal responsibility or hard work. The new generation likes the socialist idea of getting paid more, working less, or not working at all. Instead, they want to depend on the government to support them. Young people are growing up without respect for adults and without honoring their parents. Video games and movies of today are full of violence and sexuality. These have changed the mentality of many Americans, especially young people, because they do not practice moral principles. Every day we see morality diminish on television programs and immorality, senseless violence, and bad extremist behavior increase. All these are a part of the moral wrongdoing that has infected our whole nation. Political correctness is widespread in every aspect of our lives.

Christians are a part of this problem. It is estimated that 75% of the population in America claim to be born-again Christians. They have the power to elect good people to govern them. Instead, they choose to protect their interests. They wish to live without standards and biblical convictions. A few years ago, a popular American TV show asked every pastor and priest to inform their congregations about what happens to persecuted Christians. The show told them to make calls and try to persuade the President and the White House to help stop the persecution of Christians around the world, especially by the radical extremists. The tragedy was that not many pastors and priests responded because they did not want to become involved. Perhaps, if one of these pastors or priests were personally threatened, they would have wished they would have gotten involved.

Our country has become desensitized about violence and the evil things of the world today. It is no longer surprising when you hear a story about somebody committing mass murder. This happens because people worship the creature rather than the Creator. Today's society has taken the Bible and prayer out of public schools and public places and does not protect the sanctity of life. People fool themselves and pay the price. *"Be not deceived; God is not mocked: for whatsoever a man soweth, that shall he also reap" (Galatians 6:7)*. Many people today do not obey God's commandments and believe God's promises. America and the rest of the world are in turmoil because they compromise biblical principles and ignore the God of the Bible.

I once saw a beautiful picture of a frog, but after paying more attention to it, I saw it was actually the head of a horse. This is called an illusion. We see illusions in many places today. It is difficult to know the difference between what is real and what is not. The master illusionist who deceives millions of people every day is the devil, who the Bible calls *"a liar, and the father of it" (John 8:44).* A few of the devil's illusions are: "Do not waste your time to read the Bible; Do not worry there is no hell; Everyone will go to heaven; You can earn heaven with your good works; all the preachers preach the Bible, and all the churches and religions are the same."

According to the Bible, these are all not true. Deception is to make someone believe something that is not true. This is precisely what the devil does day and night. He turns the truth into lies. Jesus is the truth. He loves you and desires you to come to Him to find it: *"I am the way, the truth, and the life: no man cometh unto the Father, but by me"* (John 14:6). Only Jesus can make you free from the bondage of sin and the power of the devil. The Bible says, *"Turn them from darkness to light, and from the power of Satan unto God, that they may receive forgiveness of sins..."* (Acts 26:18). Now is the right time. Turn to God. Put your faith entirely in someone you can trust. Only Jesus Christ can save you and keep you. Only Jesus can deliver you from the devil's illusions to enjoy freedom.

❖ ❖ ❖

- "Satan himself is transformed into an angel of light."
— *2 Corinthians 11:14*

- "Satan promises the best, but pays with the worst; he promises honor and pays with disgrace; he promises pleasure and pays with pain; he promises profit and pays with loss; he promises life and pays with death."
— *Puritan Preacher and Author, Thomas Brooks*

- "Submit yourselves therefore to God. Resist the devil, and he will flee from you." — *James 4:7*

Today, America's financial problems are nothing compared with the spiritual and moral problems she faces.

77

WORLDLINESS

"Love not the world, neither the things that are in the world.
If any man love the world, the love of the Father is not in him.
For all that is in the world, the lust of the flesh,
and the lust of the eyes, and the pride of life,
is not of the Father, but is of the world.
And the world passeth away, and the lust thereof:
but he that doeth the will of God abideth for ever."
1 John 2:15-17

"Whosoever therefore will be a friend of the world
is the enemy of God."
James 4:4

*

Worldliness does not leave room for God!

Some people who go to church make mistakes because they do not give proper attention to the preachers or Sunday school teachers. For instance, one man thought that an "Epistle" was the wife of an apostle while a woman thought that "Sodom and Gomorrah" were a husband and wife. In 1 John 2:15-17, some people think the word "world" means the universe or the people of the earth because it is translated from the Greek word "κόσμος" (cosmos). The truth is that we use the term "world" in all these ways, but it is not the true meaning in this verse.

The best definition of the word "world" is in God's Word. For example, in 1 John 2:16, *"the lust of the flesh"* means sexual immorality and sensual satisfaction, *"and the lust of the eyes"* means a desire to have the best available in life, *"and the pride of life"* means to have excessive pride, arrogance, and being puffed up for what they have or for what they have done. Finally, the conclusion of the verse is that the lust of the flesh, the lust of the eyes and the pride of life *"is not of the Father, but is of the world."*

In this kind of worldly lifestyle, Christians leave out the Heavenly Father in everything they do; business, pleasure, or whatever it may be. They give all their efforts and thoughts to things of this world. They are absorbed, concerned, and involved more with worldly affairs then spiritual needs. They are so worldly-minded that they are of little heavenly good. Ask yourself, "Why is the devil called the god of this world?" Not because he made it, but because people serve him with their worldliness.

When we read magazines, newspapers, and watch TV, we discover that people are living in self-delusion and are seeking self-satisfaction. They are cheating, divorcing, lying, and stealing. They are also trying to find happiness and satisfaction in sex, money, alcohol, and drugs. Their lifestyle is full of sin, without purpose, and they are far away from God and reality. They think the way they live is normal. They are living in a dream world, and their worldliness is destroying their lives. David Wells said, *"Worldliness is what any particular culture does to make sin look normal, and righteousness look strange."*

The devil is doing a good job, not only with unbelievers but also with believers.

• Addressing a national seminar of Southern Baptist leaders, George Gallup said, "We find there is very little difference in ethical behavior between churchgoers and those who are not active religiously...The levels of lying, cheating, and stealing are remarkably similar in both groups. Eight out of ten Americans consider themselves Christians, Gallup said, yet only about half of them could identify the person who gave the Sermon on the Mount, and fewer still could recall five of the Ten Commandments. Only one in ten said they would be willing to suffer for their faith." — *Erwin Lutzer, Pastor to Pastor, page 76*

The Bible provides us with numerous examples of people involved n worldliness because they loved this world. However, there are other examples of people who were dedicated to God and chose to have a relationship with Him as their first priority. The following are a few examples of both:

Lot – From a righteous man he became "worldly" (2 Peter 2:7,8; Genesis 19:1-25).

Demas – *"Demas has forsaken me, having loved this present world, and has departed for Thessalonica..."* (2 Timothy 4:10).

WORLDLINESS

The church at Laodicea – This church was so worldly that even the ones who belonged to it felt that it was fine to live without a close relationship with Jesus Christ. (Revelation 3:15-17)

Abraham – Even though he was an extremely wealthy man, he rejected a worldly lifestyle. (Hebrews 11:8-10)

Job – He was like Abraham, a wealthy man. His priority was to have a relationship with God over his possessions. Even when all his worldly possessions were taken away from him, he still continued to honor God.

The disciples of Jesus – Some of them were rich, and some were poor men, but all of them preferred to follow and have a good relationship with Jesus except Judas Iscariot. Peter said to Jesus, *"Behold, we have forsaken all, and followed thee..."* (Matthew 19:27).

Believers must care about the Lord, spiritual things, and not things of the world. Believers must not be concerned about temporal but eternal treasures. God's Word very clearly commands us to avoid a worldly life and gives us instructions on how to avoid this great enemy. Believers need to be genuine disciples and change their thinking. They have to focus on their priorities. They can set priorities on the temporal things of the world or on the eternal. Biblical believers who become true disciples of Jesus Christ can overcome worldliness, which is the most significant adversary and destroyer of the church.

A big problem with some preachers today is that they try to catch the spirit of this age instead of trying to correct it. Many Christians try to use their own ways to reach others for Christ. One way is to become like them and become like the world. In the end, they find out that they have lost power and God's blessings because what they believe and practice contradicts the Word of the Living God. Christians who do not believe in separation are not practicing real Christianity. God wants us to reach others with His ways and not our own. Over the years, I led many people to the Lord without becoming like them or becoming like the world. Because I was different, they were attracted to what I offered them, and they wanted what I had for themselves.

The apostle John said, *"And the world passeth away, and the lust thereof: but he that doeth the will of God abideth for ever"* (1 John 2:17). Be wise. Do not play with worldliness, and do not set your heart on success, riches, position, and pleasure. All of these will disappoint you. None of these will satisfy you. They have limited time, like the Ice Hotel in Canada that only lasts for the winter, and by April it has melted. Christ alone can satisfy your heart and bring you peace and joy. Nothing else can compare with the peace and joy Christ can bring you.

Once a man asked evangelist, D.L. Moody, "Mr. Moody, now that I am converted, must I give up the world?" Mr. Moody replied, "No, you haven't got to give up the world; if you give a good ringing testimony for the Son of God, the world will give you up pretty quick; they won't want you around" *(Bible Hub.com / Men of the Bible-D.L. Moody)*. I hope and pray you will be this kind of believer, that the world will stay away from you, and that you will not blend in with the world. *"Keep himself unspotted from the world"* (James 1:27).

I'LL TELL THE WORLD, THAT I'M A CHRISTIAN

I'll tell the world, that I'm a Christian,
I'm not ashamed, His name to bear;
I'll tell the world, that I'm a Christian,
I'll take Him with me anywhere.

I'll tell the world, how Jesus saved me,
and how He gave me a life brand new;
And I know that if you trust Him,
that all He gave me, He'll give to you.

— *Hymn by Baynard L. Fox, Copyright 1958, 1963, 1986*

❖ ❖ ❖

• "Christians should live in the world, but not be filled with it. A ship lives in the water; but if the water gets into the ship, she goes to the bottom. So Christians may live in the world; but if the world gets into them, they sink." — *Evangelist, D. L. Moody*

• "I find nothing in the Bible but holiness, and nothing in the world but worldliness. Therefore, if I live in the world, I will become worldly; on the other hand, if I live in the Bible, I will become holy."
— *Evangelist, Smith Wigglesworth*

• "One of the results of worldliness is a waning enthusiasm for evangelism." — *Pastor and Theologian, Mark Dever*

• "Worldliness is destroying the church of Jesus Christ."
— *Pastor and Theologian, Joel Beeke*

78

UNGODLY ANGER

"Be ye angry, and sin not: let not the sun go down upon your
wrath: Neither give place to the devil."
Ephesians 4:26-27

"Be not hasty in thy spirit to be angry:
for anger resteth in the bosom of fools."
Ecclesiastes 7:9

*

A wise man keeps His ungodly anger under control!

In the New Testament, two Greek words are used for "anger." One is "οργή" (orge) which means, a strong feeling of displeasure, hostility, or antagonism towards someone and intends to grow in anger. The other one is "θυμός" (thymos), which means strong anger that is like a powerful engine. Anger is a significant problem. It is not restricted to any special human. It can involve any person of any age, color, race, or economic and educational background. Generally, it is a global problem. Unresolved anger can destroy marriages, cause failure of families, and impact communities and nations. It also ruins the joy and health of people. Reports from Christian counselors saw that 50 percent of people who go for counseling have problems with anger.

According to the Bible, we should realize anger is not sin at all times. One type of anger the Bible approves of is called "righteous anger" or "righteous indignation." Even God can be angry: *"And when he had looked round about on them with anger, being grieved for the hardness of their hearts..."* (Mark 3:5). Believers are also commanded to be angry: *"Be ye angry, and sin not..."* (Ephesians 4:26).

An example of biblical anger was when Jesus was angry in God's temple in Jerusalem when people had turned it into a commercial market: *"And when he had made a scourge of small cords, he drove them all out of the temple, and the sheep, and the oxen; and poured out the changers' money, and overthrew the tables; And said unto them that sold doves, Take these things hence; make not my Father's house an house of merchandise"* (John 2:13-17). This example of anger did not involve self-defense, but rather a defense of a principle. Dr. David Seamands said, *"Anger is a divinely implanted emotion. Closely allied to our instinct for right, it is designed to be used for constructive spiritual purposes. The person who cannot feel anger at evil is a person who lacks enthusiasm for good. If you cannot hate wrong, it's very questionable whether you really love righteousness."*

In 1980, I worked for a Christian publishing company as a commercial artist. My supervisor was a lady who was a non-believer. One time, another non-believing co-worker made a serious mistake and embarrassed our company. My supervisor went to the managers of the company and told them I had made the mistake. The managers called me into the office and rebuked me in front of my supervisor. I was so angry with her that in front of everybody I told her that she needed Christ in her life and that she should stop lying. I was ready to resign that day, but first I talked with my friend Jerry, a co-worker and good brother in Christ. He spent a lot of time that day, helping me calm down. Praise the Lord for this faithful brother who prayed with me and helped me decide not to resign from God's work. After a while, my supervisor came to herself and acknowledged her mistake.

"Be ye angry, and sin not..." (Ephesians 4:26**).** Anger is able to become sinful when it comes from many sinful actions like hurtful speech: *"Whose mouth is full of cursing and bitterness"* (Romans 3:14). It could also be sinful when we allow the anger to stay in us: *"Be ye angry, and sin not: let not the sun go down upon your wrath: Neither give place to the devil"* (Ephesians 4:26-27) or when we allow anger because of lack of self-control: *"A fool uttereth all his mind: but a wise man keepeth it in till afterwards"* (Proverbs 29:11).

Handling anger is an important life skill. Unfortunately, many people try to justify their anger instead of accepting responsibility for it and trying to solve it. However, the good news is that the Word of God can help us handle anger properly. We can do it in so many godly ways. For example, we can do so by returning good for evil: *"Be not overcome of evil, but overcome evil with good"* (Romans 12:21). We can also do so by using good communication to solve the problem: *"A soft answer turneth away wrath: but grievous words stir up anger"* (Proverbs 15:1) and *"Let no corrupt communication proceed out of your mouth, but that which is good to the use of edifying, that it may minister grace unto the hearers... Let all bitterness, and wrath, and anger, and clamour, and evil speaking, be put away from you, with all malice"* (Ephesians 4:29, 31).

UNGODLY ANGER

As Christians, we have to do our best to stay away from anger and try to solve the problem wisely: *"I send you forth as sheep in the midst of wolves: be ye therefore wise as serpents, and harmless as doves"* (Matthew 10:16), and do not *"cast ye your pearls before swine..."* (Matthew 7:6). Sometimes we have to understand that some people are unsafe for us. In this case, we have to forgive them and choose to stay away from them. We should do everything possible in our power to *"live peaceably with all men"* (Romans 12:18).

Sadly, we cannot control how others act or respond, but we can make the changes we need on our part. Do not let your temper explode. Do not let your temper get you into serious trouble. Venting your anger may feel good for a moment, but the blast can do irreparable damage to you and to those around you. Anger makes you say and do things you may deeply regret. Emotions are powerful and often lead to irrational decisions because it distorts judgment. Ask the Lord to show you constructive ways to channel what bugs you. Overcoming a temper is not easy to do overnight. Ungodly anger can be overcome through prayer and depending on the power of the Holy Spirit.

Remember that ungodly anger is bad for your health. It is especially bad for your heart. Recently, I read that doctors have proven that anger reduced the amount of blood that the heart pumped to body tissues even more than those who have heart disease. Dr. Peter Kaufman, acting chief of the Behavioral Medicine Branch at the National Heart, Lung and Blood Institute, said, *"It underscores the role of emotions like anger in the development of heart disease."* Lastly, *"Angry, cynical people die young. Men who score high for hostility on standard tests are four times more likely to die prematurely than men whose scores are low."* — *Bottom Line, quoted in Homemade, Feb 1989*

Stay away from anger or try to conquer it before it conquers you!

❖ ❖ ❖

- Do not say, "I cannot help having a bad temper." Friend, you must help it. Pray to God to help you overcome it at once, for either you must kill it, or it will kill you. You cannot carry a bad temper into heaven." — *"Prince of Preachers," C.H. Spurgeon*

- "We have choices when it comes to our emotions: we can master them, or they can master us." "90% of the friction of daily life is caused by the wrong tone of voice." — *Pastor and Author, John C. Maxwell*

- Anger and bitterness are two noticeable signs of being focused on self and not trusting God's sovereignty in your life. When you believe that God causes all things to work together for good to those who belong to Him and love Him, you can respond to trials with joy instead of anger or bitterness." — *Missionary, John Broger*

79

SELFISH PRIDE

*"Every one that is proud in heart is an abomination
to the LORD...he shall not be unpunished."*
Proverbs 16:5

"God resisteth the proud, but giveth grace unto the humble."
James 4:6

*

Selfish pride is your greatest enemy,
and it is a sin that God hates!

In Greek, "pride" is the word "υπεριφάνεια" and "proud" is the word "υπερίφανος." These two words mean excessive pride, arrogance, puffed up, conceited, disdain, and haughty. In Hebrews, "pride" is the word "gevah." This word means majesty, pride haughtiness, exalted, and highly exalted. The Bible tells us about two kinds of pride. One of them is when we feel good about ourselves or for others for a job well done. God does not condemn this kind of pride, and of course, it is not sinful (2 Corinthians 7:4; Galatians 6:4). God hates the other kind of pride which comes from self-love, self-admiration, and self-righteousness: *"The fear of the LORD is to hate evil: pride, and arrogancy, and the evil way, and the froward mouth, do I hate"* (Proverbs 8:13). This kind of pride is sinful because it provides resistance to seeking God: *"The wicked, through the pride of his countenance, will not seek after God: God is not in all his thoughts"* (Psalm 10:4).

Self-pride is the opposite of the spirit of humility that God seeks. *"Blessed are the poor in spirit: for theirs is the kingdom of heaven"* (Matthew 5:3). The person who is "poor in spirit" recognizes that he is unable to come to God apart from His divine and saving grace. This result brings him to

God because he depends on Him. The proud person is totally different. His pride blinds him, and he thinks he has no need of God. He even thinks God will accept him because he is special, and he deserves it. Pride is the greatest sin that keeps many people from accepting Jesus Christ as Savior and directs them to hell. Instead of boasting in the Lord according to 1 Corinthians 1:31, the proud person boasts of his own strength. He also tries to inherit eternal life with his way and not God's way. *"For not he that commendeth himself is approved, but whom the Lord commendeth"* (2 Corinthians 10:18)

Pride is the professional sin of the devil. It is a sword that wounds the one who uses it. C.S. Lewis identifies pride *as "the great sin," "the essential vice, the utmost evil, is Pride," "comes direct from Hell"* and *"the mother of all sins."* Augustine stated that *"pride is the root of every sin."* Pride is the most serious, dangerous, and deadly sin because it blinds our understanding to recognize the truth and makes us live in spiritual self-illusion and fantasy. Pride blinds us, and we are not able to see everything we have comes from God and not from ourselves. All our talents and abilities are gifts to us from Him.

Pride can destroy any person and any society. Without pride, there would never be an argument, divorce, a war, nor division within the church. Pride can delay revival, ruin homes and nations, deceive and defeat Christians, and send more people to hell than any other sin. Pride is a very deceitful sin. Everybody is contaminated with the virus of pride, and they have no idea that they are. Even the proud person is often very proud of his humility. Pride can ruin all the virtues. The proud person is capable of doing any sin. *"Pride goeth before destruction, and an haughty spirit before a fall"* (Proverbs 16:18). It is necessary for our spiritual life to fight pride. We should not permit it to enter our heart because soon, we will find ourselves a slave of Satan and his demons.

Why is pride so sinful? It is because pride blinds us, and we take credit for something God has done. Pride takes the glory which belongs to God. Anything we achieve in this world would not be possible without God empowering us. The Bible says, *"what hast thou that thou didst not receive? now if thou didst receive it, why dost thou glory, as if thou hadst not received it"* (1 Corinthians 4:7)? We have to give God the glory. If we do not, we will pay the price. *"Pride goes before destruction...Better it is to be of an humble spirit with the lowly, than to divide the spoil with the proud"* (Proverbs 16:18-19).

According to the prophet Isaiah, Satan was cast out of heaven because of pride. He had the selfish nerve to try to replace God. Because of Satan's rebellion, he will be cast down to hell in the final judgment of God. Be wise and not a fool. *"God resisteth the proud, but giveth grace unto the humble"* (James 4:6).

Pride brings shame. Humility brings wisdom. Do not toot your own horn, but be a humble person. Do not worry about getting credit for what is done. God has his own way of honoring the humble and silencing the proud. Without being humble, you cannot have grace, and without grace, you cannot have salvation. Do not let pride guide you to hell.

❖ ❖ ❖

- **"Indicators of a proud person:**

  A proud person becomes irritated when corrected for mistakes.

  A proud person accepts praise for things over which he or she has no control.

  Pride refuses to take counsel and to learn from other people.

  Pride often shows itself in competition with other people.

  Pride does not want more; pride wants more than somebody else."

  Pride will not admit mistakes. — *Dr. Adrian Rogers*

- **Self-pride is the opposite of the spirit of humility that God seeks.**

- **Pride blinds a person, and he thinks he has no need of God.**

- **Pride is the professional sin of the devil.**

- **Pride is a sword that wounds the one who uses it.**

- **Pride can destroy any person and any society.**

- **Pride blinds a person and he takes credit for something God has done.**

- **Pride takes the glory which belongs to God.**

- **Pride sends more people to hell than any other sin.**

80

WORRY AND ANXIETY

"Be careful (anxious) for nothing;
but in every thing by prayer and supplication with thanksgiving
let your requests be made known unto God."
Philippians 4:6

"Casting all your care (anxieties) upon Him;
for He careth for you."
1 Peter 5:7

*

There is a solution for worry and anxiety!

Most times, we worry about things that never happen. Worry pulls tomorrow's problems over today's happiness. Worry takes away today's joy by worrying about tomorrow. In reality, worry is a lack of faith or faith in the negative. Worry is a mental problem that drives us in a superficial and fantasy world. We worry about the unknown future which is not appropriate for a wise person. Leo Aikman said, *"Blessed is the person who is too busy to worry in the daytime, and too sleepy to worry at night."* People who worry too much and cannot sleep at night, should follow the advice of Mary C. Crowley: *"Every evening I turn my worries over to God. He is going to be up all night anyway."*

If a believer has problems with worry and anxiety that does not come from medications or medical problems, it is because he does not trust the promises of God. There is a possibility he does not know the scriptures. He may also be confused by taking the scriptures about promises and commands out of their proper context. The Bible is like a puzzle that has many pieces of different shapes and colors. We are not confused when we know the Bible as one piece, one picture, or as a complete puzzle. When we take parts of the Bible like verses, chapters, or books of the Bible alone or out of context, there is confusion. Let us check a few passages from the Bible that talk about worry. We need to pay close attention to these passages, so we do not miss the solution the Bible provides.

FIRST: Jesus in the Sermon on the Mount said, *"Therefore I say unto you, Take no thought [anxious] for your life, what ye shall eat, or what ye shall drink; nor yet for your body, what ye shall put on..."* (Matthew 6:25). If we have a problem with applying this principle, we must look at the first word, "therefore." This word points us to the previous verse which reveals the root of our problem: *"No man can serve two masters: for either he will hate the one, and love the other; or else he will hold to the one, and despise the other. Ye cannot serve God and mammon"* (Matthew 6:24). In other words, it tells us to trust the Lord for our needs. We should also serve His interests and His kingdom, instead of following the material and worldly things which increase our worry and anxiety.

SECOND: The apostle Paul tells us, *"Be careful [anxious] for nothing but in every thing by prayer and supplication with thanksgiving let your requests be made known unto God. And the peace of God, which passeth all understanding, shall keep your hearts and minds through Christ Jesus"* (Philippians 4:6,7). These verses tell us we should not be anxious. Instead, we should have peace in our hearts and minds which is achieved through prayer and by meditating on everything mentioned in the following verse, *"Finally, brethren, whatsoever things are true, whatsoever things are honest, whatsoever things are just, whatsoever things are pure, whatsoever things are lovely, whatsoever things are of good report; if there be any virtue, and if there be any praise, think on these things"* (Philippians 4:8).

THIRD: We know that the apostle Peter was fine walking on water until his attention was drawn away from Jesus to the storm. He became afraid and started to sink. The same apostle tells us, *"Casting all your care [anxieties] upon Him; for He careth for you"* (1 Peter 5:7). However, the complete instructions begin in the previous verse: *"Humble yourselves therefore under the mighty hand of God, that he may exalt you in due time"* (1 Peter 5:6). In other words, he tells us if everything does not go as planned in our life, we do not have to react with worry. Instead, we should act with humility and trust God who will exalt us in His time.

We also have to put into practice what Jesus and the apostle Paul said, *"Therefore whosoever heareth these sayings of mine, and doeth them, I will liken him unto* **a wise man, which built his house upon a rock:** *And the rain descended, and the floods came, and the winds blew, and beat upon that house; and it fell not: for it was founded upon a rock. And every one that heareth these sayings of mine, and doeth them not, shall be likened unto* **a foolish man, which built his house upon the sand:** *And the rain descended, and the floods came, and the* *winds blew, and beat upon that house; and it fell: and great was the fall of it"* (Matthew 7:24-27). *"We henceforth be no more children, tossed to and fro, and carried about with every wind ..."* (Ephesians 4:14).

The answer to worry and anxiety is to firmly anchor your faith in the rock of God and His promises. Anxiety keeps you on the sandy shores full of worry, fear, and doubt. When the storms of life hit, you start to panic. Jesus calls this foolishness. Do not allow worry and anxiety to retain control of you. When you begin to surrender and trust God and His promises, the worries and anxieties decrease. Worry and anxiety about the future can steal your joy, as well as your peace. God promises to be with you and provide you with the strength to face any problem. Trust in the Lord and show fear the way out. *"Fear knocked on the door. Faith answered, and no one was there."*— *English proverb*

ALL YOUR ANXIETY

Is there a heart o'er bound by sorrow?
Is there a life weighed down by care?
Come to the cross, each burden bearing;
All your anxiety—leave it there.

All your anxiety, all your care,
Bring to the mercy seat, leave it there,
Never a burden He cannot bear,
Never a friend like Jesus!

— *Hymn by Edward H. Joy, 1920*

❖ ❖ ❖

• "The beginning of anxiety is the end of faith, and the beginning of true faith is the end of anxiety." — *Evangelist, George Mueller*

• "Every tomorrow has two handles. We can take hold of it with the handle of anxiety or the handle of faith." — *Clergyman, Henry Ward Beecher*

• "Worry does not empty tomorrow of its sorrow, it empties today of its strength." — *Author, Corrie ten Boom*

• "Anxiety and fear are cousins but not twins. Fear sees a threat. Anxiety imagines one." — *Pastor and Author, Max Lucado*

• "Let us give up our work, our plans, ourselves, our lives, our loved ones, our influence, our all, right into [God's] hand; and then, when we have given all over to Him, there will be nothing left for us to be troubled about." — *Missionary, Hudson Taylor*

COMPASSION AND KINDNESS

"Thus speaketh the LORD of hosts, saying, Execute true judgment, and shew mercy and compassions every man to his brother."
Zechariah 7:9

"And be ye kind one to another, tenderhearted, forgiving one another, even as God for Christ's sake hath forgiven you."
Ephesians 4:32

*

Minister to others with compassion and kindness!

Three students from a theological seminary, studying the story of the Good Samaritan, planned a practical experiment. One volunteered to play the part of a victim with torn clothes, and a wounded body, and he pretended to be in great pain. The other two placed him along the path that led from the dormitory to the Bible classroom. They watched while the other students walked by him. They walked around him, ignored him, and walked away. Sadly, not one student stopped. They did not put God's truth and love into action.

The Bible teaches us a lot about compassion and kindness. In the New Testament, the Greek word for compassion is "σπλαγχνίζομαι" (splanchnizomai) which means kindness and mercy, or feel deep love and pain which comes from all the inner organs of the body which in the Greek is the word "σπλάγχνα " (splanchna). In other words, compassion is what makes a person feel pain when someone else hurts. It is more than a feeling. It is love in action.

An example of man's compassion is shown in the story of the Good Samaritan. *"But a certain Samaritan, as he journeyed, came where he was: and when he saw him, he had compassion on him"* (Luke 10:33).

Other examples refer to the Lord's compassion:

- *"But when he saw the multitudes, he was moved with compassion on them, because they fainted, and were scattered abroad, as sheep having no shepherd"* (Matthew 9:36).

- *"And Jesus went forth, and saw a great multitude, and was moved with compassion toward them, and he healed their sick"* (Matthew 14:14).

- *"I have compassion on the multitude, because they have now been with me three days, and have nothing to eat"* (Mark 8:2).

- *"So Jesus had compassion and touched their eyes. And immediately their eyes received sight, and they followed Him"* (Matthew 20:34).

Believers learn about compassion through the example of Jesus Christ and must imitate Him. The Scriptures also beg believers to show compassion and kindness in every aspect of their lives.

- *"Thus speaketh the LORD of hosts, saying, Execute true judgment, and shew mercy and compassions every man to his brother"* (Zechariah 7:9).

- *"Put on therefore, as the elect of God, holy and beloved, bowels of mercies, kindness, humbleness of mind, meekness, longsuffering"* (Colossians 3:12).

- Years ago, when the speaker of the house, Sam Rayburn, heard he had terminal cancer, he shocked everyone when he announced he was going back to his small town in Bonham, Texas. People said to him: "They have got the finest facilities in Washington, D. C. Why go back to that little town?" Rayburn's response speaks to the priceless importance of community. He said, "Because in Bonham, Texas, they know if you're sick, and they care when you die." — *J. R. Love, Rushton, Louisiana*

God has chosen us to be a family that genuinely cares for others. Make it your goal to minister with *"bowels of mercies [compassion], kindness, humbleness of mind, meekness, and longsuffering"* (Colossians 3:12).

- President Abraham Lincoln, despite his busy schedule during the Civil War, often visited the hospitals to cheer the wounded soldiers. On one occasion, he saw a young fellow who was near death. "Is there anything I can do for you?" asked the compassionate President. "Please write a letter to my mother," came the reply. Unrecognized by the soldier, the Chief

Executive sat down and wrote as the youth told him what to say. The letter read, "My Dearest Mother, I was badly hurt while doing my duty, and I won't recover. Do not sorrow too much for me. May God bless you and Father. Kiss Mary and John for me." The young man was too weak to go on, so Lincoln signed the letter for him and then added this postscript: "Written for your son by Abraham Lincoln." Asking to see the note, the soldier was astonished to discover who had shown him such kindness. "Are you really our President?" he asked. "Yes," was the quiet answer. "Now, is there anything else I can do?" The lad feebly replied, "Will you please hold my hand? I think it would help to see me through to the end." The tall, gaunt man granted his request, offering warm words of encouragement until death stole in with the dawn. — *Source Unknown*

The question to you and me is: "Are we willing to put into practice what we learn in the Bible?" God's grace treats us with compassion and kindness and blessings far beyond what we deserve. Make sure our attitude towards others does not disqualify us from being an effective representative for Christ. Communications are important. To speak nicely and kindly does not hurt our tongue. If we want to help and make a difference in someone's life today, we have to do it with kindness. Watch God's love melt that icy heart. God will bless us for our kindness in ways that will surprise us. Harsh words and uncaring actions turn people off, and we harm ourselves. We have to treat others with kindness if we want to stand out as ambassadors of the King.

• In the country church of a small village, an altar boy serving the priest at Sunday mass accidentally dropped the cruet of wine. The village priest struck the altar boy sharply on the cheek and in a gruff voice shouted: "Leave the altar and don't come back!" That boy became Tito, the Communist leader of Yugoslavia. In the cathedral of a large city, an altar boy serving the bishop at Sunday mass accidentally dropped the cruet of wine. With a warm twinkle in his eyes, the bishop gently whispered: "Someday you will be a priest." That boy grew up to become Archbishop Fulton Sheen. And Rev. Gregory Oravec adds: "Oh, the power of words, be they written or spoken!" — *Rev. Gregory Oravec / preachhim.org*

This story reminds us that our words and actions can turn the next generation on or turn them off, to the Lord. Because it is easy to influence young people regarding the things of God, one event can change them for a lifetime. We have to watch carefully what we say and do because they imitate us as good or bad examples. *"Let the words of my mouth, and the meditation of my heart, be acceptable in thy sight, O LORD, my strength, and my redeemer..."* (Psalm 19:14).

LET ME GIVE

I do not know how long I'll live
But while I live, Lord, let me give
Some comfort to someone in need
By smile or nod, kind word or deed.

And let me do whatever I can
To ease things for my fellow man.
I want naught but to do my part
To "lift" a tired or weary heart.

To change folks' frowns to smiles again.
Then I will not have lived in vain
And I'll not care how long I'll live
If I can give ... and give ... and give.

— *Author Unknown*

❖ ❖ ❖

- "It takes a true believer to be compassionate."
— *Author, Arthur H. Stainback*

- "Kindness has converted more sinners than zeal, eloquence, or learning." — *Hymn writer and theologian, Frederick W. Faber*

- "Kindness is the language the deaf can hear, and the blind can see."
— *Writer and humorist, Mark Twain*

- "People don't care how much you know until they know how much you care." — *President, Theodore Roosevelt*

- "To the world, you might be one person, but to one person you might be the world." — *Dr. Theodor Seuss Geise*

- "Too often, we underestimate, a kind word, a listening ear, an honest compliment, or the smallest act of caring; all of which have the potential to turn a life around." — *"Dr. Love," Leo Buscaglia*

PATIENCE AND ADVERSITY

"And not only so, but we glory in tribulations also:
knowing that tribulation worketh patience."
Romans 5:3

*

Patience only grows in the soil of adversity!

A tourist once visited a cathedral where an artisan was working on a huge mosaic. A vast empty wall was before the artist, and the tourist asked, "Aren't you worried about all that space that you need to fill up and how you will ever finish it?" The artist replied simply, "I know what I want to do each day. I mark off the spot I want to complete in the morning and focus on getting that done. I don't worry about what lay outside that space. I believe if I take it one day at a time, one day, the whole mosaic would be finished." As Christians, we have to live day by day and wait on the Lord for tomorrow to direct our paths. We do not have to be impatient and try to finish the mosaic of our lives in one day and especially in times when we go through tribulations.

I have served the Lord all my Christian life. I have had more trials and tribulations than many others. Since 1996 I have experienced many significant trials. My first wife died unexpectedly from a heart attack just before Valentine's day. A few years later, I was diagnosed with thyroid cancer and had to undergo two life-threatening surgeries in which the doctors removed a total of fifty tumors and lymph nodes. Some years later, I had two more surgeries to remove topical benign carcinoma from two different places on one of my legs. I also had cataract surgery on both of my eyes and surgery on one of my shoulders. My second wife also had several serious operations. Through it all, my faith in the Lord continues to grow, as well as my patience. Steve Klipowicz said, *"The Lord knows the way through the wilderness. All you have to do is follow."* Now every time any unexpected, unpleasant situation comes into my life, I do not worry and panic. Instead, I patiently wait for it to pass. With a positive attitude, I wait to see what good will come from it for God's glory. The Lord cares for and blesses the ones who love Him. *"And we know that all things work together for good to them that love God, to them who are the called according to his purpose."* (Romans 8:28).

Even though I had two successful surgeries on both my eyes a few years ago, there were problems with the prescription my doctor gave me for my glasses. I had to wait patiently for more than four months to fully understand the goodness coming from this situation. The Lord placed four doctors and the manager of the glasses laboratory in charge to solve the problem. He gave me the opportunity and time to witness to them. The Lord died for them and paid for their sins too-and He is concerned about their souls. During this situation, all of these people became good friends of mine.

The Greek word for patience is the noun, "υπομονή" (hypomone) and the verb "υπομένω" (hupomeno). Both of these words comes from two words, "υπο-μονή" (hypo-mone) and "υπο-μένω" (hupo-meno.) The first-word, "υπο"(hypo) means "under," and the second word in the noun means patience, endurance, constancy, steadfastness, perseverance, forbearance, longsuffering, and slowness in avenging wrongs. The second word in the verb means to last, remain, abide, obey, accept, wait, stay courageous, and endure under suffering. Therefore, patience means to have the ability and capacity to accept the delay. It also means to wait and face unavoidable or unpleasant circumstances with a good spirit. In Greek, the most profound meaning of patience means a person must not only have the patience for a limited time, but it must become his lifestyle and part of his character to help in every adversity he faces.

I learned through the years that patience is the ability to wait, accept the delay, stay courageous, and endure when troubles and suffering come our way. We should not worry or become frustrated, anxious or angry. Patience is the ability to put our desires and plans on hold for a time, and have the ability to keep a good attitude while waiting. Patience is a priceless and rare virtue and must be part of our lifestyle. Being a patient person is essential.

I taught my children that if they want to avoid problems and succeed in all areas of their lives, they must be patient people. Even my dear son-in-law, an intelligent and educated American, learned from my daughter some excellent and meaningful Greek words, including patience "υπο-μονή" (hypomone). Now every time he is facing stress, frustration, or trials, he remembers the significant meaning of this Greek word. It helps him to better manage and overcome the unpleasant situations he may face. He is proud to use it. He often reminds me of that word when we have family gatherings or have a serious conversation.

Do you have a mountain staring you in the face? Try bringing it down to size. No matter the obstacle facing you, patient endurance will bring you success. When you experience trials and tribulations, do not panic. Be strong in the Lord. Strong winds make for strong trees. The Lord uses the trials and stresses of life to purify your motives. Only through testing can the Lord perfect the character of Christ in you. God allows suffering and trials in your life to develop character and maturity. When life begins to bug you, thank the Lord. Recognize that God is working His goodwill for you in spite of your trials. When God brings you into deep waters, He does not intend to drown you but to cleanse you.

In adversity, you usually want God to do a removing job when He wants to do an improving job. Always remind yourself that God loves you more than anyone, and He has a reason to have you go through trials. Remember, sunshine comes after the thunderstorm. Patience is one of the fruits of the Holy Spirit. It gives you the ability to do what you can do for today and trust God for tomorrow. Learn to wait on the Lord patiently. Sometimes it may be difficult to wait on the Lord, but it is worse to wish you had. Patience is a Christian grace of exceptional quality which is highly valued by God Himself. Patience can only increase in the soil of adversity. We need to wait upon the Lord and continue walking patiently ahead in both joys or trials without giving up until the time we are in glory.

Our problem is many times we do not wait upon the Lord. We forget it is through faith and patience we obtain God's promises. Usually, in times of affliction, we meet the sweetest experiences of God's love. God's first concern is our growth, and that is why He often holds back success until the time we have learned patience. The Lord teaches us this lesson through the discipline of waiting. Keep in your mind that the Christian life is not always a convenient, pleasant, and comfortable life, without trials and tribulations, but it is a fulfilling and satisfying life. *"These things I have spoken unto you, that in me ye might have peace. In the world ye shall have tribulation: but be of good cheer; I have overcome the world"* (John 16:33). Christian, never give up but keep up because *"Winners never quit and quitters never win."* — *Vince Lombardi*

> God has not promised skies always blue,
> Flower-strewn pathways all our life through;
> God has not promised sun without rain,
> Joy without sorrow, peace without pain.

PATIENCE AND ADVERSITY

Refrain:
But God has promised strength for the day,
Rest for the labor, light for the way;
Grace for the trials, help from above,
Unfailing sympathy, undying love.

— *Hymn by Annie Johnson Flint, 1918*

❖ ❖ ❖

• "God's way of answering the Christian's prayer for more patience, experience, hope, and love often is to put him into the furnace of affliction."
— *Clergyman, Richard Cecil*

• "A clay pot sitting in the sun will always be a clay pot. It has to go through the white heat of the furnace to become porcelain."
—*Mildred Witte Struven*

• "The Diamond is a piece of coal that performed well under pressure."
— *Author Unknown*

• "Adversity makes men and prosperity makes monsters."
— *Writer, Victor Hugo*

• "There are times when God asks nothing of his children except silence, patience, and tears."
— *Author, C. S. Robinson*

• "Patience is the companion of wisdom."
— *Theologian and Philosopher, Augustine*

• "Many men owe the grandeur of their lives to their tremendous difficulties."
— *"Prince of Preachers," C. H. Spurgeon*

• "One minute of patience, ten years of peace."
— *Greek proverb*

COURAGE AND ENCOURAGEMENT

"Let no corrupt communication proceed out of your mouth,
but that which is good to the use of edifying,
that it may minister grace unto the hearers."
Ephesians 4:29

"Now we exhort you, brethren, warn them that are unruly,
comfort the feebleminded, support the weak,
be patient toward all men."
1 Thessalonians 5:14

*

With courage, encourage those who are in need!

A Pastor's sermon once went considerably longer than usual. After he finished, most of the parishioners greeted him with excitement. Except, one man who paused and said, "Pastor, your sermon was really refreshing." As the minister broke into a big smile, the man completed his comment by adding, "I felt like a new man after I woke up!"

Pastors are human, too. Their lives are affected by both the people who love them and the people who do not. To be a pastor is a difficult job. God called your pastor to be a pastor in your church. He is not there to entertain you but to keep watch over your soul. He will give an account for your soul according to Hebrews 13:17. Show love, honor, respect, and appreciation, for what he does for you. Make His life a little easier by doing that. Encourage him and let him know how thankful you are that he is your pastor. Instead of complaining and trying to find faults, start praying for your pastor. Make sure to go to church this coming Sunday

Your presence will encourage your pastor. He will feel better when he does not have to preach to an empty chair.

The apostle Paul gave the following encouraging advice to Timothy. *"But thou, O man of God, flee these things; and follow after righteousness, godliness, faith, love, patience, meekness"* (1 Timothy 6:11). Timothy was a young man with a lot of responsibilities in leading the church in Ephesus. By nature, Timothy was a fearful and shy man. For this reason, the apostle Paul encouraged him by telling him: *"For God hath not given us the spirit of fear; but of power, and of love, and of a sound mind"* (2 Timothy 1:7). He was not energetic, and he also suffered from health issues. According to what Paul recommended, it may have been a gastric problem: *"Drink no longer water, but use a little wine for thy stomach's sake and thine often infirmities"* (1 Timothy 5:23). After all, Timothy often felt that he was at the end of his rope. Maybe you know what that feels like. Paul did not discourage him. Instead, he lifted him up and said to him, *"O man of God."* He did not say to him, *"Young man, you are sick, and with your problems, you will not make it."*

There was once a time when I felt my pastor's heart was very heavy due to an issue at church. I sent him a short note by email to encourage him. You will never know how much my encouraging words meant to him. Those words helped lift him up, and he was extremely thankful. Through prayer, the Lord answered and delivered our church from that difficult situation.

If you are a minister, and you are in a difficult situation, do not be discouraged. Do not become overwhelmed. Every time you feel down, turn to the Lord for help and strength. Believe in His promises. Practice them in your ministry and in your life. God does not lie. Everything He says is true, and He will do everything He says. *"I am with you always, even unto the end of the world. Amen"* (Matthew 28:20), *"For he hath said, I will never leave thee, nor forsake thee. So that we may boldly say, The Lord is my helper, and I will not fear what man shall do unto me"* (Hebrews 13:5-6), and *"With God all things are possible"* (Matthew 19:26). If God calls you to serve Him, you are able to say with confidence like Paul, *"I can do all things through Christ, which strengtheneth me"* (Philippians 4:13). If God calls you to serve Him, you are one of His men. You belong to the company of Moses, Samuel, David, Elijah, Paul, and many others from the past until the present.

Remember that in addition to your pastor, your pastor's wife also needs your prayers and encouragement. She is the first person in his life who must support and encourage him. The wife of a man in God's ministry has a high calling and mission, but it is also a great responsibility, influence, and great blessings. Her proper spirit can help or destroy her husband's work. A few years ago, I met a pastor who told me that he had left his ministry and started a secular job. When he introduced me to his wife, it did not take me long to figure out that she was the reason he had left God's work. From her dress to her hairstyle, it was easy to see she was not content and was trying to compete with the world. She thought money would make her happy and prosperous. She was involved in selling life insurance to make a lot of money and to satisfy her carnal desires. From what I understood, the Lord did not bless her with a lot of money.

If you are a minister's wife, be content with what God gives to you and your husband. If not, you will be the devil's target. If God has called your husband to serve Him, you must be his best partner in his work. Your husband needs your love, help, prayers, encouragement, and support. For this reason, God has called you to be a minister's wife. The Lord never blesses pastors or ministries when husbands and wives do not work together as a team to glorify Him.

• There is a story about a group of frogs who were traveling through the woods, and two of them fell into a deep pit. All the other frogs gathered around the pit. When they saw how deep the pit was, they told the two frogs that they were as good as dead. The two frogs ignored the comments and tried to jump up out of the pit with all of their might. The other frogs kept telling them to stop, that they were as good as dead. Finally, one of the frogs took heed to what the other frogs were saying and gave up. He fell down and died. The other frog continued to jump as hard as he could. Once again, the crowd of frogs yelled at him to stop the pain and just die. He jumped even harder and finally made it out. When he got out, the other frogs said, "Did you not hear us?" The frog explained to them that he was deaf. He thought they were encouraging him the entire time. — *Author unknown*

From all the situations mentioned above, we see how important it is to have the courage to stand up and encourage others. There is power in every encouragement you give. "Encouragement" means to use inspirational and motivational comments with grace to have the ability to give someone support, confidence, and hope. Courage is the boldness that makes you stand up and speak. It is bravery, resistance to fear, and doing what you are afraid to do without intimidation. According to Ernest Hemingway, *"Courage is grace under pressure."*

If you know someone whose life is going down the drain, do not let fear keep you from helping with encouraging words. *"Death and life are in the power of the tongue..."* (Proverbs 18:21). Be a person of courage. An encouraging word to someone lifts him up and helps him make it through the day. However, negative and destructive words to someone who is down is dangerous and can kill him emotionally or physically. Using words of encouragement can go such a long way. Encouragement costs you nothing. It is priceless for others to receive. From this day forward, think before you speak. If you are a Christian, do not forget to encourage yourself with God's Word and His unconditional love.

> "Flatter me, and I may not believe you.
> Criticize me, and I may not like you.
> Ignore me, and I may not forgive you.
> Encourage me, and I will not forget you."

> — *William Arthur Ward*

THE POWER OF WORDS

> A careless word may kindle strife;
> A cruel word may wreck a life.
> A bitter word may hate instill;
> A brutal word may smite and kill.

> A gracious word may smooth the way;
> A joyous word may light the day.
> A timely word may lessen stress;
> A loving word may heal and bless.

> — *Author unknown*

❖ ❖ ❖

• "Courage is doing what you're afraid to do. There can be no courage unless you're scared."
— *American fighter in World War I, Edward Vernon Rickenbacker*

• "One man with courage makes a majority." — *President Andrew Jackson*

• "No one is useless in this world who lightens the burden of anyone else." — *Writer, Charles Dickens*

• "You will never do anything in this world without courage. It is the greatest quality in the mind next to honor." — *Greek Philosopher, Aristotle*

84

HONESTY AND INTEGRITY

*"Let me be weighed in an even [honest] balance
that God may know mine integrity."*
Job 31:6

"Every man shall kiss his lips that giveth a right [honest] answer."
Proverbs 24:26

*

Be a person with honesty and integrity!

D r. George Sweeting wrote about the desperate need for honesty in our culture. He referred to Dr. Madison Sarratt who taught mathematics at Vanderbilt University for many years. Before giving a test, the professor would admonish his class something like this: "Today I am giving two examinations--one in trigonometry and the other in honesty. I hope you will pass them both. If you must fail one, fail trigonometry. There are many good people in the world who can't pass trig, but there are no good people in the world who cannot pass the examination of honesty." — *sermonillustrations.com*

According to doctor and author, Spencer Johnson, *"Integrity is telling myself the truth. And honesty is telling the truth to other people."* Honesty and integrity in our society today are being compromised by people everywhere. The statistics are very shameful. For example, only 56% of Americans teach honesty to their children. Additionally, 65% of high school students cheat on important tests, as well as lie to their parents and teachers. Many adults are not honest with their spouses, friends, relatives, business partners, and other people. Finally, 24% of adults say they would keep the cash if they found a wallet with $1,000 and a much higher percentage of young people would keep the money.

HONESTY AND INTEGRITY

Years ago, a physician appeared on network news and proclaimed, *"Lying is an important part of social life, and children who are unable to do it are children who may have developmental problems."* — *Our Daily Bread, Sept. 23, 1991*

This physician certainly had no moral or biblical way of thinking in this situation.

There was a blind girl who hated herself because she was blind. She hated everyone, except her loving boyfriend. He was always there for her. She told her boyfriend, "If I could only see the world, I will marry you." One day, someone donated a pair of eyes to her. When the bandages came off, she was able to see everything, including her boyfriend. He asked her, "Now that you can see the world, will you marry me?"' The girl looked at her boyfriend and saw that he was blind. The sight of his closed eyelids shocked her, she hadn't expected that. The thought of looking at them the rest of her life led her to refuse to marry him. Her boyfriend left in tears and days later wrote a note to her saying: "Take good care of your eyes, my dear, for before they were yours, they were mine." — *Author unknown*

• Abraham Lincoln made the great speech of his famous senatorial campaign in Springfield, Illinois. The convention before which he spoke consisted of a thousand delegates together with the crowd that had gathered with them. His speech was carefully prepared. Every sentence was guarded and emphatic. It has since become famous as "The Divided House" speech. Before entering the hall where it was to be delivered, he stepped into the office of his law-partner, Herndon. Locking the door, so that their interview might be private, took his manuscript from his pocket, and read one of the opening sentences: "I believe this government cannot endure permanently, half slave and half free." Herndon remarked that the sentiment was true, but suggested that it might not be good policy to utter it at that time. Lincoln replied with great firmness: *"*No matter about the policy. It is true, and the nation is entitled to it. The proposition has been true for six thousand years, and I will deliver it as it is written." — *Author unknown*

Abraham Lincoln was a man of honesty and integrity. When he was president, he said, *"I desire so to conduct the affairs of this administration that if at the end, when I come to lay down the reins of power, I have lost every other friend on earth, I shall at least have one friend left, and that friend shall be down inside me."* Many of the people who govern us today are not like President Abraham Lincoln. Sadly, they are tempted to compromise their honesty and integrity for political gain. Pray for them so they will not compromise their honesty and integrity for the sake of our country.

• As a new born-again Christian, I cashed my check at the grocery store on a Friday night. The clerk made a mistake and gave me more than the amount of my check. She not only gave me the dollars but also gave me the amount of the cents in dollars. Instead of ninety-eight cents, she gave me ninety-eight dollars. When I got home and recounted the money, I found I had $98 extra. Even though I could have used the money for my family, I felt from the Holy Spirit that the right thing to do was to return the extra money. My wife also agreed with me that the extra money did not belong to us. For these reasons, I drove back to the store that evening and gave the money to the store manager. During the next six months, I received a promotion, three raises, and an extra week of vacation from the company in which I worked. The rewards were all given to me by my superiors because they admired my professionalism, hard work, and honesty.

I hope you are an honest person. I also hope you have a good reputation for honesty. God wants Christians to be known for their honesty and integrity. One pathway to intimacy with God is through honesty. If you expect God's blessings, tell the truth like it is, and do not try to cover it up. When you are honest, it is more than not lying. It means that you love the truth, you tell the truth, you speak the truth, and you live the truth.

Remember that character is a victory. It is not a gift. Character is what you are when nobody is watching. *"For God shall bring every work into judgment, with every secret thing, whether it be good, or whether it be evil"* (Ecclesiastes 12:14). By telling the truth and living with integrity, you gain peace of mind and a clear conscience that are worth a lot more than anything else. It is good to teach your children that in whatever they do, they must please the Lord. That is what I taught my children, and I am pleased that they have followed my advice and experienced God's blessings in their lives!

❖ ❖ ❖

- "Honesty and integrity are absolutely essential for success in all areas of life." — *Motivational speaker, Zig Ziglar*

- "Integrity is not a 90 percent thing, not a 95 percent thing; either you have it, or you don't." — *Author, Peter Scotese*

- "Honesty is the first chapter in the book of wisdom." — *President, Thomas Jefferson*

- "Honesty doesn't always pay, but dishonesty always costs." — *Law professor, Michael Josephson*

85

DEATH

What happens when you die?

*

*"And when Jesus had cried with a loud voice, he said,
Father, into thy hands I commend my spirit:
and having said thus, he gave up the ghost."*
Luke 23:46

*

Make sure you are prepared to meet death one day!

Unless our Lord Jesus comes first, each one of us will die one day. The subject of death is relevant to every person. Nobody likes to think or talk about death, but it will certainly happen to us sooner or later. We frequently remember those who have gone before us. We ask ourselves: "What happened to them? Where are they now?" One day I will die too, but when? God is the only one who knows when you or I will die. For example, our friend's brother died suddenly at the breakfast table. It was on a Sunday morning while he had a cup of coffee in his hand. My first dear wife died unexpectedly at a young age. It happened without any warning and right in front of my eyes as we talked in our family room. One day I will leave family, friends, and loved ones behind, and so will you. What have you done to be ready for it? The answer to what you need when you face death is in Jesus' words: *"Father, into thy hands, I commend my spirit"* (Luke 23:46). We notice Jesus mentioned four important words – Father, hands, commend, and Spirit.

The following is a question for you: "Are you ready to commend your Spirit into God's hands?" You will only be prepared if you are a

Christian, and you depend on God's promises. Christ will never leave Christians lost in the midst of eternal darkness. The Bible says, *"To be absent from the body, and to be present with the Lord"* (2 Corinthians 5:8), and *"Blessed are the dead which die in the Lord from henceforth"* (Revelation 14:13).

ALL THE WAY MY SAVIOR LEADS ME

All the way my Savior leads me
O the fullness of His love!
Perfect rest to me is promised
In my Father's house above.
When my spirit, clothed immortal,
Wings its flight to realms of day
This my song through endless ages:
Jesus led me all the way;
This my song through endless ages:
Jesus led me all the way.   — *Hymn by Fanny J. Crosby, 1875*

The apostle James said, *"Whereas ye know not what shall be on the morrow. For what is your life? It is even a vapour, that appeareth for a little time, and then vanisheth away"* (James 4:14). If you are not a Christian, do not be a fool. Life is more fragile than you think. You never know when your life will be over because death never respects age, lifestyle, special times, or circumstances. You could die at a time when you never expect it just as my wife and our friend's brother. We were thankful knowing that both of them were prepared to meet death and "The fear of death follows from the fear of life. A man who lives fully is prepared to die at any time." — *Writer and humorist, Mark Twain*

❖ ❖ ❖

- "He who provides for this life, but takes no care for eternity, is wise for a moment, but a fool forever."— *Archbishop, John Tillotson*
- "The day which we fear as our last is but the birthday of eternity." — *Philosopher, Lucius A. Seneca*
- "You cannot pass a day devoutly unless you think of it as your last." — *Christian Monk, John Climacus*
- "Eternity to the godly is a day that has no sunset; eternity to the wicked is a night that has no sunrise." — *Businessman, Thomas Watson*

PREPARE FOR THE JOURNEY OF DEATH!

86

FEAR OF DEATH

"Fear not; I am the first and the last:
I am he that liveth, and was dead; and, behold, I am alive
for evermore, Amen; and have the keys of hell and of death."
Revelation 1:17,18

*

There is deliverance from the fear of death!

People today experience terrorist attacks, gunfire, suicide bombings, earthquakes, severe weather, terminal illnesses, economic problems, and many other things that put fear in people's hearts. Nevertheless, there is good news. There is an antidote for this fear, which we learn about in the Bible. The Greek words used for fear are "φοβέω, φοβίζω" (phobeo) verb and "φόβος" (phobos) noun. These mean to be afraid or to be struck with fear. These words are used many times in the New Testament.

The phrase *"fear not"* is found in Luke's gospel. It is impossible for a man to be free from fear because of his sinful nature, apart from God. Isaiah 57:20,21 states,

"But the wicked are like the troubled sea, when it cannot rest, whose waters cast up mire and dirt. There is no peace, saith my God, to the wicked."

The only ones free from fear are those who have been "born again" through faith in the Lord Jesus Christ. Jesus, as the "Prince of Peace," brings peace and not fear into man's heart. On the other hand, the sinful man is unable to free himself from fear and always lives in fear. Of all things men fear, the greatest is the *"fear of death"* (Hebrews 2:15). Anyone has reason to fear death if he has never been saved by grace and washed in the blood of Jesus Christ. *"And as it is appointed unto men once to die, but after this the judgment. It is a fearful thing to fall into the hands of the living God"* (Hebrews 9:27, 10:31).

Many things in the world can bring fear to the human heart. Some of them are fear of war, terrorism, and rejection. Some fears are logical, and some are foolish, but all are very critical for the ones experiencing them. The good news is that the gospel of Jesus Christ can set us free from any kind of fear. The first time FEAR came into the world was when Adam sinned and said to God, *"I heard thy voice in the garden, and I was afraid, because I was naked; and I hid myself"* (Genesis 3:10). The Bible also refers to FEAR for the second time in Genesis 15:1 when *"the word of the Lord came to Abram in a vision, saying, Fear not, Abram: I am thy shield, and thy exceeding great reward."* The Lord always provides protection for us and reminds us in Psalm 23:4, *"Fear no evil."*

In the New Testament from the lips of Jesus, we hear several times the words "fear not" or *"be not afraid."* The apostle Paul also reminds us:

- *"For God hath not given us the spirit of fear; but of power, and of love, and of a sound mind"* (2 Timothy 1:7).

- *"We may boldly say, The Lord is my helper, and I will not fear what man shall do unto me"* (Hebrews 13:6).

Even though the greatest fear is the fear of death; the Lord still delivers us from it. He has already conquered death. He makes it very clear to us: *"Fear not; I am the first and the last"* (Revelation 1:17).

Death is not the end for every person. God's Word says that after we die, each of us will be in heaven or in hell forever (Luke 12:4,5; John 14:1-3). When our physical death takes place, our eternal destiny will be forever sealed. The worst fear anyone could ever have is to spend all eternity in hell. We can escape this because Jesus died on Calvary's cross for our sins. He carried all the judgment that we deserve. Now, God offers salvation to everyone who will confess his sins to Him and will trust Christ as his personal Savior. We must never forget that we cannot be free from fear until our sins are forgiven. *"In whom we have redemption through his blood, the forgiveness of sins, according to the riches of his grace"* (Ephesians 1:7).

Thursday, December 21, 1899, after cutting short a Kansas City crusade and returning home in ill health, D. L. Moody told his family, *"I'm not discouraged. I want to live as long as I am useful, but when my work is done, I want to be up and off."*

The next day Moody awakened after a restless night and in careful, measured words he said, *"Earth recedes, Heaven opens before me!"* His son, Will, concluded his father was dreaming. *"No, this is no dream, son. It is beautiful. If this is death, it is sweet. There is no valley here. God is calling me, and I must go."* — Moody, December 1993, p. 70

What a wonderful experience that was to walk through death without fear because Jesus had delivered him from the fear of death. If you are not a Christian, keep all these things in mind and do not let the fear of death rob your living hope. Jesus overcame death, and He is there for you. Whether you live or die, God will deliver you as he did for D.L. Moody and others. Accepting the LORD is a one-way ticket to heaven. Do not be a fool. Prepare for the journey of death. Fear is contagious. Do not let this deadly disease get a foothold in your life and in your heart. Trust the Lord Jesus and live a full life each day!

❖ ❖ ❖

- "Our God is the God from whom cometh salvation: God is the Lord by whom we escape death." — *Priest and theologian, Martin Luther*

- "Fear not death for the sooner we die, the longer we shall be immortal." — *Founding Father of the U.S., Benjamin Franklin*

- "Live in Christ, live in Christ, and the flesh need not fear death." — *Pastor and Author, John Knox*

- "And deliver them who through fear of death were all their lifetime subject to bondage." — *Hebrews 2:15*

- "Yea, though I walk through the valley of the shadow of death, I will fear no evil: for thou art with me... " — *Psalm 23:4*

FEAR NOT, DEATH IS CONQUERED!

- D.L. Moody used to say there are two ways to go to heaven: first class and coach. Coach is Psalm 56:3, *"What time I am afraid, I will trust in You."* First-class is Isaiah 12:2: *"Behold, God is my salvation; I will trust and not be afraid."* How are you traveling?

Do not let fear steal the opportunity to be valiant for God!

87

BIBLICAL DEATH

"Verily, verily, I say unto you,
He that heareth my word, and believeth on him that sent me,
hath everlasting life, and shall not come into condemnation;
but is passed from death unto life."
John 5:24

*

Biblical death
is to come under the judgment and condemnation of God!

The Bible tells us a lot about death and especially what happens after death. In reality, there are two kinds of death - the physical and the spiritual death. The physical death is when the soul is separated from the body, and the spiritual death is when the soul separates from God. As part of creation, God made many different living beings, including animals and human beings. Both have a physical life, but only humans have a spiritual life. Humans have a soul. When they die physically, their soul lives forever in heaven with God or in hell with the devil.

Just as we have two kinds of death, we have two kinds of life: physical life and spiritual life. We can be spiritually dead but physically alive. *"And you hath he quickened, who were dead in trespasses and sins"* *(Ephesians 2:1)*

When Adam and Eve sinned by disobeying God's command, they instantly lost their spiritual life and came under the penalty and the condemnation of God. *"In the day that thou eatest thereof thou shalt surely die"* (Genesis 2:17). This is biblical death in the Bible. As sinners, we are all spiritually dead before we get saved, but after our salvation we are spiritually alive. We can see this clearly in John 5:24:

"Verily, verily, I say unto you, He that heareth my word, and believeth on him that sent me, hath everlasting life, and shall not come into condemnation; but is passed from death unto life."

Jesus does not talk here about physical death but spiritual death. Biblical death is to come under the judgment and condemnation of God. All of us, by nature, live with the thought of death being ahead of us. In other words, we live until we die. *"It is appointed unto men once to die, but after this the judgment"* (Hebrews 9:27). This would not be a good life, to pass from life to death and then to judgment. This would be a dark, horrible, terrible, and unspeakable future, but Jesus speaks in John 5:24 about a person who has passed from death to life. Pastor and author Colin Smith, said, *"What we know is a life where death is ahead of us, but Jesus speaks of a life where death is behind us, a life where the judgment and condemnation of God lies not in the future but in the past!"*

This is possible because when the Son of God went to the cross, He paid for our sins. When we believe in Him, we become free from judgment and condemnation. This means we pass from spiritual death into spiritual life because of Jesus.

"There is therefore now no condemnation to them which are in Christ Jesus, who walk not after the flesh, but after the Spirit." (Romans 8:1)

This is GOOD NEWS for a believer in Christ who has passed from death to life. We used to think that life with death and judgment was before us. Jesus speaks here about eternal life, which is life with death and judgment behind us. He speaks of spiritual life and death and not of physical life and death.

Now, when a believer dies physically, he will be away from the body, and he will be in glory with the Lord. This is much better by far. *"We are confident, I say, and willing rather to be absent from the body, and to be present with the Lord"* (2 Corinthians 5:8).

In this world every day, thousands of people are passing from life to death, but Jesus came so that, through faith in Him, we may pass from death to life! If you did not know this GOOD NEWS, I hope you feel excited now to tell others. Tell others what real life is. Before, you thought that death and judgment were ahead of you. Now, as believers in Christ, you know that eternal life is ahead of you because Jesus said,

"Verily, verily, I say unto you, He that heareth my word, and believeth on him that sent me, hath everlasting life, and shall not come into condemnation; but is passed from death unto life" (John 5:24)

❖ ❖ ❖

- "Verily, verily, I say unto you, If a man keep my saying, he shall never see death." — *John 8:51*

- "For as the Father hath life in himself; so hath he given to the Son to have life in himself;" — *John 5:26*

- "For as the Father raiseth up the dead, and quickeneth them; even so the Son quickeneth whom he will." — *John 5:21*

- "Without Christ, we live life with death and judgment before us. With Christ, we live life with death and judgment behind us."
— *Pastor and author, Colin Smith*

- "It is better for me to die in behalf of Jesus Christ, than to reign over all the ends of the earth."
— *Martyr and Church Father, Ignatius of Antioch*

- **We have two kinds of life: physical life and spiritual life.**

- **We have two kinds of death: physical death and spiritual death. The physical death is when the soul is separated from the body, and the spiritual death is when the soul separates from God.**

88

DIE IN THE LORD

"Then said Jesus again unto them,
I go my way, and ye shall seek me, and shall die in your sins:
whither I go, ye cannot come."
John 8:21

"And I heard a voice from heaven saying unto me, Write,
Blessed are the dead which die in the Lord from henceforth:
Yea, saith the Spirit, that they may rest from their labours;
and their works do follow them."
Revelation 14:13

*

Do you want to die in your sins or die in the Lord?

When we are young, we do not want to hear about death. We live under the idea that death is only for old people. Like it or not, we will all die one day by accident, illness, or old age. According to the Word of God, every person who has ever lived will die in one of two ways. Jesus said, *"I said therefore unto you, that ye shall die in your sins"* (John 8:24), and *"Blessed are the dead which die in the Lord"* (Revelation 14:13).

When a person leaves this world, he will either die in his sins, or he will die in the Lord. To die in his sins means that he will bring his sins into death with him. This would be the most tragic and horrible thing. To die in the Lord means that he will be separated from his sins because the Lord bore them for him. This will be the most wonderful and glorious event for this person.

When Christians enter heaven, *"their works do follow them."* (Revelation 14:13) and do not go ahead of them. Jesus said, *"I go to prepare a place for you"* *(John 14:2)*. Jesus goes first and opens the door of heaven, which is His home and the home of all Christians. Those who follow Him enter in the presence of the Lord and their works follow them. For this reason, when a Christian, a true follower of Christ dies, we say: "He went to be with the Lord." If he is not a Christian, we cannot say that.

If you are a Christian and have children, it is a good idea to take them to a funeral of someone they do not know well and use the opportunity to talk to them about death. This is very important for you to do. Your children will realize the importance of death, and it will give them the opportunity to think about making the right decision for their own eternal destiny.

When death is near to your friend or loved one who does not believe in Christ, you can say to them something like this: "Soon you will be going to another world. There is a world that is very dark because Christ is not there. Also, there is a world that is full of light, love, peace, and joy. This is possible, because Jesus is there, who is the light. Jesus said,

I am the light of the world: he that followeth me shall not walk in darkness, but shall have the light of life. (John 8:12).

This is a time for honesty. I know you have not followed Christ, but it is not too late to change. Christ died for sinners like us. Ask Him for mercy. Ask Him to forgive you, cleanse you, and carry your sins as He carried the sins of others."

Dear Reader, no one likes to think about death, but it is inevitable. If you are not a Christian, you have to know that the Bible tells us that your soul will still have to face God after you die. Jesus died for you, so you might enter the final judgment in hope. Make your peace with God now. I am glad that I made this decision as a young man after being presented with the clear gospel of grace for the first time to me by a man of God. I feel sorry for people today who reject God's grace when others or myself present the gospel to them. If you are one of those people, I encourage you to come to Jesus Christ at this time, and ask Him for forgiveness of your sins and the gift of eternal life. Choosing your eternal destiny is the most critical decision of your life.

People die every day. They either die in their sins, or they die in the Lord. If you die today, will you die in your sins, or will you die in the Lord? I pray you will make the right decision!

❖ ❖ ❖

• "He whose head is in heaven need not fear to put his feet into the grave." — *Minister and Author, Matthew Henry*

• "The man who lives daily with the thought of death is to be admired, and the man who gives himself to it by the hour is surely a saint." — *Pastor, and Author, Gary Thomas*

• "For whether we live, we live unto the Lord; and whether we die, we die unto the Lord: whether we live therefore, or die, we are the Lord's." — *Romans 14:8*

• "Whenever loved ones die, we grieve, but if they were believers, we also celebrate because they are with Jesus. One day, we'll see them again in heaven." — *Dr. Charles Stanley*

❖

DIE IN THE LORD!

Get Jesus.

It's

Hell

without Him

89

THE HEAVENS

"The heavens declare the glory of God;
and the firmament sheweth his handywork."
Psalm 19:1

"O LORD, how manifold are thy works!
in wisdom hast thou made them all..."
Psalm 104:24

*

God has created the heavens for His glory!

We know from the Bible that God has spoken to people like Adam, Eve, Noah, Abraham, and many others. God can speak to people, even audibly, if He desires. Maybe you are wondering: Does God still speak to us today? Yes, He does in a variety of ways. One of them is revealed in His created world through nature. *"The heavens declare the glory of God; and the firmament sheweth his handywork. Day unto day uttereth speech, and night unto night sheweth knowledge. There is no speech nor language, where their voice is not heard"* (Psalm 19:1-3). Everything that God has made has been created for His glory. This includes you, me, wildlife, angels, and the universe. The colors God uses in His creation are impossible for the best artist or the best camera to reproduce. Even though God gave me artistic talent, I was never able to match His glorious colors.

When we see a magnificent view of the Milky Way or look at Saturn and other planets through a telescope, we are astonished at the wonders of God. When I slept outside on the farm at night as a teenager, I saw countless numbers of stars. Later on, I read that scientists have discovered thousands upon thousands of galaxies; each containing millions of stars. This must make us reverence and fear God who created this gigantic universe and called it the work of His fingers, and He called them all by their names.

- *"When I consider thy heavens, the work of thy fingers, the moon and the stars, which thou hast ordained"* (Psalm 8:3).

- *"He telleth the number of the stars; he calleth them all by their names"* (Psalm 147:4).

It is impossible for man to know how many stars there are or the name of every star as God does.

- *"Mine hand also hath laid the foundation of the earth, and my right hand hath spanned the heavens: when I call unto them, they stand up together"* (Isaiah 48:13).

- *"He hath made every thing beautiful in his time: also he hath set the world in their heart..."* (Ecclesiastes 3:11).

- *"In whose hand is the soul of every living thing, and the breath of all mankind"* (Job 12:10).

In Psalm nineteen, God talks to us about Himself through nature. He mentions the heavens, as well as the day and the night, which tell about God's glory. They even do this without actual speech. The natural revelation has the ability to reach every person and every place in the world. It is so powerful that it is impossible to ignore. The sun goes from one end to the other end of heaven, and everybody feels the heat, even the blind person who cannot see it. This Psalm tells us that not only do *"The heavens declare the glory of God"* present, but the natural revelation continues, and we can receive brand new every day.

Several years ago, many pastors from all around the country attended a pastor's conference at the church we attended. At that time, I made a slide presentation entitled *"The Heavens Declare The Glory of God"* for my pastor to use at the conference. My pastor also gave a copy of this presentation in CD format to each pastor who attended. The CD could serve as an educational tool for teaching in their churches, in Sunday schools, as well as in their Christian schools. My son later invested time to convert that presentation into two videos. This enabled me to make them available on the internet free of charge to the public.

God is the creator, owner, and controller of all things. All things were made for His glory. As the heavens display the glory of God, let us as the children of God do the same!

❖ ❖ ❖

- "Nature is God's greatest Evangelist."
— *Pastor and theologian, Jonathan Edwards*

- "Lovely flowers are the smiles of God's goodness."
— *Politician, and Philanthropist, William Wilberforce*

- "Some people, in order to discover God, read books. But there is a great book: the very appearance of created things. Look above you! Look below you! Read it. God, whom you want to discover, never wrote that book with ink. Instead, He set before your eyes the things that He had made. Can you ask for a louder voice than that?"
— *Theologian and Philosopher, Augustine*

- "God dwells in His creation and is everywhere indivisibly present in all His works."
— *Pastor and author, A.W. Tozer*

- "Because God created the natural — invented it out of His love and artistry — it demands our reverence."
— *Scholar and Author, C.S. Lewis*

"The heavens declare the glory of God"

Psalm 19:1

90

GOD'S POWER

"That your faith should not stand in the wisdom of men,
but in the power of God."
1 Corinthians 2:5

"Jesus answered and said unto them,
Ye do err, not knowing the scriptures, nor the power of God."
Matthew 22:29

*

Depend on God's power, not your own!

Many Christians have a desire to serve the Lord but feel they are not qualified or do not possess the necessary requirements. The problem they have is not the qualifications, but the lack of faith in the Lord and in His power. They are not committed and have not yielded their lives to Him. They live in fear, and they are not able to defeat the enemies of doubt and discouragement in their lives. They need to take the small and most important first step by faith, and that is to trust the "Omnipotent" and "Faithful God" of the Bible. I know people who did that, and they have never been the same because God performed miracles in their lives.

Some of them became pastors, missionaries, Christian school teachers, successful Christian businessmen, good spouses, and parents. I saw people who came to the Lord that had bad marriages restored, others recovered from alcohol and drug addiction, homosexuality, idolatry, pornography, and many more sinful behaviors. I saw the Lord change alcohol into new furniture, new cars, and new homes for people who recovered from alcoholism by the power of our Creator. While D.L

Moody was in England, he heard Evangelist Henry Varley say, *"The world has yet to see what God can do through a man who is totally yielded to Him."* Moody was delighted by these words and replied to himself, *"By the Grace of God, I will be that man!"* By Moody yielding his life to the Lord, millions of people have been blessed through his ministry and are in glory, because of him.

We do not need special abilities for us to be used of God and see His power. God wants our availability. God wants only a heart loaded with grace and a soul prompted by love. Let us be faithful and surrender to the Lord. *"The greatness of man's power is the measure of his surrender"* (William Booth, founder of the Salvation Army). When we meet the faithfulness of God with our faithfulness, God can use us in a mighty way and make the impossible possible, with His mighty power.

● In August of 2001, tests showed that I had three malignant tumors in my neck and nearby chest area. My surgeon told me, "Even God can't help you." He did not want to be involved in my case because it was very serious, and there was a possibility I could die during the operation. My unshakable faith in God and the prayers of believers gave me strength and peace as I faced this difficult situation. *"The just shall live by his faith"* (Habakkuk 2:4). When we put our cares in God's hands, He puts His peace in our hearts. This is exactly what happened. His peace and presence never left me.

The prayers of my loved ones and believers from around the world were answered. The surgery lasted for many hours. Everything went smoothly, and there were no complications. It is unbelievable but true. The surgeon found and removed a total of 35 tumors and lymph nodes, and 18 of them were malignant. Because there were no complications during the surgery nor afterward, they sent me home the next day. I was even without pain. My surgeon said, *"Now you are in God's hands."* This was the best place to be, in the hands of the "Omnipotent" and "Faithful God" and of the Great Physician, my Lord, and Savior Jesus Christ.

● When I finished college in my home country of Greece, I had to serve two years in the military like everyone else. After my basic training, I served in the armed forces as a secretary in the office of a four-star general. One afternoon, I had orders from the General to finish writing an important assignment. Because of that, I was late for dinner. I explained to the Sergeant who was in charge of the meals why I was late, but instead of excusing me, he punished me. He sent a request to the General to approve his punishment for me to serve two extra days in the army. If that punishment had been recorded, it would have smeared my military records, which were outstanding up to that time. Because I had obeyed the orders of the General, I did not have to fret about what would happen. I had peace in my heart. When the papers for my punishment arrived in the General's hands, he refused to sign them. The Sergeant became angry and told his superior that he was going to offer his resignation. The General said to him that he would approve and sign the resignation if he asked for it in writing. Finally, the Sergeant gave up. He did not resign, and his orders for my punishment were never recorded in my military records. So, I did not have to serve the two days at the end of my two years of service. Additionally, the General awarded me with an honorable discharge one month early due to my good behavior. He even gave an order for all the army libraries to carry the first book I wrote when I was eighteen years old and published while I was in the army.

Do you depend on God's power in your life? Do you live by faith every day? None live so peacefully and pleasantly as those who live by faith. The Lord Jesus Christ must be your help for today and your hope for tomorrow. Do not worry and fear for tomorrow; God is already there for you. If you live by true faith, you do not have to be afraid of anything. Be thankful to the Lord for all your trials because through them, He is increasing your faith and purifying your Christian character.

What problems do you have? No matter what holds you in bondage, do not give up. God can liberate you. Do not fret. Obey God's orders and depend on His power to deliver you from any bondage. With God's power and your courage, the opportunities are unlimited. Do not follow the devil. Obey the Lord. Nothing is impossible for the Lord. As your four-star general, He has the power to override any of the devil's charges against you. Be ready to walk free as a child of God because *"greater is he that is in you, than he that is in the world"* (1 John 4:4).

Our generation of Christians desperately needs to consider and experience again the power of God.

THE POWER OF GOD

"The pow'r of God is just the same today,
It doesn't matter what the people say;
Whatever God has promised
He's able to perform:
And the pow'r of God is just the same today."

— *Hymn by Frederick A. Graves, 1899*

❖ ❖ ❖

- "God loves with a great love the man whose heart is bursting with a passion for the IMPOSSIBLE." — *Founder of the Salvation Army, William Booth*

91

MIRACLES

"Thou art the God that doest wonders [Miracles]:
thou hast declared thy strength among the people."
Psalm 77:14

"Behold, I am the LORD, the God of all flesh:
is there any thing too hard for me?"
Jeremiah 32:27

*

Even today, miracles are performed by the power of God!

A miracle is an action or an event that contradicts known scientific laws. A miracle is a remarkable and unbelievable event in the physical world. It is greater than all known human or natural powers and is said to be supernatural and a work of God. A miracle is something beyond man's power. The Old and New Testament are full of miracles performed by God and by His people, prophets, and apostles. The gospels in the New Testament record thirty-seven miracles Jesus did during His earthly ministry. According to the scriptures, He did a lot more. *"And many other signs [Miracles] truly did Jesus in the presence of his disciples, which are not written in this book"* (John 20:30).

The main Greek words used to describe our Lord's miracles are " δύναμις " (dynamis) which means mighty power of God, "σημεῖον" (semeion) which means sign for spiritual truth, "τέρας " (teras) which means giant, colossus, remarkable and amazing, and "ἔργον" (ergon) which means "works." Ergon is used in the New Testament for both miracles and ordinary deeds of Jesus. The primary purpose of Jesus' miracles was to teach and prove who He was and what He could do. In Jesus' miracles, we see clear evidence that He was Lord over life, death, sickness, nature, sin, and the devil. The greatest miracle was His resurrection from the dead and the guarantee that one day He will also raise all the believers from the dead.

Even today, the Lord accomplishes miracles. We experience them in our lives and in the lives of others. According to Princeton Religion Research Center's Emerging Trends, 82% of adults mostly agree or completely agree with the statement, *"Even today, miracles are performed by the power of God."* However, one requirement is needed to receive a miracle from God - we have to believe because *"With God all things are possible"* (Mark 10:27). The Lord did many miracles in my life. Some of them I have mentioned under the subject, "Testimonies of faith." The first testimony titled "God's Miracles in my Life" I have printed in a tract, which has been distributed to thousands of people around the world.

Years ago, we attended a large church that had many successful ministries and an energetic senior pastor. At that time, my first wife, Georgia, found a job for a Christian woman from our church at the place she worked. About a year later, the lady developed a tumor in her pancreas. She had surgery at a specialized hospital about an hour's distance from our home.

A few days after the surgery, the hospital tried to contact her husband because she had taken a turn for the worse. She was placed in intensive care. Her husband was on his way to take their son to a Christian college in another state. The hospital was not able to reach him, so they called her work and informed them of her situation. After the sad news my wife called our pastor and then me at my work. I told my wife to leave her work immediately. We drove together to the hospital.

When we arrived at the hospital, we found our pastor already there. We all went into her room. She looked totally hopeless, but I took hold of her hand and prayed. I told her, by faith, not to worry because the Lord would heal her. Afterward, we went back to the waiting room where my pastor was going to pray. Before he prayed, he told me that I should not have said that she would be healed for sure. He said that only a few minutes earlier, her doctor told him that she would possibly not make it. His words really bothered me, but I did not respond or argue with him out of respect. For several days, I prayed on my knees and with tears, asking the Lord to have mercy upon her and her family.

Every time I prayed, I had peace in my heart and a clear answer that she would recover. Many people from our church lost hope, but they continued to pray. It was sometime later that she eventually recovered from her near-death experience and was actually able to return to work. PRAISE THE LORD!

Do not limit the power of the Lord. Take advantage of the access you have to God. As a child of the King, you can enter into His presence to seek His help in time of need. *"With God all things are possible"* (Matthew 19:26). Do you believe this with all your heart? Faith grows as your vision of God's greatness increases. The Bible tells us in Ephesians 3:20 that God can do more than we ask or imagine. The Lord always honors our faith, and as a result, miracles happen. God's promises are true when we put Him and His work first in our lives. The work of faith is in our hands. The blessings and work of miracles are in God's hands.

The miracle of an individual's *"regeneration"* happens frequently today when a person is born again. This is an amazing work of divine creation. Imagine a person who was *"dead in trespasses, made...alive together with Christ"* (Ephesians 2:1-5). This person has been born again, not by natural birth, but *"born of the Spirit"* (John 3:3,8). All of his life changes, especially his heart. God *"hath delivered us from the power of darkness, and hath translated us into the kingdom of his dear Son: In whom we have redemption through his blood, even the forgiveness of sins"* (Colossians 1:13,14). Also, God says that *"he hath made him to be sin for us, who knew no sin; that we might be made the righteousness of God in him"* (2 Corinthians 5:21). All the true Christians have been saved by God's grace through faith in Christ and have been *"created in Christ Jesus unto good works"* (Ephesians 2:10)

I BELIEVE IN MIRACLES

"I believe in miracles
I've seen a soul set free,
Miraculous the change in one
Redeemed through Calvary.
I believe in miracles
For I believe in God!"

— Hymn by Carlton C. Buck and John W. Peterson

It is a real miracle when a person who is going on his way to hell, instead is going on his way to heaven because of God's love and forgiveness. This miracle happens any time a person sincerely turns to Christ for forgiveness and salvation. I experienced this miracle a long time ago, and I hope it has happened or will soon happen to you as well, if you ask it from Jesus Christ.

❖ ❖ ❖

• "I never have any difficulty believing in miracles, since I experienced the miracle of a change in my own heart.
— Theologian and Philosopher, Augustine

• "Faith does not operate in the realm of the possible. There is no glory for God in that which is humanly possible. Faith begins where man's power ends." *— Evangelist, George Mueller*

92

VALENTINE'S DAY

"My beloved is mine, and I am his..."
Song of Solomon 2:16

*

On Valentine's day, celebrate the deepest love possible!

For hundreds of years, people all over the world have celebrated Valentine's Day. This day brings to our mind images of hearts, greeting cards, flowers, and candy. Many think, "Oh! Another commercial holiday for companies like the greeting-card companies to make money." Indeed, they do. Reports tell us that men (15%) and women (85%) send Valentine's cards. According to statistics, around 1 billion Valentine's Day cards are sent every year in the United States. That makes Valentine's Day the second most popular day for sending cards, after Christmas, which has over 2 billion cards sent each year.

Valentine's Day is a pagan holiday, but it is an opportunity for Christians to focus on what love is all about. We must remember that to live without love is not to live at all!

• Some people celebrate Valentine's Day without knowing about the man whose life the holiday honors. Historians give us many stories about Valentine, but the common one is that he was a young minister who lived in Rome in the third century. Emperor Claudius II was in power at that time, and he recognized that the single men made better soldiers than the ones with wives and families. Because of that, he banned young people from marrying. Valentine disobeyed the Emperor's order and from compassion for couples in love, continued to perform wedding ceremonies in secret. He also continued to preach the gospel. Finally, Valentine was arrested and put into prison where he fell in love with the jailer's daughter who he intended to marry. Valentine started to write the most beautiful and passionate love letters and assured her of his great love for her. On the date set for his execution, he sent the last epistle to his sweetheart, which he signed: "From Your Valentine." On February 14, 269, young Valentine was put to death, martyred for Jesus Christ. Ever since, people everywhere have been moved by the kindness, the compassion, and the devoted love of this heroic young man, not only to the young lady, but to the Lord.

- One story tells us about an old man who got on a bus on February 14th, carrying a dozen roses. He sat beside a young man. The young man looked at the roses and said, "Somebody's going to get a beautiful Valentine's Day gift." "Yes," said the old man. A few minutes went by, and the old man noticed that his young companion was staring at the roses. "Do you have a girlfriend?" the old man asked. "I do," said the young man. "I'm going to see her right now, and I'm going to give her this Valentine's Day card." They rode in silence for another 10 minutes, and then the old man got up to get off the bus. As he stepped out into the aisle, he suddenly placed the roses on the young man's lap and said, "I think my wife would want you to have these. I'll tell her that I gave them to you." He left the bus quickly. As the bus pulled away, the young man turned to see the old man enter the gates of a cemetery. — *By Preaching Point*

Valentine has inspired us to express our feelings for our loved ones by putting them in writing for our own "valentines." The most remarkable expression of Valentine's love was his action to obey God and serve his fellow man, which cost him his life. Valentine's Day is a celebration of the deepest love possible. Not only between a man and a woman or between a person and God, but between God and man. Jesus Christ gave His life so you and I can know His passionate love. On February 14, we have an opportunity to show what real *"agape"* love is (1 Corinthians 13; 1 John 4:8) and think about God who gave His all for the sake of love. What will you say when Jesus says, "I love you. You are mine. Your name is written upon My heart. Your life is in My hands. I am always with you *'even unto the end of the world...'*, *'I will never leave thee, nor forsake thee.'* I gave My life for you that you might live forever with Me. The only thing I ask you in return is your love. Be My Valentine!"

The question for all of us is, "How will we be celebrating Valentine's Day?" For the early church, this was not a time of erotic longings, but it was a celebration of God's love. In this time, when biblical standards of love are under attack, God's standards are something to fight for...even to die for!

❖ ❖ ❖

- "The strongest evidence of love is sacrifice." — *Writer, Caroline Fry*

93

MOTHER'S DAY

"And thou shalt teach them diligently unto thy children,
and shalt talk of them when thou sittest in thine house,
and when thou walkest by the way, and when thou liest down,
and when thou risest up."
Deuteronomy 6:7

*

A mother's love and prayers can change your life.

Every year in the United States, we celebrate "Mother's Day." In 1914 President Wilson signed the first Mother's Day Proclamation, setting aside the second Sunday of May to be observed *"as a public expression of our love and reverence for the mothers of our country,"* even though we should show love, honor, and reverence to her daily. In some other countries "Mother's Day" is celebrated on different days and dates. The role of a Mother is defined as "a female parent," "the half of the Father-Mother team," "the one who gave birth to you as a child." She is the one who took care of you from a baby to an adult, with a special touch, unconditional love, and with many unimaginable sacrifices.

Cardinal Mermillod said: *"A mother is she who can take the place of all others but whose place no one else can take."* A mother's love puts the needs of her children above her own. She loves them unconditionally, not only with words, but also with actions. A mother's love does not have limits for her children. When we become adults, we begin to really appreciate her more. I remember my mother who is with the Lord now, more than ever, especially for all the sacrifices she made for me. She was not an educated person. She also did not give me many hugs or tell me thousands of times that she loved me while I was growing up in a small village. Instead, her love was unconditional and sacrificial with many actions, and not with empty words. She did the best in her power for me. She had a fear of God even though she did not have a lot of biblical knowledge. As a religious person, she prayed for me all the time. The reverence and fear of God she had in her heart was a huge influence on me. This was so important in my life, and because of that, I had a desire to know more about God and become closer to Him. She was very proud of me, as I was of her. I am grateful to the Lord who gave me the opportunity to lead her to the LORD, according to the Bible, the last time I got to see her on this earth. Both of us as born-again Christians rejoiced for the goodness and grace of our LORD!

Remember that each heart of a child is shaped according to his mother's love and prayers.

Someone asked a mother whose children had turned out very well, the secret by which she prepared them for usefulness and for the Christian life. Without hesitation, she said,

- "When in the morning I washed my children, I prayed that they might be cleansed by the Savior's precious blood.

- When I put on their garments, I prayed that they might be arrayed in the garments of salvation and in the robe of God's righteousness.

- When I gave them food, I prayed that they might be fed with the Bread of life.

- When I started them on the road to school, I prayed that their faith might be as the shining light, brighter and brighter to the perfect day.

- When I put them to sleep, I prayed that they might be enfolded in the Savior's everlasting arms."

No wonder her children were early led to a saving knowledge of the Lord Jesus Christ, and became adornments to the doctrine of God our Saviour in all things!

What a joy to that mother's heart when *"her children rise up and call her blessed."* Now *that her* secret is an open one, may hosts of other mothers follow it. *(Letourneau Tech's Tetourneau Now/Ministry I.J.F.P.)*

- I heard about what happened to a man when he was a teenager. Before his mother went to work, she gave him some things to do around the house. When she left, he got involved with his friends and forgot all about his mother's orders. When she came back from work, he was scared to death of her because he knew from other similar situations, what would happen to him. However, this time his mother took him to his bedroom, put her arms around him and started weeping and praying. She asked the Lord, again and again, to make him a godly boy. Her prayer changed his life from that day forward when he was in his mother's arms of love. *"Or despisest thou the riches of his goodness and forbearance and longsuffering; not knowing that the goodness of God leadeth thee to repentance?"* (Romans 2:4)

• I read in a magazine once that a couple in Canada had a boy without ears. Because of his appearance, his classmates made fun of him. A donor was found while attending college, and a successful transplant operation was performed on him. After that, he was so happy with his appearance. A few months later, he received the sad news that his mother had died. When he was at the funeral, his father told him how his mother loved him. Afterward, he brushed back his wife's long hair to reveal she had no ears because she had given them to her son whom she loved so much. *"Charity [love] suffereth long, and is kind;... Beareth all things, believeth all things, hopeth all things, endureth all things"* (1 Corinthians 13:4-7)

Dear precious mother, "Do you want to leave a legacy of faith?" Then MAKE SURE YOU SHARE THE LORD WITH YOUR CHILDREN! Whether they are young or grown, you have a powerful influence on the beliefs of your children. Eighty or a hundred years from now it will not matter in what house you lived, what car you drove, or how much money you had in your bank account. The world will be different because you were important in the life of your CHILDREN!

Dear precious friend, "Where is your mommy? How much do you love and appreciate her while she lives?" After their mommy dies, many kids will say how much they loved her, and remember her, and even put flowers on her grave. Yet, they never showed their real love and appreciation in words and deeds while she lived. Possibly, they never told her sincerely, even one time, "I love you, Mommy." Try not to be like them, but make sure you express your appreciation for her in thought and deed not only on Mother's Day, but every day. Think about the sacrifices your mother has made for your sake. Be sure to thank her for all she has done for you. Women who raise children have a special place in God's heart. Let your mother know she has one in yours!

❖ ❖ ❖

• "Of all the rights of women, the greatest is to be a mother."
— *Writer and Philosopher, Lin Yutang*

• "Men are what their mothers made them." — *Lecturer and Philosopher, Ralph Waldo Emerson*

94

FATHER'S DAY

"Hearken unto thy father that begat thee..."
Proverbs 23:22

"The father of the righteous shall greatly rejoice:
and he that begetteth a wise child shall have joy of him."
Proverbs 23:24

*

A Christian father is an instrument in God's hands!

On Father's Day, we celebrate fathers and appreciate the influence they have on our homes and society. Father's Day is celebrated in the U.S. on the third Sunday of June, but in other countries, the date is different. According to *Wikipedia,* "The first Father's Day was celebrated June 19, 1910, in Spokane, Washington" by a Christian woman, Sonora Smart Dodd. She "was the daughter of American Civil War veteran William Jackson Smart and was responsible for the founding of Father's Day." Later, "In 1966, President Lyndon B. Johnson signed a presidential proclamation declaring the third Sunday of June as Father's Day. In 1972, President Nixon established a permanent national observance of Father's Day to be held on the 3rd Sunday of June each year."

Even though the Bible does not mention Father's Day, God has always recognized and honored fathers throughout history. It also speaks clearly about many of the responsibilities and privileges of fathers. From the beginning, the Bible mentions the role of the father for Adam, Noah, and later Abraham who become a "father" to Israel through whom all people would be blessed. God told him, *"A father of many nations have I made thee"* (Genesis 17:5), and God honored him for his fatherhood. The Lord commands us to honor our fathers. *"Honour thy father and mother; which is the first commandment with promise; That it may be well with thee, and thou mayest live long on the earth"* (Ephesians 6:2,3).

The Law of Moses instructs fathers, and the most important are the words of Deuteronomy 6:2,5-7.

"That thou mightest fear the LORD thy God, to keep all his statutes and his commandments, which I command thee, thou, and thy son, and thy son's son, all the days of thy life; and that thy days may be prolonged. And thou shalt love the LORD thy God with all thine heart, and with all thy soul, and with all thy might. And these words, which I command thee this day, shall be in thine heart: And thou shalt teach them diligently unto thy children, and shalt talk of them when thou sittest in thine house, and when thou walkest by the way, and when thou liest down, and when thou risest up."

This tells us that fathers must have knowledge of the Bible, study it, teach it to their children, and be involved with their children every day.

Israelite fathers had to work hard to instruct their children in the ways of the Lord for their own healthy spiritual development. The obedient father had the responsibility to follow the commands of the Lord and the duty to practice Proverbs 22:6: *"Train up a child in the way he should go: and when he is old, he will not depart from it."*

This means the father and the mother must give the first training to a child. This is so important in his early years before he receives more education from outside of the home. In the New Testament, we find instructions for fathers. *"And, ye fathers, provoke not your children to wrath: but bring them up in the nurture and admonition of the Lord"* (Ephesians 6:4). The first part of this verse is cautioning advice and tells the fathers not to irritate or require extreme behavior from the child because this will only promote evil in the child's heart. The second part of this verse encourages fathers to educate the child about the Lord and His Word. It provides wisdom and helps them come to salvation and the knowledge of the Savior Jesus Christ.

In Matthew 7:9-11 we read, *"Or what man is there of you, whom if his son ask bread, will he give him a stone? Or if he ask a fish, will he give him a serpent? If ye then, being evil, know how to give good gifts unto your children, how much more shall your Father which is in heaven give good things to them that ask him?"* This verse includes a father's determination to care, provide, and love his children, and also speaks of God's role as a Father.

The Christian father is an instrument in God's hand. The instruction and discipline must be that which God commands. A father must nurture, protect, provide, comfort, understand, forgive, teach and discipline his children in a responsible way with love. Martin Luther said, *"Keep an apple beside the rod to give the child when he does well."* Christian discipline is needed to enable the children to grow up with devotion and reverence for God, respect for parents, teachers, public authorities, and live by biblical convictions and standards.

A good father is known by the Lord. *"For I know him, that he will command his children and his household after him, and they shall keep the way of the LORD..."* (Genesis 18:19). A godly father is to be an example to his children by serving the Lord *"As for me and my house, we will serve the LORD:"* (Joshua 24:15) and be an honorable man. *"The just man walketh in his integrity: his children are blessed after him"* (Proverbs 20:7).

- *"All scripture is given by inspiration of God, and is profitable for doctrine, for reproof, for correction, for instruction in righteousness: That the man of God may be perfect, thoroughly furnished unto all good works"* (2 Timothy 3:16-17).

A father's primary responsibility is to educate his children with the Scriptures and teach them God's truth. This way, the Scriptures will take roots and help them later in their earthly lives and Christian journey. Bible teacher Arthur W. Pink said that fatherhood is at the same time "responsibility and privilege." This means that the children are not only a father's responsibility but also a father's privilege. The father teaches his children, models the Christian life for them, disciplines them, and prays for them. The Bible declares, *"Lo, children are an heritage of the LORD: and the fruit of the womb is his reward. As arrows are in the hand of a mighty man; so are children of the youth. Happy is the man that hath his quiver full of them: they shall not be ashamed, but they shall speak with the enemies in the gate"* (Psalm 127:3-5). Children are a gift from God and should be cherished, encouraged, loved, and supported by fathers. Christian fathers, remember that your *"Children are not casual guests in your home. They have been loaned to you for the purpose of loving them and instilling a foundation of values on which their future lives will be built."* — Dr. James Dobson

❖ ❖ ❖

- "And he shall turn the heart of the fathers to the children, and the heart of the children to their fathers..." — *Malachi 4:6*

- "Do you know how you measure a dad? By measuring the emotional and spiritual health of his family. Look at his children and you'll discover what kind of dad he likely is." — *Dr. Adrian Rogers*

- "A truly rich man is one whose children run into his arms when his hands are empty." — *Author Unknown*

95

THANKSGIVING

"O give thanks unto the LORD; call upon his name:
make known his deeds among the people."
Psalm 105:1

*

God wants Thanksgiving to be our lifestyle, not just a day!

Every year in the United States, we celebrate Thanksgiving. The "First Thanksgiving" was celebrated by the Pilgrims following their first harvest in the New World in October of 1621. After that, the New England colonists were used to regularly celebrating "thanksgiving," days of prayer to thank God for different blessings such as military victory or the end of a drought. Later, Thanksgiving was celebrated nationally on and off since 1789 when Congress requested a proclamation by President George Washington. Finally, it has been celebrated as a federal holiday every year since 1863, when, during the American Civil War, President Abraham Lincoln initiated the first annual National Day of Thanksgiving with the following statement: *"I do, therefore, invite my fellow citizens in every part of the United States ...to set apart and observe the last Thursday of November next as a day of thanksgiving and praise to our beneficent Father who dwelleth in the heavens ..."* Now, Thanksgiving, or Thanksgiving Day, is a public holiday celebrated on the fourth Thursday of November.

Sadly, today, for many Americans, THANKSGIVING DAY is a day off, and a day for good food and drinks and not about thanking God for all the blessings He has given to them. Lots of Americans, even Christians, do not use the name of GOD, CHURCH, or CHRISTIANITY publicly because of fear and political correctness. For example, a fourth-grader stood up in his public school class, giving a report concerning the origins of the Thanksgiving holiday. Here's how he began: "The pilgrims came here seeking freedom of you know what. When they landed, they gave thanks to you know who. Because of them, we can worship each Sunday, you know where." — *by J. Michael Shannon, Preaching.com*

"I have always thought it would be a blessing if each person could be blind and deaf for a few days during his early adult life. Darkness would make him appreciate sight silence would teach him the joys of sound" *(Helen Keller, born deaf and blind)*. Her beautiful words make me think and ask, "Do we really appreciate all the precious gifts and blessings that God gives us each day? Or do we complain and get frustrated by the problems we face without seeing all these are sent from the hand of a loving God?"

As His redeemed children, our lives must overflow daily with gratitude for His gracious salvation, even in the midst of trials. Remember that God rules everything in His creation, such as the sun, moon, stars, wind, and rain. Not even one drop of rain falls without God's command. Jesus reminds us that not even a sparrow falls to the ground without the Father's will (Matthew 10:29). Think of how much more He cares for us!

Worship the Lord today with other believers. You have been blessed with the freedom to publicly declare your gratitude and praises. Do not let political correctness keep you from giving credit to whom credit belongs. We have to realize that all our blessings come from God. We have to appreciate and be thankful to Him for meeting our needs. We have to be thankful for His goodness because everything we have comes from His loving hands. It is good and appropriate for us to say on Thanksgiving Day and every day a "THANK YOU" to God for all the material and spiritual blessings He gives to us. *"In every thing give thanks: for this is the will of God in Christ Jesus concerning you"* (1 Thessalonians 5:18).

God does not want Thanksgiving to be an event on our calendar; He wants it to be our lifestyle. If you are not a Christian, this is the best time for you to tell God: "I'm sorry for my sins. I now turn from my sin and, by faith, receive You Jesus as my personal Savior. Come into my life, forgive my sins, and save me. I'm thankful for Your mercy to me. In Your name, I pray. Amen." After your prayer, show your appreciation on Thanksgiving and every day of your life by thankfully living for Jesus Christ. You will be forever thankful that you did.

"Make a joyful noise unto the LORD, all you lands.
Serve the LORD with gladness:
come before his presence with singing.
Know that the LORD he is God:
it is he that has made us, and not we ourselves;

we are his people, and the sheep of his pasture.
Enter into his gates with thanksgiving,
and into his courts with praise:
be thankful unto him, and bless his name.
For the LORD is good; his mercy is everlasting;
and his truth endures to all generations." — *Psalm 100*

❖ ❖ ❖

• "Thou who hast given so much to me, give one more thing- a grateful heart." — *Theologian, George Herbert*

• "Be grateful for all things at all times. That is the secret of a happy and productive life." — *Dr. Adrian Rogers*

• "When we are ungrateful, the heart of God is saddened, the Holy Spirit is grieved, and the joy of the Lord is quenched within us." — *Co-founder of DaySpring Cards, Roy Lessin*

Christians have a lot to be grateful for.
Jesus Christ suffered and died for their sins.

Have you thanked God lately?
Be thankful for what you do not have
as well as what you do have!

God does not want Thanksgiving
to be an event on our calendar;
He wants it to be our lifestyle.

96

GODLY MARRIAGE

*"And Adam [man] said, This is now bone of my bones,
and flesh of my flesh: she shall be called Woman,
because she was taken out of Man.
Therefore shall a man leave his father and his mother,
and shall cleave unto his wife: and they shall be one flesh."*
Genesis 2:23-24

*"Submitting yourselves one to another in the fear of God.
Wives, submit yourselves unto your own husbands,
as unto the Lord. Husbands, love your wives, even as Christ also
loved the church, and gave himself for it. Nevertheless let
every one of you in particular so love his wife even as himself;
and the wife see that she reverence her husband."*
Ephesians 5:21, 22, 25, 33

*

A godly marriage takes three to really work!

R uth Bell's parents were missionaries to China. When Ruth was a teenager, they sent her to school in Korea. She intended to become a missionary like her parents and minister to the people of Tibet.

When Ruth was at school, she gave some serious thought to the kind of husband she must consider. As she tells in her book *" A Time for Remembering,"* she listed these particulars: *"If I marry: He must be so tall that when he is on his knees, as one has said, he reaches all the way to heaven. His shoulders must be broad enough to bear the burden of a family. His lips must be strong enough to smile, firm enough to say no, and tender enough to kiss. Love must be so deep that it takes its stand in Christ and so wide that it takes the whole lost world in. He must be active enough to save souls. He must be big enough to be gentle and great enough to be thoughtful. His arms must be strong enough to carry a little child."* From what we know, Ruth Bell never became a full-time missionary in Tibet, but she found a man worth marrying: the well-known evangelist Billy Graham, and as his wife, she became a missionary to the whole world. For many years, they had a beautiful, happy, Christ-centered marriage which became an excellent example to many others. God always honors the ones who put Him in the middle of their marriage.

Today, many marriages fall apart. Most couples yearn for greener pastures. They think a new home, car, and other material things and worldly affairs will make their marriage better and happier. Do not be fooled. Circumstances do not bring happiness; commitment does. Take some valuable time today and let your spouse know that you love him or her, and you are glad God brought you together. Marriage is the most satisfying, most strengthening, and most lasting human relationship on this earth. Marriage is the most intimate, humbling, loving, and self-sacrificial relationship between human beings.

Marriages struggle to survive when the Lord is missing from their marriage. Marriage takes three to work. You can have a good marriage when Christ's spirit controls your life, and you practice His teachings. Numerous times I say to my wife, "Thank you for being a good wife." Her response is usually, "Thank you for helping me to be a good wife." Yes! Learn to obey the Lord's commandments if you want your marriage to be blessed, *"Likewise, ye husbands, dwell with them according to knowledge, giving honour unto the wife, as unto the weaker vessel, and as being heirs together of the grace of life; that your prayers be not hindered"* (1 Peter 3:7). Learn to love your wife like Jesus loved His church. *"Husbands, love your wives, even as Christ also loved the church, and gave himself for it"* (Ephesians 5:25). When a husband practices these verses, and the wife practices verses like this: *"Wives, submit yourselves unto your own husbands, as unto the Lord"* (Ephesians 5:22), both will experience a fruitful and blessed marriage.

If you are a young Christian man or young Christian lady, and you are looking for a lifetime partner to have a happy and blessed marriage, you have to choose a person who loves and serves the Lord. The most important thing in marriage is for both to have faith in God and Jesus Christ. When you have faith, everything is possible. If your mate loves you and loves the Lord, then he or she also loves others and wants to help them. Commit to one another and ask God for His love for each other. Put Christ in the center of your marriage. A successful marriage takes three to really work...two people plus the Lord. This is wonderfully described by Perry Tanksley in his poem:

MARRIAGE TAKES THREE

I once thought marriage took
Just two to make a go,
But now I am convinced
It takes the Lord also.

And not one marriage fails
Where Christ is asked to enter.
As lovers come together
With Jesus at the center.

But marriage seldom thrives,
And homes are incomplete,
Till He is welcomed there
To help avoid defeat.

In homes where Christ is first,
It's obvious to see,
Those unions really work,
For marriage still takes three

- "And the LORD God said, It is not good that the man should be alone; I will make him an help meet for him." — *Genesis 2:18*

- "Two are better than one; because they have a good reward for their labour. And if one prevail against him, one shall withstand him; and a threefold cord is not quickly broken." — *Ecclesiastes 4:9,12*

- "Except the LORD build the house, they labour in vain that build it." — *Psalm 127:1*

- "Don't marry the person you think you can live with; marry only the individual you think you can't live without." — *Dr. James Dobson*

- "Marriage: Trust is the start of it, joy is a part of it & love is the heart of it." — *Hallmark Cards*

- "A perfect marriage is one in which "I'm sorry" is said just often enough." — *Author, Mignon McLaughlin*

- "A good marriage is the union of two forgivers." — *Ruth Bell Graham*

- "To keep your marriage cup overflowing with love. Whenever you're wrong admit it and whenever you're right, shut up." — *Poet, Ogden Nash*

- "A good marriage would be between a blind wife and a deaf husband." — *Philosopher, Michel de Montaigne*

97

CHILDREN AND GRANDCHILDREN

"And thou shalt teach them diligently unto thy children,
and shalt talk of them when thou sittest in thine house,
and when thou walkest by the way, and when thou liest down,
and when thou risest up."
Deuteronomy 6:7

"Train up a child in the way he should go:
and when he is old, he will not depart from it."
Proverbs 22:6

*

To reap a harvest for eternity,
invest in your children and grandchildren now!

All parents strive to raise good children. Some are successful, and some are not. I always tried to raise good children, and I am thankful to the Lord for all His help. In 1970, when I was a very new Christian and before I had my first child, a dear old Christian saint quoted to me the verse above, Proverbs 22:6, from the Bible. Also, I attended a special training seminar at our church about the importance of child training and Christian education. These had a good influence on my Christian character and helped me as a father in training my two wonderful children.

By the grace of God, my wife and I made it a priority to use godly ways in raising our children even if it cost us time, money, and many other sacrifices to make this important investment. For example, when our children were small, we never used babysitters for us to go out and have a good time. One of us worked days, and the other nights to keep them always with us. We stayed away from unnecessary expenses, and we always gave them the best education we could afford by sending them to the best private Christian schools, colleges, and universities. They also attended great Bible believing churches with us, as well as when they were attending college.

Our first priority was always to direct them from their earliest years to the Lord for their salvation and to love and serve Him. Today, we are glad to see that they have developed tender hearts. If we saved the money we spent on them, we could have had a vacation home and many material goods. Yet, material things meant nothing to us compared to developing godly character in our children. Our sacrifices were great, but nothing compared to the character we see in our children today. We never regretted one minute of our time or one penny of our expenses. When growing up, my children thought I was a very strict father, and they did not like some things. Now that they have their own families and are raising their own children, they think differently and are more appreciative. Today, they and their spouses follow God's ways for their own children, and by the grace of God, they have become successful.

My children are grown now, but I still love them enough to give them godly advice. My children and I are not perfect, but with God's help, we strive to become better and better each day. When my children were teenagers, the pastor asked me to come up to the pulpit and tell the congregation the principles I followed in raising my children. Another time when I was soul winning with our assistant pastor who had small children, he asked me for advice as well. He was a humble and wise man who took my advice and raised wonderful children.

A few years ago, the University of Illinois held a special reception that honored my son and gave him an award for the most successful High Technology Engineer under forty years of age. Sometime later, one of our friends who after having seen my son's professional biography and picture, wrote to me: *"What a wonderful son you have raised! May he always bring glory to the name of our Lord and Savior. May God bless his family..."* Yes, the glory always belongs to the Lord. I give all the credit to Him. Without His help, wisdom, and direction, it would have been impossible to raise good children and please my Savior.

My son once sent me a Father's Day card, that said, *"Along the way, step by step...there were footprints, big and strong, right when I needed them, that's made all the difference, Dad. Thanking God for you on Father's Day and Always...You have a very special place in my heart. We have shared together the blessings of God"* (Philippians 1:7). My daughter sent me one that said, *"You're the kind of father God wants for every family - a father who cares, gives, and shares...and is happiest when he sees those he loves the most walking closer to the Lord. Happy Father's Day Dad!."* Also, my grandson, after his high school graduation, gave his testimony in front of all the church; and among other things, he told how I led him to the Lord at an early age and how much influence I had upon his spiritual life. Being a good parent and grandparent is the best occupation we have. Our children and grandchildren are a gift to us. How we raise them is our gift to the world. Kids can learn to read and write in school, but the character is determined and developed from their parents!

Many times in my ministry, I give principles for parents to follow in raising children with good Christian character. Many of the principles are not popular today. I always use the Bible and real-life experiences - not fiction. In this case, my son's and daughter's professional successes did not only depend upon their intelligence, education, and hard work, but also on their Christian character. They have been a good example to their professors in college and to their superiors at work. I am glad and proud of the good Christian values they follow which are not easily found in the society we live in today. *"He that walketh uprightly walketh surely: but he that perverteth his ways shall be known"* (Proverbs 10:9).

Be careful of what you are letting into your home. It may end up destroying your children. God has placed you as the gatekeepers for your family. You need to be extra diligent. Do not allow unsavory literature, videos, or other "adult" materials into your home. Such things may seem harmless, but they can eat your family alive. Today, children can be frightened by the threats and anxieties of our world. Teach them to fear the Lord instead. Tell them how the God of the Bible can keep them safe. Times may have changed, but He has not. Today's families are walking through a minefield. Nevertheless, there is a future for families who are obedient to God. If you desire to see your kids come to Christ, call on the healing power of Jesus. God honors the prayers of the parents. He will turn the hearts of your children if you first turn your heart to Him!

One time, my pastor told me that a father visited our Christian school with his five-year-old son. Before they left, the father asked the son, *"Would you like to come to this school?"* This is a problem today. It is easier for parents to have children than for children to have wise parents. It is harder to raise parents than children. When I was a boy, I was afraid to go to elementary school because my older brothers had scared me about the teacher. I even told my mother, *"It's better to die than go to school."* I am glad that my mother did not listen to me, but instead took me to school. Parents, what are you teaching your children? Children usually learn more from actions than from words. Make sure your life is a good example for them as Charles Spurgeon stated: *"Train up a child in the way he should go — but be sure you go that way yourself."* The reality is that people may disbelieve what you say, but they will always believe what you achieve.

Parents, do not forget *that "Children are an heritage of the LORD..."* (Psalms 127:3), and God chose you to be responsible for the godly training of your children. *"For I know him, that he will command his children and his household after him, and they shall keep the way of the LORD, to do justice and judgment..."* (Genesis 18:19). Are you leading or losing your children? God has called parents to shape the attitudes of their sons and daughters. Love your children enough to show them how to live. Make sure you have no regrets when you look back.

❖ ❖ ❖

- "With divorce and dual careers, parents spend 40% less time with their children than parents did a generation ago."—*Evangelist, Charles Colson*

- "Committed fatherhood would do more to restore a normal childhood to every child, and dramatically reduce our nation's most costly social problems, than all of the pending legislation in America combined." — *National Fatherhood Initiative*

- "Parents wonder why the streams are bitter when they themselves have poisoned the fountain." — *MD and Philosopher, John Locke*

- "To train a boy in the way he should go you must go that way yourself." — *Evangelist, Billy Sunday*

- "Every one of our children will be brought into the ark, if we pray and work earnestly for them." — *Evangelist, Dwight L. Moody*

- "Each day of our lives we make deposits in the memory banks of our children." — *Dr. Chuck Swindoll*

- "No one ever finds out what he believes in until he instructs his children." — *Missionary, Francis Xavier*

**Talk to God about your children before you talk
to them about God.
Spend time with your children.
They need your presence more than your presents.
Anything you do not teach your children, someone
else will, and you may not like the lessons.**

98

TED'S TESTIMONIES OF FAITH

Prayer
accomplishes miracles when we pray in faith!

*

"Let us therefore come boldly unto the throne of grace, that we may obtain mercy, and find grace to help in time of need."
Hebrew 4:16

*

GOD'S MIRACLES IN MY LIFE!

By Ted Matamis,
Founder and Editor Of the Free International Email Ministry
"A Spiritual Note from the Bible."

It is my joy and privilege to share with you how God has worked miracles in my life. Jesus Christ saved my soul out of the bondage of sin, and later, He saved me from the deadly illness of cancer.

I was born in a small village in Greece, the country where the Olympics were started and whose language God used to write the New Testament. My parents were poor and simple people, but they were very kind and hospitable. They sacrificially provided for their children and others. They loved God and lived with moral and ethical principles.

I was raised Greek Orthodox. In the Orthodox church, I learned the first lessons of the Christian faith. Generally, I was a good boy and a good student. I studied five different languages (in addition to English, which I learned later), and I wrote my first book at the age of eighteen.

I graduated from college with a degree in Education. Later, the Department of Education prepared a scholarship for me to go to France for more studies. Regardless of all this, I was still very unhappy, and my heart was filled with emptiness.

I turned in all directions to find the truth that was missing from my heart - the truth that would satisfy me and fill the emptiness. Everything my parents, teachers, and others taught me was not enough. I feared God, and I desired to know Him better. As a religious person, I prayed and asked God to give me peace in my heart and the opportunity to help others.

After I got married in 1968, I came to the United States to earn a Ph.D. in Education that I dreamed of, but God had different plans for me. Because I had a talent for art, I received two scholarships from two well-known American art academies. After attending the academies, I started to work for large American companies and became a successful commercial artist.

I thought a wonderful family, education, a successful career, money, a lovely home, and a car would offer me the happiness and satisfaction I expected. The strange thing is, even though I began to accomplish and earn these, one by one, still, I felt unhappy and empty inside.

At this time, while I was still trying to find happiness in my life, I became very sick, and the doctors told me that I would never recover. While I was in pain and despair, God sent one of His people to me. He was a godly man who preached the Word of God in a Greek church and on the radio in the Chicago area where I lived.

For the first time in my life, somebody sat down with me, and plainly talked to me about God's love and the price that Jesus Christ paid for me on the cross. He described God's simple plan and told me that Christ died for my sins and offered me eternal life. As he unfolded God's plan of free salvation by grace, my spiritual eyes were opened. Finally, I began to understand clearly all that I had been reading in the Bible about salvation.

On March 17, 1970, I repented and by faith accepted Jesus Christ as my personal Savior and Lord. He gave me eternal life and filled the emptiness I had. The Lord put a smile on my face and peace in my heart. He performed a miracle in my life. He not only healed my soul, but He also began to heal my sick body.

My whole life began to change, and the Word of God became not just theory and head knowledge, but a transforming power in my daily life. Before, I had taught the Word of God and the Greek New Testament to my students without experiencing a personal relationship with Jesus Christ.

After my salvation, my dear wife got saved, then later, my two children. Praise the Lord! Through the years the Lord has opened many doors for me to witness to thousands of people of many different nationalities.

I have been involved in many American Christian ministries and have taught and preached the Word of God in Greek churches, schools, and on a Greek Christian radio program. The Lord gave me a passion for souls, a loving and caring heart, and made me a successful soul-winner. It has been a blessing over the years to direct thousands of souls to Him and see many of them get saved.

Since 1996, God has given me a unique and blessed ministry in the English language through the Internet, "A Spiritual Note from the Bible." The Spiritual Note, which includes a short message from the Bible, is sent out free of charge. It also contains the plan of salvation for adults and children, prayer requests, and information relating to the main subject of the Spiritual Note (testimonies, Bible verses, sermons of well-known preachers and evangelists, good Christian music, interesting Christian websites, inspirational quotes, beautiful pictures, clean humor, and more).

The Spiritual Note is received by believers and non-believers from all walks of life who have requested them. I have experienced the hand of God upon this ministry. He has helped to spread the Spiritual Note all over the world by recommendation of the people who receive it without any personal, commercial advertising or marketing. Also, many recipients have described the Spiritual Note as "the best email ministry in the world." The goal of this ministry is to glorify the Lord and help others by encouraging, comforting, teaching, inspiring, challenging, and evangelizing.

My first dear wife is now with the Lord in heaven after she had a heart attack in 1996. We had twenty-eight happy and blessed years of marriage. I am grateful to God for giving me a wonderful and blessed wife and children to help me in His ministries. Later, when I became seriously ill, God miraculously brought my second wife into my life. She is a blessed Christian lady with a kind, loving, and caring heart. Her sacrificial and supportive spirit has helped me through all of my hard times. She is a real servant of God, and we are both very pleased and happy with our marriage.

In 1999, I was diagnosed with thyroid cancer and a large tumor nearby. The thyroid and the tumor were both malignant. A surgeon removed the entire thyroid, the tumor nearby, plus fifteen malignant lymph nodes. During the next two years. I had radiation treatments. In August of 2001, tests showed another three tumors in my neck and nearby chest area. My surgeon told me, **"Even God can't help you."** He did not want to be involved with my case because it was severe, and there was a possibility I could die during the operation.

When people I knew heard this sad news, many (even some believers) raised their hands and gave up. Instead of comforting, praying, or helping me, they began to wait for my funeral. The devil used their attitude and the hard words of my surgeon to try to discourage me. Instead, as a redeemed child of God, I raised my eyes to heaven with confidence, and by faith, I told those with weak faith and negative attitudes that the Lord would deliver me from this life-threatening situation.

I believed that the Lord still had work for me to do for Him in this world. Through my internet ministry, I asked for prayers from sincere Christians and their churches around the world. A retired pastor told me he was getting up at midnight and was praying with tears for me, and a missionary wrote to me that he was praying for a miracle. As Christians, we believe the work of faith is in our hands, but the work of miracles is in God's hands!

The Lord helped me find a better hospital and surgeon. My unshakable faith in God and the prayers of believers gave me strength and peace as I faced this difficult situation. The Lord not only allowed the right doctor to perform the surgery, but He also caused my health insurance to approve coverage for all the costs of the operation, which they had earlier denied.

"The just shall live by his faith" (Habakkuk 2:4). When we put our cares in God's hands, He puts His peace in our hearts. This is exactly what happened. His peace and presence never left me. The prayers of my loved ones and believers from around the world were answered. Although the surgery lasted for many hours, everything went smoothly, and there were no complications.

It is unbelievable but true. The surgeon found and removed not only three, but a total of thirty-five tumors and lymph nodes. Eighteen of them were malignant. Because there were no complications during the surgery nor afterward, they sent me home the next day. I was even without pain. My surgeon said, "Now you are in God's hands." This was the best place to be.

I am in the hands of the Great Physician, my Lord, and Savior Jesus Christ! I am very thankful for the many miracles the Lord has done in my life over the years, and now He has added one more. I feel very well now, and the yearly follow up medical results have been normal. I know my trials in this world are not over, but I praise the Lord because, through them, He is increasing my faith and purifying my Christian character.

This temporary life is so short, and sooner or later, each one of us will meet the Lord. I hope you are ready to meet the Lord as **"Savior"** and not as **"Judge."** If you are not saved, I want to tell you something very important from my own experience. If you are far away from the Lord Jesus Christ, you will not find the salvation of your soul, real peace in your heart, or happiness in your life. Only Jesus Christ can give you a NEW LIFE and REAL LIFE. I am not promising that if you have Jesus Christ in your life, you will be without trials, but the Lord always will be there to help you.

Dear Reader, I believe with all my heart that it will not be the end for me when I die, but only a new beginning in my Father's heavenly home for eternity. Will you be there?

I encourage you, before it is too late, by faith, trust Jesus Christ as your personal Savior. The Bible says, **"Behold, now is the accepted time; behold, now is the day of salvation"** (2 Corinthians 6:2). In the quietness of your mind at this very moment, you can receive Christ's gift of salvation by sincerely praying this simple prayer from your heart:

Dear God, I know that You love me and want to save me. Jesus, I believe You are the Son of God, and you shed your precious blood and died on the cross to pay for my sins. I believe God raised You from the dead. I now turn from my sin, and by faith, receive You as my personal Savior. Come into my life, forgive my sins, and save me. In Your name, I pray. Amen.

❖

THE ORGAN

Several years ago, we gave our piano to my daughter so that she could teach her children to play. This way, her children could use their talents to serve the Lord as they grew. Because my wife played the organ in the church where we attended at that time, she needed an organ at home to practice. By faith, I told her that the Lord would give us a free organ for a Christmas present.

I believed this because first, we tried to help my daughter; second, we did not have thousands of dollars to buy an organ; and third, because my wife was going to use it to glorify the Lord. When some other people heard about this, they were skeptical and told me, "You are asking too much. Maybe the Lord will give you one for a good price, but not free."

Without giving those people any attention, I checked on the internet and found a church in our area that wanted to give their organ away for free. They wanted to give it away because somebody had donated a brand new organ to them. I was the first to respond to their ad. Possibly, others thought a free organ would not be worth anything. The organ was beautiful and in excellent condition, but it was too big for our living room.

We talked to our Pastor about the organ after we saw it. He told us that our church would take it and would give us the church's current smaller organ for free. Our church's smaller organ was like brand new. The church received the big organ; and the pastors, with a few other men from our church, delivered the smaller organ to our home without us having to pay a penny. The Lord not only blessed us - He blessed our church, too. PRAISE THE LORD!

Are you living by faith? Faith is not feeling, it is believing. Faith is not doing, it is resting. Faith is more than mere belief. Faith is deep confidence in the One you trust. This confidence is demonstrated by your actions. The Bible says, *"Without faith, it is impossible to please Him"* (Hebrews 11:6), and *"all things work together for good to them that love God"* (Romans 8:28).

Depend on God's promises. By faith leave everything in God's hands and wait to see the surprises He has for you. Maybe your test will take a little longer, but for sure, God will *"supply all your needs according to his riches in glory by Christ Jesus"* (Philippians 4:19). Take a step of faith today. The Lord will honor your faith and may even give you a free organ for Christmas!

❖

THE VENDING MACHINE

One morning in 1970, my first wife and I took a bus to pick-up some transfer papers from college. Because of a severe snowstorm, the college was closed, and only a few office staff were there. One of them told us that they would prepare our papers, but we had to wait until late afternoon. Due to the weather, we were stuck by ourselves in the waiting room all day.

We had not brought along anything to eat, and we did not really have any money for the few vending machines that were there. In fact, I only had twenty five-cents in my pocket. Just a few days earlier, I had gotten saved and was experiencing "the first love" the scriptures mention. I had faith that the Lord could do anything for us. I told my wife the money was not enough to buy food for both of us, but we would pray with faith and ask the Lord to perform a miracle.

After we prayed, we decided to buy a container of soup with the twenty-five cents. When we got soup, the quarter came back. We tried again for another soup. Again and again, the money came back until both of us had a soup, sandwich, drink, and dessert. PRAISE THE LORD!

Live by faith and believe in the power of the Lord. No matter what you face, God will help you. The Lord may not do a miracle opening the heavens to send you "manna" or control the vending machine to give you food when you need it, but for sure He will find a way to supply all your needs. *"For they were about five thousand men. And he said to his disciples, Make them sit down...Then he took the five loaves and the two fishes, and looking up to heaven, he blessed them, and brake, and gave to the disciples to set before the multitude. And they did eat, and were all filled..."* (Luke 9:14, 16, 17)

NEW JOB

In the summer of 2001, I told my wife to resign from her job. She was not happy there because of her Christian convictions. I told her that the Lord always honors a person who lives with Christian convictions, and He will have something better for her. By faith, I also told her with peace in my heart that she would find another job within four weeks.

The first three weeks, we found many jobs opportunities, but they were far away from home. The fourth week I told her to apply for a job that was only two and a half miles from home. She felt that she was not qualified, but she sent her resume anyway. When the personnel director called, she asked her to come the next day for an interview and to take a test that would last about four hours. At first, she felt it would be a waste of time, but I told her with confidence and faith not to close the door. Instead, allow the Lord to close the door if it was His will.

The next day as she went for the interview, I prayed sincerely that the Lord would be praised and glorified in this situation. The test took her only twenty minutes, and all the people who interviewed her liked her personality and her qualifications. The position they advertised was not for her, but they hired her immediately for another and better position with much better pay and benefits. PRAISE THE LORD!

Are you living by faith or by sight? Depend on God's promises. No matter what problems come your way, God will help you. The Lord may not do a miracle by giving you a good job, but for sure, He will find a way to supply all your needs according to his riches in glory by Jesus Christ. I recommend that you walk by faith and step out of the boat, and you will discover the thrill of walking on the water as Peter did! *"And when Peter was come down out of the ship, he walked on the water, to go to Jesus"* (Matthew 14:29).

❖

OUR FIRST HOUSE

In 1972, my first wife and I began to look for a house to buy close to our church and to the company where my wife and I both worked. One of us worked at night while, the other one worked during the day, so one of us could be home to take care of our daughter, our first child. Because there were no houses for sale in the area we were looking, I went door to door and asked if the homeowners were thinking about selling their house.

Not a single person had an interest in selling their house except for one lady. She told me that she had cancer and was in the process of getting a divorce. She also said that possibly they would sell their house in the future. I gave her my phone number and told her to give me a call when they were ready to sell the house.

We really liked that house very much. Since a few months passed and we did not hear anything from the lady, we made an offer on a single-family home we really did not like much. The night we went to the realtor to find out if our offer was accepted, I told my wife that before we go to the office, let us pray for the Lord to do His will. We prayed, sincerely and earnestly. After our prayer, we went inside. The first thing we heard from the realtor was, "You lost the house. Another person got it because he made a cash offer and not a loan."

As human beings, we were disappointed. I told my wife, "The Lord closed the door for a reason. Let us go home and see the next door He will open." When we got back, we could hear the phone ringing as we opened the door. I rushed in and picked up the phone. Can you imagine who it was? It was the lady who I had given my phone number a few months ago.

She told me that she and her husband decided to sell the house for an excellent price. This house was a hundred times better than the other one. It was a newer brick house with two apartments. We purchased the house and lived there free because we were able to rent out one of the apartments. PRAISE THE LORD! The Lord gave us a good lesson-not to close the door before He closes it.

❖

OUR SECOND HOUSE

In 1975, we had two children and were looking to sell the first house to buy a single-family home for our children with plenty of room in the backyard to play. My first priority was to find a house close to a specific church that had a Christian school where I wanted to send my daughter and my son. This was in a nice suburb of Chicago. For a year, we looked for the right house.

This time, we did not rush after we learned a good lesson from the first house. Finally, the Lord opened a door. It was a house that was almost brand new. A young family had built it, but they wanted to sell because the man of the house found a better job in a different state. The man had already moved, and his wife was trying to sell the house.

We liked the house very much. It had everything we were looking for, plus a lot more. The only problem was that it was very expensive. My wife and I felt that the Lord had this house for us, but we needed a miracle for us to buy it. I gave a much lower offer than the asking price. The realtor tried to tell us that we would lose this beautiful house. One Sunday, after our morning church service, we stopped to see the house again. We did this before heading to a Greek church in Chicago where I preached on Sunday afternoons.

The realtor again tried to push us to give a better offer. He told us that this is your last opportunity. He told us that, next Sunday there will be an open house, and somebody else will take it. My wife and I without hesitation and with faith told him, "If this house is for us, the Lord will keep it." We left to go to church and continued to pray for this house.

The next Sunday, which was in the month of April, they had the open house. Believe it or not, during those hours it unexpectedly began to snow. As a result, nobody went to the open house. Because they needed to move, they accepted my low offer. After that, the Lord brought a buyer who bought our first house at a good price. We got the house the LORD had for us. PRAISE THE LORD! I have been living in this house since 1976. If somebody does not experience miracles, it is because he does not believe in miracles. For me, God's miracles are not unusual anymore.

The Lord also challenged the faith of the realtor, who questioned our attitude and faith at that time. Later, when we had him, his wife, and his five children for dinner, he openly admired us for our faith and he admitted that his faith was weak.

❖

LADY IN THE HOSPITAL

Many years ago, we attended a large church that had many successful ministries and an energetic senior pastor. At that time, my first wife, Georgia, found a job for a Christian woman from our church at the place she worked. About a year later, the lady developed a tumor in her pancreas. She had surgery at a specialized hospital about an hour's distance from our home.

A few days after the surgery, the hospital tried to contact her husband because she had taken a turn for the worse. She was placed in intensive care. Her husband was on his way to take their son to a Christian college in another state. The hospital was not able to reach him, so they called her work and informed them of her situation.

After the sad news, my wife called our pastor and then me at my work. I told my wife to leave her work immediately. We drove together to the hospital. When we arrived at the hospital, we found our pastor already there. We all went into her room. She looked totally hopeless, but I took hold of her hand and prayed. I told her, by faith, not to worry because the Lord would heal her.

Afterward, we went back to the waiting room, where my pastor was going to pray. Before he prayed, he told me that I should not have said that she would be healed for sure. He said that only a few minutes earlier, her doctor said to him that she would possibly not make it. His words really bothered me, but I did not respond or argue with him out of respect. For several days, I prayed on my knees and with tears, asking the Lord to have mercy upon her and her family.

Every time I prayed, I had peace in my heart and a clear answer that she would recover. Many people from our church lost hope, but they continued to pray. It was sometime later that she eventually recovered from her near-death experience and was actually able to return to work. PRAISE THE LORD!

Please do not limit the power of the Lord. Take advantage of the access you have to God. As a child of the King, you can enter into His presence to seek His help in time of need. *"With God all things are possible"* (Matthew 19:26). Do you believe this with all your heart or just with your mind? Faith grows as your vision of God's greatness increases. The Bible tells us God can do more than you can ask or think (Ephesians 3:20).

❖

OUR FAITH'S NUTRITION

Many times, people have admired my faith and asked me, "How can we have your faith?" or "How can our faith grow?" To grow your faith, ask the Lord to help you with this. If the Lord gives you trials in your life, do not complain. These are the best nutritional foods for your faith. Through them, your faith is tested and grows. Faith grows by obeying and trusting Christ even when you do not know what He is doing. Faith grows by seeing that Christ is not limited by the weakness of your faith. *"According to your faith be it unto you"* (Matthew 9:29), and *"Now unto him, that is able to do exceeding abundantly above all that we ask or think..."* (Ephesians 3:20).

When I was a new Christian, I met some older Christian men and ladies who had strong faith, and I admired them. I always prayed, and I asked, Lord, give me more faith." The more I asked, the more trials and difficulties I had in my life. I almost came to the point of telling the Lord, "I do not want any more faith." However, before getting to that point, I learned my lesson-that through my trials, my faith increased by obeying and trusting in the Lord. Today, I know that my trials in this world are not over. Nevertheless, I praise the Lord because, through them, He is increasing my faith and purifying my Christian character. PRAISE THE LORD!

Are the storms of life making you feel down? The next time you feel queasy with fear, remember to call upon the Lord. He is with you. He is greater than any storm you face. When the strong winds blow and the storm rages, remember to look up!

❖

WHAT HAS PRAYER DONE?

"Prayer has divided seas, rolled up flowing rivers, made flinty rocks gush into fountains, quenched flames of fire, muzzled lions, disarmed vipers, and poisons, marshaled the stars against the wicked, stopped the course of the moon, arrested the rapid sun in its great race, burst open iron gates, conquered the strongest devils, commanded legions of angels down from heaven. Prayer has bridled and changed the raging passions of man and routed and destroyed vast armies of proud, daring atheists. Prayer has brought one man from the bottom of the sea, and carried another in a chariot of fire to heaven; what has prayer not done!"— Dr. Ryland

If you want to be used by the Lord, dedicate yourself in prayer today and be willing to follow Him, no matter what the cost!

If You Need A Sign from GOD, STOP & PRAY WITH FAITH. This Is It!

99

PERSONAL TESTIMONIES

GOD'S ABUNDANT GRACE...
IN OUR DARKEST HOUR!

*The following personal testimony was in my church's
nationwide Christian magazine.*

*

Ted Matamis lost his wife to a heart attack
in February 1996.
This is his story about his darkest hour.

It was a typical night for us. My daughter taught in a Christian school about four hours away from us, and my son was finishing his engineering degree at the University of Illinois. With both the children gone, we were enjoying some time by ourselves. My wife had met some girlfriends, and when she returned home, we sat in the family room and talked. We had gone through a lot together for twenty-eight years, both of us coming from Greece to America. We came to this country with only one suitcase of clothes and another of books.

Through a series of miracles, we both heard the gospel. I will never forget the night I trusted Jesus Christ as my personal Savior on March 17, 1970. Suddenly, the emptiness that I had felt all my life was filled. Less than a month later, my wife came to the Lord. Together, we learned the Word of God. Together, we were baptized. Together, we prayed. Together we raised a fine son and daughter. Together we served the Lord. I always felt so blessed that we were partners in Christ. I smiled at Georgia as she sat on the sofa across the room. We talked about Valentine's Day coming up, and I mentioned to her a funny story I heard on a Christian radio station. As we continued, she said she felt dizzy. Concerned, I stood and went over to her just as she fell backward onto the couch. I rushed to call 911.

The darkest day of my life was when I stood next to this wonderful lady who was my wife. This person, my sweetheart for twenty-eight years had left. That night I was alone in my house. My neighbors had invited me to stay with them, but I said I wanted to spend the night with the Lord. The loneliness and shock I felt were incredible. My life had changed 180 degrees in a few hours. The only way that anyone can go through something like this is to be prepared ahead of time. The verses I had memorized came to me in my most difficult moments. His promises, His presence, His counsel, His strength-all were there for me that night. I cannot explain how real the Lord was to me.

I still miss Georgia. The pain sometimes gets so bad I think I cannot go on. Then, the Lord shows his faithfulness, and somehow, I gain strength. I know she is with the Lord who loves her more than anyone. It was a comfort to me that my children also believe this. My son told me he knew he would see his mother again.

Three souls were saved at the funeral, and I know there were others saved who did not indicate it. My daughter said afterward, *"Daddy, Mom left three people on the earth, but she took three souls with her to heaven."* Both of my children gave me strength even though it was a great shock to them as well.

My neighbor Johnny was an elderly man whose wife had died from cancer. Georgia always wanted to help him, so we had him over two or three times a week for dinner. Both of us tried to do our best to help him physically, emotionally, and spiritually. Because we loved him, we continually tried to witness to him, but he did not listen to us. Even after he suffered a stroke, he did not want to hear the gospel.

After Georgia died, I called him to come over to my house for lunch. I witnessed to him again, and this time, he was ready. He accepted the Lord and said to me, "I would like to go where your wife went and where you will go."

The Lord is our help for today and our hope for tomorrow. I am not pretending that there are not times that are very difficult; still, the Lord is always there for me. If you are reading this and you are without the Lord, I encourage you to trust Him as your personal Savior. It is the only way you can go through terrible times. I could never thank Him enough for all that He has done for me.

I WAS GREEK ORTHODOX

As a young boy, I feared God and desired to know Him better. As a Greek Orthodox, I was a religious person who prayed and asked God to give me peace in my heart and the opportunity to help others. While I was a college student in Thessalonica (Thessaloniki) Greece in 1965, I read the Sunday sermon of Dr. Spiros Zodhiates in the worldly magazine, "Romanzo." I liked the sermon and mailed in a request for the free Christian literature they offered. The manager of the LOGOS bookstore in Athens, Greece, Mr. George Konstantinidis, sent me the gospel of John, the Daily Bread, and a few Christian tracts. I liked all of them and even had them on my table and showed them to all of my friends who visited me.

While I was in the Greek army for two years, the other soldiers and I received the New Testament, through the ministry of Dr. Zodhiates. Later, when I came to the United States, the weekly radio messages of Dr. Yerasmus Zervopoulos made an impression on me. In 1970 when I met Dr. Zervopoulos, it did not take long for him to lead me to the Lord. Over the years, God used many other people to plant and water His seeds in my heart.

Are you a faithful ambassador of Christ? God did not call you to do everything, but only to do your part in the body of Christ. It does not matter where God calls you to work whether it is in your local church, in your own ministry, in the ministry of Dr. Zodhiates, Dr. Zervopoulos, or Dr. John Doe. You still have the responsibility to plant a seed or water it. Never worry about the increase; that belongs to God. *"I have planted, Apollos watered; but God gave the increase"* (1 Corinthians 3:6). Do your part the best you can and leave the results to the Lord! Remember: *"Every man shall receive his own reward according to his own labour."* and *"We are labourers together with God..."* (1 Corinthians 3:8,9).

❖

GOD'S GUIDANCE

In August of 2001, tests showed that I had three tumors in my neck and nearby chest area. My surgeon at that time told me in his office, "Even God can't help you." He did not want to be involved with my case because it was very serious, and there was a possibility that I might die during the operation. From the conversation I had with him, I also learned more information about my first surgery in 1999 when he had removed the entire thyroid, the tumor nearby, and fifteen malignant lymph nodes.

From either laziness or carelessness, he had left all the rest of the cancer without cleaning it out entirely. He used the excuse that the radiation would take care of it. I believe because of that, he felt guilty and tried to recommend that I go to another hospital. When I asked him, "Why?" he said that he took out only the tumors he could see with his eyes — nothing else, and the other hospitals used better methods for detection.

I lost hope and all confidence in him. I went and talked with the specialist who had recommended him. Before I met with the specialist, I asked the Lord to help me and give me His wisdom and guidance as I faced this serious situation. First, I asked the specialist to recommend someone for a second opinion, so he suggested an excellent surgeon who was a professor of surgery at a well-known university.

Second, I asked if there was any other way besides using only his eyes for the surgeon to possibly see if there were more tumors in addition to those that were on the CAT scan. His answer was not satisfactory and almost the same as my first surgeon. I then told him that the day before I had the CAT scan in the hospital, they had given me a radioactive pill to help them see the tumors in the pictures. I asked him why not talk to the surgeon and ask him to consider giving me two or more radioactive pills the day before the surgery. I told him I believed that these pills would help the surgeon to see more clearly, not only these tumors to remove, but also others also if they existed.

My doctor and my second surgeon discussed my suggestion and decided to give me ten radioactive pills the day before my surgery. Because of that, the surgeon found and removed a total of 35 tumors and lymph nodes. Eighteen of them were malignant. Now, everything is history. By God's grace, I am alive, and my doctor and surgeon use the same surgical procedure to do other surgeries to help save the lives of other people. PRAISE THE LORD!

Do you have your back against a wall? Do not lose hope. There may be an answer you have not considered. Ask the Lord for the gift of wisdom and trust His guidance. Seeing things from God's perspective may be the first step on your ride to the top!

❖

TWO TEENAGERS

I once had the privilege to give biblical advice to two Christian teenagers: Mark and John. I gave them the same basic Biblical advice and shared my own Christian experience. I believed that if they followed my instructions, they would become good Christian men and successful in society.

Mark was wise and accepted my advice. He worked hard and made many sacrifices. He started attending an excellent Bible-believing church. He went to the best Christian school in his area and later one of the best universities in the U.S.A. He earned his bachelor's and master's degree in engineering. At thirty-one years old, he has a respectful senior engineering position in a large corporation. He loves and serves the Lord and gives generously to God's work. He always keeps in touch with me and is a very loving and appreciative person.

On the other hand, **John** was a foolish and proud person. Even though he said everything I told him made sense, he followed his own desires and ways because it was easier. He dropped out of school early, became involved with the wrong crowd, and married at a young age - even before he had a job. He started to take drugs, divorced and left his beautiful wife and daughter. Today, John is in jail, suffers from hepatitis and AIDS, and is not expected to live long.

Do you need some directions? Are you in a situation in your life where the road seems a bit confusing? Be wise. Do not follow your own desires but seek godly counseling and follow God's directions. You will never regret and worry when you are in God's will. It is better to be a good Christian and successful engineer than to be in jail and dying. Never forget, God's directions are always the best.

❖

TWO FRIENDS

For many years, I have known two good men: Jim and Jerry. They were very good friends. Both attended the same Sunday school and Christian school. Later, Jim graduated from a liberal Christian college that compromised in many areas. Jerry graduated from a conservative Christian college that did not compromise with the Word of God. After graduation, both men lived in the same town and started families.

Jim took his family to a large church that compromised with the Word of God using worldly music and unscriptural programs to attract young people to the church. It only took a short time for Jim to become lukewarm and stop serving the Lord. His children also turned very worldly and did not even respect their own parents.

Jerry, on the other hand, chose to go to a smaller church that did not compromise with the Word of God and always used godly music. The church had a Christian school and soul-winning program. Jerry and all his family were involved in the work of God. Jerry's children graduated from the Christian school. Most of them went on to good Christian colleges and now serve the Lord full-time. Even his children that graduated from public universities continued to serve and be on fire for the Lord. All of Jerry's kids have respectful positions in the community and beautiful families. They also love, respect, and take care of their parents, who are now in their old age. Even the kids that live out of town take two weeks off every year from their jobs to take care of the needs of the elderly parents and their property.

Are you being tempted to compromise your faith or morals? Do not give in. Do what is right as Jerry did. God calls His children to walk the highway of holiness. You and your family's spiritual future depends on t he tough choices you make today. Maybe you will need to make some sacrifices, but you will never regret doing what is right. Be wise like Jerry. Today, Jim regrets the unwise decisions he made, which all started a long time ago when he chose the wrong college and church.

❖

THE PLANE TREE

When I was in grade school, my teacher gave us a project to do. We had to plant trees all over my village. I planted a "plane" tree in the center of the village. I was responsible for taking care of this tree for a long time. Now, it is a massive tree over 65 years old. Under the tree, the village put nice tables and chairs that were available to everybody. The elderly people especially enjoy the shade of the tree, and they play games there.

For many years, I was far away from my country. The last time I was in my village was at my father's funeral. For the first time, I understood that the people of my village honored me by referring to this tree by my name. For many years, the people said to one another, "I will meet you by Ted's plane tree." In Greek, which is my first language, my name, "Theodoros," means "God's gift." At that time, I was the only person in my village with this name.

The people told my father, "God gave us a nice gift through God's gift." My father was proud to hear my name mentioned each time, even though I was not around. After all, I felt good too because my people were able to enjoy the beauty and the shade from my tree for so many years.

Do you wonder if what you are doing will ever make a difference? Do not give up hope. Continue to help others and serve the Lord. The Lord promises that one day, you will receive rewards in heaven, and you will feel good just like I felt good about "Ted's plane tree." *"As we have therefore opportunity, let us do good unto all men..."* (Galatians 6:10).

❖

THE HOMELESS OLD MAN

One rainy day, a homeless old man sat on a bench underneath a tree outside of a department store. The Holy Spirit led me to walk over to meet him and to witness to him. He had only a bicycle full of his belongings and a piece of cheese that he was eating. He did not complain about the rain or seem to be envious of other people. To each of my questions, he answered with a positive attitude.

When I asked if he needed anything and offered to help him, he told me, "Thank you, God gives me more than I need." He smiled and gladly accepted what I told him about the Lord and right away started to read the tract "The Simple Plan of Salvation," that I gave to him. As I was leaving, I was reminded of how many people in this world, even many Christians, who have a lot more than he does and still constantly complain about everything.

Are you a source of a negative attitude and complaints? Check out what you have been saying lately. Your words have a powerful influence on you and those who listen to you. Find ways to give praise or appreciation. Let an attitude of gratitude dominate your conversations. Be positive. The finest test of character is in the amount and power of gratitude you have. Do not complain because God put thorns on roses. Instead, praise Him for putting roses on thorns.

❖

CO-WORKERS, NOT COMPETITORS

One of the goals of my ministry is to inspire people in many areas, especially Christians. We have witnessed this, and we are very pleased. One area has been that many Christians have started forwarding the Spiritual Note to the people on their email list. This has become a big blessing to them and to their friends. Over the years, several others have started their own email ministries, and I helped them as much as I could.

One time, a Christian wrote to me and told me, "'So and so' will become a competitor of yours..." Oh, my friends, if all Christians in the world started email ministries, they would make my day. I would see that as a great blessing, not competition! It is hard to believe that a person who calls himself a Christian would think that way about another ministry. The Christian must have the fruits of the Holy Spirit, and not the works of the flesh-one of which is "envy."

So often, it disappoints me to see similar situations between Christians, pastors, churches, and other Christian organizations. In private, many of them talk negatively about others, instead of being quiet, helping, praying, and cooperating. They should be co-workers for the same cause and promoting God's Kingdom, instead of their own agenda with pride. In the end, they develop trouble, and God's blessings are not upon them.

If you are a redeemed child of God, you must be a wise servant by helping other Christians, and not by competing and promoting your own agenda. It is time for you to examine yourself and check your Christian condition, motives, and actions. You must walk in the Spirit and not in the flesh. *"Be not deceived; God is not mocked: for whatsoever a man soweth, that shall he also reap"* (Galatians 6:7). *"Humble yourselves in the sight of the Lord, and he shall lift you up. Speak not evil one of another, brethren..."* (James 4:10-11).

❖

I LOVE AMERICA

I love the country where I was born very much, but I have a special love for America. America is the country where I have spent most of my life. My wife told me many times, "You love this country more than others who were born here."

I have studied and visited many countries of the world, and I have found that no other country is like America, even with all her mistakes. The freedom and opportunities offered in this country to every individual are unexplainable.

Young American do not take for granted what you have. If you do not believe me, just go to any of our neighboring countries and then come back afterward and talk with me. America has helped most of the other countries of the world in various ways over the years, but she still has the most enemies. Millions of Americans have died to offer freedom and peace to other countries. I believe that without America, the world would be in worse condition than it is today. The Lord still has mercy on this country despite all the wrong things that have happened lately because there are still many sincere Christians who cry out to the Lord every day. American Christians also send and support more missionaries around the world than any other country.

Remember our founding fathers and their sacrifices. They gave us the Declaration of Independence and the U.S. Constitution, which made this country great in the short time of its existence. Also, remember all those who are serving in our military all over the world, our veterans, and the ones who gave their lives for our freedom. Even if you are not an American, I encourage you to pray for this country. Thank you, God bless you, and God bless America!

AFRICA

Many times, I receive messages from underdeveloped countries where the people do not have their own computers but must go to the public library's computers to read the Spiritual Note. They also make copies and share them with others and use them in their Sunday schools and churches because they do not have Sunday school materials or even Bibles.

One time, I found out that the workers in one factory in Africa used their own time to read the Spiritual Notes on the factory's computers. I was surprised when I got a message from their supervisor. All of these workers became better people and more productive workers. The Lord works in mysterious ways to spread the gospel and give opportunities to the people to accept Him as their personal Savior.

❖

ENCOURAGING COMMENTS

Every day, we receive many gracious and wonderful messages from people around the world that encourage us. With love, concern, and appreciation they tell us how each part of the Spiritual Note has blessed them, their loved ones, and friends by teaching, encouraging, challenging, inspiring, and evangelizing them. Some of them feel they cannot do without the Spiritual Note because it is for them the only weekday email ministry in the world with so many various uplifting Christian materials. This ministry has helped many of them make the most important decision in their lives: accepting the Lord as their personal Savior.

We always appreciate the kindness and prayers of people because we really need them every day. By the grace of God, the Spiritual Note has ministered freely to many people since 1996. Only a couple times have we received messages lacking in kindness and good manners that have disappointed us. *"But in all things approving ourselves as the ministers of God...by kindness... by love unfeigned"* (2 Corinthians 6:4,6), and *"He hath shewed thee, O man, what is good; and what doth the LORD require of thee, but to do justly, and to love mercy, and to walk humbly with thy God?"* (Micah 6:8)

God's grace treats you with kindness and blessings far beyond what you deserve. Make sure your attitude towards others does not disqualify you from being an effective representative for Christ. Communications are important. If you would like to make a difference in someone's life today, do it with kindness. Watch God's love melt that icy heart! God will bless you for your kindness in ways that will surprise you. Harsh words and uncaring actions turn people off, and you harm yourself. Treat others with kindness if you want to stand out as an ambassador of the King.

❖

NOT OVERNIGHT

Christians often think that witnessing to people all over the world through my ministry, "A Spiritual Note from the Bible" happened overnight. Not so. It did not happen instantly. First, I witnessed to my own family, then my neighbors, and then the people of my community, state, and country. Later, the Lord opened the door to other countries.

For example, my first wife accepted the Lord as her personal Savior in our living room about a month after my own conversion. My daughter accepted the Lord in our church, my son in our dining room, my son-in-law in our living room, and my two grandchildren in my office. One of my neighbors accepted the Lord as his personal Savior in our kitchen, a teenager in my car, a lady in the parking lot of a bank in my neighborhood, an old man in a hospital and a young man and older man in their houses in a town near us.

Since becoming a Christian in 1970, the Lord has allowed me to witness to more and more people further and further from my own home with the help of the Internet. The Spiritual Note was first prepared for my own children and then for our friends. Later, it became available to the world. The message was first called "A Spiritual Note from Dad," then "A Spiritual Note from Ted, " and finally " A Spiritual Note from the Bible." As you can see, the full inspiration of "A Spiritual Note from the Bible" did not come overnight. It was developed, reshaped, and maintained from a lifelong relationship and trust in the Lord.

"But ye shall receive power,
after that the Holy Ghost is come upon you:
and ye shall be witnesses unto me both
in Jerusalem, and in all Judaea, and in Samaria,
and unto the uttermost part of the earth."
Acts 1:8

TESTIMONIES
FROM MEMBERS OF MY FAMILY

Testimony
by my beloved second wife, Deanna

I was born and raised in northern Wisconsin. Although my parents did not attend church, they allowed me as a small child, to walk up the hill from our home to attend a little Baptist church. Later, when we moved to Milwaukee, I attended a Bible church along with my mother and my younger sister.

When I was twelve years old, I went to a Summer Bible Camp, where I made a decision to accept Jesus Christ as my personal Savior and Lord. After high school, I attended Technical College and received a secretarial and accounting degree. After graduation, I worked as the secretary for the Student Counselor in the same college. Later, I worked in banking as well as doing payroll and accounting for other companies. In all my Christian life, I served the Lord faithfully and consistently with the talents He gave me including teaching Sunday school and playing the organ in several churches I attended.

My first dear husband and I had five children. We all regularly attended a Baptist church where my husband, along with my children, played guitar and sang in the church. By the grace of God, we sent our five children to a Christian school, and later I homeschooled. We were heartbroken when my husband was diagnosed with a terminal blood disorder at the age of forty-one, the same year, our oldest daughter entered Bible College.

After I had been a widow for fifteen years, I saw my second husband's testimony on the internet, where he said he was a born-again Christian and he did not compromise with the Word of God. That caused me to send him an email with a short message and with the subject "encouraging words" and encouraged him never to give up, but continue with his ministry the "Spiritual Notes" which were a blessing to me.

As a result, we began corresponding and getting to know more about one another. Finally, the Lord allowed us to meet, first as friends, and later the Lord laid it upon our hearts to get married. Before we were married, my future husband was diagnosed with thyroid cancer, and instead of running away, I wrote to him and said, "Ted, now is the time to serve the Lord together."

The Lord honored that desire and has blessed our marriage and our service for Him since 1999. By the grace of God, my beloved husband and I have experienced His miracles in our lives even through the many trials and tribulations He has allowed us to experience. *"Ye are of God, little children, and have overcome them: because greater is he that is in you, than he that is in the world"* (1 John 4:4).

❖

Testimony
by my beloved daughter Magdalene

I had the privilege of growing up in a Greek Christian home. Both of my parents came from Greece and became "born-again Christians" shortly after coming to America. I accepted Jesus Christ as my personal Savior and was baptized when I was seven years old.

While attending a Christian college to become a math teacher, I claimed Philippians 1:6 as my life's verse: *"Being confident of this very thing, that he which hath begun a good work in you will perform it until the day of Jesus Christ."* It was this verse that enabled me to have the faith and strength to achieve the goals that God had and still has in store for me.

In February 1996, I had to face my greatest fear—losing a close loved one. On the day of my 25th birthday, I found out that my Mom had died unexpectedly. It was very hard to understand why God would allow something like this to happen when I had earnestly prayed for years for this NOT to happen, but the Bible says, *"HIS ways are not OUR ways."* Each year, my birthday is a reminder that my mom's work for God had come to an end, but my work for Him is to continue.

As a Christian school teacher, I was not accustomed to much money, fame, or material possessions; however, my Mom used to remind me that I was making "eternal investments" which were worth a whole lot more. Today, I strive to continue making those "eternal investments" with all my math students and especially with our son and daughter. My husband and I try to set a good example to our family and to others. Each of our family members knows that God is very important to us. We make it a point to go to church together, pray together, teach, witness, give, and be hospitable. Just as the Bible says in Joshua 24:15, *"But as for me and my house, we will serve the Lord."*

My husband and I are very grateful for all of the many blessings that God has given us. God is so good!

Testimony
by my beloved son-in-law Bryan

As a young man growing up, I was taught to obey my parents, do well in the classroom, develop good sportsmanship on and off the field, and take advantage of what life has given to me. It took over twenty years of my life to realize that something else was missing. Something that was far larger and more important than just being a good sport or even doing well in the classroom as an engineering student. Jesus Christ was missing from my heart.

I had thought all the while growing up that I was a Christian. I went to Sunday school and church each week and had been baptized as a child. That's all before I met my future father-in-law who taught me the real meaning of being a Christian, and what it means to be obedient to the Lord. It's then that I realized that all this time, I had not been living my life as a true Christian. At that time, I accepted Christ as my personal Savior and later followed with scriptural Baptism.

After I was saved, you could not imagine the weight that had been lifted off of me, and I felt overwhelming peace in my heart. Since then, I got married and now have two beautiful children. Jesus Christ has blessed my family in so many ways. Knowing what Jesus means to me, and how important He should be in each of our lives, I have to make sure that my children continue to grow up with a loving heart and commitment to Him. Each will know what it means to be a Christian, and I hope that both will be able to see His power and love through my wife and me.

It has been amazing to see how the kids have grown with such servant hearts. One summer, the Lord opened up an opportunity to send my daughter on a missions trip to Mexico with her youth group at church. Although I felt a bit uneasy about sending her to a foreign country in an area known for criminal activity, I felt compelled by the Holy Spirit to let her go. Through the trip, my daughter was able to experience the power of Jesus Christ "first hand." The Lord even provided her and the entire group protection for the week. Through this experience, I learned that the Lord protects His children no matter where they serve Him.

Another major decision that the Lord continued to work on me for several years was in making a decision on where my kids would go to college. I had always thought my kids would graduate from a Christian school, but then go off to a local or state college of their choice. However, the Lord worked on my heart yet again. I was not all that familiar with Christian colleges and was a bit concerned about what types of education would be offered.

Over summer several years ago, while vacationing in Florida, I took my family to Pensacola Christian College to visit the campus. After only a few hours on campus, I just knew that the Lord was telling me this is where our kids should attend college. We met some of my wife's friends while on campus and attended the church that Sunday. We felt so welcomed there.

To help cement our decision, the Campus Pastor from Pensacola Christian College came to our home church as a guest speaker just two weeks after we visited the campus. We had no idea that he was visiting our church. To make a long story short, we helped enroll our son at Pensacola Christian College. Nothing can make a parent more spiritually proud than to see his son or daughter grow in Jesus Christ.

I am looking forward to seeing what God has in store for both of my children. I love my parents and thank them for all that they have done; however, just like me, they also need to learn what it means to be a Christian and how to be saved. Please pray that someday I will also be able to lead my parents and the rest of my family to Christ. *"The word of our God shall stand forever"* (Isaiah 40:8).

❖

Testimony
by my beloved grandson Tyler

I got saved when I was seven years old when my Papou (grandpa in Greek) told me about Jesus. He is a Greek teacher and even teaches me Greek sometimes when I go to his house. Papou was raised in Greece, and later in his twenties, he moved to America. He has told me numerous stories about all the things that are different in Greece compared to being here in the United States.

He was introduced to biblical Christianity when he was in college, but he did not get saved until he came to the United States. One of the greatest things that he has taught me is the importance of prayer. When Papou prays, he includes every minute detail. He has so much faith in God and is an excellent example to me. I am so thankful that he prays for me every day. He even surprised me by traveling a long distance to come to my high school graduation. The day before my graduation, when I arrived back home, he opened the door. I was in shock! I was so glad that my grandparents came to my graduation.

I am blessed to have been raised in a Christian home. God has blessed me with great parents, grandparents, and friends. God has also blessed me with a good Christian school and church, where I learned about the Bible. After hearing a sermon at one of our chapels while I was in high school, I realized that I had doubts about my salvation. I had never mentioned this to my parents or to my grandpa. After the message was over, I went back to find a teacher who helped me with scriptures to settle my doubts. I have never had any doubts since that day when I experienced assurance of my salvation. My favorite verse is Psalm 119:105. *"Thy word is a lamp unto my feet, and a light unto my path."* I like this verse because I know that God will help me make decisions through my life's journey.

I am now a current underclassman in college. I have since learned that even though I am on the bottom rung of college, I have been able to make many great friends with most of them being upperclassmen. I still have some friends from home, but I knew I would have to step out of my comfort zone and be social to make new friends. I overcame that fear and met a lot of great people and made new friends, but now, the next fear to overcome is speaking in front of people. I have realized that I cannot do everything on my own; God is the shoulder that I need to lean on when I fall and need help. He is always there and will help. Even though I am just one student of many at college, I still sometimes feel alone, but I know that God is always right there for me to talk to. My first year at college was overall successful, and I cannot wait for what God has in store for me in the upcoming years!

Thank you to everyone who has helped me grow and come closer to the Lord day by day!

❖

Testimony
by my beloved oldest granddaughter Alexandra

When I was five years old, Papou (grandpa in Greek) led me to the Lord on Christmas Eve, 2007. Over the past several years, I had struggled with doubts about my assurance of salvation, and I never truly knew if I was saved. I had never mentioned this to my parents or to my grandpa. In October of 2016, I had the privilege of going to a revival at my school. On the last day of the revival, the Lord was really tugging at my heart. I realized that day that I needed to completely settle my doubts and make sure of my salvation. I have never had doubts since!

When I was a junior in high school, God blessed me with the opportunity to go on a missions trip to Mexico. That trip opened my eyes. It made me realize how blessed I truly am. As an American, we can often take so much for granted. The Lord softened my heart, and I was burdened for the people of Mexico. We were able to see many people saved, and I was able to be a tiny part of the great work that God did that week in Mexico.

I am beyond blessed that God has placed me in such a wonderful family. I have had the privilege of attending a Christian school and going to a great church. God has given me the ability to play the flute and memorize the scriptures. I love the Lord, and I love serving Him with the talents He has given me. God has been so good! My life verse is Ephesians 3:20 because everything I am able to do is because of God. I cannot do anything without Him, and He can do things beyond what we can imagine as long as we have faith in Him. *"Now unto him that is able to do exceeding abundantly above all that we ask or think, according to the power that worketh in us"* (Ephesians 3:20).

❖

Testimony
by my beloved son George

I was very fortunate to be raised in a Christian home and accept Jesus Christ as my personal Savior at an early age. Although my parents were not wealthy, they provided my sister and me with all the necessities of life. They worked day and night (sometimes alternating shifts) so that we would have a comfortable and healthy life. Most importantly, my parents taught us the best they could on how to serve God. I even had the privilege of attending Christian schools all the way through high school and going to church every Sunday. At times, I did not always agree on the way my parents did things. However, now, I can look back and see how much my father and mother loved and cared about us.

I had some challenging times (being on my own, going to engineering school), but the most difficult time for me was when my mother went to be with the Lord when I was a Junior in college. I remember my mother telling me, "One day, you will look for me, but I won't be around, and then you will know what I meant to you." I took those words for granted when I was young, and now I can look back and see exactly what she meant. She sacrificed so much for her family, and she never took time for herself. Although my mom is not here on this earth anymore, her funeral was able to touch many lives in revealing her true Christian testimony.

That same year in 1996, my dad started an email ministry that has blessed thousands of people by sharing the gospel of Christ. My Dad is an inspiration to me spiritually, where he has devoted 100% of his life to do whatever the Lord has called him to do. I have a wonderful stepmom that supported my Dad even through the severe medical problems that he has gone through over the last several years. Not only am I fortunate to have wonderful parents, but I am also blessed to have a wonderful sister.

In 1999, my dad was diagnosed with thyroid cancer. After four years and two surgeries, my dad finally recovered. It was a difficult time for my dad, my sister, and myself. During that time, I was able to see how the Lord used his life in so many positive ways. The Lord showed me how we need to take life more seriously and not take things for granted.

I do not have a life-changing story that brought me to Christ; instead, my testimony is to share the wonderful things that God has done in my life and what he continues to do. Because of the strong Christian background in which I was raised, I am able to look back and thank God that I did not fall into a sinful lifestyle that would have hindered my Christian testimony. Since I am not perfect in any way, I do need to work every day on getting closer to God. As I get older, I can appreciate more and more what God has done for me.

Sometimes, we look at other people and envy the things they have. However, we should not think that way. An important verse that I take very seriously is Proverbs 30: 7-10: *"Two things have I required of thee; deny me them not before I die: Remove far from me vanity and lies: give me neither poverty nor riches; feed me with food convenient for me: Lest I be full, and deny thee, and say, Who is the LORD? or lest I be poor, and steal, and take the name of my God in vain."* God has a purpose and plan for each one of us. When I am in doubt about certain things (or when the devil tries to put me down), I try to think of what God has done in my life. Remember, there are so many people that have it much worse than we do. Our job is to glorify God and spread the Good News to everyone. By doing this, people will accept Christ and live a life that would glorify and honor Him.

Over the years, God has been good to me by allowing me to travel, work, and live throughout the world. Once while living in Japan, I had a neurological problem because of lack of sleep. It was frightening at the time, but my father helped support me and got me back on my feet. During that difficult time, I needed to refresh my walk with Christ by trusting Him. While I was seeking medical attention back in the United States, I met my soon-to-be wife, who has always supported me and has been by my side ever since. We have a wonderful ten-year-old daughter, and she attends a Christian school and loves the Lord.

Sometimes life may not seem fair, but when we all really think about it, God really takes care of his children. He may put challenges and occasionally difficult circumstances in front of us, but He will always guide us through it. For this, we must always be thankful and strive to fulfill God's calling in our lives no matter what it may be.

❖

Testimony
by my beloved daughter-in-law Tiffanie

I was born and raised in Alaska, in a good home with wonderful parents that loved us and did whatever they could for us. I am the middle child and only girl. My brothers were both very active in sports and kept our family very busy. We were members of the Mormon Church and were active until we moved to California in my freshman year of high school. After we moved, things were different. We started looking at other churches, but it never felt like we were in the right place. Eventually, as a family, we stopped going to church except for attending the typical Christmas and Easter services.

There was a turning point in my life when I was about twenty-six years old. I was going through several personal issues and was really struggling. My older brother was also going through some issues of his own that resulted in him going into a Christian based rehabilitation program called "Teen Challenge." That program opened both my brother's and my eyes. I was able to witness God's work through my brother and watch him change. He had accepted Christ as his personal Savior and was baptized on New Year's Eve. After my brother went through this amazing change, I too accepted Christ, and I tried to live a life that would please God.

Several years later, I met my future husband on a Christian website. I know that God brought us together. At that time, he had accepted an assignment overseas that was going to last for at least three years. We truly had a long-distance relationship! During that time, we learned a lot about each other, including our families, lives, and our relationship with God. The Lord gave me the patience to see what was best. When he finally returned from overseas, we were married a year and a half later.

We recently moved to another state, and we are looking forward to the opportunities of service that God has for us. We have a beautiful daughter who is 10 years old and attends a Christian School. It brings me so much joy, as a mother, to watch our daughter grow in her faith and knowledge in the Lord. We like to be active with our local church and children's ministries. I was a leader in our AWANA kids program. Being able to work with children is a wonderful experience. I have the pleasure of watching how God helps the children blossom and seeing them get excited to share God's word.

Throughout my life, I have had some ups and downs, but through all these experiences, God has always been there to support me and get me back on track. I continuously need to pray and seek God's guidance. I have so much to be thankful for what God has done and will continue to do in my life. He is truly amazing. *"O give thanks unto the LORD; for he is good; for his mercy endureth for ever"* (I Chronicles 16:34).

❖

Testimony
by my beloved youngest granddaughter Makenna

I am in 4th grade. I was born into a Christian family. My parents started teaching me about the Bible when I was just a baby. I accepted Christ when I was six years old. Knowing God is with me, I pray throughout the day and ask for Him to help me. I know that when I make mistakes, Jesus forgives me so that I can learn from my mistakes and become a better person.

I currently attend a Christian school. God has given me the opportunity to sing in my Christian school choir, attend AWANA, and learn every day about Christ. Our school motto is "taking every thought captive to Christ." This means in everything we do, Christ is the center of all. I also love to write, draw, and swim. I pray one day, God will use my talents to serve Him. My favorite verse in the Bible is John 3:16. *"For God so loved the world, that he gave his only begotten Son, that whosoever believeth in him should not perish, but have everlasting life."* I am so happy that God is so good to me.

"For I am not ashamed of the gospel of Christ:
for it is the power of God unto salvation
to every one that believeth."
Romans 1:12

PERSONAL TESTIMONY
By Ted Matamis

I WILL NEVER FORGET THE SACRIFICES
MY FATHER MADE FOR ME!

Dad,
Thanks for giving me
the finest things in life,
your time,
your care,
your love,
and teaching me
to love God!

"The father of the righteous shall greatly rejoice:
and he that begetteth a wise child shall have joy of him."
Proverbs 23:24

I believe, like me, that each of you has special memories of your father. I miss him very much. I think of him all the time and especially on Father's Day. My father was not a person with a lot of education. He did not even finish grammar school. He spent his life as a farmer, but he was brilliant, kind, compassionate, thoughtful, generous, hospitable, hardworking, and had a great sense of humor. His dream was to see his three sons have a better life than him, and he accomplished that by making many sacrifices.

During my high school years, from the age of twelve until eighteen, I lived by myself in a rented room in a larger town where the high school was located far from our village. I will never forget the sacrifices my father made for me. In the winter, on rainy and snowy days, he brought me food and wood for my fireplace to keep me warm. He spent three hours traveling with his mules to come where I was living, going through mountains and dangerous places. He did not have a lot of money, but he gave me 50 drachmas (about $1.50 at that time) a month to buy some food and kerosene for my lamp.

He loved all his sons very much. I was the youngest son. I had his father's name. He also had a special relationship with me, as Jesus had with the apostle John. My father was always proud of me because I never broke his heart with a bad attitude or embarrassed him in front of anybody, especially in the schools where he sent me. When people told him that my name was in the newspapers with good comments about my progress in school, it made his day. While I was in the army for two years, he voluntarily published my first book in Greece, which I had written before going to college.

I respected, honored, and loved my father very much. I never questioned him. I never talked back to him. I never considered myself above him in knowledge or experience. I never criticized him to anyone. To me, he was next to God. He became my hero, my friend, and my best counselor. When I was far from home, he regularly wrote wonderful letters to my family and me until the time he passed away.

My father never took Bible courses, but he loved God and had a fear of the Lord, both of which he passed along to me. He always took me to the church and taught me everything he knew about God and Christianity. He had a tender heart for the Word of God. Every time he heard someone preach in the church, he would shed tears.

The last time I visited my home country with my family, he came with a taxi to the airport to give us a ride to our village. When we left, he came to say goodbye at the airport. He felt so proud to be around us and to introduce us to his friends who did not know us.

My father asked me to help him on the farms in the summertime when I was home, but he never asked me for financial help. He always told me that he had more than enough and worried more about me because I had a family and more expenses. Still, because of my responsibility as a son, and out of love and appreciation, I supported him and my mother regularly. That was one of the priorities for both myself and my wife. Now, as I look back, I wish I would have been able to do more for them. Because of the Lord and them, I am who I am today, and I am extremely grateful.

When I got the bad news that he had a stroke at the age of 82, I took an airplane back home, went to the hospital, and spent the last days of his life with him. When I witnessed to two other patients who were in the same room and encouraged them to accept the Lord as their personal Savior, I felt that my father participated in our conversation. Even though he was not able to talk to me, tears flowed down his face until his last breath as he died in mine and my brother's arms.

He always agreed with me in our spiritual conversations and responded to the gospel as compared to my mother, who resisted. After his death, my mother became more receptive, and I was able to lead her to the Lord after 20 years of continually praying.

When both of them passed away, it cost me a lot. It took several years for my grief to lessen in my heart because most of my life, I lived far away from them. I believe that I will see both of them again one day and walk together with them on the golden streets of heaven. In the meantime, I have a special place at my home, planted with beautiful flowers in their memory.

My father's priority was his family, and he wanted his family to know that they always came first, no matter what. This made him a hero to me. He put others first, then himself.

Fathers, your children need you. Your love and sacrifices will make all the difference in their lives. Take time to invest in them. Especially, show love to your children with actions and not only with words. Your first priority must be to teach them about the Lord and encourage them to accept Him as their personal Savior. After that, teach them to love and serve the Lord. The father who fears the Lord also enjoys God's presence, wisdom, direction, and blessings all his life.

*

The Bible says to love others, but when it comes to father and mother, it says to honor them:

- "This is my commandment, That ye **LOVE** one another, as I have loved you."— *John 15:12*

- "Husbands, **LOVE** your wives, even as Christ also loved the church, and gave himself for it;" — *Ephesians 5:25*

- "Thou shalt **LOVE** thy neighbour as thyself." — *Matthew 22:39*

*

- "**HONOUR** thy father and thy mother: that thy days may be long upon the land which the LORD thy God giveth thee."— *Exodus 20:12*

- "**HONOUR** thy father and thy mother, as the LORD thy God hath commanded thee; that thy days may be prolonged, and that it may go well with thee, in the land which the LORD thy God giveth thee." — *Deuteronomy 5:16*

- "**HONOUR** thy father and thy mother: and, Thou shalt love thy neighbour as thyself." — *Matthew 19:19*

- "**HONOUR** thy father and mother; which is the first commandment with promise;" — *Ephesians 6:2*

100

YOUR TESTIMONY

*"Jesus...saith unto him, Go home to thy friends,
and tell them how great things the Lord hath done for thee, and
hath had compassion on thee."*
Mark 5:19

*"Be ready always to give an answer to every man that asketh
you a reason of the hope that is in you..."*
1 Peter 3:15

*

Your testimony can change someone's life, even the world!

Anxiety and uncertainty at a global level have caused many to re-examine what is truly important in life. Many realize that today's high-technology and high-stress leads to frustration and hopelessness. Some find happiness in the pursuit of pleasure, possessions, or in relationships, but soon understand that this type of satisfaction is only temporary. We believe that God taught us in His own Word, the Bible, that if we want to find lasting peace and joy in life, we must have a relationship with Him through Jesus Christ. *"Come unto me, all ye that labour and are heavy laden, and I will give you rest"* (Matthew 11:28).

For some people, God's presence in their life is real, and this relationship is a source of significance and purpose. The following two testimonies examine the lives of these kinds of individuals and their relationship with God providing an answer to those seeking true fulfillment in life. If you are searching for answers to life's most difficult questions, I encourage you to read them.

- A friend of mine once told me about a man named Mark, who had irresponsible parents, and they were the worst examples in the town. Their kids always made trouble and lived like pigs, even eating food out of the garbage. When everybody in the town saw them, they thought these kids will never change, but Mark did. There came a day when he heard the powerful message of the gospel of Jesus Christ, and he made the decision to get saved. He repented of his sins, believed in Jesus Christ, and accepted Him as his personal Savior and Lord! Not long after that, the Lord called him to become a preacher. A part of his ministry was first to reach his family for Christ. As a result, most of them got saved. One day, Mark was at the funeral of a relative. One couple who were there had not seen him since he was saved. They spoke with him and were amazed at the change that had taken place in his life. They thought all of this change he had made by himself. However, Mark said to them, "I really didn't change myself, but Christ, who is in me, brought all the changes in my life."

- World-famed pianist Arthur Rubenstein took aback prime minister Golda Meir and a national audience once when he professed his faith in Jesus Christ over Israeli television. According to a report in the Mount Zion Reporter, the incident took place while Mrs. Meir was interviewing the American-Jewish virtuoso. She asked him to name the "greatest event in your life." "When I received Yeshua Harnashiach [Jesus the Messiah] into my heart," he replied. "Since then, my life was changed. I have experienced joy and peace ever since." The report went on to state that at the comment, Mrs. Meir leaned back in her chair with an expression of complete surprise! — *Donald Deffner, Seasonal Illustrations, Resource, 1992, p. 80*

Christian and follower of Christ, when was the last time you shared about the Lord? If you want to win others to Jesus, try inviting them to meet your Savior. A life totally dedicated to Christ is an impressive, dynamic, and powerful testimony. Christianity is a personal relationship with God and not a mere set of beliefs. Tell them how God has made a difference in your life. Your personal testimony can have a powerful impact on others. I have my own experience with that. Before I became a Bible-believing Christian, many good Christian testimonies had amazingly affected my spiritual life. These testimonies were more powerful and touched me even more than inspirational sermons.

As a new Christian, my spiritual father asked me to preach several times while he was away from his church, rather than having others with more experience preach at the church. He told me, *"I want you to preach because you have a good testimony."* I did not seriously analyze his comments at the time, but later, I understood what he meant and what he wanted to accomplish. I started to appreciate some people with good Christian testimonies more than those with experience because people are affected more by the godly living of a person than the words coming from their lips.

The beautiful thing about sharing your own testimony is that you do not have to know all the answers. The Bible teaches us this with the story of the man born blind to whom Jesus gave his sight. He was asked many questions, to which he responded, "I don't know." But there was one thing the mockers were not able to discredit when he told them. *"One thing I know, that, whereas I was blind, now I see"* (John 9:24).

A Christian must love God above everything else and love others more than himself if he desires to live his life as a testimony for Jesus Christ. A believer must share what Jesus has done in his life and serve God and others. As a result, he will reflect the life-giving power of Christ more and more into a dark world. When your efforts of godly living, agree with the words coming from your mouth, your testimony will be recognized as true.

Live for the Lord each and every day. Take advantage of your opportunities to share Him. The next time you have the chance, be bold. Soon, they will want to meet the Man who turned things around for you. God can use your testimony in amazing ways to change the world. Your words can change your neighbor, a country, or a continent. Do not limit God, and He will not limit you!

THANK YOU, LORD, FOR SAVING MY SOUL

"Thank you, Lord, for saving my soul
Thank you, Lord, for making me whole
Thank you, Lord, for giving to me
Thy great salvation so rich and free."

— *Hymn by Seth and Bessie Sykes, 1940*

❖ ❖ ❖

• The most powerful testimony is a Godly life. Christians, only in this life, can share with unbelievers their story of a changed life!

• "If lips and life do not agree, the testimony will not amount to much." — *Dr. H.A. Ironside*

• "Throughout the world, in nation after nation, men and women have died for their Christian faith. The very least we can do is live for our faith." — *Author Unknown*

Dear Lord,

I want to take a moment, not to ask for anything
from you, instead, I want to simply say
from the bottom of my heart,
THANK YOU
for saving my soul!

THANK YOU
for all the trials and joys you allowed
in my Christian journey!

THANK YOU
for the privilege of serving you!

THANK YOU
for my honorable father and mother!

THANK YOU
for two godly wives, one of which is with you!

THANK YOU
for my two wonderful Christian children
and their Christian spouses!

THANK YOU
for my beautiful and sweet grandchildren
who are saved by grace!

www.ingramcontent.com/pod-product-compliance
Lightning Source LLC
Chambersburg PA
CBHW021959090426
42811CB00001B/86